TRACKING POP

SERIES EDITORS: LORI BURNS, JOHN COVACH, AND ALBIN ZAK

In one form or another, the influence of popular music has permeated cultural activities and perception on a global scale. Interdisciplinary in nature, Tracking Pop is intended as a wide-ranging exploration of pop music and its cultural situation. In addition to providing resources for students and scholars working in the field of popular culture, the books in this series will appeal to general readers and music lovers, for whom pop has provided the soundtrack of their lives.

Listening to Popular Music: Or, How I Learned to Stop Worrying and Love Led Zeppelin
by Theodore Gracyk

Sounding Out Pop: Analytical Essays in Popular Music
edited by Mark Spicer and John Covach

I Don't Sound Like Nobody: Remaking Music in 1950s America
by Albin J. Zak III

I Don't Sound Like Nobody

I Don't Sound Like Nobody

· REMAKING MUSIC IN 1950s AMERICA ·

Albin J. Zak III

The University of Michigan Press · *Ann Arbor*

2013   2012   2011   2010   4   3   2   1

A CIP catalog record for this book is available from the British Library.

Library of Congress Cataloging-in-Publication Data

Zak, Albin.
    I don't sound like nobody : remaking music in 1950s America /
Albin J. Zak III.
        p.   cm. — (Tracking pop)
    Includes bibliographical references, index, and discography.
    ISBN 978-0-472-11637-9 (cloth : alk. paper)
    ISBN 978-0-472-02454-4 (e-book)
    1. Music—United States—20th century—History and criticism.
2. Music trade—United States.   I. Title.

ML200.5.Z35   2010
781.640973'09045—dc22   2010014120

• FOR *Leo Treitler* •

Contents

Acknowledgments

I've been at this project for several years during which I've amassed debts to many individuals and institutions. Early financial support came in the form of grants from the University of Michigan School of Music Faculty Research Fund and the University of Michigan Office of the Vice Provost for Research. University of Michigan Senior Vice Provost Lester Monts provided further invaluable assistance. I also received generous support from the Centre for the History and Analysis of Recorded Music, which took me to London at the invitation of Nicholas Cook to present some of my research at the inaugural Art of Record Production conference. One of my research projects involved reading a couple of decades' worth of *Billboard,* which kicked off with some very helpful initial indexing by Stephanie Heriger. I am grateful to the university libraries and librarians at Michigan, Harvard, Columbia, Memphis (Tennessee Valley Collection), Buffalo, Syracuse, and Albany, along with the New York Public Library and the great cooperative known as Interlibrary Loan, for access to sources and all-around helpfulness. I would single out in particular Daryl Bullis at the University at Albany and Charles Reynolds at the University of Michigan, whose above-and-beyond research assistance was matched only by their cheerful collegiality.

Many writers—critics, scholars, biographers, historians—have kindly given of their time and expertise. For their many tips and insights, I thank Bruce Jenkins, Dave Marsh, Jas Obrecht, Joel Selvin, Colin Escott, Susan Schmidt Horning, Walt Everett, John Covach, Richard Carlin, and Marv Goldberg. Conversations early on with recording veterans Jim Dickinson, Larry Levine, Dave Gold, Stan Ross, Roland Janes, Earl Palmer, Cosimo Matassa, and Carol Kaye gave me a tangible connection to the time I wanted to write about. These interviews were a key step in bringing the book's vast, diffuse topic into focus. Nourishing talks with friends and colleagues are vital in the otherwise solitary research and book-writing process. Thanks to Alex Stewart, Travis Jackson, Andy Flory, John Howland, Nancy Newman, Matt Malsky, Michael Long, Serge Lacasse,

Mark Spicer, Gabriel Solis, Rich Crawford, Phil Ford, Eric Santos, Peter Schmelz, Mark Clague, Daniel Worley, Thomas Bass, Simon Zagorski-Thomas, and John Prihoda for sharing ideas, sources, stories, tunes, and jokes. I owe a special debt of thanks to Bill Shea. Expert in the repertory, historiography, and technological issues of postwar pop music, he read the entire manuscript and returned it with copious annotations. I'm grateful for his interest and willingness to share his knowledge, and the book is certainly better for it.

Acquisitions editor Chris Hebert, who first brought me in to the University of Michigan Press to propose and ultimately coedit the Tracking Pop series, has been my trusted reader and sounding board. I have relied on his eye, ear, and literary intelligence throughout the process. Press director Phil Pochoda was an early supporter of both the series and this book. And my series coeditors, Lori Burns and John Covach, have been, as they remain, a pleasure to work with. I appreciate the feedback from the anonymous readers whose comments led me to further refine the manuscript, and the editorial precision and general helpfulness of the press's editorial and production staff.

Research trips require room and board. Cynthia Thomas, Andrew and Maria Zak, and John and Jitka Wiley shared their homes and fine company over many days and nights. Since I wrote this book while serving as chair of the Music Department at Albany, logistical support has been critical. For the reliable daily assistance that allowed me time to write, I am deeply indebted to Bernadette Socha, whose official title of Music Department secretary hardly begins to describe her role. Finally, for all-around support, my family—parents and siblings, my wife Victoria, and my daughter Sally—have been, as ever, true blue. My heartfelt thanks to all who helped me get from there to here.

Introduction

The story of American popular music in the 1950s has about it the feel of absurdist fiction. Even the bare outline is strange to recount: how the nation drifted away from its love affair with the grand tradition of big band swing music and into a period of musical nihilism; how once stable conventions of musical style and practice were overwhelmed by tides of aimless novelty; how inanimate musical objects—records—became the most common medium of musical experience; how young, unschooled musicians rose almost overnight to positions once reserved for those of the highest professional attainment; how entrepreneurs with little experience of the music business and just as little capital competed effectively with large and powerful corporations; how the whims of teenagers exerted a deciding aesthetic and commercial authority in the music marketplace; how popular music came to both reflect and contribute to changes in America's social and cultural fabric; and how beneath a surface of apparent trivia ran a deep current of transformation.

Several historical accounts have mapped aspects of the fifties' musical terrain. Among these, the early standouts are Arnold Shaw's *The Rockin' Fifties* (and its complement, *Honkers and Shouters*) and Charlie Gillett's *The Sound of the City,* which take an encyclopedic approach to the decade's tumultuous music business. By contrast, Glenn Altschuler's *All Shook Up,* Michael Bertrand's *Race, Rock, and Elvis,* and Brian Ward's *Just My Soul Responding* concentrate on the music's role in social history. Philip Ennis crafts a useful hybrid of the two approaches in *The Seventh Stream,* which will make an appearance in my chapter 4. And James Miller, in *Flowers in the Dustbin,* offers a critical account from the perspective of a longtime rock music journalist with a scholarly turn of mind.

Despite these commendable works, I was drawn deeper into the topic by a host of unanswered questions. The problem might be summarized in a single illustrative musical contrast: compare Bing Crosby and the Andrews Sisters' "Ac-Cent-Tchu-Ate the Positive" to the Byrds' "Mr. Tambourine Man," top-tier pop hits in 1945 and 1965, respectively. Though separated by a mere twenty years, these records bear stark differences in their conceptions of songwriting, performance style, rhythmic feel, instrumentation, arranging, and record production. How does their historical proximity square with such unqualified contrast? What explains such a rapid reorientation of the pop mainstream? How was the musical economy and its lingua franca so transformed? The rise of rock and roll—the unlikely, upstart, music industry party crasher—has long provided the pat answer. But the emergence of rock and roll itself poses yet more questions. What sort of market turmoil would admit largely amateur and inelegant records into the company of the industry establishment's pop finery? How could inexperienced, overnight stars eclipse Crosby and Sinatra? What public mood encouraged such widespread aesthetic revolt? The postwar period was clearly a watershed for American pop music, but what were the causes and what changes accrued to the nation's public soundscape and its musical consciousness?

These are the broad questions that impelled this book. The clues to the story would certainly lie in the era's hit records—those that managed to stake a place in the public ear and heart—which have over time evolved from entertainment commodities to historical documents. While myriad events shaped the postwar musical climate, the key catalyst was sound recording. As collaborative artworks, records represent the spectrum of pop music's artists and artisans: songwriters, arrangers, performers, producers, and sound engineers. As commodities they fueled the ambitions and imaginations of entrepreneurs and offered the general public—with each retail purchase or jukebox selection—the opportunity to make known a personal aesthetic choice. As historical witnesses, they report what went into their making and give us an accurate account of what captured the contemporary ear. As radio programming, they are mass media; on a phonograph, they provide the soundtrack to an individual life. Operating in all these capacities, records in the postwar years fueled a cultural dynamism beyond anyone's control. They enabled, even fostered, a revolution and then remained to provide their own account of what had happened.

The early signs of upheaval were apparent in the waning position of swing era jazz. The swing era (from roughly 1930 to 1945), which spawned and sustained the big bands, was a time of extraordinary artistry in American popular music. It was a period when popular song and cutting-edge jazz merged to form a sophisticated entertainment music that delighted both connoisseur and casual fan. Its conventional practices amounted to a common language shared among composers, arrangers, performers, and a broad musical public. There was an ever-expanding body of repertory that included a core of canonic standards. Performance practices demanded a high level of technical competence. The idiom represented the artistic aspirations of a generation of gifted musicians even as it was embraced across the social spectrum as the most popular music in the land. It was "a style and aesthetic of jazz," wrote Gunther Schuller in his epic account, *The Swing Era,* "which reflected a preponderance of American popular taste." It was "the only time in its history when jazz was completely in phase with the social environment, and when it both captured and reflected the broadest musical common-denominator of popular taste in the nation."[1]

In the wake of the swing bands' exit from pop's center stage, there arose an unprecedented traffic in recordings of diverse idiom and provenance. Each week saw the release of more than a hundred new records, infusing the market with a rambunctious energy the industry could scarcely control. While the nation's common soundtrack had long been shaped by forces in New York and Hollywood, records now issued from almost every region of the country and were aimed at almost every kind of audience, a musical Babel reflecting the nation's own unruly cultural mix. In their day, the prominent bands were relatively stable musical institutions whose life cycles lasted at least several years. A hit record, on the other hand, might catch the public fancy overnight, often fading just as quickly in a universe of records vying for the public ear—like stars burning at differing intensities, flickering on and off at random, and sometimes shooting across the sky.

Swing was the culmination of a popular music tradition that stretched back to the early nineteenth century and included a wealth of entertainment music: society orchestras, "military" bands, a multihued solo piano repertory, singing groups of all sorts, Broadway shows, Tin Pan Alley songs, and Hollywood films (both silent and talkies). The common thread among all of these was music notation, a technology that, in the form of song sheets and arrangements, captured musical thought and provided a medium for commodification. Swing jazz, of course, also included improvised music making, but its tunes and arrangements were squarely within the written tradition. There was, meanwhile, a new technology abroad—sound recording—that captured not only musical thought but action. As such, it had the potential to change the concept of music "writing" altogether to include sound as an element of music inscription. For centuries, while notated music was rendered anew with each performance, its only enduring form was on the page. No ephemeral instance of a piece could claim to *be* the piece. Sound recording, however, blurred the historical distinction between writing and performing, ascribing to sound the same fixed, defining qualities as notes, rhythms, and words. This de facto reality took some time to sink in, for it required a rethinking of age-old ideas.

I begin with an account of the music industry's early difficulties in coming to terms with recordings, and, in one way or another, the theme is a recurring one throughout the book. While records were a key factor in reshaping postwar pop—removing most barriers that had historically confined certain music to certain audiences and affording record makers a nimble medium for creative experiment—it took many years of contentious wrangling for their potential to be unleashed. Publishers, performing rights societies, record companies, radio networks, government agencies, and individual musicians and their collective union all tussled in the courts over questions of records' value and purpose. A slippery conceptual problem underlay the debate. For while mundane financial concerns drove the negotiations and court battles, the persistent difficulty in arriving at lasting agreements lay in the new technology's alchemic power to reshape the very nature of music and, in turn, its role in society and the marketplace. Musical sound had never before known permanence and its corollary, repeatability. The far-reaching ramifications of this new status whittled away at the structures of the musical economy as old attitudes persisted in vain attempts to force recordings to behave according to historical precedent. The rapid evolution of record production and reception in the postwar years reflected a dawning realization that sound recording's transformative potential was already at work on the public mind. Its power, in the end, was irresistible; it was time to embrace the machine as a musical partner.

While the postwar marketplace suddenly teemed with upstart record labels releasing music unfamiliar to the mainstream, the effects of the new recording culture also disturbed long-established habits at the major labels. Chapter 2 focuses on what was widely referred to (by some enthusiastically, by others derisively) as the "new sound," a new pop wave that diverged markedly from the swing ethos. Mainstream pop records reached new levels of artifice as it became common to manipulate sound using various electronic techniques, to invent ad hoc instrumental ensembles and outlandish arrangements, and to record songs that, by Tin Pan Alley standards, fell in the category of novelty—trashy, throwaway amusement. In a decade filled with critical controversy, dire predictions of cultural demise, and a persistent wish for a return of the high-pop big bands, records like Frankie Laine's "Mule Train" and Johnnie Ray's "Cry" were among the initial wave of hit records to raise the alarm. The critical consensus held that sound recording was meant not to invade and manipulate real world musical experience but to document it and make it portable; studio trickery was an unseemly affront to musical intelligence. Mitch Miller, Columbia's head of A&R (artists and repertoire) for pop singles, was a perennial whipping boy, yet he was also the most successful record producer of the time. What were widely dismissed by his critics as "gimmicks" he saw as creative innovation, and with the public's enthusiastic acceptance he spearheaded a blasphemous conception of record production that prized novelty of song, arrangement, performance, and sound.

While the effervescent tricks of record making proved enormously popular, the public mood also suggested a more encompassing notion of novelty that included a curiosity for the wonders of unfamiliar musical idioms. Taking advantage of this demand were the hustling independent record men who tenaciously pursued hits in places the musical establishment had rarely explored. Chapter 3 moves off the industry's beaten paths to where hustlers pursued unheralded performers and rushed them via records onto the national stage. As the discs spun over the airwaves, they reached audiences no one even knew existed, adventurous young listeners with surprisingly catholic tastes. Music by black performers, their voices unvarnished for mainstream sensibilities, increasingly inhabited the same market as mainstream pop stars. Records by young performers more spirited than skilled spun alongside the best efforts of seasoned entertainers. Production standards no major label would tolerate seemed only to add a poignant charm to rough-hewn discs made in garages and storefronts.

As record buyers behaved unpredictably, industry veterans faced the ongoing conundrum explored in chapter 4: crossover. Markets had long been organized to cater to specific social and regional groups. But when large numbers of records spilled out of their intended markets in response to unexpected audience demand, the system grew volatile. Guesswork, luck, theft, creativity, and plain accident all played a part in navigating the industry's ongoing tumult. Ultimately the dynamism, in both the industry and the broader society, produced a generation of young musicians for whom an eclectic universe of records was the chief frame of musical reference. Theirs was a sensibility infused not only with a multitude of stylistic idioms but a willingness to mix those styles indiscriminately, which the recording medium deftly accommodated. In "writing" records, recording teams could forge collages of divergent performance styles that redefined the notion of authenticity.

Elvis Presley's Sun sessions illustrate the point. True to the spirit of his famous quip (this book's title), each record is a mixture of country and R&B elements, but none is really country or rhythm and blues. No less than Mitch Miller's efforts, they are imaginary concoctions hatched in a recording studio. In his spectacular popularity and his embrace of music across the pop spectrum, Presley came to symbolize the spirit of the time. His run of number-one concurrent hits on the pop, country, and R&B charts was unprecedented and remains unmatched. But if his achievement was unique in its commercial impact, it was also a sign of a broader movement. Before rock and roll was an idiom, it was a process of absorption, revision, and fusion of disparate influences. Presley, like his peers, became a rock and roll star by immersing himself in the rock and roll process, that is, by embodying the era's haphazard convergence of musical dialects.

Chapter 5 pauses to reflect on technology's role in the systemic shakeup. Since its invention, sound recording had been dedicated to the faithful rendering of musical events. Unlike filmmaking, recording was seen not as a creative endeavor but a craft subservient to music making. Records certainly had an existence apart from the performances they contained, but they had no identity of their own; they were representations. The idea made sense as long as recordings aimed to produce snapshots of music as performed in concert halls and nightclubs. But after the war pop music producers became fascinated with creating music in recording studios that existed nowhere else. The artifice that recordists had sought to disguise was instead put on display, pressed into the novelty project. Further, among indie firms that produced records under all sorts of makeshift conditions, fidelity was a moot concept. Surprisingly, the public readily accepted records that sounded nothing like anyone's real world acoustic experience, records that in effect presented listeners with an aural fantasy. Taken together, the artifice and lo-fi sounds meant that records had to be either accepted as things in themselves or dismissed as musical gibberish.

The final two chapters follow the evolution of the pop mainstream in the latter half of the fifties and the early years of the sixties as a climate of accelerating ferment brought forth yet another new wave—rock and roll—sweeping aside the previous one. Unlike country or R&B, rock and roll never had its own tracking charts for radio, jukebox, and retail. The music struck a turbulent industry such that it took up residence on the pop charts alongside mainstream stars before anyone even knew what it was. The most experienced hands in the music business and music press struggled to fathom a rapidly shifting terrain deluged by a disorienting rush of sound. At first, the term *rock and roll* appeared to describe no distinct musical style; it was only an alternative word for *R&B*. On the other hand, records such as the Orioles' "It's Too Soon to Know" (1948) or Don Howard's "Oh, Happy Day" (1952), which seemed to have no place among the day's pop hits, signaled unexplained disturbances. As such anomalies accumulated, most associated with young performers and audiences, they took on an irresistible momentum. Because they came onto the scene at random, they brought to the mainstream an unpredictable diversity of sound and style that gradually evolved into a musical idiom unlike its predecessors.

Throughout the book I cite from contemporary accounts in newspapers, magazines, and the trade press. In the first years of the rock and roll explosion (1955–57), we see a remarkable degree of confusion in defining the style features of the new music and conflicted speculation about its significance and the musical economy's future course. Adding to the problem of seeing where things were headed, rock and roll did not immediately take the stage from its pop predecessors. The sales charts of the late fifties were a motley collection of rock and roll and older pop styles with ample evidence of cross-pollination. Rather than a battle between distinct musical idioms, the market was a free-for-all grab for audience share, one record at a time. The new sounds pointed in no particular direction, yet, paradoxically, it was the era's unfocused meandering that fueled its revolutionary thrust. In a period filled with unlikely events, perhaps the most improbable was that the mosaic of disparate recordings accumulating in the public soundscape would ever coalesce into a coherent language. When it finally did, its rhetoric reflected its mixed heritage. The book ends with the Beatles' stunning arrival on the world stage, a crystallizing moment that showed, finally, that the previous decade's chaotic clamor was in fact the sound of genesis.

I was drawn to this story some years ago, initially interested less in the music per se than in its historical situation as the immediate precursor to sixties rock, which decades later remains an enduring force in pop music. The sixties rock musicians who raised record making to a new height of creative accomplishment grew up on fifties rock and roll. Its early icons, though mostly eclipsed from the sixties sales charts, were regularly invoked as founding figures. An exploration of these origins promised a deeper understanding of the classic rock era and, perhaps, the nature of its pervasive influence.

But as I made my way through the topics and characters, the music gradually claimed its rightful, central place. Over years of listening to records across the pop spectrum, I was seduced by their whimsical detachment from acoustic reality and cultural roots, their willful contrivance. Whatever their differences, the records shared something fundamental. For the most part, these were not faithful documents of any existing live performance culture but artworks unto themselves created in short bursts of interaction among members of recording teams. I was struck by their radicalism, their bold break with the past not only in terms of musical style but in an unabashed marriage of music and technology that other idioms resisted or disguised. As I better understood the conceptual significance of fifties production practices, their connections to the rhetoric of sixties record making became quite concrete. The aesthetic space and creative energy for rock's brilliant eruption in the sixties was opened up and primed by developments in the previous decade. It was not only the fifties' songs and artists that lingered in pop's collective consciousness but an entire musical worldview.

Understanding the sea change in postwar pop music, then, calls for an exploration of the full range of its bustling traffic in hit records. The disc market best illustrates the wrenching transition from swing to rock because it represents all participants—performers, writers, producers, record firms, publishers, fans, deejays, critics, jukebox operators, and recording engineers. Records' mass popularity across a diverse social cross section asserted cultural values arrived at in a largely democratic process, with music fans' record purchases, jukebox selections, and radio station requests counting as votes taken at the grass roots. Fans registered their preferences in a market of songs and sounds. Because records contained both, they conveyed a sense that song and voice were of a piece. That self-evident yet extraordinary idea formed an inescapable undercurrent of musical life, driving changes no one really understood and upending long-standing aesthetic, social, and commercial conventions. This book, at its core, is the story of that idea.

ONE

Records on the Radio

*It amuses me to recall that when we first started spinning
disks on the air the record companies were almost
unanimous in their opposition to this new medium of
entertainment.*
　　　　　　　　　　　　—MARTIN BLOCK

· 1 ·

In the cultural churning of postwar America, radio, the nation's great
public medium, was in the midst of big changes. When wartime restrictions were lifted in 1946, applications for broadcast licenses soared and
new broadcast outlets sprang up across the country. By decade's end, the
number of licensed stations had more than doubled, from 943 to over
2,000. At the same time, the national radio networks and advertising
agencies, which for nearly two decades had substantially controlled programming nationwide by linking stations and feeding programs coast-to-
coast over telephone lines, were turning their attention to television, as
were the stars who had made radio such a successful entertainment
medium. In 1949, network advertising revenues began what would prove
an irreversible decline.[1] The increased numbers of stations coinciding
with dwindling network programming caused a splintering that saw individual stations, much as in radio's pre-network infancy, forced into
greater self-reliance. With fewer network feeds of big-budget, live drama
and music productions, along with the ads from their large corporate
sponsors, programmers renewed their focus on the local markets lying
within range of their signals.

As station directors worked to attract audiences, which, in turn, attracted the spot advertisements for local products, recordings of popular
music proved invaluable. The discs were plentiful, they were relatively
cheap to acquire, and they were popular with the public. (Immediately
following the war, record sales exploded, with Columbia reporting a
sales increase of 850 percent from 1945 to 1946 and all of the other large
companies registering profit increases of at least 100 percent.)[2] Moreover,
records offered flexibility to programmers seeking to build and hold an

audience. It was a simple matter to add or remove a record from a station's playlist. Attuned to local tastes and trends, and free of network scheduling and strictures, radio stations became more nimbly responsive. Using records, they could tailor their offerings to create a particular station identity or quickly respond to listeners' requests. Further, the boom in record sales led to dozens of start-up record companies specializing in regional or ethnic styles that broadened and enriched programming possibilities. With programmers, record hustlers, and the listening public joined in what one radio historian has described as a headlong dash "into the wide-open field of electronic entertainment and salesmanship," the public soundscape took on a dynamic effervescence.[3]

While the years of network-dominated radio, the so-called Golden Age, had produced a certain coast-to-coast consistency in programming at the most powerful and prestigious stations, the airwaves had always had the potential for exuberant eclecticism, the sort of dizzying mix the Radio Act of 1927 sought to contain. In radio's earliest days, the medium was both a maverick's paradise and a marketing free-for-all. Another historian tells us that in Texas alone, between 1921 and 1927, "dozens of radio stations were established by individuals on their back porches, newspapers wanting to increase circulation, universities as experiments in classes, churches to spread their messages, electronic and department stores to sell receivers and give buyers something to which to listen, hotels for publicity, entertainment parks and movie theaters for publicity, and many others, including, interestingly enough, automobile repair shops."[4] Once the government began imposing regulations and networks assumed a veneer of corporate decorum, some broadcasters set up shop in Mexico, beaming their signals back across the border with high-powered transmitters five times more powerful than the strongest U.S. signals. Beyond regulatory control, stations such as XERF and XERB broadcast their programming as far as Washington, Michigan, and New York with 250,000-watt transmitters. In the signal were the voices of faith healers, astrologers, preachers, cowboy singers, and various snake oil merchants, all mixing it up in a surreal potpourri of disembodied sound.

In the postwar era, with the waning of the large networks' power and influence, American radio entered a period of decentralization that saw a resurgence of some of the local color that had characterized its early years. With at least a hundred records released each week, there was a vast pool to draw from, with musical styles and idioms to appeal to nearly every taste. There was, of course, the great pop mainstream. But there were also record labels specializing in gospel music, Yiddish music, Mexican music, blues, hillbilly, polka, and more. Whatever demographic the station and its sponsors catered to, there were records to fill the bill. The radio dial provided access to an abundance of cultural expression that made the airwaves a pluralistic cornucopia. In the hands of a free spirit such as Memphis deejay Dewey Phillips—whose show ranged from Sister Rosetta Tharpe to Hank Williams—records enabled the kind of cultural blend that America promised yet rarely delivered. Radio freed listeners from the social constraints associated with live music making. One need not go to a strange or forbidden neighborhood to hear its music or to come up with an admission fee. The radio could take a listener to musical worlds of wholly unfamiliar yet fascinating sounds, jostling one another as they perched side by side on the dial. Choosing one station or another was entirely at the discretion of individual listeners.

But in its Golden Age, radio would have been in a position neither to foster nor to capitalize on this kind of grassroots dynamism. Recordings, both the medium and the fuel for the emerging upheaval, had been consigned to specific functions, secondary to and far less prestigious than live programming. As a matter both of economic self-interest and opinions about what constituted quality entertainment, the New York–based networks had consistently upheld the view that the live broadcast was radio's gold standard and records were a poor, second-rate programming choice. Moreover, networks were not alone in opposing broadcast recordings. Although it would come to seem as though radio and records were made for one another, the marriage initially faced widespread resistance.

· 2 ·

In 1946, Bing Crosby, coming off "a long, fat decade" as the era's biggest musical star, was ready for a change.[5] In addition to his unsurpassed success as a recording artist and his popularity as a film star, his radio show, *Kraft Music Hall,* was the preeminent variety show of its time, offering a mixture of music, comedy, and chummy conversation between Crosby and a who's who roster of celebrity guests. But Crosby was tired of the rigid schedule of weekly live shows. Why, he wondered, couldn't the show be recorded, "transcribed," and broadcast from disc? As things stood, Crosby was tied to the studio in New York, and the performances had to be repeated to accommodate East and West Coast time zones. Recording several shows at once, and holding them for later broadcast, would free up his time. More important, he insisted, the show could be made better. Recording more material than was necessary to fill the half-hour time slot, the production team could cull the best "jokes, gags, or situations . . . the solid stuff that played big."[6] Songs could be recorded before the show and again in front of the studio audience. The best take could be edited, "dubbed," into the final transcription. The show would also benefit from a freer use of improvisation, which would add a feeling of spontaneity, while retaining editorial control. Any of the ad-libs that didn't work could simply be cut out of the final product.

Both the show's sponsor, Kraft Foods, and the NBC radio network that aired it were dead set against Crosby's idea; in their view, recordings were simply no substitute for the real thing. Recordings did not sound as good as a live broadcast, they argued, and lacked the sense of unique occasion. The network had vast resources in equipment, performers, engineers, studios, and sponsor revenue that individual radio stations could not match, and its ability to offer big stars in real time set network programming apart from locally produced fare and certainly from recordings. A recording of the show would put the network in the position of being little more than a middleman between the advertisers and the radio stations, with little to distinguish it from the transcription services that sold packages of recorded material. The slippery slope could only lead to disaster, a prospect neatly summarized in a brief *New York Times* announcement: "If Mr. Crosby's transcription arrangement works out in practice . . . it may set a trend for other stars to seek similar arrangements. . . . Needless to say, some quarters in radio do not relish the prospect, since the 'live' program . . . is the heart of the network's raison d'être."[7]

The network's long-standing policy against broadcasting recorded sound had its roots in attitudes that arose in the 1920s, when the epithet "canned music" was used, as one radio man has phrased it, "to imply all the shabby elements of third-rate broadcasting."[8] In the early 1920s, as the federal government struggled to come up with policies governing radio broadcast frequencies, the use of phonograph records as program material was prohibited for stations seeking a Class B license, which allowed a station significant power and a spot in the prime frequency range. There was no value to the public in cluttering the limited airwaves with sounds that could be obtained in other ways. "Phonograph records . . . had no real value as entertainment or instruction," wrote David B. Carson, in a memo dated January 27, 1922, to the assistant secretary of commerce. Carson, who was commissioner of the Bureau of Navigation, which administered the Radio Act of 1912, further claimed that broadcasting records "threatened to . . . interfere with the higher classes of service."[9] Later that year the office of the secretary of commerce (at the time Herbert Hoover) announced first that "mechanically operated musical instruments [phonographs, piano rolls, and music boxes] may be used only in an emergency and during intermission periods in regular programs." Soon thereafter, the rule was further tightened to stipulate that "the use of mechanically operated instruments is prohibited."[10] Stations seeking Class B licenses, which included most large stations that would eventually comprise the infrastructure of the networks, already relied to a great extent on live talent. With the new rules in place, they stopped playing records altogether.

The issue was far from settled. The Radio Act of 1927 created the Federal Radio Commission (FRC), which continued to tussle with the problem, its evolving rules reflecting the sense of treading unfamiliar new territory. While the commission recognized the complexity of the issue—the fact, for example, that stations in "smaller towns and farming communities" had less access to live "program resources"—it was concerned above all "that the limited facilities for broadcasting should not be shared with stations which give the sort of service which is readily available to the public in another form." Furthermore, in the commission's view, "the real purpose of the use of phonograph records in most communities is to provide a cheaper method of advertising for advertisers who are thereby saved the expense of providing an original program." The prospect of allowing stations to use records to constrain advertising rates, thus keeping "some other stations . . . out of existence which might put to use . . . original program material," was something the commission was keen to avoid.[11] In the end, the FRC created regulations, set forth in a series of General Orders, that left a degree of wiggle room. Playing records on the air was not expressly forbidden, but the general view remained that they were a poor substitute for live performances. For those with the means to produce original shows, then, it made sense, in terms both of status and avoiding governmental entanglement, simply to avoid broadcasting phonograph records.

Crosby, of course, was not asking to play records on the air. What he wanted was to record transcription discs of his program. Transcription discs, unlike mass-market 78 rpm records, were recorded specifically for radio broadcast. They were not sold retail, and their format was different from the consumer products. A 78 contained recordings made in wax, which had been transferred to a master plate for mass production; transcription discs were themselves recording media capable of recording, playback, and duplication. They had less surface noise than 78s, and, because of their large size (sixteen inches) and relatively slow 33 1/3 rpm speed, they could hold more program material, up to fifteen minutes per side. They were used widely in the production of local programming, advertising spots, and air checks and served as a distribution alternative to the networks' telephone lines. One of the first syndicated radio shows, *Amos and Andy,* which originated at Chicago station WMAQ, was distributed on transcription discs before being picked up for live broadcast by NBC. In the 1930s, there were four major transcription services dedicated to recording and leasing discs, including recordings of network programming.

Transcription discs, however, had their own contentious history, different from but related to that of broadcast records. The government's concern centered on truth in advertising: the public was to be fully informed of what they were hearing. Again, rules and attitudes evolved throughout the 1930s. The language of the 1929 FRC General Order 78 required that transcriptions be preceded by an announcement: "This program is an electrical transcription made exclusively for broadcast purposes."[12] While this made a regulatory distinction between mass-market records and recordings made specifically for radio use, many broadcasters considered the language cumbersome and confusing. It was also disruptive since it was required at the beginning of every side of recorded programming even if this meant interrupting the program flow. The announcement rule was amended in the 1932 FRC Rules and Regulations, which replaced the General Orders, allowing the announcement to be streamlined and written in such a way as to fit into the program in the least intrusive way. Again, however, the suggested language was vague and open to interpretation. One suggestion, for instance, was to announce, "This is a mechanical reproduction," a term that might fit either a record or a transcription. In response to criticism, FRC commissioner H. A. Lafount articulated the spirit of the regulation in a statement of February 13, 1932. "It is my personal view," he wrote, "that no attempt should be made to 'fool the public' in the announcement of phonograph records. . . . [E]very ordinary record performed must be described in clear terms each time it is played. There should be a distinction, however, between phonograph records and transcriptions made exclusively for broadcast purposes."[13]

Of greater concern to broadcasters and production companies than the announcement language was the requirement that it precede the playing of each side of recorded programming. The World Broadcasting System, one of the largest transcription services, hired a former FRC commissioner, Judge Ira E. Robinson, to lobby on its behalf to change the rule to one announcement at the end of the program so as not to prejudice listeners with an opening disclaimer. He argued that under the current Rule 176, transcriptions were "stigmatized in a class with more ordinary phonograph records; advertisers [are] fearful that the public do not appreciate phonograph records and stations [are] fearful that their credit before the Commission is harmed by the use of anything but live talent."[14] The argument continued through the formation of the FRC's successor, the Federal Communications Commission, which was created by the Communications Act of 1934. Finally, on January 28, 1936, the FCC issued a revision of Rule 176 that acceded to World's argument that recorded programming should not be broken up every fifteen minutes yet at the same time undermined Robinson's plea for transcriptions' special status. In essence, the rule placed all programming on an equal footing so long as the public was furnished an accurate description of the medium involved, stipulating, "Where a transcription is used it shall be announced as a 'transcription' . . . and where a phonograph record is used it shall be announced as a 'record.'"[15] The FCC ruling injected some common sense into a debate fraught with misrepresentations based on competing commercial interests. Finally, the "ordinary" phonograph record now stood alongside other program material as, if not equal in status, at least a legitimate broadcasting choice. Clearing the government's hurdles, however, was only the beginning.

· 3 ·

During the 1930s and early 1940s, the music industry at large struggled to come to terms with new technologies that rapidly permeated its fiber. The competitive wrangling was confused; stances shifted as the factions lurched forward in an unfamiliar world where allies and adversaries could be difficult to discern and positions could change overnight. Musical performance had always been restricted to a particular time and place, available only to those present. Sound recording and broadcasting had overturned this historical fundamental and, in turn, changed the rules and procedures by which profits were generated and distributed. The first half of the twentieth century saw a near continuous series of court battles attempting to reconcile new realties with established practices. Cases were argued in matters of property rights, labor rights, fair trade, monopoly, privacy, and anything else that could conceivably be analogized with what was acknowledged to be an unprecedented cultural and legal situation. The parties included an alphabet soup of organizations, most newly formed—including ASCAP, NAB, MPPA, SPA, NAPA, AFM, MMG, and IRNA—as well as individual artists, radio stations, record companies, and the networks, all competing with one another for advantage on a tumultuous cultural frontier.[16] The music business in the electronic era, *Time* magazine told its readers, had become "a huge and complicated industry in which the artist, the advertiser, the salesman, and the inventor fought ceaselessly for expression and profit."[17]

Although commercial self-interest lay at the core of the various parties' positions, even such elemental motives rested on shifting sands. Record companies, for example, the two largest of which were owned by radio networks (RCA Victor by NBC and Columbia by CBS), went through a period in which they opposed broadcasting their products. If people could hear records for free, the argument went, why would anyone buy them? "The use of our commercial records by small broadcasters," one RCA Victor executive wrote in a 1933 letter to NBC president David Sarnoff, "injures the sale of our records."[18] To offset the perceived sales impact, the companies sought to extend their product rights beyond the point of sale. With no legal foundation, they simply asserted the right, printing such phrases as "For Home Use Only" and "Not Licensed for Radio Broadcast" on their records. When broadcasters ignored the prohibition, lawsuits followed, yielding conflicting opinions. But if the courts sent mixed messages, the market gave clearer guidance. By the mid-1940s, there was no doubt that a radio broadcast, far from a giveaway, was actually a record company's best promotional tool for selling its products. The firms wasted little time in reversing their stances, and instead of serving radio stations with summonses they plied them with free records and sundry incentives in the hope that the stations would play their records as often as possible. Amid such volatility, the courts were repeatedly asked to mediate disputes using interpretations of laws that never envisioned the problems that electronic media now presented.

The property rights sought by record companies for their recordings had been granted to owners of song copyrights before the advent of radio. In 1897, the Copyright Act underwent one in a series of revisions that extended to musical works the same protection afforded dramatic works in the previous revision of 1856, asserting that "any person publicly performing or representing any . . . musical composition for which a copyright has been obtained, without the consent of the proprietor of said . . . musical composition . . . shall be liable for damages therefor."[19] In other words, copyright holders were due payment not only for sales of their properties but also for their use. A further revision in 1909, by which time it was clear that recordings and piano rolls were sources of substantial profit, included protection for musical works presented through mechanical media. The problem, however, was enforcement. There were no practical means for individual copyright holders to track all the performances of their properties let alone to combat unauthorized ones. The solution, many writers and publishers felt, was to form a performing rights society on the model of European ones such as the Société des auteurs, compositeurs et éditeurs de musique (SACEM), which was founded in France in 1871. Such societies acted as central licensing agencies, representing their members in fee negotiations, collections, and matters of enforcement. They collected royalty payments for the use of their members' musical properties in concert venues, hotels, nightclubs, recordings, and films, anywhere the music turned up, and distributed the money to members according to an agreed-upon scheme.

The American Society of Composers, Authors and Publishers was formed along these lines on February 13, 1914, by a group of 170 writers and 22 publishers. Its expressed purpose was

> to protect composers, authors, and publishers of musical works against piracies of any kind; to facilitate the administration of the copyright laws for the protection of composers, authors, and publishers of musical works; to promote and foster by all lawful means the interest of composers, authors, and publishers of musical works, and to grant licenses and collect royalties for the public representation of the works of its members, and to allot and distribute such royalties.[20]

While ASCAP was an important step forward for copyright holders, it was not entirely a model of solidarity. In the intensely competitive and uncertain climate of the time, songwriters and publishers, historical adversaries, felt impelled to start their own associations in addition to their ASCAP membership; the Songwriters Protective Association and the Music Publishers Protective Association were their respective representatives.

In its early years, as ASCAP struggled to carve out a power base, suing the likes of hotels, restaurants, and dance halls to enforce copyrights, the organization saw radio as an ally in promoting its members' music and allowed the struggling new medium free use of the music. But by 1923, unable to resist what was developing into a potential licensing bonanza, it began charging radio stations a blanket fee for broadcasting ASCAP members' music, which amounted to all of the most popular Tin Pan Alley, Broadway, and Hollywood tunes of the day. The next seventeen years were marked by repeated battles between ASCAP and radio's trade group, the National Association of Broadcasters, both in negotiating sessions and in the courts. Finally, in 1940, in response to a new ASCAP contract that would double licensing fees to 7 percent of broadcasters' gross receipts, the broadcasters started their own performing rights organization, Broadcast Music, Inc. (BMI)—40 percent of whose stock was soon acquired by NBC and CBS—and called for a ban on all ASCAP-licensed music.

At the time ASCAP had a virtual monopoly on mainstream pop music but had shown little interest in other idioms. Indeed, the membership rules and distribution formulas were such that most songwriters and composers outside the Tin Pan Alley mold were either denied membership or paid minimal royalties. To join, a writer had to be "regularly published" and sponsored by at least two members of the board and then seek approval from the membership committee.[21] In an organization dominated by a Tin Pan Alley songwriting aesthetic and the habits of New York publishing houses, outsiders, even a country music celebrity like Gene Autry, had a difficult time being admitted. Autry, in Senate testimony, recalled having "many numbers listed in folios, on records . . . and in those days they were considered big hits, but I still never could get into ASCAP." It was "a historical fact," he continued, "that writers and publishers of this kind of music were not admitted to ASCAP in any substantial manner." It was only after several years of movie stardom that Autry was finally admitted. As he found out, however, membership was no guarantee of royalty payments. "Even those of us who were admitted to ASCAP," he stated, "found that the ASCAP royalty distribution system . . . did not result in any substantial economic rewards to the writers and publishers of what I call country music."[22] The problem was that the distribution rules stipulated that only live performances on network radio programs counted toward royalty payments. The music for those performances was drawn overwhelmingly from the Tin Pan Alley song catalog.

The various shenanigans afoot in 1940 led the Justice Department to file antitrust charges against all concerned: ASCAP, BMI, NBC, and CBS. All parties soon settled by consent decree and negotiated new agreements. But the landscape had changed dramatically. In BMI, ASCAP now had a competitor throwing open the doors to the vast diversity of the nation's musical expression. Not only did BMI accept all kinds of music; it paid royalties on all aired performances, whether live or recorded, on networks or independent stations. All writers now had a conduit into the mainstream industry, which allowed country music, rhythm and blues, novelty pop, and finally rock and roll to compete with Tin Pan Alley songs over the same airwaves. Eventually ASCAP would adapt, but its diehard members would blame BMI for many years to come for what they saw as its poisonous influence on popular music. "I don't see how it can escape the charge," lyricist and impresario Billy Rose told a House Antitrust Subcommittee in 1956, "that it is responsible for rock-and-roll and the other musical monstrosities which are muddying up the airways."[23] Looking back from 1961, several musical light-years away from 1940, the trade weekly *Billboard* published an editorial that recognized the founding of BMI as a watershed moment.

> In our generation, the most profound change to come upon the music scene undoubtedly was the formation of Broadcast Music, Inc. The creation of BMI set up a chain reaction of developments which brought to American music a richer repertoire and a broader base. In a phrase: Tin Pan Alley is now the United States of America.[24]

While ASCAP's tough stance with broadcasters was in part a matter of greed, it also reflected a belief that radio's value in promoting songs was a two-edged sword sowing instability in the music production and marketing system. The incessant radio play that could turn a musical property into a quick best seller often diminished longer-term sales as its popularity waned before the sheet music had a chance to fulfill its market potential. The concern was expressed by lyricist and ASCAP president Gene Buck in 1936 in terms of a general malaise at the changing nature of public reception. He worried that the popular tunes of the day were becoming increasingly disposable, complaining that "In the old days, prior to radio broadcasting, it took three or four years for an American song to sink into the hearts of the people. Today, with more than 600 broadcasting stations, the popularity of any song, no matter how splendid it is, lasts no more than six weeks."[25] Buck's was a not uncommon fear of the rapid and apparently uncontrollable changes the music profession faced in its confrontation with technological evolution. In barely three decades of commercial sound recording, the national soundscape had changed from one inhabited by occasional music—at a band concert, a church gathering, a nightclub—to one where music poured from speakers dotted in their millions throughout the fabric of daily life.

Star performers had a similar property rights complaint to the record companies when it came to broadcasts of their recordings, although it was a matter of contention who, the company or the performer, should have the dominant claim against the broadcasters. While the Copyright Act of 1909 had addressed recordings, it did so only in the context of the music and words they contained, not the performances or the sounds of the records themselves. Once again, technology forced a reevaluation of long-standing ontological concepts. Because musical performances had never been functionally equivalent to written texts—that is, they had never been fixed, durable items—the idea of protecting them by copyright opened new legal territory. Performers were paid a fee to make records, and if they possessed sufficient star power they earned royalties on record sales, not by statute but by contract. Radio, however, complicated matters. The new medium allowed records to be used not simply for the enjoyment of those who purchased them but for the profit of a radio station playing them repeatedly, trading on the stars' names and their work without further compensation. Furthermore, the practice put musicians in competition with themselves both for radio work and audience share. Bandleader Fred Waring complained that at times his radio performances aired opposite his records. "I felt it unfair," he said, "for them to have our records playing in competition to us, and it was a growing menace to all performers."[26]

Seeking a remedy, many of the most popular bandleaders and singers, including Waring, Crosby, Paul Whiteman, and Guy Lombardo, formed the National Association of Performing Artists. Waring was elected president, and the organization, in the course of many court battles, pursued a claim of ownership rights for recording musicians. Reasoning that "the typical purchaser does not buy a record of just a song; he buys a record of someone's interpretation of that song," Waring aimed, through NAPA, "to add to the copyright law *the Right of Interpretation*."[27] His suit against radio station WDAS in Philadelphia in 1935 made its way two years later to the Pennsylvania Supreme Court, where the majority opinion, written by Judge Horace Stern, sided with Waring. Stern's opinion began with an acknowledgment of the unprecedented twofold problem posed by the combination of records and radio.

> The problems involved in this case have never before been presented to an American or an English court. They challenge the vaunted genius of the law to adapt itself to new social and industrial conditions and to the progress of science and invention. . . . Sound can now be mechanically captured and reproduced, not only by means of the phonographs for an audience physically present, but, through broadcasting, for practically all the world as simultaneous auditors.[28]

The court struggled to read the technological evidence using analogies with existing case law, but, concerned "adequately to do justice under current conditions of life," it was ultimately forced into untested waters.[29] Considering the question of whether "the performer's interpretation of a musical composition constitutes a product of such novel and artistic creation as to invest him with a property right therein," Stern looked to the market for practical guidance. Moving away from the general question of principle, he drew a distinction among performers based on their marquee value. Unlike rank-and-file musicians, star performers' "enduring fame" and "financial rewards" proved that their "interpretations definitely added something to the work of authors and composers."[30] He more than once referred to the Waring band's deal with the Ford Motor Company for $13,500 per radio show. He also found, as a matter of common sense, that the "Not Licensed for Radio Broadcast" label, far from the restraint of trade the other side alleged, was in fact "not unreasonable. . . . It was intended to effect a legitimate purpose," marking not only a musician's right to fair compensation but also a practical distinction. "Uses of the records on phonographs and for broadcasting purposes are so radically distinct," he wrote, "as to belong practically to two totally different fields of operation."[31]

But along with his comments on market value and practical use, Stern also waded, wittingly or not, into a long-standing aesthetic debate concerning the dualism of musical composition and musical performance. An idea well established among connoisseurs of classical music held that a musical work's enduring identity lay in the web of musical relationships represented in a composition's written score. Any given performance of the instructions contained in the score was an instance of the work but not the work itself, a concept reflected tacitly in both the copyright law and the sheet music business. But Stern declared:

> A musical composition in itself is an incomplete work; the written page evidences only one of the creative acts which are necessary for its enjoyment; it is the performer who must consummate the work by transforming it into sound. If, in so doing, he contributes by his interpretation something of novel intellectual or artistic value, he has undoubtedly participated in the creation of a product in which he is entitled to a right of property, which in no way overlaps or duplicates that of the author in the musical composition.[32]

The idea that a musical composition is an incomplete work was aesthetically startling and legally, as it turned out, well ahead of its time. Musical works had gained their status as enduring art through the technology of musical notation. Writing music down freed it from its evanescent nature and put it on a par with literary works, a concept borne out in the common term *music literature*. Stern, however, insisted that written music was only a template requiring a sounding representation in order to fulfill its artistic expression. From this singular perspective, musical works were by nature collaborative projects.

A second justice, Judge George Maxey, concurred "in the conclusion of the majority opinion but not in all its rationale." He ignored, in particular, the aesthetic aspects and flatly disagreed with Stern's unfair trade argument. Maxey framed his opinion narrowly, setting aside the question of value, monetary or aesthetic, and homing in on what he saw as "the invasion of an ancient right." Referring to Stern's opinion, Maxey asserted that "a plaintiff's right to such protection in a court of equity depends [not] on whether his production constitutes 'a novel and artistic creation' which 'elevates interpretations to the realm of independent works of art.' . . . I think plaintiff's right which was invaded by defendant was his right to privacy, which is a broader right than a mere right of property." In Maxey's opinion, arguments about value or ontology were beside the greater point. The broadcast of records when it had been expressly forbidden amounted to "old fashioned eavesdropping brought up to date with the aural assistance of modern devices." And, he reminded the court, "at common law eavesdropping was considered such an invasion of people's right to privacy that it was treated as something even baser than a civil wrong, to wit, a crime." The analogy was unassailable, he believed. "There is no moral or legal difference," he wrote, "between tapping telephone wires for the purpose of 'listening in' than there is in using for broadcasting a phonograph disk made by plaintiff in defiance of the maker's injunction written across this disk, to wit: 'Not licensed for radio broadcasting.'"

Commingling property rights and privacy rights, a groping court implicitly acknowledged that answers to such questions were elusive. (A later court decision would characterize Maxey's privacy argument as a "strange assertion.")[33] Yet despite Maxey's protest that his concurrence with Stern's opinion was based on entirely different logic and better-established precedent, in a roundabout way it accorded with the spirit of Stern's thinking. For in privileging the record's sounding elements—its performances—by invoking the analogy of a private telephone conversation, Judge Maxey was saying that the expressive act itself was due protection equal to that afforded copyright owners. Together, the two opinions set forth a conceptual framework for thinking about records and broadcasting that was novel not only in legal circles but in musical ones as well: a record's content was a totality of all its elements—song, arrangement, and performance.

Waring's victory held only for Pennsylvania. His larger plan was to bring about new revisions of the nation's Copyright Act, and his big stick was to be the lawsuit filed by attorneys for Paul Whiteman in New York City against W.B.O. Broadcasting, owner of the New York station

WNEW, "prohibiting the use for broadcasting purposes of any phonograph record, made and created by the plaintiff and his orchestra."[34] This was to be NAPA's "banner suit in that [Whiteman] was the most important musical artist of the day," Waring recalled.[35] He was confident that a win would provide the ammunition he needed to move a new copyright law through Congress. The suit, argued on principles of common law property rights, which provided a more flexible context for interpretation than any existing statutes, produced a mixed result. The trial judge, Vincent Leibell, agreed with the contention that Whiteman was by his "peculiar interpretations of musical compositions a creative musical artist." Furthermore, "The fact that Whiteman contributed something in addition to that which was already the subject of a copyright, the musical composition itself, cannot in any way detract from his right to protect what is his property, over and above existing property rights of the composer."[36] But in an unfortunate wrinkle for the musician's side, it was discovered that Whiteman's contract with RCA Victor had assigned rights to his records to the company. As the case went forward, Whiteman withdrew his suit and RCA named him, along with W.B.O., as defendants in the case, essentially claiming that any ownership rights the court declared to exist belonged to the corporation. It was a blow to Waring, losing his publicity shot with Whiteman, but in the end Leibell's decision upheld the principle Waring was fighting for. Leibell ruled against the broadcaster, and, even though he found that all of Whiteman's property rights had passed to RCA, Whiteman, too, was granted an injunction based on the unfair competition argument.

All parties appealed. Whiteman sought to recover his property rights, W.B.O. sought to void the injunctions altogether, and RCA, although it had won the case, appealed Judge Leibell's refusal to recognize its property rights in the records themselves. (The latter, in Leibell's judgment, was one of the case's "most controverted issues." Indeed, the nature of a record's content—which fuses musical composition, performance, and sonic rendering—presented an unprecedented and fundamental problem. Despite an acknowledgment of the firm's contributions—its recording engineers, facilities, and expertise—Leibell decided that the answer to the question of "whether or not the part played by RCA Victor Company in the recording of Whiteman's interpretation and renditions constituted such intellectual and artistic contributions as to vest in RCA a common law property right in what went on the record" was no.)[37] The appeal came before the Second Circuit Court of Appeals, which reversed the lower court's decision on July 25, 1940, in an opinion written by the renowned jurist Learned Hand. In short, as the *New York Times* reported later in the year after the Supreme Court declined to review the case, the decision held "that any common-law property rights ended with the sale of the records."[38]

Hand acknowledged the novelty of the case, saying it was

> only in comparatively recent times that a virtuoso, conductor, actor, lecturer, or preacher could have any interest in the reproduction of his performance. Until the phonographic record made possible the preservation and reproduction of sound, all audible renditions were of necessity fugitive and transitory; once uttered they died; the nearest approach to their reproduction was mimicry. Of late, however, the power to reproduce the exact quality and sequence of sounds has become possible, and the right to do so, exceedingly valuable.[39]

But, less impressed with its conceptual ramifications than the Pennsylvania court, Hand situated the case within a frame of strict legal reasoning. It had been long established, he pointed out, that the work of an "author" was "not limited to words" and that "the monopoly of the right to reproduce" such works "has at times been stated as though it extended to all productions demanding 'intellectual' effort." He allowed that "for the purposes of this case we shall assume that it covers the performances of an orchestra conductor, and—what is far more doubtful—the skill and art by which a phonographic record maker makes possible the proper recording of those performances upon a disc." Hand was willing to grant Whiteman's "intellectual" contribution as conductor the same legal status as a composer's or writer's so long as it was in the context of a live radio broadcast. Performances captured on records, however, fell in the category of "chattel," and "restrictions upon the uses of chattels," the judge wrote, "once absolutely sold are at least prima facie invalid."[40]

Distinguishing between live and recorded performances, Hand made room in the argument for the Copyright Act—precisely what the original suit had avoided because it undermined the common law property claim. The result was a kind of legal catch-22. Copyright, Hand explained, is a trade between an author and the government in which the author is granted a monopoly for a period of time, after which that individual "dedicates" his or her work to the public domain. Because records were not subject to copyright, however, they could not fulfill the bargain. If their use was restricted after sale, it would amount to a "perpetual monopoly," which would be "contrary to the whole policy of the Copyright Act and of the Constitution." The only protection for performers' recordings "must be found in extending statutory copyright to such works."[41] Since no such statute existed, Whiteman's work, though privileged as intellectual property, had no legal protection in its recorded form.

Copyright revision would come up repeatedly in Congress throughout the 1940s under the rubric of "interpretation," but nothing ever developed past the point of committee hearings and debate. Squaring both the practical and conceptual ramifications of sound recording with existing legal principles and statutes proved a thorny and persistent problem. In 1955, reviewing the confused situation, Harvard law professor Benjamin Kaplan wrote that "copyright law, precisely because it has taken shape around the model of a book communicated to the public by multiplication of copies, has experienced difficulty, not to say frustration, with cases where communication is by performance or representation." The problem was bigger, he argued, than individual court cases could handle. "Better than any solution open to the courts (or to state legislatures acting severally)," he concluded, "would be a proper rewriting of the Copyright Code to take care of the question of phonograph records."[42] The rewriting would not come until 1972.

After the Hand decision, things became increasingly difficult for NAPA as members began making their own separate deals. "Our enemies began working on our members," Waring said, and adversaries were spread throughout the industry: "the broadcasting stations, the disc jockeys, the publishers, the record companies, and even ASCAP, who feared that we would invade their rights and split their take."[43] By 1947, Whiteman himself was moonlighting as a celebrity disc jockey. He acknowledged that many found the idea "strange," but, as he explained in his book, *Records for the Millions,* although he "had won fame as King of Jazz and enjoyed a musical reputation far above that of the average platter spinner," he did not "consider a career as a disk jockey a step down in any sense." Whiteman was a pragmatist through and through. Although he received no royalties for his early RCA Victor recordings, he embraced the medium because, as he put it, "[R]ecords were my best bet for putting my band over." In the postwar years, he changed his earlier position on broadcasting discs because he realized that "nowadays it's the disk jockey who accounts for the greatest success of a vocalist or name band."[44]

· 4 ·

The most single-minded opponent of broadcasting records, indeed of records period, was the American Federation of Musicians president

James Caesar Petrillo, one of the most powerful labor leaders of the 1940s. "A scratch of his pen on the bottom of a one-paragraph letter," wrote *New York Times* radio editor Jack Gould, "usually has reverberations from the recesses of Tin Pan Alley to the halls of Congress."[45] For Petrillo, the issue was simple: canned music meant less work for the members of his union. All the proof he needed was provided by the advent of the sound film and the corresponding decline in theater orchestras. He was not about to let the same thing happen to musicians' radio jobs. He viewed transcribed performances of any sort as threats because once a musician's work was bought and paid for it could be used countless times without further compensation. Whether the music turned up on radio, jukebox, film, or a wired music service like Muzak, if no one was actually playing the music as it was heard, it meant a musician was not working. The struggle was, in Petrillo's words, the latest chapter in "the endless conflict between labor and machinery."[46] For Petrillo, battling on the side of labor was a sworn duty.

Amid rapid industrialization in an increasingly urban society, American musicians had begun banding together in the 1850s for mutual support and protection. Like other workers, they found in the rising union movement of the latter nineteenth century a network of fraternal solidarity that helped to offset the inequities and unpredictability of capitalist individualism. In 1886, several local unions from large eastern and midwestern cities banded together to form the National League of Musicians (NLM). Over the course of the next decade, competition developed between local chapters that sought affiliation with the larger labor movement represented by the American Federation of Labor (AFL), formed also in 1886, and those that viewed musicians' work as special and distinct from the likes of "stovemolders" or "shoemakers," as one union president put it.[47] The latter view prevailed for a time, reflecting the dominance of musicians from large eastern cities like New York and Philadelphia who made their living playing primarily classical music and viewed themselves as performing artists not laborers. The rough and tumble of the AFL—its tactics, politics, and social class—was a world apart from the "Silk Hats" that controlled the NLM.[48]

By 1896, the differences among NLM members led to the formation of a new association, the American Federation of Musicians, which within a few years had asserted complete control and driven the NLM out of existence. The change had aesthetic, as well as political and social, ramifications. The new union was more democratic than the NLM, more representative of all its members across the country, whatever sort of music they played. Increasingly, union leaders came to appreciate the effectiveness of other unions' coercive strategies. Exploiting the relative lack of sophistication in labor matters among the venues employing musicians (hotels, theaters, saloons)—especially their lack of a cooperative trade organization to counter the union—the AFM succeeded in establishing a significant presence in American labor in the first two decades of the twentieth century. While the AFM was more representative of its general membership than the NLM had been, there were still various internal stresses, including racial discrimination and the monopolistic practices of a well-connected elite. But in matters of competition between its members and any forces that threatened their livelihoods, the union was of one mind.

Joseph Weber, the union's president from 1900 to 1940, favored a measured approach to accommodating technological changes he viewed as inevitable. He worked actively but increasingly ineffectively to control the impact on musicians' employment caused by the rapidly evolving electronic media. Finally in 1937, responding to the increasing militancy of AFM members facing a complex array of powerful forces from across the electronic entertainment industry, Weber modified his long opposition to hard-line tactics, and at the AFM national convention in Louisville the union began developing a comprehensive plan for dealing with radio (networks and their affiliates, as well as independent stations), record companies, and film studios, which carried the coercive threat of strike action. The so-called National Plan of Settlement had mixed success among the various industries, but in radio it was, at first, remarkably effective. The union rules required, for example, that radio stations maintain staff orchestras with numbers corresponding to the station's size and location regardless of how much the orchestra was actually needed. When network affiliates balked, the union threatened to strike the parent network. Keen to avoid any work stoppage, the networks pressured their affiliates to accept the union's terms.

At first the National Plan was mutually beneficial, as union members saw their pay rise along with broadcasters' profits in the last two years of the decade. But when Weber sought to expand musicians' benefits to reflect the industry's record earnings, broadcasters refused to renew the agreement. Moreover, the Justice Department threatened to file suit against the union, alleging restraint of trade. In January of 1940, facing opposition from both the government and a determined radio industry, the AFM withdrew the plan and canceled its threatened strike. Later that year a restive membership elected Petrillo at the AFM convention in Indianapolis. He had a well-earned reputation as a tough, effective leader who had run the Chicago local through the 1920s and 1930s. As a teenager he had played "strictly a business trumpet," which summed up his pragmatic and egalitarian attitudes toward music and musicians. In the mind of a man whose immigrant father dug sewers in Chicago, there was no "difference between Heifetz and a fiddler in a tavern."[49] His commitment to musicians' employment was as unyielding as his autocratic nature, and under his leadership the union would become more confrontational than ever.

Petrillo is best remembered for ordering the recording ban that began on August 11, 1942, and continued until November 11, 1944. With the exception of V-Discs recorded for exclusive distribution among the armed forces, all instrumental music recording stopped (vocalists were not union members). Petrillo had convinced even such former holdouts as the Boston Symphony Orchestra to join the union, and when the ban went into effect he controlled practically every professional instrumentalist in the country. The ban was a battle royal, the Waring dispute writ large. The tactics, of course, were entirely different, as were the aims. The stars of NAPA sued radio stations to protect their records, which they saw as intellectual property. In the process, they sought to gain further compensation for their already lucrative efforts. Petrillo took on the record companies to secure more jobs and job security for rank and file union members, and would have been happiest had recording magically ceased altogether.

The record and broadcast industries—which in the cases of Columbia and RCA Victor were one and the same—set about a well-financed public relations campaign to smear Petrillo at every opportunity. Newspapers and Congress, some of whose members also owned radio stations, were easily swayed by charges that Petrillo was unpatriotic, selfish, and despotic. But the union chief held his ground, performing brilliantly in congressional hearings with a mix of evasive savvy and homespun little-guy humility. He painted union members—who recorded V-Discs at no charge, bought many thousands of dollars in war bonds, and served in uniform in large numbers—as patriotic citizens exemplifying the best in American aspirations for fair dealing in the face of corporate power. When he politely refused even President Roosevelt's plea to end the strike, the president pressed the matter no further.

Jack Kapp, president of Decca records, settled first in September of 1943. Unlike Columbia and Victor, Decca had no radio network to sustain revenues, nor did it have the additional concern of the other two firms that accommodation now would mean tougher negotiations on the next radio contract. Kapp agreed to pay the union a royalty on each record sold, the monies to be distributed among locals across the country and paid to musicians in return for performing in free public concerts. Capitol records followed a month later, but Columbia and RCA Victor held out for another year before capitulating. Petrillo proclaimed it "the greatest victory for a labor organization in the history of the labor movement," but, despite the overheated rhetoric from all sides, the recording ban turned out to be little more than a temporary inconvenience to the industry.[50] It was yet another front, representing another perspective, in the futile struggle to control the fallout of sound recording. Unlike earlier battles among wealthy corporations, associations, and individuals, the AFM ban concerned the everyday lives of common working musicians striving to come to terms with an unstoppable force that was both alluring and potentially threatening. The situation, however, was more complex and ambiguous than Petrillo allowed. Some two-thirds of union members, all of whom benefited from the royalty fund, did not earn their primary living through music and rarely if ever recorded. For the top professionals who made records and many of whom opposed the ban, the settlement amounted to a redistribution of earnings accrued from their work. Perhaps the greatest, and certainly the most unforeseen, irony in the whole affair was that what the union resisted with all its might would soon be the very thing to create opportunities for new generations of musicians who saw recording as their primary ticket from obscurity to the big time.

· 5 ·

Despite the opposition to his transcribed radio hour, Crosby eventually prevailed, signing with a new sponsor, Philco, and a new network, ABC (formerly NBC's Blue Network). The first "Canned Crosby" show, as a *Newsweek* headline called it, aired on October 16, 1946.[51] In order to allay any concerns about deceiving the public with electronic chicanery, the show was introduced with the announcement "transcribed in New York City" along with the date. The featured guest was Crosby's film partner, Bob Hope. The clash between the biggest singing star of the time and the powers behind one of the era's most popular shows, which, of course, triggered intrigue among competing suitors, all made for a good spectacle on Radio Row in New York City and beyond. But the principle at stake, along with the timing of the dispute, made the outcome more than simply a win for Crosby. It had already been noted by *New York Times* reporter John Hutchens in 1943 that the networks' conventional arguments concerning canned programming were specious. In fact, based on transcribed shows he had heard on the British BBC network, he believed that transcriptions made for "better broadcasting, more decisively in the public interest, including," just as Crosby argued, "the fact that the transcribed program, polished and edited, very often represents a superior performance in the acting and the writing."[52] Crosby's widely publicized success in legitimizing prerecorded shows affirmed a dawning realization among broadcasters, record companies, performing rights organizations, and the AFM that rapidly changing entertainment technology was something more profitably exploited than opposed. The recording/radio marriage was further consummated when recordings of radio shows, complete with dubbed-in laughter, began appearing in the retail market. "It was only a matter of time after Bing Crosby's pioneering experiment with transcription of his radio shows before someone would make a similar one on commercial records," the *New York Times* reported in 1947.[53]

The long and conflicted opposition to recorded music on the air would become a distant memory, the reasons for the argument largely forgotten. The battles that had been waged with a certain passion in the 1930s and early 1940s waned, and Petrillo's renewed recording ban in 1947 (which many recording musicians skirted surreptitiously) was short-lived. Soon thereafter, the networks would turn their attention to television, and, as one of Crosby's chief *Music Hall* writers, Carroll Carroll, summed up the situation, for the radio shows that had entertained the country through economic depression and war, "there was nowhere to go but down."[54]

Carroll also noted in the Crosby affair another development with long-term significance. In 1947, a year into his new show, Crosby became interested in magnetic tape, which he had been introduced to by engineer Jack Mullin. Mullin, while serving in the Army Signal Corps, had come across the Magnetophone tape machine in Germany following the war. Manufactured by the Algemeine Electrizitäts Gesellschaft (AEG), the Magnetophone was the most advanced recording device of the time, relatively lightweight with reliable recording media and a clean sound. Crosby was impressed. He bought an interest in the fledgling Ampex Corporation, whose engineers, with Mullins's help, built one of the first American tape recorders, the Ampex 200. Mullin went to work on Crosby's show in the capacity not only of recordist but of postproduction editor, "creating the craft of tape recording," as he put it. He learned to splice together bits of various performances, dub in canned laughter, and use "tight editing to take out offending material," all of which were accomplished far more efficiently than with disc recording.[55] "Anybody with even the tiniest knowledge of broadcasting," Carroll wrote, "could see the potential of this new and versatile way of recording. But it was Bing, with his stake in the tape, who used the muscle of his box office power to force it onto the network-dominated broadcast industry."[56] The machine that Carroll reckoned "changed the face of radio broadcasting" would also change the face of record making.[57] As Crosby's two-decade reign entered its final phase, he unwittingly helped to sow the seeds of the brewing musical revolution that would spread via recorded sound across the nation's airwaves and supplant his kind.

When word began leaking out in the spring of 1947 that Decca, the last of the major-label holdouts, would begin servicing radio stations with dedicated promotion departments and free discs, it was clear that a new, industrywide promotion system had taken shape. Thanks to president Jack Kapp's staunch opposition, Decca was slow to recognize the value of investing in radio promotion for its products, but now *Billboard* reporter Joe Carlton, who had followed the story for some time, reckoned that "the entire record industry ha[d] surrendered to the hit-making powers of the disk jockey."[58] The record firms were finally beginning to understand that the expense of servicing radio stations was small compared to broadcasting's powerful promotional effect. And instead of inhibiting sales, as they had earlier feared, broadcasting records was a sales-enhancing advertising tool. Bands, which had relied on remote broadcasts to advertise their live appearances, found that by 1947 they, too, got better promotional results from broadcasts of their records. Bands began employing advance men "to contact platter pilots and set up a constant barrage of platter plays, personal appearances, and other promotional gimmicks. In short," Carlton concluded, "records make bands."[59]

In his 1935 autobiography, *Ten Years before the Mike,* radio announcer Ted Husing proudly insisted that in the early days at RCA's WJZ in New York, "We never played phonograph records into *our* mikes, but always gave the public genuine acts."[60] By the 1940s, attitudes toward recorded programming had swung 180 degrees. Now canned music itself had an aura of the "genuine." It was not a substitute for the real thing; it *was* the real thing—not a replacement for live music, or a stand-in, but something different altogether, a piece of shellac with a soul of its own. Capitol developed "a field staff especially employed to do nothing but give disks away—with extra-added salesmanship intended to get air play."[61] Capitol was among the youngest of the majors, founded in 1943 by Glenn Wallichs, Johnny Mercer, and Buddy DeSylva. The company understood from the outset that radio play was an essential element of sales, and its deejay-centered promotion network was the industry's most sophisticated and successful. But the older firms were adapting quickly to the new ways, with Columbia and RCA Victor preparing to launch in 1948 "gigantic new platter-promotion-via-radio programs to the tune of hundreds of thousands of dollars." Columbia sponsored its own *Columbia Record Shop* program, emceed by Fred Robbins, which ran on 538 stations, and planned to increase purchases of "sponsored spots to some 144 spinner programs thruout the nation." An "initial $100,000" was earmarked by RCA Victor to service disc jockeys with records and promotional packages. Even Decca, "originally the most reticent of the diskers spinner-wise," was "quietly expanding" its efforts.[62]

With records' new status came new roles for the men who played them. Known by an array of colorful descriptive terms—platter pilot, tallow turner, wax whirler, disc jockey—they became entertainers and power brokers cultivating unique personae that both sold their sponsors' products and enthusiastically hyped the music they played. The most successful early disc jockey was Martin Block, who began presenting his *Make Believe Ballroom* in 1935 on New York's WNEW with the visionary blessing of station manager Bernice Judis. The show's name, borrowed from Al Jarvis, whose own disc show had begun two years earlier on Los Angeles station KFWB, acknowledged openly its ersatz content. But Block's manner gave it the feel of something genuine. He worked the microphone, as former radio man Philip Eberly noted, like two other contemporary masters of the medium, Franklin D. Roosevelt and Bing Crosby, using it to create an imaginary intimacy connecting him with his audience.[63]

Although WNEW was not affiliated with any network, Block's presentation of an array of popular music interspersed with his patter and salesmanship proved a successful counter to the networks' endless daytime soap operas. He addressed his listeners as "you folks," his people. He spoke to the performers whose records he played, although they were present only in his imagination. He crafted illusion and laced it with empathy. When advertising fur coats, wrote a *New York Times* reporter, "he does not urge fur coats on his feminine listeners. His voice merely carries an undertone of fervent sympathy for any woman who does not have a fur coat."[64] In this understated way, ad-libbing conversation with the ether in a soft, purring voice, he sold everything from diet pills to war bonds. By the end of the decade, he had some two million weekly listeners, with nineteen sponsors paying $325,000 a year for airtime. In 1947, *Billboard* reported his potential weekly earnings at "close to $14,000—for spinning records."[65]

Adding the extraneous "for spinning records" quip suggested bemusement on the part of the reporter not unlike that expressed by a 1939 article in *Time,* where a description of Block's "talent" required scare quotes.[66] But if the rise of the disc jockey occasioned initial head-scratching, it showed, as Block argued, that "the public has unquestionably changed its mind about listening to records." He pointed to national surveys that found "many instances" of disc shows outdrawing live programming.[67] *Billboard*'s 1949 "Special Disk Jockey Supplement" acknowledged unequivocally the industry's new order.

> The very existence of this poll, the fact that so much effort should be expended upon it, the fact that it enjoys such wide acceptance in the trade— all point to one overall theme: The importance of the disk jockey to the multi-faceted music business.
>
> The jockey, circa 1949, is a maker of tunes, a seller of records. His judgment merits the consideration of artists and repertoire men, of record manufacturers, distributors and dealers. What he says and believes can affect the writer of songs. His word is of moment to talent agencies, ballroom operators, bookers.[68]

As Block's example made clear across the industry, the successful deejay was far more than a platter spinner. He was a skilled salesman using art as a tool of commerce, just like the record companies that supplied his library. But more than this he was a new kind of performer. Jockeys were creatures of the electronic age, using records, microphones, and broadcasting to forge a new kind of expressive practice rooted in technology. They projected personalities and conjured atmospheres that enlivened the records they played as they fostered among their listeners a sense of virtual community. As their ranks grew, disc jockeys took on new power in the music industry, many rising to celebrity status. Such figures as Dave Garroway, Bob Poole, Steve Allen, Dewey Phillips, Al Benson, Dick Hugg, Bill Randle, and Alan Freed entered into a media pantheon whose members both sold products and increasingly influenced popular taste. Musicians, too, got into the act. Besides Whiteman, such stars as Tommy Dorsey, Kate Smith, and Duke Ellington all took turns at the mike as wax whirlers.

· 6 ·

With radio stations across the country spinning ever more records, and jukebox operators buying a million records a week by 1949, the country was awash in recorded sound. As the fifties unfolded, the trend only accelerated. "No age," a *New York Times* reporter worried in 1956, "has run greater risks of being overwhelmed by musical overabundance."[69] Disc jockeys guided their listeners through the plenitude, highlighting records they particularly liked or were, in one way or another, induced to play. They served, Block wrote, "as a record buying guide for the listening public."[70] Records were now radio's primary programming vehicle, and, with programming decisions and policies no longer concentrated in the nation's entertainment capitals, the airwaves teemed with an abundant sonic pluralism. Among these musical hosts were a few African American men, many disguising their diction in order to keep listeners focused on their professionalism rather than their ethnicity, which was linked in the radio world to the likes of such stereotyped black imitators as Freeman Gosden and Charles Correll, the white actors who starred in *Amos and Andy.* The black deejays' sensibilities and perspectives were distinctive, however, and their presence on the radio made for a cultural integration of the airwaves far more progressive than American society at large.

In 1929, Jack L. Cooper went on the air in Chicago with the *All-Negro Hour.* The show first aired on November 3 at 5:00 p.m. on radio station WSBC, a low-power independent that specialized in programming aimed at the city's various immigrant communities, all supported by advertising for local businesses. The program's content included comedy routines, musical numbers, and religious segments, including remote broadcasts from local churches. Instead of the black stereotypes that were the rule at the networks—whether it was white minstrels affecting black caricatures or the occasional black actor playing some loosely imagined archetype such as Eddie Anderson's Rochester on the *Jack Benny Show* (which radio historian William Barlow has called a "mix of the faithful servant and the urban Zip Coon")—the *All-Negro Hour* presented authentic African American voices expressing a range of cultural values and issues of interest to its black listeners.[71] The station's 250-watt signal barely reached beyond Chicago's South Side, but Cooper, whose many hats included writer, actor, announcer, salesman, and, beginning in 1932, deejay, was an ambitious and clever entrepreneur. In addition to producing programming financed by his own sponsors, he bought blocks of airtime and sold them piecemeal to other black programmers, whose broadcasts included music, religious programming, sports, and so forth. He not only controlled an increasing amount of time on WSBC, but he eventually began broadcasting over several other stations in the city, establishing an air presence for black-appeal programming, including news and public affairs, that was unmatched anywhere in the country.

In 1946, a feature story in *Ebony,* a new magazine published in

Chicago by John H. Johnson that focused on the interests of African American readers, took note of the new roles blacks were playing on Eddie Cantor's, Danny Kaye's, and other network shows, breaking from such caricatures as Ernestine Wade's Sapphire on *Amos and Andy* or Lillian Randolph's Birdie on *The Great Gildersleeve* and performing as singers, actors, and comedians whose ethnicity was secondary to their talent and skill. "Into the world of kilocycles," the article claimed, "has come a new cycle—a cycle of tolerance and understanding that has cracked the crudities of classic caricature which for years has been radio's unwritten rule."[72] The following year, the magazine ran another radio spread, this time featuring the success of black disc jockeys. Cooper received particular notice as the "highest paid negro in radio."[73] It was noted as well that the Chicago area had the most black deejays in the country, although fifteen others were identified in ten markets from New York to Seattle. The reporter took the view that disc jockeys had

> crossed up the color line in radio more than any development since Marconi invented the gadget. White discmen cater to colored fans and vice versa. Most successful jockey, Martin Block, advertises his show in a Los Angeles negro newspaper and virtually all of the colored spinners have big white audiences.[74]

While the reporter's evidence was mostly anecdotal, it was undeniable that the faceless character of the medium allowed for a cross-cultural traffic still forbidden elsewhere by custom or law. And the jocks' identities were often a mystery to listeners. Harold Jackson, of Washington D.C.'s WOOK, reported receiving a phone call from a listener "protesting his playing of 'jig' music," evidently unaware that Jackson himself was black.[75]

The numbers of black deejays grew exponentially after the war. There were over a hundred by 1949, including such widely influential figures as Al Benson in Chicago and Nat D. Williams in Memphis. In 1948, Williams had begun broadcasting on WDIA and was so successful that the station gradually adopted a format aimed entirely at black listeners, the first station in the country to do so. The move saved the struggling station from bankruptcy and allowed it, in 1954, to make the jump to fifty thousand watts of broadcast power and from daytime-only operation to nearly round-the-clock programming (4:00 a.m. to midnight). The station's turnaround was but one piece of evidence of the black buying power trumpeted in an article that appeared in the advertising trade publication *Sponsor* in 1949 entitled "The Forgotten 15,000,000." The article, which highlighted WDIA, pointed out that African Americans' incomes in 1946 totaled some twelve billion dollars and that most black households owned radios yet few national advertisers were taking advantage of the potentially lucrative market.[76] With the Great Depression well past and postwar prosperity widespread, blacks with money to spend asserted a new activism whose cultural and political dimensions were reflected in resurgent markets.

As significant as it was for black deejays and black appeal programming to gain a foothold on the nation's airwaves—in effect, making the sounds, ideas, and passions that circulated in geographically circumscribed and socially segregated black urban ghettos available to whoever chose to tune in—there were other, more far-reaching electronic avenues of African American influence on the postwar mainstream. Recordings by black performers were also broadcast increasingly by white deejays in radio markets around the country, putting the music within reach of virtually any listener. As part of their on-air personae, many white jocks affected a version of black street vernacular, creating an impression of hipness, which, in turn, conferred a mantle of authority, a sense that these men understood the music and, in a sense, lived its ethos. As black deejay Eddie Castleberry recalled thinking of such jocks as Dewey Phillips, Zenas Sears, and John Richbourg, "My God, them guys—they *know*—they're hip!" The impression was such that Castleberry and his peers "thought the guys *were* black."[77]

One of the first to send the music far and wide into the ether was Gene Nobles at Nashville's WLAC, a fifty-thousand-watt clear-channel station whose nighttime signal could blanket the eastern half of the United Sates and reach into the Caribbean. The station was a CBS affiliate that, like so many others, had added disc jockeys to fill time left vacant by cutbacks in network programming. Nobles began broadcasting rhythm and blues records on a lark in the fall of 1946 at the request of a group of black university students. To everyone's surprise, fellow deejay Hoss Allen later recalled, "people started writing in from El Paso to Richmond, and from Detroit to New Orleans, and from the Bahamas and all over," begging for more.[78] The station's management approved Nobles's request to change the format of his show from pop to an exclusively black music lineup, and he secured sponsorship from Randy Wood, who was looking to advertise his mail-order Randy's Record Shop, which became the show's name. (Wood would use his mail-order profits to found Dot records, one of the most successful independent record firms of the 1950s. Ironically, since the sound of *Randy's Record Shop* was the sound of black music, Dot became the label of Pat Boone, the Fontane Sisters, and other white performers who recorded versions of such hits as Little Richard's "Tutti Frutti," Fats Domino's "Ain't That a Shame," and the Jewels' "Hearts of Stone," which sounded anything but black.) Nobles would be joined at WLAC by two more of radio's legendary white R&B deejays—Bill "Hoss" Allen and John Richbourg—in a lineup that nightly blanketed its broadcast area with the latest in black music.

The unexpected yet resounding success of black music programming was due in part to a hunger on the part of blacks for such styles as blues and boogie-woogie—earthier than big band swing—which had been sparsely represented on the airwaves. Country music was at least as baffling and distasteful to network executives in New York as rhythm and blues, but it gained a much earlier widespread air presence via two NBC affiliates: Chicago's WLS (*National Barn Dance*), which went to 50,000 watts in 1931; and Nashville's WSM (*Grand Ole Opry*), which did so in 1932. As disc jockeys took over radio programming, country music's proven popularity made spinning country discs a simple choice. But demand for black popular music was little understood and poorly served by white station owners and program directors, which is why successful experiments airing black records met repeatedly with pleased astonishment. When the music suddenly appeared on powerful stations capable of reaching listeners who had never heard Jack Cooper or Eddie Honesty in Hammond, Indiana, or Bass Harris in Seattle, a long-contained passion met its object of desire and a waiting audience responded with abounding, and lucrative, appreciation. But this was only part of the story. Over the years, WLAC's black fans numbered in the millions but so, it turned out, did whites. And while the cultural trappings and sensibilities that produced the songs and performances were remote from most whites' everyday experience, the black sounds emanating from their radios spelled delight, novelty, exuberance, exoticism, and a good time, all of which were irresistible to a restless new generation seeking an identity apart from that of their parents. As radio exposure grew for rhythm and blues records, they rapidly claimed a place on the national stage, exerting unprecedented influence on a market whose increasingly unpredictable behavior was akin to a gathering storm.

The man who would follow Martin Block as the country's most famous record-spinning personality was Alan Freed. The difference in program material between *Make Believe Ballroom* and the rhythm and blues of Freed's *Rock 'n' Roll Party*, which cemented his status when he began hosting it on New York station WINS in 1954, encapsulated the changes under way in the record and radio industries. As much as Freed came to symbolize controversy and cultural upheaval, however, neither the job of deejay nor the music he took to calling rock and roll was in his sights when he began his career. His path to the top was fueled by a combination of ambition, charisma, and happenstance; he was, as a *New York Post* feature put it, "an 'accidental' disk jockey."[79]

In 1945, as a twenty-four-year-old news and sports announcer at WAKR in Akron, Ohio, Freed was pressed into deejay service one evening when the regular deejay failed to show up in time for his show. Reportedly, Freed went from his sports report, without prior notice and within five minutes, to presenting the records the station engineer instructed him to play. A satisfied sponsor called station owner S. Bernard Berk to say what a fine job Freed had done. Berk had hired Freed based on a chance meeting; he was impressed with the sound of Freed's voice and thought he would make a good announcer. Now Berk took the sponsor's call as a confirmation of his own hunch about Freed's ability. He gave Freed the job of hosting the record show, called *Request Revue,* and within two years it became Akron's most popular. Freed had his first taste of celebrity as he was recognized around Akron due to his promotional appearances, many of them in schools. He presented his show before a live audience of wildly enthusiastic high school students, among them his own retinue of bobby-soxers.

Freed's primary passion was career advancement, for which the boom in independent radio provided a wide and open road. But he was also a genuine music lover. He had grown up with music, both in the Freed family home and the Salem, Ohio, school system where he played trombone in the marching band, the orchestra, and a dance band, the Sultans of Swing. He had a vast collection of classical recordings and was an avid fan of the swing era bands. Part of his charismatic appeal lay in his feel for the music he played, which was borne out in his lively interaction with the records. After he moved to Cleveland and began spinning rhythm and blues records, he shouted along with the music—"Go, man, go" or "Yeah, man, yeah"—and beat time with his fist on a telephone book. As his chief competitor in Cleveland, Bill Randle, put it, "[H]e was an incredibly involved performer who lived every beat of every note of the music he played."[80] But despite his success in Akron, or more likely because of the hubris it engendered, Freed was out of radio by 1950. Following a forced departure from Akron, he found himself working at Cleveland TV station WXEL introducing the afternoon movie after a failed attempt at hosting a late-night television record show. His move to Cleveland was the result of acrimonious contract negotiations with Berk, to which Freed had responded by taking a job at a competing Akron station, WADC. Berk invoked a contract clause prohibiting Freed from broadcasting within a seventy-five-mile radius for one year after leaving WAKR and was granted an injunction effectively barring Freed from the Akron market, which was as far as his celebrity extended.

Freed found his way back to radio through another chance encounter in early 1951. While drinking at Mullins Bar on Euclid Avenue in Cleveland, he met Leo Mintz, owner of Record Rendezvous, a retail record store whose sizable African American clientele had alerted Mintz to the R&B market's robust growth. Along with letters, telegrams, and phone calls to radio stations and their sponsors, as well as coins dropped into jukeboxes, everyday individuals were exerting a growing influence on the nation's culture market through their record purchases. While the industry sought to influence consumer tastes through all manner of sales gimmicks, the market was becoming an unruly, teeming mass of contradictory signals that record men watched like hawks, ready to pounce on any whiff of a perceived trend. Mintz had started his shop on Prospect Avenue in 1939 with the idea that it could be something of a music center where fans could gather and share, as well as purchase, their favorite music. He put the records in bins, rather than behind the counter, so customers could browse. He installed listening booths so they could preview records. And he hosted in-store appearances by celebrity performers. The shop provided an excellent window on local tastes, and Mintz's success proved his skill at tracking his customers' preferences.

When he met Freed, Mintz had long been a sponsor on Cleveland station WJW, advertising Record Rendezvous, and he helped Freed land a job at the station spinning classical records. Mintz, however, had another idea, this one more difficult to sell. He wanted to sponsor a radio show devoted entirely to the music his customers demanded, further driving his store's R&B sales boom. Rhythm and blues was a relatively new name *Billboard* assigned to the market category known formerly as "race," a catchall term that included any musical style marketed primarily to blacks. The music Mintz was interested in specifically was a rollicking style that lent a gospel fervor to such popular genres as boogie-woogie and jump blues. With fewer instruments, the textures were leaner than those of the big bands. The rhythmic fabric had something of the swing feel, but it tended to shuffle and lean harder on the second and fourth beats of the bar—the backbeats. The sound had an unpolished, loose-limbed, party atmosphere about it, often reinforced by the sounds of hand claps and lyrics laced with references to drinking and sex. The voices—Joe Turner, Ruth Brown, Wynonie Harris—shouted and cried with abandon. The featured solo instrument was usually a saxophono but, unlike such jazz players as Lester Young, Coleman Hawkins, or

Johnny Hodges, the R&B stars—Big Jay McNeely, Red Prysock, Big Al Sears, Gil Bernal, Joe Houston—took a simpler approach to melody and harmony. They emphasized the horn's noise, its barely tamed growl and honk, creating textured surfaces shaped by slides and slurs and grainy shards of sound. The records had an overall loudness whose spirited presence issued from loudspeakers like a sonic eruption.

Freed apparently knew something of this music but not much. He heard its appeal, but he was skittish about programming such rough and lusty material devoid of the controlled pop craftsmanship of Nat Cole or the Mills Brothers, which had long proven itself in attracting a large white audience. How large an audience could he hope to attract with a show dedicated exclusively to the music played on jukeboxes in inner city black neighborhoods? Freed's biographer, John Jackson, has argued convincingly that Freed's story of seeing young white record buyers (who he referred to in a coded way as "kids . . . not only from the immediate neighborhood but from all parts of town") in Mintz's shop buying R&B records, alerting him to the existence of a crossover audience, amounted to a revisionist invention.[81] In earlier accounts, Freed had acknowledged that he assumed his audience would be overwhelmingly black and that the show was "more Leo's idea than mine."[82]

His assumption was entirely within the realm of conventional wisdom and was confirmed when he began hosting concerts and dances whose audiences were almost entirely black. They were also huge, as a startled Cleveland would learn following Freed's overrun Moondog Coronation Ball at the Cleveland Arena in March of 1952. Though accounts vary, at least six thousand people beyond the arena's capacity of ten thousand showed up for an R&B revue advertised almost exclusively on Freed's show. If Mintz's R&B sales were up, the boost came not from young whites but from young black Clevelanders expressing with cash their enthusiasm for the rocking R&B music. Mintz assured Freed that he would advise him, tell him what to play, and sponsor the show. He would be, in effect, Freed's boss. Freed finally went along, and immediately his showmanship took over. He threw himself into the identity of a character he called Moondog, shouting along with records and pounding out the beat. And if the initial idea was to tap into the surprisingly large black audience for R&B, within a year it had become apparent from request letters and cards that came "from all parts of town" that the audience was expanding in an unexpected way.

Freed's move to New York was risky. There were, by 1954, at least a dozen black deejays broadcasting rhythm and blues in the New York market, though typically on low-power stations. So-called good music remained the city's standard fare, and WINS's bid for Freed was precipitated mostly by its desperate financial straits. (The station's only profits came from broadcasts of New York Yankees baseball games.) Freed had earlier established a tentative presence in the New York area when station WNJR in Newark, New Jersey, began broadcasting transcriptions of his shows. His stature rose significantly when he brought one of his live R&B revues to Newark's Sussex Avenue Armory in the spring of 1954 and the trade papers witnessed up close the fabulous box office numbers he had put up routinely in the Midwest. "Not since the hey-dey of the swing bands," *Billboard* reported, "has a dance in the East created such excitement or pulled so strongly."[83] The program director at WINS, Bob Smith, became convinced that Freed was the man to lift the station from its financial doldrums, and, although the station manager, Bob Leder, was reluctant to sign a man who sounded on air like an unhinged personality, Smith persuaded him to bring the deejay to New York. Within months, Freed had won over the city's teenagers—doing his act, playing the records—and given R&B a fifty-thousand-watt platform in the entertainment capital of the world. The accidental deejay had become the "Pied Piper of rock 'n' roll," and with his New York ascendancy "the dial setting for radio station WINS became one of the things that was not to be touched in a home that housed a teen-ager."[84]

To some extent deejays were pied pipers, leading their listeners through the music of the day. The disc jockey, wrote *Billboard* editor Paul Ackerman in 1957, had become "the nation's Number One practicing musicologist," bearing "a greatly expanded set of responsibilities . . . to keep abreast of developments in repertoire, music publishing, record manufacturing and distribution and all the other facets entering into the overall music scene."[85] If a deejay had some interest in a particular record—whether idealistic or pragmatic—he or she could affect its fate in the market by playing it repeatedly. As John Richbourg put it, if he believed in a record he would "lay on that sucker til something happened."[86] But jocks were also open to grassroots suggestion. The public's letters and phone calls—centered on records and the passions they stirred—formed a collective voice engaged in an ongoing dialogue with the deejays.

Enumerating the factors in deejays' programming decisions elicited in its first annual disc jockey poll in 1947, *Billboard* cited various influences, including its own charts and reviews, sponsors' requests, contents of local jukeboxes, and record company promotion. There was, however, one common theme: "[P]ractically all the jockeys said a combination of [listener] requests and their own judgment was a basis of the programming of the shows."[87] One of the most successful disc jockeys in the country, Bill Randle of Cleveland station WERE, stated plainly, "I've got news for you. . . . [M]ost of all I'm with the public. I give them strictly what they want."[88] And, although at the height of his fame Freed appeared to command the musical world of teenagers, he knew that it was the energy flowing between him and his audience that made it all work. "As long as the kids want rock 'n' roll, I'm going to give it to them," Freed wrote in 1956, "and as soon as they indicate they want something else, I'm going to give them that."[89]

The conflicts of the 1930s and 1940s surrounding the evolving interface of music and technology came down in each case to money and power. Performing rights organizations, musicians' union, radio stations and networks, record companies, and government all vied for some measure of self-serving, top-down control over a rapidly changing set of circumstances that proved impossible to corral. But by the 1950s, disc jockeys and their listeners were shifting the balance of power toward the street and the airwaves, where records—accessible and affordable to all—circulated in unprecedented numbers. With records ubiquitous on radio, canned music became the nation's daily bread. Twenty-four hours a day, the country hummed with musical emanations as the two electronic media together cultivated a new mode of musical traffic heading to no one knew where.

TWO

Shifting Currents
in the Mainstream

They should build a statue to Mitch Miller at 57th and
Broadway. . . . He was the first great record producer in
history.
                                          —JERRY WEXLER

Mitch, out. . . . Don't you ever come into the studio when
I'm recording again.
                                          —FRANK SINATRA

So many gimmicks, so little music.
                                          —BING CROSBY

· 1 ·

By 1955, it was clear that a new musical trend centered in the social
worlds of teenagers had taken solid shape. The signs were many.
Through radio and jukebox exposure, the market for rhythm and blues
records had grown substantially, surprising many industry veterans.
Black voices, unvarnished for mainstream tastes and disseminated for the
most part by small regional labels, were moving beyond their intended
markets, filtering into the broader culture through their popular appeal
in the vastly numerous audience of white teenagers. A young country
singer with the curious name Elvis Presley was electrifying young southern audiences with a style unlike anything found among his fellow entertainers on the *Louisiana Hayride* radio show. Chuck Berry's first single,
"Maybellene," an odd combination of country groove overlaid with
R&B swing, and Fats Domino's ambling New Orleans shuffle, "Ain't
That a Shame," were both top-ten pop hits. And Bill Haley's "(We're
Gonna) Rock Around the Clock," which became explicitly associated
with youth culture through its appearance in the film *Blackboard Jungle,*
spent twenty-four weeks on the pop chart, eight of them at number one.
    Yet even as this new wave of music gained momentum, most of the
year's biggest hits came from mainstream pop singers recording for large

labels with international distribution and promotion networks. These records, however, were markedly different from those that had defined the pop mainstream only a few years earlier. While the major labels and their producers were slow to grasp the nature and power of the growing rock and roll groundswell, they sought freshness and novelty in ways of their own. The once reliable instrumental conventions of the 1930s and 1940s—big bands both sweet and swinging, jazz combos, Hollywood orchestras—were no longer to be expected. They became dialects in a broader language of record making whose rhetoric relied more on surprise than expert handling of conventional devices. A successful record might just as well feature a couple of strumming guitars and some simple backing vocals, like Dean Martin's "Memories Are Made of This" (Capitol), as a full orchestra, like Doris Day's "Secret Love" (Columbia). Waning, too, were many of the best-known vocal stars: Dinah Shore, Dick Haymes, the Andrews Sisters, the Mills Brothers, even Crosby. In their places were new voices: Eddie Fisher, Frankie Laine, Johnnie Ray, Rosemary Clooney, Mary Ford. Novelty was king, and, more than ever before, making a successful pop record was a matter of creative experiment, often featuring odd style combinations and quirky arrangements. Selling records had always been a marketing crap shoot, but now the game had new players and a newly evolving set of rules.

The situation was volatile and confusing to an industry whose marketing plans had been developed according to certain established verities like the demographic makeup of particular markets and generic categories of musical style. In *Down Beat*'s 1954 disc jockey poll, respondents, unable to neatly classify several hybrid pop hits, grouped them together under the "novelties" rubric. "The mambo, country-western, and rhythm-blues influences of 1954," noted the magazine's editors, "helped obscure formerly clear cut ideas of what constitutes a novelty, with Bill Haley's 'Shake, Rattle, and Roll' (Decca), Rosemary Clooney's 'This Ole House' (Columbia), and Vaughan Monroe's 'They Were Doin' the Mambo' (RCA Victor) emerging high in the novelty division." The deejays were "reluctant to acknowledge these influences on the pop market," the editors speculated, and so "grouped them all as novelties in the absence of separate classifications." Yet their reluctance was itself confusing. For while the inauthentic R&B, country, and mambo records were consigned to the novelties division, a record of equal artifice—the Crew Cuts' "Sh-Boom" (Mercury)—made the top-ten lists both in Best Vocal Record (defined as the "straight vocal classification") *and* Best Novelty Record categories.[1] The deejays' failure to recognize that all such records pointed to a transforming pop mainstream reflected the stylistic topsy-turvy pervading the musical economy.

In a 1953 *New York Times* review of new major-label releases, the jazz/pop critic John S. Wilson noted with disapproval that "popular music has been going through a frantic search for what recording people consider 'new sounds' in recent years."[2] The search produced many curious stylistic hybrids of the sort that stumped the disc jockeys considering the hits of 1954, and the trend was accelerating. By the end of 1955, among the top-selling records of the year were three quasi-folk songs— "The Ballad of Davy Crockett" (Bill Hayes), "The Yellow Rose of Texas" (Mitch Miller with His Orchestra and Chorus), and "Sixteen Tons" (Tennessee Ernie Ford)—and a number of covers of R&B hits by Georgia Gibbs, the Fontane Sisters, the McGuire Sisters, and Pat Boone, none of which bore much trace of R&B style but nevertheless demonstrated the broad appeal of R&B songs. The pop music mainstream was succumbing increasingly to what were widely characterized as "gimmicks"—tricks of song, arrangement, performance, and sound whose peculiar thrill might fleetingly impress a fast-moving market.

The so-called mainstream of American popular music describes a broad nexus of entertainment and commerce, each reinforcing the other in an unending process of large-scale cultural production, dissemination, acquisition, and use. The designation "mainstream" reflects, first of all, market dominance from coast to coast. Historically, to traffic in the mainstream was to play on a national stage unimaginable without the distribution power of the radio networks, Hollywood film companies, and the largest record labels. Because its geographical centers were New York and Los Angeles, the mainstream bore something of a generic urban polish, eschewing regional colloquialisms except for the occasional novelty song. But while the stream and the sales chart that tracked it tended toward Tin Pan Alley–type songcraft, any song in any style that could be marketed successfully on such a vast scale could claim a place. Bob Wills and his Texas Playboys put nine records on the pop charts in the 1940s; Louis Jordan and his Tympani Five managed nineteen. Still, while country or R&B acts had a sporadic presence, crooners such as Bing Crosby, Frank Sinatra, Perry Como, Dick Haymes, and Nat Cole; songbirds such as the Andrews Sisters, Ella Fitzgerald, and Dinah Shore; and the big bands of Benny Goodman, Tommy Dorsey, and Glenn Miller ruled the pop charts throughout the 1940s. The voices were silken and fine, with an unforced jazz inflection and a worldly intimacy. The songs were chiefly the products of Tin Pan Alley tunesmiths, whose output had nourished the nation's pop canon for decades. The instrumental textures were familiar—bands, combos, and orchestras, all reproduced in high-quality audio. Countless records conjured an image of effortless execution, paragons of high-class musical professionalism.

But in the postwar cultural clatter, things were changing. In September 1951, *Billboard* reported that "Crosby, the Andrews Sisters, Dick Haymes, and other of the staples have slowed to a walk." Overtaking them was a rising "youth movement . . . sparking a most extensive search for new talent." A headline conveyed the trend's magnitude—"Newcomers Blast Veterans Off Polls"—and the report noted that "not in a decade has youth taken such a fast grip on the hit lists." Record companies were so impressed by the trend that they now devoted "the most conspicuous portion of their time and budgets . . . to the development of new blood."[3] Among the newcomers were Tony Bennett, Rosemary Clooney, and Guy Mitchell at Columbia; Mario Lanza, April Stevens, and Eddie Fisher at RCA Victor; and Les Paul and Mary Ford at Capitol. (Paul, of course, had long been famous as a guitarist on radio with Waring's orchestra and then Crosby's. His status as a newcomer owed much to his newly successful collaboration with Mary Ford.) Before there was an inkling that the musical stew brewing at small, independent companies across the country would ever amount to real competition, the majors were pressing their own innovations in response to an audience seeking fresh young stars.

Despite some temporary retrenchment, which led *Billboard* to report in May 1954 that "the youth movement that swept pop records only a few years ago appears to have dissipated," the public's hunger for new acts continued to grow.[4] A year later *Billboard* editor Paul Ackerman reported on the publication's front page that record buyers were "more prone . . . to accept new artists than at any period within recent memory." Of the forty-eight records that appeared on the best-selling singles chart in the first few months of 1955, twenty-seven "were made by artists whose pop acceptance was nil or minor a year ago." The range of artists now included such newcomers as Nappy Brown, LaVern Baker, and Pat Boone, as well as performers who were either making pop record comebacks, such as Georgia Gibbs, or showing a new pop assertiveness, such as Sarah Vaughan, Johnny Ace, and Tennessee Ernie Ford, who were better known as jazz, R&B, and country stars, respectively. "The pop market is apparently wide open for new talent," Ackerman observed, for "pop record buyers are indicating a wider range of taste." He noted further that "labels which have scored heavily in the new artist sweepstakes are those which have been most experimental" and that "one interesting aspect of the picture is the great amount of novelty material cut by these new artists."[5]

Fresh voices were not the only new sounds in the hit parade; songs, arrangements, and records themselves were showing signs of change as well. The conventions of musical form, melody, and harmony manipulated with deftness and subtlety by the masters of Tin Pan Alley were increasingly replaced by a simpler, more straightforward kind of song—unambiguous and instantly hummable. In the place of the big bands that had accompanied so many pop singers of the 1930s and 1940s, ad hoc groups began appearing on records, one-off ensembles put together in a recording studio for a particular session or even a single song. And records, often the results of elaborate feats of construction, increasingly gave the impression of unique sonic artifacts, with exaggerated reverb, overdubbed performances, sound effects, and instrumental balances controlled electronically by recording engineers. With its unabashed mingling of music making and electronic legerdemain, record making was becoming, on a smaller scale, like making movies.

· 2 ·

In criticizing the trend toward novelty pop records, in which "tune and talent have frequently been secondary to accompaniments that snap, crackle or pop, [and] singers who gasp or shriek," Wilson named Mitch Miller as "one of those most responsible for the present interest in sounds *per se*."[6] Miller was a classical musician by training, an oboist who had earned a degree at the Eastman School of Music in his hometown of Rochester, New York. After graduating, he moved to New York City and became one of the premier players in town, a first-call soloist for such conductors as Reiner, Stokowski, and Beecham, his sound characterized by Virgil Thomson as "warm and laughing and sensuous, faun-like and wholly without acidity."[7] By his midthirties, after years of crisscrossing Manhattan, moving from one engagement to another and rushing at night to catch the last ferry home to New Jersey, he had played everything and reached, at $17,000 per year, what he considered the limit of his earning potential as a performing musician. So when, in 1947, the renowned A&R man, John Hammond, offered him a position as record producer at Keynote Records, Miller struck out on a new career path.

Miller began by producing classical repertory, but with Mercury Records' acquisition of Keynote he was soon assigned to pop sessions as well. It was a task he was happy to take on, having played all kinds of music during his years as a New York session player. He had long tenures with both the Andre Kostelanetz radio orchestra and the CBS orchestra, which played classical, pop, and dramatic music (Miller played on the famous Orson Welles Mercury Theater production of *War of the Worlds*), and he augmented this with a variety of freelance work around town. As a musician and then a producer, he moved easily between the popular and classical worlds. "I never compartmentalized it in my own mind," he said. "The same rules apply. You know—taste, musicianship, balance, get the best sound out of the artists."[8] In a postscript to a 1952 "Blindfold Test," conducted by Leonard Feather for *Down Beat* magazine, Miller declared that "musical snobbishness is one of the curses of the music business. Many of the most eloquent things have been said very simply and the simplest things are the hardest to say well."[9] Moreover, he pointed out in a *New York Times* essay of his own, simple songs speaking to common themes had historically accounted for the biggest hits.[10] And aside from pop music's everyman appeal, its open invitation to musical experiment fascinated Miller. In the changing pop landscape, the possibilities appeared boundless. "Let's face it," he declared, "pop music is the most. It's audacious. You can try anything once. Even twice."[11]

Miller quickly made his mark in the pop world with a series of Frankie Laine recordings, three of which—"That Lucky Old Sun," "Mule Train," and "The Cry of the Wild Goose"—reached *Billboard*'s number-one spot within a six-month span from October 1949 to March 1950. The brisk sales lifted Mercury, a young and struggling Chicago-based label, from its financial doldrums and raised Miller's own capital significantly. In February 1950, he moved to Columbia, lured for twenty-five thousand dollars a year plus expenses by executive vice president Goddard Lieberson, a former Eastman classmate and himself a producer and composer with definite ideas about making and selling records. Lieberson made it clear that Columbia was aiming for a change of direction in its record production policies. "Hereafter," he proclaimed in announcing Miller's appointment, "more emphasis will be placed on selecting the right artists for the right tune and an imaginative, creative effort to produce the best records possible will be made at the main source of every successful record—the recording studio." Lieberson moved to synchronize corporate policy with market trends that had been emerging with increasing clarity. A successful record required not only a good performance of a good song but also a distinctive overall character, which, in turn, required a creative approach to production. "A record is in a sense like a play," Lieberson said. "It requires a beginning, a denouement and an end."[12]

Miller's position as A&R chief of Columbia's flagging pop singles division involved all the duties of record production—finding songs, matching them to performers, deciding on musical treatments, and supervising recording sessions. The wisdom of Lieberson's choice became apparent almost immediately. Within months, Laine followed Miller to Columbia and joined a roster that would grow to include Guy Mitchell, Doris Day, Johnnie Ray, the Four Lads, Rosemary Clooney, Jo Stafford, Tony Bennett, Johnny Mathis, and many more of the famous hit makers of the day, as well as star arrangers Percy Faith and Ray Conniff. Some, like Stafford, found new chart life after a period of commercial decline, but most were new to the national pop soundscape. "We were all unknown quantities," recalled Guy Mitchell of Columbia's hit-making upstarts. "Miller made us."[13] In 1951, *Time* reported that "in just 18 months, [Miller's] guesses and general savvy have upped Columbia's pop record sales more than 60%." Though not mentioning Miller by name, an April 1952 *Billboard* article comparing sales among major labels in the first quarter of the year noted that Columbia, despite having released the fewest records, had "garnered many more entries on the best-seller chart than any other firm." The company's "pop-disk primacy" was measured in a 12 percent success rate, with 13 best sellers out of 108 sides released. Columbia's closest competitor was Mercury at 6 percent.[14] By 1953, Miller had produced over 50 hit recordings for Columbia artists, and between 1950 and 1956 he was associated with records that sold some 80 million copies. *McCall's* magazine called him "The Man Who Makes Money Records," and a 1956 feature in the *Saturday Evening Post* billed the bearded Miller as "The Shaggy Genius of Pop Music."[15]

Miller was an idea man, not a songwriter or nuts-and-bolts arranger but a conceptualizer and the ultimate authority in the studio. He selected songs with specific voices in mind and coached singers in directions that often led away from their habitual comfort zones; he chose arrangers, invented ensembles, and suggested stylistic directions for the musical treatment; and he edited songwriters' work, calling for changes in lyrics or music that he felt would improve a song's chances in the marketplace. In the studio's control room, he collaborated with the session engineer (in particular Frank Laico, a longtime studio partner), selecting microphones for specific singers and instrumentalists and presiding as the ultimate judge on matters of sound and balance. Above all, he was the figure responsible for etching into a record's grooves a lively personality. "To me, a record is a psychological experiment," Miller told an interviewer in 1952. The aim of the experiment was to engage listeners with a musical and sonic thrill. "Excitement is everything," he said. "It's what has made the record business what it is today." Excitement stemmed from high-spirited productions featuring some kind of unusual twist. Any trick of performance, instrumentation, arrangement, or sonic treatment was acceptable "so long as it [made] the result more palatable to the ear." A pop record's success relied on making a sonic impression that stood out from the day to day or the conventional. Flights of sonic fancy were the delights Miller offered listeners, and, although his critics were many, no one could argue with his success. Using the studio to construct miniature audio dramas, he reckoned that he and his team had "captured something entirely new in the recording field."[16]

Miller conceived of records *as* records, which meant standards of live performance were not to be confused with those of studio artifice. He claimed never to have seen Tony Bennett perform before signing him to Columbia. Bennett's taped performance was enough. Miller believed that a performer's impact onstage was not necessarily a good measure of his or her recorded persona. He auditioned by demonstration record because he thought it the best way to gauge a performer's intuitive ability to bring life to a record, transmuting his or her physical expression into an arresting electronic persona. "Looking at an act doesn't mean anything," he insisted. "If it's good on the floor, it's not necessarily good on records. And by looking you can easily be influenced in the wrong way."[17] Sam Phillips, another producer who understood both the affective and ontological differences between records and live performances, would later take the same approach with Elvis Presley: "We'll just set up an audition," he told guitarist Scotty Moore, "and see what he sounds like coming back off of tape."[18]

Frankie Laine, Francesco Paolo LoVecchio, was among a new breed of postcrooner pop voices—chesty, declamatory, emotive, and early on often mistaken for black. In his own characterization, Laine reckoned he was "not a crooner" but rather "a singer who shouts." In 1947, after years of scuffling around the lower reaches of the entertainment industry as a singer, marathon dancer, emcee, and occasional songwriter, he finally, at age thirty-four, had a hit record on Mercury called "That's My Desire." The record's success was a sign of changing times in the industry. The likes of Crosby and Sinatra developed their initial national presence through associations with popular bands—Whiteman and Tommy Dorsey, respectively—prior to their first hit records. Such was the well-worn path to stardom. But Laine was a complete unknown nationally when "That's My Desire" hit. His club dates had been sporadic, and his few radio appearances were strictly brief, local affairs. When he signed his record deal with Mercury, he had just been laid off at the defense plant in Burbank where he worked the swing shift. It was one of many jobs he had held to keep body and soul together. Yet now a single record, out of the blue, propelled him into the public ear and eye as though an overnight success.

Laine recounted his stylistic development as a series of chance epiphanies whose impact he grasped only in retrospect. As a boy growing up in Chicago he came across Bessie Smith's "Bleeding Hearted Blues," a "strange record," he remembered, found in a pile of mostly classical discs left behind by a former inhabitant of his family's home on West Schiller Street.[19] With his young musical imagination bounded by his church choir and the movies, the blues record caused him "cold chills and an indescribable excitement."[20] In its grooves he heard a mysterious, captivating allure unlike anything in his everyday life. Later, on a truant afternoon trip to the movies, it was Al Jolson in *The Singing Fool* that captured his fancy. "Without knowing what was happening," he recalled sitting mesmerized through two successive screenings. As a teenager, he began regularly attending shows at Chicago's Merry Garden Ballroom, where he heard Mildred Bailey with the Whiteman band. Her rendition of Hoagy Carmichael's "Rockin' Chair" proved a revelation far beyond her recorded performance, which he already knew and loved. "Once I heard her in person," he stressed, "it became *my* song and she became *my* singer." Also at the ballroom he encountered "an explosion of dynamite" in the form of Cab Calloway, whose dynamic performance style "absolutely gassed" young Laine. "It shook me up and propelled me in the direction I was going without my knowing where I was going."[21]

When he signed with Mercury, Laine was a jazz singer, and his phrasing on "That's My Desire" bore the mark of one of his greatest admitted influences, Billie Holiday. (Among his early Mercury sides were several songs Holiday had recorded, including "Georgia on My Mind," "All of Me," and "God Bless the Child.") But when Miller took on pop production at Mercury, he moved Laine in a new direction. The jazz, by this time a music of venerable tradition but waning popular appeal, was replaced with a rootless new hybrid hatched in the recording studio. To Laine's ears, the first of the Miller-produced Mercury hits, "That Lucky Old Sun" by southern songwriters Haven Gillespie and Beasley Smith, had the hint of a "Western flavor."[22] The lyric was a straightforward, plainspoken yet eloquent expression of daily travail and a prayer for deliverance. The arrangement began with a simple accompaniment of strummed guitar, evoking a country-folk ethos befitting the song's working-man protagonist. After the first A-section, a choir of voices added the decidedly nonfolk character of a Hollywood soundstage complete with exotic harmonic touches that clashed with the song's simple harmonic framework. Violins, woodwinds, and brass followed, filling out the arrangement with the sounds of a symphony orchestra, the guitar chugging along all the while. With an incisive rhythmic attack, Laine cloaked the protagonist's sadness in a vigorous stoicism evoking what Miller called the "blue collar singer . . . who understands what it means to sweat and to make a living, and who pounds his pillow with frustration."[23]

If Laine thought "Lucky Old Sun" an unfamiliar yet intriguing "change of pace," his next hit, "Mule Train," shocked him when Miller first played him the song.[24] "Jesus Christ, you can't expect me to do a *cowboy song!* I'll lose all my jazz fans," Laine protested.[25] But whatever his impression of "Mule Train," he could not deny the fact that of the fifteen songs he himself had chosen for the recording sessions that produced "That Lucky Old Sun," the best any of them managed in the marketplace was as that record's B-side. Impressed with Miller's commercial instincts, Laine dropped his initial opposition and took a further step in a "western" direction. To his surprise and delight, he glimpsed the record's appeal firsthand in what amounted to a public premier, standard for films but almost unheard of for a pop record. Having received a pre-release copy of "Mule Train" during a run of shows in Detroit, Laine offered his closing night audience a choice between his usual closing number, the popular "Shine," or an audition of the new record. When the audience clamored for the record, Laine "sat down by the footlights" while the theater filled with disembodied sound. When it was over, the crowd erupted with shouts of "Play that record again!" and Laine was convinced that all was well.[26]

"Mule Train" was a piece of programmatic sound painting featuring hoofbeats, lyrics that repeat "clippity-clop," and shouts of "Get along, mule! Get along!" followed by the crack of a whiplike sound. Laine's voice, bathed in a spacious reverb suggesting the vastness of a western landscape, was accompanied by guitar, accordion, the incessant woodblock emulating mules' hooves, and several male voices repeating an ostinato grunt. Laine sang with good humor and gusto, feigning a vaguely rural accent on words like "gee-tar" and "to-bac-cee" as he listed characters—cowboy, rancher, miner, the Reverend Mr. Black—whose lives would be touched by the various items the mule train was hauling. The song, a kind of imaginary cowboy concoction, was written by three Hollywood songwriters during a car trip across the desert between Las Vegas and Los Angeles. It had attracted enough attention as a demo to have already been recorded by Vaughn Monroe, Gordon MacRae, and Tennessee Ernie Ford (and would yet be covered by Bing Crosby), but Laine's version was the first to be released and the biggest seller. Although Laine's earthy vocal captured the song's spirit, it was no doubt the record's overall feel—its novel sonic setting of images familiar to average Americans and central to the national imagination—that won it such a large audience.

The last of Laine's trio of number-one Mercury hits was folksinger Terry Gilkyson's "The Cry of the Wild Goose," a song whose free-spirited protagonist ("brother to the old wild goose") was compelled to a life of wandering. For this production, Miller called again for male voices and guitar, but this time the evocative tone painting fell to a brass section of horns, trumpets, and trombones whose intermittent bleating emulated the call of the wild goose. Perhaps, too, since the brass parts often sounded like hunting calls, they carried a hint of danger, reflected metaphorically in the protagonist's internal conflict, "torn between the security of a home, a woman's love and the urge to move on," as a record company advertisement put it. The agitated arrangement and rushing tempo, along with Laine's own troubled yet urgent performance, conveyed contradictory impressions of resoluteness and ambivalence. Once again, Miller produced a minidrama in the form of a one-off piece of processed folk music, what Laine himself called "pseudo-folk."[27] The record company, of course, touted the record more grandly; it could not "be classified simply as popular music," the advertisement read, for it was "folk poetry at its purest."[28] Indeed.

Each of these records was something of an oddity, a unique musical statement made of recognizable references but exemplifying no established genre or style. They were musical tableaux concerned primarily with their own narratives; style and sound acted according to each track's expressive conception. They shared, however, a common idea: Miller's pop records were not meant to be transparent representations of musical events belonging to a specific time and place but, rather, independent artifacts capable of establishing a palpable presence wherever they turned up in the ever more cacophonous modern soundscape. Recording, for Miller, was not simply a means of making portable snapshots of the music that, night after night, filled clubs, theaters, radio stations, and dance halls around the country. It was a creative medium distinct from other kinds of musical activity. His early fifties Columbia recordings were collages of musical style and technological sound sculpting that aimed, each one, to achieve an identity of its own even as it highlighted the artist and the song. There was no typical Miller texture. "I would have an image in my mind," he told an interviewer, and all production decisions—from song choice to performer to arrangement to electronic processing—were based on achieving that image.[29]

Laine noticed from the outset that Miller "demonstrated a talent for setting off voices in original, if not downright quirky, musical settings," often using what Jerry Wexler called "bastard instruments."[30] French horn was one of the unusual timbres Miller favored. Another was harpsichord, whose appearance in a barrelhouse role on Rosemary Clooney's breakout hit, "Come On-A My House," was a source of widespread critical bemusement. But Miller liked the effect so well he made it a fixture of Clooney's subsequent up-tempo hits. Miller took style elements from various idioms as off-the-shelf objects, combining them according to creative whim in mismatches aimed at evoking what he called "the sweet surprise," catching the audience's attention with unlikely combinations and juxtapositions.[31] Stylistic authenticity was irrelevant. The idea, rather, was to make the record an idiosyncratic confection all of whose parts contributed to the overall narrative. In answer to the question, "When is a gimmick not a gimmick?" Miller said, "When it's an essential part of the record. A gimmick is only a gimmick when it has failed to complete the conception of a record."[32] In other words, the record as a whole transcended any subset of its parts.

Miller's production philosophy proved dizzying to the industry, breaking with high-pop conventions in ways many found outrageous and tasteless yet selling records at an astounding pace. The records that "dominated the vocal hits" of the early fifties, wrote a *Down Beat* reporter, were little more than a "rash of whispering-screaming-bellowing styles, over-produced records, multiple recording methods, pseudo folk tunes, and other such phony gimmicks."[33] And in addition to such unseemly melodramatic stunts, an unsettling eclecticism was turning the pop mainstream into a hodgepodge. In a 1953 feature on Miller in the *New Yorker,* Robert Rice characterized contemporary pop records generally as pieces of "fast-selling musical bric-a-brac" that included

> almost all types of rhythmic noise—new songs, old songs, show songs, drinking songs, plantation songs, Hawaiian songs, cowboy songs, Venezuelan songs, operetta songs, Elizabethan songs, college songs, Yiddish songs, Stephen Foster songs, holy songs, cradle songs, songs of the South African veldt, and even songs by William Saroyan.[34]

All in all, it was a fair account of Miller's own catalog.

· 3 ·

Johnnie Ray was another performer on Miller's roster who shot to instant stardom on the strength of a single record. Ray was born in 1927 and grew up in the small town of Dallas, Oregon, where he began playing piano in early childhood. Music in the family home included his father's fiddle playing—"cowboy songs, mountain folk songs," his sister Elma recalled—and the records his sister brought home.[35] Elma, a devoted pop fan and aspiring singer, introduced her little brother to the likes of Ellington, Holiday, and Pete Johnson, whose boogie-woogie style he learned by ear. He also sang and played in church. When the war came, the family moved to Portland where Ray attended high school and, despite an accident that left him severely hearing impaired, began performing as a singer, pianist, and actor. He also wrote songs. He was hungry for show business, "a burning ambition," he called it, "something like a calling."[36] In his early twenties, with a rough year in Los Angeles under his belt, he headed east, making it as far as Ashtabula, Ohio, where he wound up broke and scrambling for any lounge gig he could find.

In early 1951, Ray found his way to Detroit where a couple of show business friends, a comedy team, had secured him an audition at the Flame Show Bar where they had been performing. The club was a prominent black-and-tan nightspot in an all-black section of the city. Although the clientele was mixed, the performers were mostly black and included many such top names as Louis Jordan, Dinah Washington, and T-Bone Walker. Al Green, the Flame's powerful floor manager, and Maurice King, leader of the house band, the Wolverines, were impressed enough to offer Ray a two-week contract to close the show following the night's main event act.[37] Green also signed Ray to a personal management contract. Ray became close friends with LaVern Baker, who opened the show each night. Baker and King advised Ray nightly in stagecraft, and as his performances became more confident he began performing with abandon. Immersed in black nightlife, and with a responsive audience, his tendency toward unrestrained expression was liberated. Like Laine, he was a white man proffering a degree of public emotion to which the pop mainstream was unaccustomed. Although most of the audience left after the headliner finished, those who stayed took notice, and Ray was rewarded with a two-week contract extension.

In a return engagement at the Flame a few weeks later, Ray was approached by Danny Kessler, A&R chief at Okeh, Columbia's newly revived R&B subsidiary. Kessler was in Detroit to promote records and see LaVern Baker, whose reputation as "Little Miss Sharecropper" had spread beyond the Midwest. But Dearborn deejay Robin Seymour alerted Kessler that he should also stick around to check out the piano player who closed the show. Baker was riveting, as Kessler expected. He signed her to Okeh, although her tenure on the label would be brief (she sang on three of six sides recorded by the Wolverines). In Ray, however, Kessler found something utterly unexpected. "Out came a white kid wearing a hearing aid, who played the piano," Kessler recalled.

> There was no name introduction. I really didn't know this was the kid Robin was talking about—I assumed he was talking about a black singer. But I was probably more overwhelmed with what I heard and saw than by anything else I had ever encountered artistically in my life.[38]

Kessler offered Ray a contract the next day, just after Ray received a letter of rejection from Voyle Gilmore at Capitol, to whom he had sent a demo disc. ("Capitol was the groovy label I wanted to be on," Ray said. "They had Kay Starr, Peggy Lee, Stan Kenton, Nat Cole.")[39] Ray's first Okeh recording was a slightly delirious performance of one of his own songs, "Whiskey and Gin," accompanied by the Wolverines in an arrangement by turns raucous and suave. As with Laine, many listeners mistakenly took Ray's emotional delivery as a sign of blackness, although that impression said more about perceptions at the time than about the singer's actual style, which might best be described not as black but as histrionic. Dramatically emotive performances, whatever the stylistic particulars, suggested blackness simply because the collective mind had no other way to identify them. Or if not black, then perhaps it was female, as the Columbia sales team guessed when they heard the recording. "Finally I convinced them," Kessler recalled, "that she was a boy, and then I had to break the news that she was a white boy."[40] The epitome of white male drama in the 1940s was the smoldering Frank Sinatra, who upped the heat ante on the likes of Crosby, Como, and Haymes. But Sinatra's was a slow burn, an artful intensity. He was not about to reveal all in shouts of uncontrolled feeling. Ray, by contrast, would make a career of holding nothing back.

"Whiskey and Gin" did not make the national charts, but it attracted some regional attention, notably in the bellwether Cleveland market where influential disc jockey Bill Randle was an enthusiastic supporter. (Randle would later help to break the young Presley north of the Mason-Dixon Line.) The stir caught Miller's attention, and he set about producing Ray's next recording session. Among the songs Miller selected was a piece of honky-tonk weltschmerz called "Cry," written by Churchill

Kohlman, a man whose songwriting efforts had yet to deliver him from his job as a night watchman in a Pittsburgh dry-cleaning establishment. The song, like so many others, came to Miller in the form of a recording, stacks of which he auditioned weekly. It expressed an unabashed romantic grief and counseled listeners who found themselves in similar straits to bare their torment—"Go right on baby and cry!" The sentiment was perfect for Ray's stylized delivery, and Miller's production focused entirely on the voice. The accompaniment was sparse and gimmick free—the Four Lads on vocal harmony and a demure rhythm section that included a warmly rounded electric guitar sound and celesta. The gimmick was Ray's performance, a vivid display of emotional distress that flirted with caricature. Apparently overcome and at the brink of despair, he bellowed, dragged the beat, and stretched consonants as though he could barely get the words out of his mouth. The act was both flamboyant and forlorn, and the press had a grand time coming up with characterizations and epithets; the "prince of wails" moved his audiences with his "tortured tonsiling," his "shriek of anguish," his "lacerating threnody."[41]

"Cry" b/w "The Little White Cloud That Cried" was released on November 11, 1951. It sold a million copies in eight weeks and two million by April of 1952 when the *New York Times* classical music critic, Howard Taubman, weighing in with a rare public comment on pop music, wrote a piece suggesting that the degree and swiftness of Ray's spectacular success perhaps signaled that he was more than simply "another of a series of phenomena thrown up by a frenetic branch of the entertainment business."[42] While the A-side was the record's biggest hit, spending twenty-seven weeks on the *Billboard* pop chart, eleven of them at number-one, the B-side, another of Ray's own songs, was a hit in its own right, charting for twenty-two weeks and peaking at number-two. The record was also a hit among R&B record buyers. "Cry" spent fifteen weeks on the R&B chart, peaking at number one; "The Little White Cloud That Cried" managed four weeks, peaking at number six. The record's astonishing sales prompted a move from Okeh to the parent label, Columbia, and by the end of his first year as a recording artist Ray had sold five million records. In a flash, he had gone from an unknown singer lucky to make 150 dollars a week to a world famous celebrity commanding 5,000 a week at New York's Copacabana and 10,000 a week at the Paramount. He was greeted at airports by mobs numbering in the thousands at tour stops throughout Europe, and *Down Beat* reckoned he had "established himself as the phenom of the music-record business of the second half of the century."[43] The latter half of the century would yet produce record sales barely imaginable in 1952. But Ray's example of instant and extravagant success achieved by an unknown young performer would become a common story throughout the industry in the coming decade. And all who followed this path would attain their initial success through records.

Accounting for the response to "Cry" left many observers at a loss. The "phenomenon," as Ray's popularity was routinely referred to, was credited largely to the mysterious enthusiasms of teenagers, although, as Taubman noted, there were few of these to be seen at the Copacabana. But if it seemed unlikely that the newest generation of bobby-soxers alone accounted for Ray's vast international popularity, his success was nevertheless evidence of a new, postswing audience as yet little understood by music industry veterans and critics. Ray and his audience, Taubman wrote, were noteworthy because they reflected "a significant aspect of the country's cultural pattern," which was by then three decades in the making.[44] Like it or not, "the appeal of the crooner and shouter" could not be "argued . . . laughed or deplored away," for what was once "a trend ha[d] hardened into a tradition." More than "caprice or sentimentality," such performers expressed "something for the youngster that is all but inexpressible to him or her." The microphone was "rod and staff" for evoking such "inchoate yearnings," a tool of electronic alchemy. It gave preternatural substance to a singer's most intimate utterance and converted the sound into electric current that flowed, finally, into the records that "transported [listeners] out of their everyday existence into a dream world full of bittersweet beauty."[45]

Looking back, Miller pointed out that "Johnnie Ray's unique way of sobbing through a song, his impassioned musical plea to his audience to 'Cry' hit exactly right at the time of the Korean war." In this context, "Ray's records reflected the uncertainty young people felt in an anxious era, their inability to make plans for the future."[46] It was true that sentimental romantic songs historically had seen some of their greatest popularity during wartime, but Miller probably got the idea from Taubman, who had expressed much the same opinion in trying to fathom Ray's appeal. "If one may hazard a guess," he wrote, "one would suspect that this young man's style speaks for young people beset by fears and doubts in a difficult time. His pain may be their pain. His wailing and writhing may reflect their secret impulses."[47] The reasons for Ray's popularity surely varied widely, but it was a telling sign of the times that an attempted explanation of the performer's charisma left an experienced critic looking not to musical criteria but to the mood of the enraptured audience.

Many of the new mainstream pop singers of the early fifties were themselves ambivalent and uncertain about the changing state of pop music. Frankie Laine, Patti Page, Rosemary Clooney, Kay Starr, Tony

Bennett, and so many other contemporary pop singers who made their names with novelty items—which included songs borrowed from the country and R&B repertories—were schooled in jazz singing. Pop music paid the bills and provided a thrilling celebrity ride, but jazz was their deepest influence and greatest love. In magazine interviews during the years of Tony Bennett's early pop successes, he repeatedly asserted his preference for jazz over his pop hits, which he characterized as "filled with gimmicks."[48] "When you walk into the record studio, the tempo goes bouncy, bouncy ball—and we make hit records," he told critic Nat Hentoff in 1954. But he longed to get back to the jazz standards and "away from the commercially stylized records we've been making."[49] Kay Starr insisted that she had been "brought up to be a jazz singer" but "with a little daughter to support . . . had to get commercial." She harbored no illusions about her pragmatic choice. "Am I happy?" she mused to a *Down Beat* reporter. "Now, what do you think? . . . Do you think I like to sing a song like 'Hoop-De Doo'? Or imagine anyone going up and saying 'I loved you while the fiddles played'—fiddles!"[50]

Hentoff, always on the lookout for the jazz in pop, knew from transcription discs that Patti Page could swing in ways rarely evident in her commercially released recordings. So in a 1952 interview he asked "if she were getting tired of all the echo chambers and the kind of songs she has to sing on records." Page answered "incisively" that she was certainly "not tired of making money" but her own favorite listening ran to Ella Fitzgerald, Louis Armstrong, and the *Jazz at the Philharmonic* albums. She went on to offer a curious assessment of the contemporary audience.

> About songs, though, it is true that great songs aren't being written as often as they were 10 or 15 years ago. And when a great song does come along, it doesn't sell.
>
> I guess the reason may be that years ago, the people who bought records were interested in a better quality of song. They enjoyed music and were of all ages. Today the record buying public is mostly composed of the younger people and their interests aren't especially musical when they buy a record.

In an attempted clarification, she explained that extramusical factors such as a performer's image excited the young fans whether the singer "sings well or not." One "young male artist," a "good friend" she insisted, was "selling just hysteria. He's not singing."[51] In the summer of 1952, the Johnnie Ray implication could have been lost on no one. But extramusical factors had always been part of a fan's attraction to a star. Crosby, Sinatra, Holiday, Cole, all sold a persona as well as a voice and a song. It was not so much that the young pop fans were not interested in the music on a record but, as mounting evidence suggested, that the audience's idea of music was changing.

· 4 ·

In 1950, arranger and orchestra leader Gordon Jenkins emerged as one of Decca's top-selling stars, catching the public's fancy with a stylistic brew both nostalgic and novel. His success was based on something of a conceptual formula: repackaging familiar stars or songs in unusual settings, producing a musical mixture made not of new stylistic materials but of unfamiliar combinations of existing ones. In a series of collaborations fostered by Decca A&R chief Milt Gabler, Jenkins was paired with figures so well known as to be iconic in the pop pantheon, stars like Louis Armstrong and the Andrews Sisters. Gabler was well up to the project, for "over the decades," as Atlantic producer Jerry Wexler put it, "he truly understood the natural art of bending and blending genres."[52]

Along with John Hammond, Gabler was a colossal figure, striding through successive eras of popular music recording stretching from 1920s jazz to 1960s rock. He started out in the twenties as a high school student working in his father's radio store, the Commodore Music Shop on Forty-second Street in Manhattan. Selling records at the shop began as a sideline, along with "sporting goods, novelty goods, tricks and jokes for parties," but in the early thirties Gabler began stocking custom jazz reissues on his own Commodore label.[53] By 1938, when Gabler began producing sessions for original Commodore recordings, the shop had become a well-known hub for jazz record collectors, critics, and musicians. In 1941, Jack Kapp, well aware of Gabler's producer instincts, hired him at Decca, where he was joined by Jenkins in 1945.

In the first half of 1950, Jenkins had three top-ten recordings: "I Wanna Be Loved" (with the Andrews Sisters), "Bewitched," and "My Foolish Heart," each "tricked out with sobbing, throbbing violins and choruses of female voices" in "big, lush arrangements," as *Time* described them.[54] "I Wanna Be Loved" was the last of the Andrews Sisters' top-ten hits (number one, in fact), and, like their 1949 number-one "I Can Dream, Can't I," another Jenkins arrangement, it marked a stylistic departure. On dozens of hits, from their breakout "Bei Mir Bist Du Shoen" (1938) through the war years and after, the sisters married tight ensemble harmonies with an irresistible rhythmic snappiness. Their zest was one of the things that made them such successful foils for a laid-back Crosby in their string of hit collaborations. The Jenkins charts, however, were notably unswinging affairs featuring his characteristic chromatic violin and choral lines underpinned by straightforward harmonic progressions spelled out clearly in the bass line. The music had the atmosphere of a nostalgic film score, and in fact Jenkins was unapologetically old-fashioned in his aesthetic ways. "I think of Gordon as a museum piece," recalled composer/arranger Johnny Mandel. "He embraced the music of the Twenties and Thirties, and nothing else ever reached him quite the same way. His orchestrations, harmonies, everything dated back to those times and he never changed his style."[55] In a 1951 *Down Beat* blindfold test, in which his impression of Stan Kenton's recording of Pete Rugolo's modernist *Mirage* was that "it's just not music," Jenkins himself mused, "sometimes I wonder whether I've lost touch with things."[56]

But if he brought forward the sounds of earlier pop eras, Jenkins was also an ambitious and innovative pop composer who wrote extended works that combined elements of classical tone poem and Broadway musical in a new genre invented for sound recording. With such pieces as *Manhattan Tower, Seven Dreams,* and *California,* Jenkins produced true concept albums that brought together a range of styles from schmaltz to blues. (Johnny Cash's "Folsom Prison Blues" is largely an appropriation of Jenkins's "Crescent City Blues" from *Seven Dreams.*) His musical motto was a chromatic inflection—a repeated half-step fall with the accent on the upper note, which studio musicians recognized as the "Gor-don Jen-kins" motif—that exuded a faux exoticism.[57] Yet there was also an essential simplicity to Jenkins's work, an intelligibility that the public grasped easily and in numbers. The chromaticism was an artifact of a decorative surface; the highfalutin sounds of strings and choirs brought to mind not the classics but the populist sentimentality of countless Hollywood films. From his chord progressions to the limpid piano lines he played on such recordings as Peggy Lee's "Be Anything (But Be Mine)" or his own "Homesick, That's All," there was a directness to the Jenkins style. His was a pop modernism imbued with sentimental nostalgia, a stylistic ambivalence whose commercial success evinced its resonance with the public mood.

Jenkins was largely self-taught, with a fine ear and musical smarts developed in his childhood home in Saint Louis, where his father was a church organist. A high school dropout unaware that there were such things as orchestration manuals and treatises, he prowled the local union hall in Saint Louis pestering musicians to learn the ranges of instruments. In 1928, at eighteen, he landed his first arranging job with one of the city's most prominent outfits, the Joe Gill band, where by his own admission he "made a ton of mistakes" but earned the bandleader's indulgence. Gill could see that the young man "had something" and so tolerated the trial and error of an apprentice's on-the-job training. Jenkins went on to a job in the local Fox Theater, which still had a large orchestra for film accompaniment, working with "a very sympathetic conductor who," Jenkins recalled, "would let me try any arrangement I wanted, and if it didn't come off, I could try something else." Writing for the pictures, he learned to fashion music that underscored drama, emotion, and narrative, a skill he would put to use in the recording studio.

Jenkins reckoned that these early jobs "beat any school in the world" for learning the ropes as a professional composer and arranger and preparing him for the coveted position of arranger in the Isham Jones Orchestra—"the greatest sweet ensemble of that time or any other time," he called it—which he took in 1932.[58] He stayed on after Jones retired in 1936 and leadership of the band's alumni cooperative passed to Woody Herman. He also wrote arrangements for the likes of Benny Goodman, Paul Whiteman, and Kostelanetz as he rose to the top of his profession, becoming music director for a string of network radio shows culminating with the Dick Haymes Show, which featured both songs and what Jenkins called "mini-operas."

In September of 1949, four years after signing with Decca, Jenkins wrote charts for a Louis Armstrong session featuring versions of "That Lucky Old Sun" and "Blueberry Hill." The latter was originally recorded by Gene Autry in 1940, although it was best known in the 1941 Glenn Miller version. The collaboration fulfilled a desire Jenkins had harbored since first hearing Armstrong in 1925. At the session, by his own admission, Jenkins "went all to pieces," becoming so excited that he "brought in an arrangement to the date with more junk in it than a 3rd Ave. antique shop."[59] He pruned the arrangements at the session, but they remained replete with orchestral and choral shadings. As he had with the Andrews Sisters, Jenkins repackaged Armstrong in an alien stylistic milieu in which Armstrong's iconic jazz persona was only part of a larger set piece, his elastic phrasing clearly arising from some other musical place than Jenkins's scripted orchestra and chorus (prominently featuring the "Gor-don Jen-kins" motif). Although both men were grounded in earlier styles, their singular musical meeting produced something essentially modern, conceived and realized in the new musical hothouse of the recording studio.

In the second half of 1950, Jenkins continued his hot streak with the Weavers, another case of a mixed stylistic marriage in which once again his anachronistic style produced an unexpected result. This time, however, the singers were not established stars with a widely known stylistic legacy. Rather, it was the musical idiom they represented that was treated to Jenkins's eclectic revision. The Weavers were a quartet of folk revivalists—Pete Seeger, Ronnie Gilbert, Lee Hays, and Fred Hellerman—who performed their own arrangements of traditional folk songs, as well as newer songs from the urban folk repertory by such writers as Woody Guthrie and Huddie Ledbetter. Seeger had gained some notoriety in the late 1930s as a member, along with Guthrie, of the Almanac Singers. And in 1948 he had campaigned with Progressive Party presidential candidate Henry Wallace. But the Weavers only began to capture a general audience when they became regulars at Max Gordon's Village Vanguard in Greenwich Village in the winter of 1950. After a slow start, the shows began selling out regularly as the residency went on month after month. The group displayed "electrifying vim," "amazingly gutty harmonies," "pure excitement of sound," and a "seemingly endless repertoire . . . with plenty of variety," as a *Down Beat* reviewer put it.[60] In the audience, night after night, sat Jenkins "alive with energy," Hellerman recalled.[61] Jenkins admired the group's lively yet unaffected music making, which struck him as deeply genuine. (In 1963 he wrote to Hays saying that he still had the Weavers' original demo tape for Decca and that he played it often, remembering fondly the Vanguard shows "where music, talent and truth had such a wonderful blending.")[62]

The Weavers signed with Decca after some intense lobbying on Jenkins's part. Decca A&R chief Dave Kapp had little confidence in the group's commercial potential, especially given the folk scene's socialist leanings. Moreover, *Down Beat* reported, the label was grappling with "the problem of how to fit them into the commercial picture" since they could not be "departmentalized as hillbillies, blues and rhythm, or pop."[63] Kapp finally relented but only when the group alerted Jenkins that they were on the verge of signing with Miller at Columbia. Jenkins insisted to Kapp that he would record the group one way or another even if he had to pay for it himself, and, although Kapp saw it as little more than financial folly, he reluctantly indulged his star arranger.

The American folk revival of the 1930s and 1940s bore a guileless aura seemingly antithetical to the glitzy polish of major-label pop music. With an emphasis on the plainspoken expression of age-old themes, the music represented a "wide human procession," as Carl Sandburg phrased it in the introduction to his folk song collection, *The American Songbag,* "as ancient as the medieval European ballads brought to the Appalachian Mountains" yet "as modern as a skyscraper, the Volstead Act, and the latest oil-well gusher." As a commodity, folk music had only a marginal market presence, but this only heightened its image of authenticity and connectedness to a mythical past and enduring tradition. Its resonance was not dependent on mass marketing for, as Sandburg put it, the music came "from the hearts and voices of thousands of men and women."[64] When the Weavers performed their first reunion concert at Carnegie Hall in 1955—after landing on the House Un-American Activities Committee's blacklist and falling from the pop firmament—Sandburg contributed liner notes to the recording in which he wrote, "The Weavers are out of the grass roots of America. I salute them for their great work in authentic renditions of ballads, folk songs, ditties, nice antiques of word and melody."[65]

But their collaborations with Jenkins were anything but "authentic renditions." Like so much else in the pop landscape of 1950, the records were confections, with songs and performances dressed in lavish and idiosyncratic garb. Compared to the music a listener would have heard at the Vanguard shows, the Weavers' Decca recordings were in a style whose provenance was more Hollywood than heartland. On each track, Jenkins took a different approach, treating the songs like scripts to be enacted according to their own unique character. The first single was "Tzena, Tzena, Tzena," an adaptation of an Israeli song that he set to the brassy sound of a Gershwin musical, heightening the Weavers' rollicking tempo and rhythmic verve with exuberant orchestral and choral flourishes bordering on the madcap, humorously punctuated with the insistent "Gor-don Jen-kins" motto. The track's momentum was irresistible in its toe-tapping catchiness, and, although Jenkins filled every available bit of musical space with bustling commotion, he managed almost miraculously never to overpower the singers or their instruments.

The record's B-side was a version of Huddie Ledbetter's "Goodnight, Irene," which opened with a tear-jerking violin melody that set a wistful mood evoking a past musical time. Jenkins had a natural affinity for the sentimental underscore, and on "Goodnight Irene" he aimed to ply the heartstrings with a sweet-sad nostalgia. Most of the arrangement that followed was far more demure than "Tzena," but there was one choral/instrumental section early on that set an oddly exotic tone, a vocalise that melded chorus and instruments in a texture of otherworldly strangeness. Again, the folksingers and the studio orchestra and chorus coexisted in bizarre juxtaposition. How to take the campfire sing-along commingled with what sounded an alien siren call? All of the track's main elements exuded a sense of musical times past, but in their electronic fusion they became a modern pop collage, a concoction without precedent.

The record was released in June, and to nearly everyone's astonishment both sides became runaway hits, selling over two million copies. Ronnie Gilbert recalled hearing "Tzena" on jukeboxes everywhere as she traveled across the country on her honeymoon. Seeger noted a similar ubiquity with "Goodnight, Irene." "The summer of 1950," he remembered, "no American could escape that song unless you plugged up your ears and went out in the wilderness someplace."[66] The scene typified the growing upheaval in the pop mainstream. The songs, one by two members of the British Army's Palestine Regiment, another by a black Texan songwriter with a violent past, both sung by a group of left-wing folksingers accompanied by a slick New York City studio orchestra playing a species of 1930s Broadway/Hollywood music, were nationwide hits. It was, as Gilbert put it, "unthinkable." In her estimation, the Weavers, and the nation along with them, "were wandering through this maze of mainstream music, not knowing where the heck we were going, what we were doing there, or if there was a way back."[67] For Seeger, who had dropped out of Harvard in 1938 to lead the life of a left-wing troubadour, the moment was both heady and disorienting. As he recalled it, "1950 was a rare opportunity to hear myself coming out of a jukebox. It happened then, and in 1951, and never again. All I could do was laugh; it was so unexpected. I remember once hearing my voice, and all I could do was roll on the floor with my heels in the air. I felt as though I was Eliza the flower girl, suddenly being dressed up in a gown and taken to the queen's ball."[68]

The Jenkins-Weavers collaborations produced a number of sides— "Around the Corner (Beneath the Berry Tree)," "Old Paint (Ride Around, Little Dogies)," "Wimoweh (Mbube)," "So Long (It's Been Good to Know Yuh)," "The Midnight Special," "Lonesome Traveler"— each of which married folk simplicity and pop extravagance in paradoxical revisions of familiar tropes. The spareness and apparent sincerity of the folk idiom became the subject of pop pageantry and production-number spectacle, and the interaction brought forth something new. The Weavers would have only a brief moment of commercial success before their names began to appear in anticommunist publications such as *Red Channels* and *Counterattack,* and in February 1952 they were accused before the House Un-American Activities Committee of membership in the Communist Party. In 1954, Decca dropped the group, and their records went out of print after a run of eleven charted hits, six of them Jenkins arrangements. But their Decca sides left an indelible mark on the pop soundscape of the early 1950s, adding to the mix yet another strand of peculiar musical styling born not in performance venues but in a recording studio.

Peggy Lee came to Decca from Capitol in 1952. She had come up with an unusual version of Rodgers and Hart's "Lover," which she was performing in her nightclub act and wanted to record. But Capitol, with Les Paul's 1948 version for overdubbed and processed electric guitars already in its catalog, refused. When Gabler heard Lee perform the song at the Copacabana in New York, he wooed her to Decca with a promise that recording "Lover" would be the label's first priority. He assigned Jenkins to the arrangement, and, although Jenkins would ultimately judge the result a bit frenetic even for him, the melodramatic rapture he brought to the work was well suited to Lee's conception. The idea had come to her as a general hunch about the dramatic potential inherent in combining a layered Latin percussion section and a series of rising stepwise modulations.[69] She cast about for a song suitable for such treatment and settled on "Lover," which had first appeared in the 1932 film *Love Me Tonight* (with different lyrics). The song was a waltz whose melody and harmonies descended steadily by half steps through the first six measures of each A-section, an unusual chromatic device that, combined with Hart's lyrics suggesting the passionate yet fraught transport of transgressive love, gave Lee suitable material with which to cast her fevered musical spell.

The first thing the Lee-Jenkins version did was to do away with the lilt of the waltz meter, substituting a quick four. The track's introduction began with a repeated sixteenth-note chromatic turn nervously spun out by agitated violins followed by the full orchestra featuring an abrasive trumpet riff and impelled by a hyperactive Latin percussion section, all echoing around the resonant Pythian Temple recording venue. The introduction offered no hint of the song to follow, and Lee's entrance sounded a disoriented delirium oddly incongruous with the orchestral setup. She seemed to follow her own tempo, slower than the rest of the orchestra, dragging out the waltz remnants against the orchestra's rushing tempo. In the first of the track's three thirty-two-bar choruses, Lee stuck to the melody while the orchestra wove a fairly sparse texture. With each chorus, however, she became increasingly unhinged. As the key moved up with each repetition, she abandoned the melody as written, infusing her improvisation with melismas and microtonal swoops and repeating words with rhythmic agitation. As her performance seemed to succumb to a rising desperation, Jenkins's arrangement followed suit in a through-composed narrative mirroring the singer's growing histrionics.

The record sold over a million copies in the summer of 1952 and was followed by another, more modest hit in Cole Porter's "Just One of Those Things," cast in a similarly frenzied style. The track is a surpassingly strange piece of pop music—edgy, tense, and overwrought, yet clearly a big hit with the public. In a *Down Beat* editorial, Ella Mae Morse, a terrific singer herself and Lee's former label-mate at Capitol, took Lee to task over the record, chiding her for following a trend Morse attributed to Johnnie Ray: cartoonish, emotional exaggeration. "I thought she must be kidding," wrote Morse. "I kept waiting for Mel Blanc to come in and start purring like a cat or quacking like a duck." Worse, the record was a symptom of a more general trend. "Everybody's shouting," she complained, adding that she looked forward to the time when singers would once again "start relaxing and singing the way they feel, instead of trying to force things."[70]

Fran Warren, another singer Morse singled out for criticism, responded several weeks later in the same magazine. She pointed out first that her own loud singing was a result of proper voice training and her work in unamplified musical theater. With regard to "Lover," she supposed that Morse was simply confused. It was not belting on Lee's part that gave the record its manic effect; rather, the "background by Gordon Jenkins was overwhelming," she wrote. Warren agreed that Johnnie Ray was not a singer. "He has no voice and the worst intonation," she wrote. He was, however, an effective "stylist" with a talent for "showmanship," and she ended with the wish that "some of the older singers wouldn't worry so much about the styles of the younger kids in the music world." What was happening was "exciting to a lot of people," she reminded her fellow thrush, "whether we like it or not."[71]

· 5 ·

Like Mitch Miller, the guitarist Les Paul was an innovative record producer who appreciated the value of a gimmick. He integrated the most advanced electronic trickery of the time into his arrangements of material ranging from ballads to rhythm numbers to country songs, all of which, in his hands, became novelty items. Paul was as much enthusiastic tinkerer and electronic hobbyist as accomplished guitarist and arranger. With equipment he modified or built himself and recording techniques of his own devising, he used overdubbing and electronic effects to create records of astonishing artifice. His first solo hit was an instrumental version of "Lover" (1948), on which he overdubbed eight guitars manipulated variously to create a range of electronically tailored timbres. The record's B-side, "Brazil," was also a hit. Both tracks later appeared on an album collection Capitol released in 1950 called *The New Sound!* a phrase that caught on in the press and came to signify the new wave in record making. Here was music, the album's liner notes proclaimed, "to satisfy that mood for a fresh approach." For the forward-looking music fan, the album contained music that was "understandable, melodic, free from dissonant 'modernisms' . . . and yet unusual enough to halt conversation in even the most sophisticated gatherings."[72]

But like novelty songs and idiosyncratic arrangements, such electronic artifice came in for regular criticism from traditionalists, most of whose pop sensibilities were tempered by a jazz ideology that righteously distinguished musical substance from sonic distraction. Even positive reviews of Paul's work contained hints of skepticism about their musical value. His technical accomplishments were impressive, but what did it all add up to? As a "combined performance and technical achievement," read a *Down Beat* review, "Lover" had "few parallels." But the reviewer could not resist a seemingly trivial caveat, writing, "You may disagree with the four-note tag . . . from a purely musical standpoint."[73] A *Metronome* reviewer found the track "Carioca," a top-twenty hit, "a great mechanical feat" but added that "musically it's a good deal less."[74] When Paul began recording with Mary Ford, he used the same "layer-cake" overdubbing techniques, only now on the voice parts as well as guitar.[75] Paul and Ford's biggest hit of all, "How High the Moon," which was the country's number-one record for nine weeks in 1951, brought this from *Down Beat:* "All *Moon* needed was to have a Les Paul version of it to kill it for all time. He's now taken care of that detail in a sometimes-funny satire in which he mixes bop clichés, banal riffs, hillbilly twangings and the multiplied voice of Mary Ford. Not for tender ears."[76]

In 1952, *Metronome* editor Barry Ulanov wrote a mostly admiring feature on Paul that nevertheless took care to distinguish between his virtuosic musicianship and his "juke box success." Ulanov aimed to let readers know that Paul used his hands "musically as well as commercially," and "buried under a flood of praise—and nickels" that had anointed him the "new King of the Jukes" lay a background of "serious achievement."[77] While Paul's was not "the kind of gimmick that dies out with one or two, or even half a dozen successful records," neither was it "a trick that [could] bask forever in such high esteem." The gimmick's "eventual failure," Ulanov concluded, was to be cheered at least as much as Paul's pop success, for it "might bring back a great soloist."[78] The implication of a mutual exclusivity was clear.

Miller's critics, too, complained of what they perceived as a substitution of beguiling sound for musical substance. "Miller's unique contribution to the trade is his ability to make pretty bad songs sound pretty good, by means of musical-*cum*-electronic hocus-pocus," wrote Rice in the *New Yorker* feature.[79] In a similar formulation, the *New York Times'* John S. Wilson wrote that "a song became 'good' only if it could be matched with a gimmick" and furthermore "under Miller's influence, normal voices took on awesome, doom-filled proportions, gunned up by echo chambers, multiple taping and the endless use of sound gadgetry."[80] Miller's one-time champion, John Hammond, was especially put off by Miller's use of sonic enhancements such as reverb. In a jazz recording initiative for Vanguard Records that he characterized as a "return to natural sound," Hammond sought to redress what he perceived to be the sonic excesses that had moved pop records away from transparent sonic representation, observing, "Mitch Miller's a great guy, but ever since about 1948, when he started playing tricks with sound—making those horrible echo-chamber recordings for one thing—all the record companies have been knocking themselves out to achieve phony effects. . . . Anyhow, we're fighting all that electronic fakery."[81]

Ulanov, too, characterized Miller's methods as dehumanizing flimflam. In an editorial titled "Mitch the Goose Man," he wrote, "Borrowing a trick or two from the army engineers, Mitch applied camouflage to the efforts of singers willing to lose their identity to the sound-effects man." For Miller, of course, the interface of music and technology was now fundamental to modern record production. His method, which Ulanov grudgingly admitted was "a new art . . . now in the ascendancy in the record business," brought together singer and sound effects man in a new kind of collaborative project.[82] But Ulanov's real complaint seemed aimed at the very nature of the new pop aesthetic. While his general comments focused on the easy targets of sound effects and reverb, his inclusion of "Cry of the Wild Goose" in the editorial suggested a broader concern, for that record had no sound effects, just hypercharged brass and an earnest male chorus accompanying an ersatz folk song. It was not camouflage, but the musical mélange itself, that disquieted the listener seeking some measure of identifiable stylistic authenticity.

The criticism that swirled around the new approaches to record production was set against an aesthetic backstory in which the fading swing ethos remained the symbol of American pop music's Golden Age. Adherents everywhere passionately advocated and expectantly awaited its resurgence. The postwar trade press carried persistent speculation over the ultimate fate of the swing bands, which by the early 1950s teetered near extinction. *Down Beat,* acknowledging such general factors as "diversified audience taste" and "overplay given vocal recordings by disc jockeys," determined to get to the bottom of the story by following and reporting regularly on a newly formed "laboratory band" led by Roy

Stevens.[83] But while the project generated many articles and editorials throughout 1950, nothing more specific was ever pinpointed, for the causes were diffuse. The competition from broadcast recordings proved a constant source of erosion through the late 1940s, with remote broadcasts of live band engagements falling in popularity as more and more stations switched to disc jockey shows.[84] And with fewer and fewer venues willing to post the guaranteed sums demanded by big-name bands, along with cutbacks in profit shares, financial pressures took an ever greater toll.

But there were also aesthetic clashes between musicians and a public whose tastes and attitudes were changing. When *Billboard* conducted a survey of amusement park venues in 1947, for example, it was learned that, in addition to financial considerations, owners had heard from their patrons that " 'brassy, jam-type' bands are out, and orks must offer a little showmanship and entertainment over and above dispensing of dance rhythms." Bands playing in a sweet style, "sugar orks," were preferred by a majority of respondents, and demand was slight for bands playing primarily "swing, rhythm or jump" styles.[85] Singers, once the bands' occasional adornments, had become the stars, and audiences were demanding more ballads and slow dances. In 1948 several colleges, their students miffed at bandleaders' refusals to take their song requests, put a "three-ballads-out-of-four" clause into the orchestras' contracts.[86] In a bid for survival, and noting the success of the Spike Jones comedy orchestra and its wildly popular "music depreciation revue," many bands began to include novelty gimmicks of their own to keep up business. "Even the extremists in musical righteousness" lent a touch of vaudeville entertainment to their acts with dancers, comics, whistlers, and dramatic bits.[87]

In 1950, the record industry attempted its own rescue when RCA Victor, with great fanfare, released a set of fifteen albums called *Here Come the Dance Bands Again. Billboard* trumpeted the collection as a "New Birth for Dance Bands." It was a heroic effort for which Victor secured pledges from radio stations for an estimated ten thousand hours of radio exposure. If successful, the initiative "could conceivably revive the dance band field, which has been dormant since 1942," the year the AFM recording ban took effect and "when vocalists, under the impetus of the craze for Frank Sinatra, preempted the field from the dance maestri."[88] But despite repeated efforts and occasional glimmers of hope, the bands' revival would never come, even though as late as 1957 *Billboard* reported that "the average jock . . . longs wistfully for their return."[89] The episode was a telling reminder that the power of large institutions over public taste was not what it once was.

Sinatra had indeed done his part to eclipse swing, moving from boy singer with the Harry James and Tommy Dorsey bands to superstar swoon-inducing soloist whose collaborations with arranger Axel Stordahl regularly featured ballads in string-heavy arrangements. But Sinatra, too, was a persistent critic of the new directions in pop, especially the many novelty ditties that increasingly displaced his beloved Tin Pan Alley classics on the charts. In 1947, he began his second stint as host of the radio program *Your Hit Parade,* which gave him a front-row seat on the growing novelty phenomenon. Sinatra was obliged not only to introduce the top ten songs each week but also to perform whatever tune was in the top spot. The format caused him to suffer firsthand through such tunes as "Feudin' and Fightin'," "Too Fat Polka," and "Woody Woodpecker," all effrontery to the high-class pop aesthetic he identified with and championed.

Sinatra and Miller famously came to loggerheads when Miller took over A&R for pop singles at Columbia, Sinatra's longtime label, and their differences epitomized at close quarters pop music's aesthetic tussle. In 1945, however, they had been of similar mind, collaborating on a labor of love—a recording of concert music by Alec Wilder, who Miller had known since his Eastman days. Wilder's music was something of a classical-popular amalgam; his well-honed compositional technique lent his pop songs elegance, and his sense of the popular imbued his concert music with an accessible warmth, both of which accorded with Sinatra's high-pop principles. Sinatra suggested to Columbia's A&R director, Manie Sachs (Miller's predecessor), that the label record a set of Wilder's pieces. Sachs balked at the prospect of a financial flop until Sinatra offered to conduct the orchestra and release the record as *Frank Sinatra Conducts the Music of Alec Wilder.* According to Miller, who actively promoted Wilder's music, it was his idea for Sinatra to volunteer himself as conductor; lending the star's name to the project would allay Sachs's misgivings. Since the proposition was only a marketing ploy, however (Sinatra could not read a score let alone rehearse an orchestra), Miller prepared the orchestra before Sinatra arrived for recording. He also played the oboe and English horn solos.

The two men retained a mutual respect when Miller took over from Sachs at Columbia in 1950. On Sinatra's sessions, Miller approached his producer's role in a traditional way, as an organizing supervisor, leaving creative decisions to Sinatra and whoever was handling the arranging. With Sinatra's string of commercial disappointments in 1949–50, however, Miller, by now the hottest producer in the business, was instructed by higher-ups to take a more active role. He managed to produce a top-five hit for Sinatra with a version of "Goodnight Irene," but Sinatra resented the drift away from the classic pop songs he loved and believed in. "Hey, that's a nice tune," offered deejay Ben Heller in a backstage interview. "You wanna bet?" Sinatra retorted. And when Heller suggested that Sinatra "do a lotta songs like that," the answer was curt: "Don't hold your breath!" Sinatra's drummer, Johnny Blowers, remembered thinking, "How in the world did [Mitch] ever get him to do this?" as crowds clamored for "Goodnight Irene" at every Sinatra appearance.[90] When Miller proposed "My Heart Cries For You" and "The Roving Kind," both pseudo-folk singsong items, Sinatra flatly refused, even though the orchestra, chorus, and studio were already booked and waiting to go. (Miller went on to record the songs with the unknown Al Cernik, who, in turn, became an overnight success as Guy Mitchell with million sellers on both tunes.) It ended badly between the two men, with Sinatra accusing Miller of ruining his career, a stretch given Sinatra's many personal and professional woes at the time.

In truth, although Miller did bring Sinatra some novelty material, including the notorious "Mama Will Bark" (a duet with the early fifties television personality Dagmar, a woman with "the voluptuous curves of a Venus, the provocative grace of a young Mae West, and the virtue of a Girl Scout"), the singer's last years at Columbia also produced many recordings of songs by venerable Tin Pan Alley masters—Rodgers and Hammerstein ("Hello, Young Lovers"), Cole Porter ("I Am Loved"), Duke and Harburg ("April in Paris")—and an up-and-coming Cy Coleman ("Why Try to Change Me Now").[91] But Sinatra's high-pop recordings were not selling in the early fifties. The star with a household name who had commanded 41,000 dollars for one week of performances in Chicago in the spring of 1946 was now struggling. The public was hungry for something else. Sinatra, of course, would recover his career momentum with a move to Capitol and a fruitful new partnership with arranger Nelson Riddle. But even as he found his footing, he found, too, that the pop terrain around him continued its drift toward noisy diversity.

In the increasingly chaotic musical economy, all the old certainties were fading. New players seemed to appear daily with products that, though widely popular, were inferior according to established high-pop standards. Nor would the upheaval end with the major label pop kitsch of the early fifties, which, though lambasted for its tastelessness, was nonetheless perfectly competent in execution. There was no denying that the likes of Miller and Paul were masters of their craft. But they, too, would soon find themselves competing desperately with an even more motley stylistic brew purveyed by groups of unknown amateurs whose rough-hewn recordings swept the country like a rising tide, bewildering the mainstream pop establishment with something vaguely labeled "rock and roll." "People like me and Crosby were confused," recalled Paul in 1977, "because everything we had learned was just thrown out the window. The music world had taken a different shape and I didn't know what to do about it."[92]

Miller was resolute in his rejection of the amateurs, passing up opportunities to sign Elvis Presley, Buddy Holly, and Connie Francis. In his famously controversial speech at a disc jockey convention in Kansas City on March 8, 1958, he blasted the music of "the last couple of years" for its "paralyzing monotony." It was "not the creation of real musicians" and had "no entertainment value for anyone over fourteen," a group he characterized as "the pre-shave crowd that makes up twelve percent of the country's population and zero percent of its buying power, once you eliminate pony tail ribbons, popsicles and peanut brittle."[93] Perhaps the teenagers were not the best customers for many of the radio stations' sponsors, but they were a powerful new force in the decade's pop singles market. Only three years earlier Miller himself had written an articulate defense of the current pop trends, including the rising mainstream popularity of rhythm and blues, in which he acknowledged that it was the "millions of white teen-agers who [bought] most of the pop records in America" and that it was in the natural order that "the appeal of popular songs is primarily to young people."[94] But things had spun farther out of control than Miller could have imagined, with large numbers of records "so badly produced the listener thinks he can't tune [the station] in properly" making their way to the top of the charts.[95] Still, while he blamed rock and roll for weakening the singles market, retail figures told another story. The year would see 47 discs chalk up at least a million in sales, with 72 record firms contributing 283 singles to the pop chart, all of which were record-setting numbers.[96]

There was irony aplenty in the rapid rise of yet another generation of stars so soon after the newcomers of the early fifties had shaken pop's jazz and Tin Pan Alley foundations. The stars of the first half decade had accelerated a musical turmoil that would soon consign them to memory. There would be no going back. Although they deplored the rock and roll music that increasingly displaced them, it was they themselves whose records, gimmicks and all, had laid the groundwork for a new, vastly diffuse aesthetic whose only constant was the pursuit of distinctive recordings. Once ignited, the hunger for new records became insatiable and the trickle from small upstart labels into the mainstream became a torrent churning the booming record market. Records could be made quickly and inexpensively by almost anyone, their sounds rapidly disseminated through all kinds of outlets, both local and national. It all made for a volatile, fast-moving consumer culture in which no one could retain the kind of control major labels and publishers had enjoyed in the past. The "new sound" was any sound from anywhere that broke through the din to claim a spot on the charts.

Sinatra, in a 1948 diatribe against novelty songs, said that "if the music business is to lead the public—and actually we do lead as to the things it likes—we must give people things that move them emotionally."[97] It was a reasonable prescription except for its top-down formulation. The explosive growth in record sales brought about a far more democratic musical economy, with the public voting at local record shops, eighty-nine cents a throw. Who led who was an ever-changing question. Publishers, who had run the business for decades, were the first to feel the effects records had on songs. "A record should be a by product of publishing," one old-guard publisher lamented. In earlier times, publishers had a "concept of quality and values in songs" that helped to guide record company decisions. In the new way of things, however, publishers did not "dare publish a song until some artist perhaps likes it, or the whim of an a&r 'genius' decides it should be done with echo chambers, or a 'cracking-your-knuckles' type of arrangement."[98] The passing of control from publisher to record company—from song sheet to recording—was an internal power shift in an industry centered in New York City. But more far-reaching in its aesthetic ramifications was the diffusion of choice across the national cultural spectrum—geographic, economic, ethnic, and social—facilitated by consumers' access to a cornucopia of records.

In his 1953 autobiography, Crosby summed up his understanding of the new state of affairs in pop music.

> Those who are now in charge of production at the various recording companies tell me that to awaken popular interest in a record they've got to produce a new "sound": an unusual combination of instruments or voices which record buyers haven't heard before. If you can do this, they say, you've got a chance to turn out a hit record. It doesn't matter what the material is like or how good the song is or what it's all about, how it's done, or how it's performed. It's just whether it features an unusual sound which hasn't been heard before.[99]

In contrast to Sinatra's vehemence, Crosby was philosophical. It was he, after all, who had pushed for the transcribed radio show, he who had promoted magnetic tape recording, he who had given Les Paul his first tape recorder and encouraged him to pursue his electronic fancy. More-over, Crosby recorded all manner of repertory during his years at Decca. Jack Kapp "saw to it" that Crosby "sang hillbillies and blues, ballads and Victor Herbert, traditional songs and patriotic songs, light opera, and even an opera aria or two," all of which he was happy to do.[100] In short, Crosby had both anticipated and helped to instigate much of what was now in pop's ascendancy. But the new way was not for him. He reckoned that this musical world, where songs and performances were only com-ponents of a larger project aimed at an overall sonic impression, had passed him by. "To tell the truth," he wrote, "I don't think I'm capable of producing any new sounds. I've used up all the sounds in my system many years ago."[101]

THREE

Hustlers and Amateurs

There never was an industry. There was a collection of individual record companies run by individual people with different ethics, different morality, different needs, different greeds.

—JERRY WEXLER

We didn't sit down and figure it out with pencil and paper, we just went in and experimented.

—ROLAND JANES

· 1 ·

Wayne "Buddy" Knox was twenty-three years old when he recorded "Party Doll" in 1956. He later told an interviewer that he had written the song years earlier when he was "just a kid," maybe fifteen, entertaining himself on his parents' farm near Happy, Texas, after chores were done.[1] He traveled to Clovis, New Mexico, just over the state line, in search of a recording studio he had learned of from a fellow West Texan musician, Roy Orbison. Established for company business by the Atchison, Topeka and Santa Fe Railway in 1907, Clovis was an unlikely location for a studio, but in the postwar years such small operations sprang up in all sorts of improbable places around the country. Orbison had already made the trip across the border, and following Knox yet another young West Texan, Buddy Holly, would find his way to the studio, which was owned and operated by Norman Petty, himself a musician as well as an engineer and record producer. Here, far from the entertainment capitals of New York and Los Angeles—or any real music scene like that of New Orleans or Memphis—records were crafted in ways unthinkable in big-city recording studios. With no hourly rate or union rules to influence the process, musicians and engineer experimented at will with sounds and arrangements, the criteria for success mostly a matter of guesswork and gut feeling.

Petty was born in Clovis in 1927 and raised there in a close-knit family. The building that would one day house Norman Petty Recording Studios was a general store on West Seventh Street run by his aunt Eula and her husband. The adjacent building, which would house Nor-Va-Jak, Inc., Petty's publishing company, and serve as living quarters for him and his wife Violet, was his father Sidney's place of business, a gas station and garage where Sidney fixed cars and appliances while his wife Thelma pumped gas and kept the books. According to accounts from friends and family, before he was ten Petty had demonstrated the traits that would make him a successful record producer: a quick musical ear, a keen sensitivity to sound, and an interest in and affinity for electronics.[2] At twelve, he acquired a Wilcox-Gay wire recorder and began recording commercially, hauling the machine around to record weddings, servicemen's messages to loved ones, and political campaign material. As a teenager, he formed a band, the Torchy Swingsters, and worked as a disc jockey at Clovis station KICA, where his group also performed on the air. Following a stint in the air force, where he continued to work in radio and recording, he returned to Clovis in 1946 and two years later married his high school sweetheart, Violet Ann Brady, a classically trained pianist with whom he formed the Norman Petty Trio, with himself on organ, his new bride on piano, and Jack Vaughn on guitar.[3]

The group became a successful regional touring outfit playing a range of repertory that included both pop and country songs, all rendered in a smooth lounge-pop style. Eventually they landed a deal with X, an RCA Victor subsidiary. Their 1954 recording of Duke Ellington's "Mood Indigo," a velveteen, middle-of-the-road pop arrangement for organ, guitar, and piano with close vocal harmonies, was a top-twenty hit. Petty used his royalties to outfit a studio where the band could produce its own masters, which could then be leased to record companies. With his experience as an engineer, the move made good business sense. It also meant that the group would be free from studio time constraints and better able to control the overall quality of their recordings. But do-it-yourself recording was only the beginning, for in short order Petty opened up the studio to outside clients. When word got around that he not only made excellent recordings but also had big-time music industry contacts in New York, young musicians from across the region began making their way to his door.

While Petty's pop sensibilities were very different from those of the raw young country and rockabilly musicians who began showing up at the studio, he was well aware of the industry's relentless novelty hunt, and as a modern record producer he was quite willing to experiment with new directions in record making. At a time when the standard big-city recording session was limited by union rules and record company budgets to three hours, during which producers expected to complete four sides, finished arrangements and well-rehearsed performances were usually prerequisites to entering the studio. Petty, however, charged a flat fee for projects and let the clock run. The musicians might stay in the Petty recording/residence complex for days at a time pursuing adventurous excursions into the stylistic unknown, driven by a sense that there was something important about a record and that making one required more than just registering a musical performance. This method allowed the process time to percolate, opening space for the unexpected. Standard recording practice required music to be fully formed before recording began. But in Clovis the music took shape in what amounted to a musical retreat. The feel of the rooms, the hermetic companionship, and all the peculiarities of any given day in the recording studio became entwined with the acts of musical creation and expression.

Knox, bassist Jimmy Bowen, and guitarist Don Lanier had formed the Orchids while studying at West Texas State College in Dumas, Texas. They played mostly for personal amusement but also worked small gigs "for $5 here, $5 there, and all the beer we could drink, in little bars and joints," as Knox put it. The trip to Clovis seems to have been as much to make a souvenir as anything else, a recorded token of the band's existence. "The only thing we'd gone to Clovis for," recalled Knox, "was just to have a couple of copies of the record," with which, after cutting the acetates himself on the studio's disc-cutting lathe, Petty sent them home, reportedly after three nights of recording for which he charged sixty dollars. On the record's flip side was another Knox tune, "I'm Stickin' With You." The group was augmented in the studio by a local drummer, David Alldred, beating on a cotton-filled cardboard box (a trick Petty would later use for Buddy Holly's "Not Fade Away"), several female backup singers, and a stand-in bass player since Bowen's bass skills proved inadequate for recording. The record was nicely balanced, its clean sound a mark of Petty's refined sense of sonic detail. But the song and performance were strictly amateur: a stiff, emotionally flat vocal; sloppy ensemble; inconsistent rhythm; an inane lyric; and a melody that clung for dear life to the tonic note. Back in Dumas, however, a local record man, Chester Oliver (of Blue Moon Records), offered to press several hundred copies for local release, and the record came out on a label created expressly for the Orchids (Triple-D, named for the Dumas radio station WDDD). With some regional airplay the record became a minor radio hit around West Texas and sold a couple of hundred copies.

What happened next was as incredible as it was typical of these tumultuous years in the music business. Through Lanier's sister, who was working as a model in New York City, a copy of the record made its way to a new record label, Roulette, one of whose owners was Morris Levy. At this point, the amateurs' naive musical souvenir was taken up by one of the industry's savviest hard-core hustlers. Levy was a tough Sephardic Jew from the South Bronx cut from similar cloth to Savoy's Harold Lubinsky, King's Syd Nathan, Old Town's Hyman Weiss, and Chess's Phil and Leonard Chess. He was connected to some of New York's top organized crime figures, who he saw simply as business associates. Like all who survived in the record business, he knew how to turn records, by hook or by crook, into serious money. Because in its regional run both sides of the record had received positive responses, Roulette sensed a potential double-sided hit and split the Orchids' record in two. "I'm Stickin' With You," which had been sung by Bowen, became the A-side of a second release. With the group's name changed to the Rhythm Orchids, the records were released under the names Buddy Knox and the Rhythm Orchids and Jimmy Bowen and the Rhythm Orchids. They were Roulette's first two records, and both climbed into the top twenty on the national pop and R&B charts; "Party Doll" eventually reached number one on the pop chart.

In summary, the recording was made at a small, out-of-the-way studio and was not intended for commercial release, yet by chance it found its way to a firm two thousand miles away whose owners chose it for their debut offering. Despite the record's lack of professional songcraft, arrangement, and performances and its release on a start-up label with no track record, it rose to the top market position, pushing aside competition from the majors. Moreover, although the record was infused with white West Texas twang, it was warmly received by young black urban audiences according to all three of *Billboard*'s tracking measures: the R&B charts for retail sales, radio, and jukebox play. This set of facts would have made no sense in an earlier pop era. To members of the old guard it still made no sense, but by 1957 they had seen enough of such weird occurrences that they were hardly surprised. The unlikely series of events that led to the success of "Party Doll" and the unlikely appeal of the record itself epitomized the market's turbulence. The industry's long-standing power structure was no longer in control and the one thing record men of all stripes agreed on was that audiences' tastes had become impossible to predict.

· 2 ·

The surge in record sales that followed the war spawned fledgling record labels across the United States, recording and disseminating all manner of musical sound, anything with even the slightest potential audience. The indies' sales were tiny compared to those of the major labels, yet they sometimes managed "spectacular sales figures despite the fact that the artists and tunes were unknown, distribution spotty and exploitation funds virtually non-existent," as Bill Simon put it in a 1949 *Billboard* profile. Simon gave an admiring account of the independent record men's gumption and versatility.

> It has become more and more obvious that the gimmick makes the hit, and these indies have been able to come up with the gimmicks. The hit then makes its own distribution. The indie topper [owner], who usually acts as artists-repertoire chief, recording director, business manager and promotion man, has got out in the field to dig up new talent with that different, provocative sound. And he's kept his doors open to all sorts of new writers and performers. Since overhead is low, and he's not expected to pay the kind of fees a major pays a name artist, he can afford to take chances. And he often has the boldness and the imagination to do so. . . . They have consistently attracted the salable new talent and tunes. They have learned their field thoroughly, and maintain a close contact with the buying public. They have set up their distribution where it counts.[4]

The pioneering indies were run by resourceful, tough, and often ruthless men. Possessed of a gambler's instincts, they took big risks, betting that their shrewdness and resilience would deliver success in the face of long odds. Unlike the movies, the record business was open to almost anyone. All that was required was a recorded master, some cash, and, if one were to continue for very long, a fair amount of luck. Manufacture and distribution were contracted out to record plants and distributors around the country, which meant that much was beyond the record man's control. Promotion was a matter of relentless hustling—every day and in every way imaginable—directed toward anyone who could help sell records. Recording equipment was housed in all manner of unlikely spaces—storefronts, garages, and shacks, as well as radio stations and proper, if spartan, studios. Cosimo Matassa's J&M studio in New Orleans, the site of innumerable historic recordings, including those of Fats Domino and Little Richard, was set up in a room adjacent to his family's appliance store. Sam Phillips's Memphis Recording Service was a storefront. Bill Putnam's original Universal Recording was in an upstairs room in the Chicago Civic Opera House. Many records were recorded on location in a YMCA, church, VFW hall, or house, almost anyplace with a roof and walls.

The indies worked in a sort of parallel universe to the majors, servicing markets deemed too small to cover corporate overhead let alone deliver any substantial profit. Whereas the majors' offices were concentrated in New York and Los Angeles, indies sprouted wherever an opportunity arose. With no need to sell vast quantities, they often put out records they judged to have some sort of local appeal or parochial novelty. Their owners were opportunists, idealists, scoundrels, pirates, dreamers, tough guys, free spirits, swindlers, and quasi- and not-so-quasi-gangsters, all pursuing the next hit. Some were ethical, some were not. As they hung onto a tenuous existence, they clawed for every nickel, and of the hundreds that set out on a wing, a prayer, and a song, few survived for long. But together their energies reoriented the pop music economy; by 1957, they had achieved "virtual dominance" of the pop singles market, claiming more than two-thirds of the top-thirty singles.[5]

Aside from the obvious goal of making money, the record men's motivations and aspirations varied. Ahmet Ertegun and Jerry Wexler at Atlantic in New York City genuinely loved the R&B music they recorded at sessions with such stars as Ruth Brown, Joe Turner, Ray Charles, Clyde McPhatter, and LaVern Baker. They were connoisseurs, their taste evident in their extensive lineup of top talent. Ertegun was an avid jazz and blues record collector and owned thousands of 78s. He and his brother Nesuhi had amassed their collection while growing up in Washington, the sons of Munir Ertegun, the Turkish ambassador to the United States. With a fan's passion and no business experience, Ahmet and cofounder Herb Abramson started Atlantic in 1947 with a pledged credit line of ten thousand dollars from Ertegun's dentist. By his own assessment, Ertegun "had never done a day's work in his life" and "knew next to nothing" about the record business, yet he "had a sense of what might sell."[6] Indeed, he was repaying his dentist before he ever reached the limit of the loan. Wexler, too, was a self-described "music addict" and a "record hunter, fierce and indefatigable." Through the course of his unsettled early life, his musical consciousness developed in a "slow-cooking gumbo of New Orleans jazz, small Harlem combos, big bands, western swing, country, jukebox race music, pop schmaltz."[7] Wexler's broad musical sensibility would sustain decades of record production ranging from LaVern Baker to Aretha Franklin, Solomon Burke to Wilson Pickett, Willie Nelson to Bob Dylan.

The Chess brothers of Chicago came to America from Poland with their parents in the early 1920s. Their father, Joseph, became a scrap dealer in Chicago, and older brother Leonard, whose most valued locution appears to have been "motherfucker," worked for a time in the business. Joined by his brother Phil, he moved on to a series of ventures doing business with the black citizens of Chicago: liquor store, nightclub, record company. The brothers could see the powerful appeal of the urban blues cooking in Chicago in the late forties; it was all around them in the businesses they ran. While all they knew of music was that people would buy it, with little more than instinct, drive, and the good sense to install Willie Dixon as the operation's musical brain, they built a roster— Muddy Waters, Chuck Berry, Bo Diddley, Little Walter, Howlin' Wolf— whose influence would permeate the core of rock music. They traveled incessantly, promoting their records and always on the lookout for untapped talent. In addition to its exemplary blues catalog, which would form the foundation of the 1960s British blues revival, Chess (and its subsidiary Checker) released many seminal rock and roll records: Jackie Brenston's "Rocket 88," the Moonglows' "Sincerely," the Flamingos' "I'll Be Home," and everything by Chuck Berry.

In Cincinnati, Sydney Nathan named his label King, as in "King of them all," as he told his first artists, Merle Travis and Grandpa Jones. It seemed an unlikely ambition for a man of almost forty whose checkered résumé included "drummer, pawnshop owner, jewelry store owner, park concessionaire, and wrestling promoter." But he saw in the hundreds of thousands of transplanted southerners, called hillbillies, working at wartime production in the Cincinnati munitions plants both a ready market and potential talent pool. "We done business," he said, "because we knew how to do business. . . . We work at it as if it was the coffin business, the machinery business, or any other business." After a start in hillbilly music, Nathan branched out into R&B with Bull Moose Jackson, Roy Brown, Wynonie Harris, and many more, not because he was particularly in tune with young urban blacks but because he assessed the market and "saw a need."[8]

The music business has a long history of duplicitous characters and unscrupulous practices. Even its most legitimate corporate institutions have shown that ethics are defined by what can be gotten away with. For small companies flying under the radar somewhere off the industry's beaten paths, there were very few holds barred. Whatever was expedient in the project of making money was on the table. If it worked, for instance, to bribe a radio disc jockey by signing over a songwriter's copyright, which is how Alan Freed came to be credited as the writer of Chuck Berry's "Maybellene," that was simply part of the price (at the artist's expense, of course) of promoting the record. If artists could be convinced to accept flat fees for recording with no expectation of future royalties, or if royalties could be promised but never paid, so much the better for the record man. He, after all, put up the money for recording knowing the odds of a profitable return were considerably less than fifty-fifty. And if he got lucky, the rationalization continued, he still had to contend with distributors who by paying late or not at all turned even a hit into a potential for bankruptcy.

In addition to their freewheeling business practices, the indies demonstrated an equally unbridled and wide-ranging musical taste. In a postwar culture eager for novelty, and with a burgeoning market filled with buyers waiting to snatch up who knew what, many forged into uncharted territory where idiomatic habit gave way to freewheeling invention. The general Wild West atmosphere in which the indies operated fed an aesthetic clutter that accumulated week by week and eventually made inroads in the broader musical landscape. For while they recorded and distributed music in which the pop music establishment initially had little interest either commercially or aesthetically, in the end the indies' growing success could not be ignored. The "smaller diskery influence," *Billboard* reported in 1947, "has frequently pressured major waxeries into getting on the bandwagon."[9] As music from the margins introduced a curious pop audience to a growing array of sounds and sensibilities, the aural buffet expanded rapidly and unpredictably, increasing the uncertainty of gauging public taste.

With a flood of new records released each week, record men, struggling to draw attention to their products, sought some mark of distinction, some sign of freshness or novelty, some hook. Almost anything might do. The finer classes of music—classical, jazz, Broadway, Hollywood—partook of rich legacies that included historically informed aesthetic assumptions, critical discourse, and standards of achievement. But for producers trafficking in the nation's musical margins, recalled Cosimo Matassa, "there was no sense of history. Nobody ever felt like we were producing great art." The goal was to master not an idiom or a practice but the market. Making hits was all that mattered, which meant listeners' responses were a record man's chief guide. Matassa had an instinctual way of judging the records made in his studio. "If you transmit an emotion to the listener," he said simply, "it's a good record." It sounded a truism, "a fundamental thing," and yet it was worth repeating, for he knew from long experience how difficult it was in practice. Day in and day out, the pursuit remained "totally elusive," an uncertain business with few established criteria.[10] While a good song, for instance, had long been presumed to be the sine qua non of a successful record, it was no longer clear what a good song was. One New York publisher complained that, in the "awful turmoil" besetting the industry as the indies gained increasing market share, a song became a hit based on "its amateur unorthodoxy, its dissonance, its beat, plus a particular type of 'singing' which the kids are buying." And it was not only the songs that failed to measure up. Across the board, he lamented, the record business had become "stalemated in a period of less than mediocrity—inferior material, doubtful talent and questionable instrumentation." The future, he despaired, was "anybody's guess."[11]

In their early years in business, the independent record men knew they had little chance of competing with the major labels head-to-head in the pop market. They concentrated instead on markets underserved by the majors "such as rhythm-blues, folk, Latin-American and Polish."[12] Herman Lubinsky's Savoy label, which began operating in Newark in 1942, came out with "a series of Jewish jive records (old Jewish standards played by hot jazz men in strictly jump tempo)" before turning his attention to the untapped rhythm and blues market.[13] Art Rupe, who started Jukebox Records (later renamed Specialty) in Los Angeles in 1944, had learned in an earlier failed venture how difficult it was to compete with the majors at their own game. In aiming his records at urban blacks, he said, he "looked for an area neglected by the majors, and in essence took the crumbs off the table of the record industry."[14] Jules Bihari tried a pop roster at Modern, the Los Angeles company he started with his brother Saul in 1945, but by 1948 he, too, saw that the R&B market provided far more accessibility and opportunity. "Because of increased buying interest in race sides," Billboard reported, Modern "would henceforth concentrate solely on race records."[15] The idea was "to stay out of fields in which the majors push heavily, and concentrate on items where the majors do more or less of a token job."[16]

There were, to be sure, many black performers signed to major labels in the 1940s, but with the exception of mainstream stars like Nat Cole, Louis Jordan, or Ella Fitzgerald, the lion's share of promotional attention went to the pop performers who delivered the biggest hits. As a result, a Billboard reporter noted in the spring of 1948, the publication's "race charts show[ed] a majority of indie label platters popping up."[17] In the early fifties, the trend accelerated. In the spring of 1953, although R&B's market share trailed those of "pop, classical, kiddie, and country" at 5.7 percent, it was reported that "two or three new r.&b. labels . . . suddenly burst upon the market" each week, adding to the nearly one hundred active labels that made the field "alive, exciting and precarious."[18] By 1954, despite repeated efforts by the majors to establish a position in R&B, indies had accounted for forty-six of the fifty best-selling R&B records of the previous five years, proof enough of their "virtually complete control of the field."[19]

The indies' low overhead meant that a record would usually break even if it sold as few as five thousand copies, and the occasional hit that sold upward of one hundred thousand was a financial bonanza. Still, records with these sales numbers would not show up on the national pop chart and hardly represented competition for the majors. But in 1947 two independent releases, both novelty pop items, managed the kind of fabulous business that got everyone's attention and signaled a capricious mood in the mainstream. In mid-July, an instrumental version of an old song from the Broadway show *Ziegfeld Follies of 1913* named "Peg O' My Heart" passed the one million mark in sales, "probably the first time any independent diskery has hit the million class," *Billboard* reported.[20] The record featured Jerry Murad and the Harmonicats. It was engineered and produced by Bill Putnam, a central figure in Chicago's postwar recording scene, and released on a local label called Vitacoustic. The song was arranged for three harmonicas drenched in extravagant reverb, an unusual, attention-grabbing sonic trick. It was an example of the "material" or "drop-in" discs that *Billboard* had identified earlier in the year as the indies' best shot at the pop mainstream, records that sold on the basis of their novel appeal rather than a recognized star, something that seemed to be catching on with the "unpredictable public."[21]

Later that year Francis Craig's "Near You," on the Bullet label, had an even more spectacular success. Bullet was established in 1945 when Wally Fowler, a Nashville songwriter, singer, and music publisher, approached Jim Bulleit with the idea of starting Nashville's first record company. Bulleit was a peripatetic man with a restless spirit, far more comfortable with risk than the boredom he had felt working as a college music teacher and radio announcer. It was an easy matter, then, for Fowler to entice Bulleit into a venture of which he knew practically nothing. The two sought out Conrad Vertre "C. V." Hitchcock, a local jukebox operator and record wholesaler, as a third partner. "We talked for about fifteen to twenty minutes," Bulleit recalled, "and when I got out of [Hitchcock's] store I was in the record business."[22] In its first year of operation, with a fifteen-hundred-dollar investment from each partner, Bullet followed the same strategy as many other indies, releasing records in a "Hillbilly Series," a "Gospel Series," and a "Sepia Series." But Bulleit, who had a bachelor of music degree from Illinois Wesleyan University and "was used to big bands and orchestral music," hoped also to make a play in the pop field.[23]

Francis Craig, a pianist and bandleader, had been a fixture on the Nashville scene since the 1920s. His home base for more than two decades had been the Hermitage Hotel, where his orchestra played nightly. He also worked dances at Vanderbilt University and the Belle Meade Country Club and broadcast on WSM, an NBC affiliate. In 1938, he wrote "When Vandy Starts to Fight (the Dynamite Song)," which instantly became the Vanderbilt fight song. In short, he was a popular local musician, familiar to radio listeners within WSM's range as the leader of Nashville's premier society orchestra, but not a national figure. He had cut a few sides for Columbia in the 1920s, but nothing during the 1930s and the war years. In 1947, with musical styles changing, live radio ceding ever more airtime to records, and the band business becoming an expense fewer venues were willing to bear, the Hermitage declined to renew Craig's contract. After a final radio broadcast on May 4, he dissolved the Francis Craig Orchestra.

Earlier in the year, however, Craig had recorded four sides at WSM's Studio C, a space leased from the station by several of its employees for their fledgling recording venture, the Castle Recording Laboratory. (The name was borrowed from WSM's own handle, Air Castle of the South.) Craig approached Bulleit about making a vanity recording of "Red Rose," his signature number, which he had written for his wife Elizabeth in 1927. On the verge of disbanding his orchestra, the record was to be a keepsake, a souvenir of his years as a bandleader, and he convinced Bulleit that enough records could be sold locally to cover the cost of a session. Once again Bulleit needed little persuading. Despite his partners' wariness of the expense of a recording session with orchestra and the general difficulty of competing in the pop market, Bulleit saw the project as the firm's entrée to the big time. If Craig's expectations were modest, Bulleit had grander ideas. The session took place on January 20, nominally supervised by a young Owen Bradley, who would become one of Nashville's premier record producers. "Near You," the last side recorded that evening, was also the last tune selected, a late choice for the B-side of "Red Rose."

"Red Rose" b/w "Near You" was released on March 7. Despite Bullet's Nashville promotion, which included "several planes [flying] promotional runs dropping red roses as they flew over the city," sales were slow and airplay limited.[24] Then in early summer, out of the blue, a small record store in Griffin, Georgia, Record Heaven, placed an order for one hundred copies, a fabulous number for a small store in a small town. A deejay for the local station in Griffin, Cal Young, had obtained the record on one of his trips to visit family in Nashville where he regularly stocked up on records at his uncle's downtown record store. On his own, without any promotional push, he began to play the record's B-side, and listeners responded. The order from Record Heaven was a sign of things to come as the record broke out in cities across the South—New Orleans, Birmingham, Atlanta—and then around the country. By mid-September, the "Near You" phenomenon was in high gear. The "disk from Dixie," *Newsweek* reported, had sent shockwaves through the industry, which

> could hardly believe what it read in *Billboard* last week. Without benefit of a big-name band, and under a nationally unheard-of record label, a song called "Near You" was now No. 6 on the Honor Roll of Hits, No. 4 in Best-Selling Popular Retail Records, No. 1 in Records Most-Played on the Air, and No. 10 in Most-Played Juke Box Records.[25]

By the end of the month the record would reach the top spot in all categories. Cover versions by the Andrews Sisters (Decca), Alvino Rey (Capitol), Elliot Lawrence (Columbia), Larry Green (RCA Victor), and Two-Ton Baker (Mercury) also charted, although the original outsold all the competition.

The song, seemingly an eminently forgettable ditty, lodged in the nation's pop consciousness as the record reigned for an unprecedented seventeen weeks at number one. In a 1948 interview, Sinatra, who, as host of *Your Hit Parade,* was forced to sing the song, singled it out as symptomatic of the "decadent . . . bloodless" songs that in his mind were becoming all too pervasive. "As a singer of popular songs," he went on, "I've been looking for wonderful pieces of music in the popular vein—what they call Tin Pan Alley songs. You can *not* find any."[26] If things were not as bleak as Sinatra made out—and he did admit that great show tunes were still being written and were popular—it was certainly true that the public was going for an unusually high volume of substandard material, according to conventional criteria. But if "Near You" was musical farce, its popularity obviated such high-minded quibbles. Its success forced even high-pop standard-bearers Columbia and RCA Victor farther into the novelty craps game.

Given the public's robust appetite for such fare and the fact that in almost all cases "the success of the novelty tune [was] traceable to a record" rather than an established star, commercial prospects for the indies' unconventional A&R moves and recording gimmicks appeared promising.[27] But the impressive pop sales of "Peg O' My Heart" and "Near You" were anomalies at the time. By 1949, Bulleit's ambitions had burned through most of Bullet's profits and, unable to make any lasting inroads in the pop market, he was forced out of the company. The majors' pop stranglehold would be broken within a few years, as the definition of *pop* shifted in the indies' direction. In the meantime, however, the large firms were keen to follow up on the small labels' successes. The majors' catalogs were filled with the best of the pop tradition, but they were not constrained by aesthetic principle or ideology. If there were new trends afoot, they wanted in. They were "awakened to a quickening of the public pulse, probably stimulated by the small firms' 'song scouting.'" And sales departments impressed on their "repertoire headquarters . . . that, top artist or no top artist, it would be nice to get out first with some of the new crop of ditties."[28] In the end, however, these responses to their indie competition only furthered the market's aesthetic turmoil, which would ultimately create for them even more headaches.

· 3 ·

The power of a single record to elevate unknown musicians to instant stardom fueled the success of both indie record companies and the musicians they put before the public, who went on to greater financial reward from their live appearances. The majors, too, enjoyed the overnight success phenomenon with many of their young stars, but their aesthetic impact on the public soundscape was not as dramatic as the rude interruptions from the industry's margins. Unlike the indies, the major labels adhered to professional conventions of musical execution and record production; even their quirkiest discs had a polish to them. And most of their seemingly instant sensations had paid quite a bit of dues in the entertainment business, developing solid technical skills through years of performing in obscurity. The indies, on the other hand, put out many records by performers whose styles were far too coarse to attract the attention of the majors or, in most cases, to make any impression on the pop charts. Some of the performers, many of the vocal groups, for instance, were simply inexperienced; others, blues shouters, say, were seasoned performers but in a style foreign to the mainstream. The records' sonic quality was often deplorably rough-hewn compared to the majors' hi-fi sounds. So as these unfamiliar sounds began reaching a broad public, they disrupted conventional criteria for songwriting, performance practice, and record production, and challenged the majors not only in market share but in shaping the cultural landscape.

The harbingers of rock and roll were the young African American vocal groups of the late forties and early fifties whose styles would later become known collectively as doo-wop. At the time, their records were simply classed as rhythm and blues, a catchall rubric indicating only that the performers and likely audience were black. In fact, however, the category encompassed a variety of different styles, including the jazz-tinged Ella

Fitzgerald, the urban club blues of Charles Brown, the electrified country blues of Muddy Waters, Nat Cole's seductive croon, the Mills Brothers' fine harmonies and infectious swing, and much else. Among all of these, the doo-wop groups stood apart in several ways that would gradually define rock and roll as a distinct musical idiom and map a new kind of career path. In their youthful freshness, they exuded a naïveté bearing only the rudiments of conventional stylistic habit. Even in their sometimes risqué lyrics ("Sixty Minute Man," say, or "Work With Me, Annie"), they had an innocence not heard from the likes of a Joe Turner or Wynonie Harris, veterans of countless adventurous nights on the club circuit and many rounds with industry scoundrels. The young singers, as the critic Greil Marcus has framed it, appeared to "come out of nowhere." Their records "married black and white," and they were both "urban" and "primitive-modernist."[29] In a surprising number of cases, they produced but one successful record. The new genre "was limited largely to the one-shot artist," *Billboard* reported, one who "came equipped with his own material, including usually one good song. He was sought out far from the usual Brill Building Turf haunts of the music trade, recorded doing his own tune, and the talent lived and died on the single effort."[30]

A prime outlet for the young performers was the talent contest, such as those held at Harlem's Apollo Theater or Memphis's Palace Theater, where audience members voted for their favorites with applause and losers were "hooked" or "shot" from the stage. Radio, too, sponsored talent shows, and it was on one of these, *Arthur Godfrey Talent Scouts,* that the Orioles, a group of five young men from Baltimore, began their rise to national prominence. Lead singer Sonny Til (who assumed the nickname Sonny after his favorite record as a child, Al Jolson's "Sonny Boy") recounted how he, George Nelson, Alex Sharp, Johnny Reed, and Tommy Gaither had come together as a "street singing group," performing on the corner outside Baltimore's Avenue Cafe where they had met while performing individually on the club's amateur nights.[31] On April 26, 1948, the group, still known as the Vibra-Naires, made the trip to New York City with their manager and chief songwriter, Deborah Chessler, a young Jewish sales clerk, to appear on Godfrey's show. They came in third, but their performance generated so many phone calls that Godfrey invited them back to appear twice more on his morning show.

Chessler, armed with a few demo recordings and the group's radio exposure, was able to interest a New York record man, Sid De May, who set up a new label (It's a Natural) to market the group. At the first session, in the summer of 1948, the Orioles recorded six sides, one of which was Chessler's "It's Too Soon to Know." Like many indie releases, the record was soon put under a different label, Jubilee, which Herb Abramson had set up in 1947 to market gospel music. He soon sold out to another record man, Jerry Blaine, who subsequently partnered with De May, having meanwhile built some sales momentum for the firm not with gospel but with Yiddish comedy records. "It's Too Soon to Know" was added to Jubilee's motley roster, and within weeks it was introduced in New York by radio cohosts Willie Bryant (the 1950s "Mayor of Harlem") and Ray Carroll on WHOM. The jockeys were "riding it hard nightly" when it became the "latest boom 'Rip Van Winkle' recording to awaken in left field." By early September, the record had already sold a reported eighty-six thousand copies, and eventually it rose to number one on *Billboard*'s national Most-Played Juke Box Race Records chart and number two in Best Selling Retail Race Records.[32] Surprisingly, however, it also reached well into the top twenty on the mainstream pop chart, the first record of its kind to do so.

Chessler, who could neither read music nor play the piano, wrote songs into her memory, later singing them to a transcriber or plugging them with her own performance. "It's Too Soon to Know" came to her in an inspired moment during a dinner out with her mother at the Forrest Hotel in New York. She wrote the lyrics on the only paper available, toilet tissue from the restaurant's bathroom. The song had an oddly proportioned twenty-four-bar chorus made of two similar yet contrasting twelve-bar segments and no bridge. Its melody, with many of its most prominent notes falling a fourth, sixth, or seventh above the harmonic root, had a tenuous vulnerability about it. Though remarkably unconventional in its design, the song and its arrangement were in a style not unfamiliar to the mainstream pop audience of the late 1940s. In fact, to contemporary listeners the record would have sounded like a rough emulation of the Ink Spots, in particular their hugely successful recording of "The Gypsy" which had, in 1946, spent nearly half the year on the pop charts, thirteen weeks at number one. Both songs were slow ballads expressing a fearful romantic uncertainty, both recordings featured a seductive lead voice accompanied by sustained vocal harmony and a small instrumental group, and both had a middle section taken by a baritone voice.

But as similar as their basic resources were, the records were very different. The Ink Spots track had a refinement about it, a clean, balanced instrumental sound and subtle, almost neutral vocal harmonies. Bill Kenny's lead vocal was precise and controlled, with a diction style that sounded like the work of a Hollywood diction coach. By contrast, the Orioles track opened with a slightly ragged sounding guitar followed by

Sonny Til's sweet yet slightly ragged sounding voice, a street-corner croon with the idiosyncratic diction to match. The instruments were submerged in the far background while the vocal harmonies were louder than those of the Ink Spots, with a more pronounced vibrato and lacking the older group's seamless blend. The song's second chorus followed the example of the Ink Spots in substituting a lower voice for the lead, but in contrast to the reserved, carefully articulated spoken words of Herb Kenny, the younger group's baritone, George Nelson, sang in a gruff style reminiscent of the young Louis Armstrong. Here, then, was a record in the mainstream pop vein but coarser in sound and sung in clearly black voices of the sort rarely heard on mainstream pop radio.

The Orioles' success pointed up a puzzling, if still anomalous, aesthetic question. To one *Billboard* writer reviewing an Orioles show at Broadway's Strand Theater in May of 1951, the group was "just about as unmusical and sloppy an act as has been seen hereabouts." Yet the group's "poor man's Ink Spots routine nevertheless seemed to win the audience."[33] In a music business accustomed to professional standards in everything from songwriting to recording practices, "It's Too Soon to Know" was a warning shot, isolated at the time but prefiguring radical changes to come. The singers, without much in the way of professional experience or training, harmonized on instinct, with little theoretical knowledge of how notes fit together to make a desired sound. In what James McGowan, lead singer for the Four Fellows, called "the method of the block," a "crude, almost primitive way of learning," young neighborhood singers groped their way toward presentable arrangements with "nothing more than the sound of other groups to go on."[34] In addition to popular music, of course, what the young men had in common was the black church, where they had heard and participated in both the fervent gospel and sweetly blended jubilee styles of singing throughout their childhoods. The church, McGowan recalled, was "our first school of music."[35]

From the vocal groups' informal, trial-and-error approach emerged felicitous stylistic choices that a professional might have automatically passed over as too crude or simple-minded. On a stoop or street corner, in a schoolroom or subway station, young black men sang together, trying in part to emulate the sounds of success embodied in groups such as the Ink Spots, Mills Brothers, and Delta Rhythm Boys yet also fascinated with the sounds of their own voices resonating in harmonic textures of their own devising. The older groups had spent years on the road and in radio and recording studios refining their sophisticated yet apparently effortless styles. They were royalty, like Crosby or Sinatra. The young groups were earnest in their admiration but as green as could be. Given time, they, too, might have settled into similar habits, but they never got the chance. Almost as soon as their harmonies began to sound presentable, record men scooped them up and put them before microphones. As one reporter put it in 1954, a year when vocal groups of all sorts represented the best-selling genre of new talent, "If you've a brood of kids around the house, guard 'em closely. Chances are they'll be name entertainers via wax and footlights if the current popularity of vocal groups is any indication."[36] With the young performers' worth measured in the irrefutable terms of record sales, amateurs and pros became de facto colleagues. Rather than poor emulations, the amateurs' performances turned out to be innovative revisions. Their lack of pop sophistication was, to their young audience, a virtue, a sign of unaffected sincerity and originality.

George Goldner was a record man of impeccable instincts. Born in New York City in 1918, he began by working in the city's garment business but moved on to managing dance halls in the early 1940s. Goldner himself was an avid dancer and music fan. When his Puerto Rican wife Gracie introduced him to New York's surging Latin music scene, driven by a wave of postwar Puerto Rican migration, he became a devotee. Latin-tinged music had been an exotic fixture on the periphery of the mainstream for two decades, associated with such stars as the tango dancers Vernon and Irene Castle, the percussion-driven rumba of Don Azpiazú's Havana Casino Orchestra, and society bandleader Xavier Cugat. During the 1940s, Latin music—especially Brazilian and Cuban—gained greater mainstream popularity with appearances in Broadway musicals and Hollywood films. At the same time, stars such as the Brazilian singer and dancer Carmen Miranda, conga entertainer Desi Arnaz, and fusion bandleader Machito, with his Latin jazz Afro-Cubans, peppered the wider musical landscape with a sunlit blend of rhythmic action and sonic color. In midtown Manhattan, the Palladium Ballroom at Broadway and Fifty-third Street—"our home of the mambo," Tito Puente called it—symbolized Latin music's widespread popularity as the mambo craze spilled out of New York and swept across the country in the early 1950s.[37]

In 1948, with little more than a passion for the music and an entrepreneurial bent, Goldner decided to start his first record company. He teamed up with radio personality Art "Pancho" Raymond, a Jewish deejay who hosted a Latin music show and spoke on air in a Spanish accent, tossing in occasional phrases he remembered from his high school Spanish classes. They called the label Tico, after the song "Tico-Tico No

Fubá," a popular Latin standard written by Brazilian composer Zequinha de Abreu in 1917, with several 1940s versions circulating as "Tico-Tico" in films and recordings by Ethel Smith, the Andrews Sisters, and Carmen Miranda. Among Goldner's first signings were two stars of the New York scene who would instantly put the fledgling label on the map: the percussionist, composer, and bandleader Tito Puente; and the suave singer Tito Rodriguez. Snatching major local stars from under the noses of the big three New York record companies, Goldner demonstrated a sharp sense of taste on the street, as well as an ability to follow through with record production, marketing, and promotion. It was a package that would make him one of the decade's premier record men.

Goldner was also plagued by an uncontrollable gambling addiction—a "degenerate gambler" Morris Levy called him—which would cost him every record company he ever owned (most went to Levy), but no one could argue with his success in a crowded and competitive marketplace.[38] Years later, in 1964, when Goldner joined songwriters Jerry Leiber and Mike Stoller in founding Red Bird, his seventh successful label, it was he who picked out of a pile of acetates the one that the company would stake its future on—the Dixie Cups' "Chapel of Love," a song Leiber hated so much he had refused to work on the record in his usual capacity as Stoller's coproducer. But the pair trusted Goldner's proven instincts and released the record as their inaugural offering. It went to number one on the pop charts. (Goldner would have had a sense for the girl group sound, having produced one of the genre's breakout records in 1958, the Chantels' "Maybe.") While Goldner would remain involved in the Latin music scene through the 1950s, with Tico consistently turning out some of the idiom's finest discs, he also began noticing a new musical trend in the city. In the early 1950s, young African American vocal groups seemed to be everywhere, and Goldner launched a new label, Rama, devoted to the new rhythm and blues style pioneered by the Orioles, Ravens, Clovers, and Five Keys. One of his first signings was the Crows, a group whose limited musicianship stood in marked contrast to the Latin bands Goldner worked with on Tico, yet whose 1953 record, "Gee," would eventually become one of the seminal crop of black vocal group records to cross over to the pop chart in 1954.

The Crows were Daniel "Sonny" Norton (lead), Harold Major, Bill Davis, Gerald Hamilton, and Jerry Wittick (later replaced by Mark Jackson). They came up through the competitive street-singing scene in Harlem and in 1952 made an impressive appearance at an Apollo Amateur Night contest. They caught the attention of manager Cliff Martinez, who in turn paired them with the experienced rhythm and blues pianist and singer Viola Watkins. After some unsuccessful recordings for Jubilee, Martinez took the group to Goldner, who had by then released two records on Rama by another local group, the Five Budds. In April 1953, he produced a session at which "Gee" and three other sides were cut: "Seven Lonely Days" (which had been a hit for pop singer Georgia Gibbs), "No Help Wanted" (a country novelty popularized by the Carlisles), and "I Love You So," written, like "Gee," by group member Bill Davis with arranging assistance from Watkins. The first release was "Seven Lonely Days" b/w "No Help Wanted," a confusing pairing with Watkins singing lead on one side and Norton on the other. The record failed to make an impression on the market. A month later Goldner released the other two songs, both of which featured only the Crows, with Watkins handling piano and arranging. This record fared better than the first, but for several months after its release it sent mixed signals, with different regions of the country preferring one side or the other. In any case, neither side broke through to the national charts until the following year. It was an unusually long gestation period in the world of singles given that failure to achieve rapid success usually sapped a record's staying power in the face of a relentless weekly surge of new releases.

"Gee" was minimal in its lyric and musical content, relying for its impact on an infectiously enthusiastic performance and innocent sentiment. It had a catchy, jaunty bounce similar in feeling to the Ames Brothers' "Rag Mop," a 1951 hit in many versions. The record had a curious aspect especially common among New York City groups at the time, a mismatch between the singers and the far more experienced instrumentalists (piano, guitar, bass, drums), which gave the record an ambivalent yet intriguing stylistic orientation. The combo's natural inclination to swing was continually interrupted by a stiff, downbeat-heavy vocal riff. In each of the song's A-sections, the voices dominated except at the turnarounds, where suddenly a lightly swinging groove emerged briefly. When the harmony voices moved to sustained chords in the song's bridge, the musicians extended the swing groove a bit, and then, when the voices dropped out for the instrumental break—a jazz guitar solo—the liberated groove took flight into pure swing. With the voices' return, the heavier groove was restored. The effect was dizzying. In its stylistic collage, its juxtaposition of musical attitudes representing different realms of musical experience, the record marked a fusion effected not on any bandstand but in the recording studio.

According to rock and roll lore, the record's real chart momentum began in Los Angeles in the winter of 1954, some eight months after its release. Reportedly, popular deejay Dick "Huggy Boy" Hugg played "Gee" several times in a row on his remote broadcast from John Dolphin's twenty-four-hour record shop in order to placate an angry girlfriend after a spat. He had not thought much of the record, but knowing that she liked it he began playing it in hopes that she would hear it on her car radio as she drove home. He insisted on air that he would keep playing it until she either returned or he lost his job. The tactic worked not only with Hugg's girlfriend but the other listeners, who quickly snapped up some fifty thousand copies in the Los Angeles area. Apocryphal or not, the story is believable enough given the growing number of similarly unlikely chance occurrences defying historical practice and conventional marketing logic. In any case, the Los Angeles activity sparked a nationwide boost in sales, lifting the record ultimately to number two on the R&B jukebox chart (number six in R&B sales) and number fourteen on the pop deejay chart. "Gee" was the first of several vocal group records to show up on both the R&B and pop charts in 1954, but further underscoring its curious history and reflecting the market's shifting dynamics, its crossover path was not from R&B to pop. Although its initial showings were on regional R&B charts, the record's first national chart appearance was in pop, with R&B following a month later. Despite the excitement the record generated and the generally good quality of their four follow-up singles, "Gee" was the only hit the Crows would have, and by 1955 the group was finished.

The amateur performer teamed with the hustling independent record man was a common arrangement in cities around the country throughout the 1950s. A third character was often involved as well, a sort of musical intermediary working at myriad tasks: talent scout, rehearsal coach, bandleader, songwriter, arranger, producer, whatever needed doing to pull the project together. Robert "Bumps" Blackwell (Specialty), Dave Bartholomew (Imperial), Willie Dixon (Chess), Johnny Otis (Duke/Peacock), Jesse Stone (Atlantic), and Ralph Bass (Federal, Savoy) were among the most prominent such figures. By 1955, Goldner's third man was Richard Barrett, leader of the Valentines, whose "Lilly Maebelle," with helpful airplay from Alan Freed, was a local hit for Rama in the New York region in the fall of 1955. Around the same time, Barrett became interested in a group calling itself the Premiers, whose members caught his attention with a spirited performance of his own hit, "Lilly Maebelle." Goldner was looking to start a new label called Gee, and Barrett persuaded him to make the Premiers his first signing. (It is not clear whether the company's name was in response to the success of the Crows' record or simply a spelled-out version of Goldner's initial, G.)

Goldner had several vocal groups already, and with the city's proliferation of aspiring young singers in pursuit of instant stardom there were plenty more to choose from. His curiosity was piqued, however, when he met the group in person and realized that, even by the standards of the day, its members were remarkably young, ranging in age from thirteen to fifteen. They also had a remarkably catchy pop song, "Why Do Birds Sing So Gay," which they had written themselves. And in their youngest member, the diminutive showman Frankie Lymon, they had a striking high-tenor voice. Lymon's was not their lead voice when they came for their audition, but Goldner insisted he take over the lead role. The song's title was also changed to "Why Do Fools Fall in Love."

Goldner took the group (which along with Lymon included Jimmy Merchant, Herman Santiago, Joe Negroni, and Sherman Garnes) into Studio A at Bell Sound on Fifty-fourth Street in Manhattan in December of 1955 along with Jimmy Wright and his five-piece band. The musicians were R&B session aces whose interaction with the singers made for another rollicking musical mismatch. The rhythmic effect of using contrasting grooves—one beat heavy, one swinging—was similar to the Crows' "Gee." But in the juxtaposition of Wright's hard-swinging, bluesy tenor saxophone solo and Lymon's angelic voice there was also a contrast between an impression of naive wonder (belied, as he would later describe, by the hard facts of Lymon's young life) and grown-up sexiness.[39] It was an intersection of mature and nascent musical sensibilities fused on the recording as if it were a single thing, for in fact it was. Once again, the sound was raw, concerned more with visceral impact than clear timbres and balanced texture. The record won both R&B and pop chart success and landed the group in two Alan Freed films—*Rock, Rock, Rock* and *Mister Rock 'n' Roll*. The boys spent a heady eighteen months as topdraw pop stars, a rare feat among doo-wop groups and a ticket into rock and roll's founding canon. At the session, Wright suggested one further change, a new name befitting both the group's biography and its image: the Teenagers.

Most hit rock and roll records in 1956 were by performers in their twenties, past adolescence but close enough to remember and connect with their listeners. In the Teenagers, however, the young audience saw and heard a group of kids literally their own ages. Lymon's voice, still that of a young boy, thrilled his young fans, one of whom was the future Ronettes star, Ronnie Spector. "I was twelve years old when I first heard Frankie and the Teenagers singing 'Why Do Fools Fall in Love' on my grandmother's radio," she recalled. "Frankie had the greatest voice I'd ever heard, and I fell in love the minute that record came on." It was an "innocent little voice" with "perfect diction," and she "couldn't tell if he was black, or white, or what." All she knew was that she could not get enough. "I pressed my head into the speaker until I got Frankie going right through my brain."[40]

Doo-wop groups were everywhere in the 1950s, and it was not long before white kids got in on the act and then young women. Their youth and inexperience only intensified their audience's enthusiasm. Their lack of musical expertise, a presumptive limitation, was instead an avenue to innovation, freeing their fascination to wander among musical styles and genres, absorbing and blending whatever caught their fancy. The Teenagers' run of success was dazzling by doo-wop standards. Most groups had only one hit if any. Yet in aggregate they were a force, feeding the national soundscape with an infusion of fresh music making that brought together the airiness of pop, the grit of the urban street, and the committed emotional expression of the black church.

· 4 ·

Postwar Memphis teemed with musicians, many of whom came from the surrounding countryside and small towns of Arkansas, Mississippi, and Tennessee, where mass electrification was an unfinished project. Despite their rustic origins, however, they were acutely aware of the opportunities afforded by the modern technological marvels of broadcasting and recording. They knew radio—with its power to reach beyond their listeners among the clientele in gambling parlors, honky-tonks, and brothels—to be a useful advertising tool. Fifteen-minute shows featuring the likes of B. B. King, Rice Miller (the second "Sonny Boy Williamson"), Johnny Cash, Junior Parker, and Howlin' Wolf were regular items on WDIA, KWEM (West Memphis, Arkansas), and KFFA (Helena, Arkansas). Howlin' Wolf held forth at KWEM at three in the afternoon, alerting his listeners to where his House Rockers band would be performing on Friday and Saturday nights. "People would be there waitin' on us when we get there," recalled the band's guitarist, Willie Johnson, "if they done heard us on the radio."[41] And if radio attracted a larger local audience, records were a conduit to the big time. A successful record meant fame and bookings in faraway places, a sudden leap from the juke joints to a national stage. Moreover, it was a powerful totem, carrying musicians' names and an electronic facsimile of their expressive auras to record racks, jukeboxes, and radio stations in places they might never visit.

For label representatives from Los Angeles and Chicago, Memphis was a gold mine of available talent. Modern and Chess, through arrangements with Sam Phillips, Ike Turner, and others, scored repeated successes with Memphis musicians—B. B. King, Rosco Gordon, Howlin' Wolf, Jackie Brenston. David James Mattis, who became program director at WDIA in 1951 going by the name David James, saw in the action taking place around him an opportunity. Though owned and controlled by whites, WDIA had become a beacon for southern blacks—"like a light," B. B. King called it—and with its numerous live musical broadcasts the station was a magnet for local talent.[42] It was known as the Starmaker Station.[43] Mattis reasoned that if the out-of-towners could do so well with Memphis musicians a local record label could surely succeed by taking advantage of the talent on its doorstep. With no experience in the record business, he wisely chose, in Music Sales owner Bill Fitzgerald, a partner who happened also to own a regional distribution company, and in the spring of 1952 their new venture, Duke, was ready to go.

Although Mattis was widely credited by WDIA staff with bringing a new level of professionalism to the station—and it was under his direction that the power was boosted to 50,000 watts in 1954—his prior radio experience was fairly limited. In the 1930s, he had spent several years as a pilot flying in South America. When the war broke out, he served as a flight instructor for the army in Tuscaloosa, Alabama, and in 1944 he flew in Burma and India during the closing months of the war. When he returned to the States, he enrolled in radio school and landed his first job on station KYJK in Forest City, Arkansas, spinning hillbilly discs under the name "Cousin Jesse." But if radio was relatively new to Mattis's résumé, the record business was a leap into the unknown. He knew nothing of publishing royalties or performing rights payments let alone the mercurial workings of indie promotion and distribution. He ran seat-of-the-pants recording sessions at the WDIA studio after hours using "an old Berlant tape recorder and three inadequate microphones."[44] (In these 250-watt days, WDIA signed off at sunset.) With clean sound out of the question, the records relied on the performers' expressiveness and the audience's indulgence.

Duke's first two sessions, with the Gospel Travelers and Rosco Gordon, initiated contrasting genre-focused series: gospel and R&B. The third session was nearly aborted when Bobby "Blue" Bland, unable to read the lyric sheet Mattis had given him, showed up unprepared to sing the songs he was to record that night. Mattis, who ran the station with iron discipline, was initially livid at the prospect of wasting the session. But when he happened to overhear pianist John Alexander "diddlin' around" with Ruth Brown's "So Long" he was struck by something he "hadn't heard before." Instead of canceling the session, he wrote a new set of lyrics to the same chord changes and had Alexander improvise a new melody, altogether "a fifteen minute job," he recalled.[45] (The songwriting story is only *almost* as preposterous as it sounds, for while Mattis was not a lyricist he was an experienced scriptwriter.) The result was "My Song," released as Duke 102 under the performer's new name: Johnny Ace. Even by indie standards, the record was remarkably rough, barely demo quality. A *Down Beat* review noted that "the singing, the balance and the performance" of the accompanying band were "distinctly inferior," yet in the summer of 1952 the record spent nine weeks at number one on the R&B chart.[46] Clearly, the criteria that major labels and record critics associated with high-quality record production were of little importance to Ace's audience. Indeed, the record's deficiencies only enhanced its poignancy. The disc's plaintive sound complemented the singer's expressive performance, imparting an overall sonic affect that spoke of a world of hurt and isolation and empathy for the world's brokenhearted.

Johnny Ace was born in 1929. From childhood, he sang, along with his mother and siblings, in the choir at the Bethel African Methodist Episcopal Church in Memphis and played the piano by ear in the family home and at school. He was in most respects an undisciplined young man: a high school dropout dishonorably discharged from the navy and an absent husband and father to his teenage wife and baby. He was also uninterested in the formal musical training his mother sought for him at the suggestion of Nat D. Williams, who, in addition to star WDIA deejay, was Ace's high school social studies teacher. He found the direction that would guide his short life in the nighttime Memphis music scene, where by 1950 he was one of the loose conglomeration of musicians known as the Beale Streeters. Besides Ace on piano, the group included B. B. King on guitar, Earl Forest on drums, Billy Duncan on saxophone, and Bobby "Blue" Bland on vocal.

Ace was a good blues player and singer; he could swing and deliver a lyric with cool intensity. But in "My Song" and all his subsequent hits, he approached a rough approximation of the black crooning style of which Nat Cole was the master. Like the Orioles' "It's Too Soon to Know," Ace's record was utterly lacking in the sonic polish and stylistic sophistication of his pop elder, but with its commercial success it took its place alongside Cole's work as an alternative possibility. Ace's recordings revised a central pop archetype of the 1940s, the solo male ballad singer. The genre's urbane polish was replaced by a plainspoken tenderness, and, although the songs themselves were primitive, Ace's recorded persona made an empathetic connection with his listeners that transcended mere songcraft. His "simple and unaffected style of singing, his evident sincerity and heart," a *Billboard* obituary held, "actually started the r.&b. field on a type of song that has come to be known as a 'heart-ballad.'"[47] Ace would have eight R&B hits in the heart ballad vein, and the biggest, "Pledging My Love," crossed over to the pop chart in 1955 soon after his death from an accidentally self-inflicted gunshot wound. In a year in which *Billboard* reckoned "rhythm and blues virtually took over the pop field," it was "the pacesetter . . . the most played r.&b. record of the year."[48] "Forever my darling," the song began, and to Ace's bereft audience the soulful voice that remained on the spinning disc made the promise seem good as gold.

Mattis's run in the record business lasted barely a year. When "My Song" began to hit, Duke ran into the same cash-flow problem that plagued all start-up firms. To survive, he went into partnership with Don Robey, owner of the Peacock label in Houston and one of the most successful African American record men of the time. Mattis's brief, brutal education in the record business now accelerated. Robey was a masterful hustler—wily, gun-toting, unyielding. Randy Wood, founder of Dot and sponsor of *Randy's Record Shop* on Nashville's WLAC, cautioned Mattis about Robey and offered to join the venture himself. But Mattis, a self-described "bleeding heart liberal," was unwilling to back out on his commitment. He would be "in partnership with a black man," and he would show "that inter-racial activity could really work."[49] Duke became affiliated with Peacock in July, and by November Robey, unhappy with the muddy sound of the WDIA recordings, had moved production to Bill Holford's ACA studio in Houston and put arranging into Johnny Otis's expert hands. From Houston, Robey controlled both record production and cash receipts, and by January of 1953 Mattis "just wanted out."[50]

Coincidentally, at about the time Mattis launched Duke, Sam Phillips, a man driven by a mix of idealistic vision and raw ambition, also went into the record business in Memphis. Except for the abortive Phillips label, a partnership between Sam and deejay Dewey Phillips (no relation) that released one record in 1950, owning a record company was not initially in his plans. His main concern for the first couple of years after opening his Memphis Recording Service in January 1950 was simply staying in business, working endless hours with his committed and tireless assistant, Marion Keisker, to fulfill the company slogan: "We Record Anything—Anywhere—Anytime."

But along with the weddings and funerals, Phillips wanted to use his recording machines to capture what he called "a certain province of human emotion," which he heard in the resident blues and country singers whose voices seemed to spring from the southern earth. "When I opened the studio," he recalled, "the main thing I wanted to do was keep it open until I had the opportunity to do some of these things that I had in my mind since I was a child in Alabama."[51] Phillips had a deep affinity for the rural everyman music making he heard growing up around Florence, Alabama, "all the music of the country people—black blues, hillbilly, and spirituals." Born in 1923, Phillips often pointed to the Depression years of the thirties as a time when he began to perceive the vital role music played in the lives of everyday people. It was an awareness he carried with him for the rest of his life.

> There were two types of downtrodden people back then. There were the black field hands and the white sharecroppers. It was impossible in those days not to hear and grow to love all the music of oppression and the music that uplifted people—blues, country, gospel, all of it—either in the fields, or the black women doing their chores, or on a weekend. One man in particular, Uncle Silas Payne, an old black man, taught music to me. Not musical notes or reading, you understand, but real intuitive music.[52]

After recording and leasing several records that hit on the R&B charts, including Howlin' Wolf's "How Many More Years" (Chess, number four), Rosco Gordon's "Booted" (Chess, number one), and Jackie Brenston's "Rocket 88" (Chess, number one), Phillips took the risky plunge of starting his own Sun Records in 1952, a leap of faith for which he had a "lack of time, lack of know-how, and lack of liquidity."[53] (Jim Bulleit was Phillips's partner for a time.) It was perhaps a dim prospect that he would ever make money selling Joe Hill Louis or Harmonica Frank Floyd records, but he was determined to capture these raw, primitive, nearly bygone sounds, which, to his ear and mind, seemed to exude a timeless expressive essence. The core of his company's ethos, even as it moved from rural blues to rockabilly, from limited sales to the top of the pop chart, had little to do with technical polish or professional pedigree. Phillips meant to cut through the abstraction of musical notes arranged and learned and controlled for calculated effect. He listened to anyone who came seeking an audition, always on the lookout for what sounded to him natural, spontaneous, unaffected.

"These artists who came to Sun," Keisker recalled, "many of them were not even musicians. They had guitars but most of their playing was done in their own homes or on their back steps or something, and they had no styles, they had no techniques. Most of them had their own songs; many of them were composed right there in the studio in front of a microphone."[54] As Carl Perkins's drummer, W. S. Holland, put it, "We could do what we did and that's all we knew to do."[55] Roland Janes, who played guitar in the studio's house band, stressed that, while there was a clear intention to make records that sounded "different," that might somehow stand out in the market, "For the most part, we were just—I don't know—cotton-patch-into-the-studio head musicians, just playing, you know, by feel."[56] And Jack Clement, in a wry summary of his work as a Sun engineer and producer, said, "We didn't know all the things you couldn't do, so we went ahead and did them and some of them worked."[57] Phillips gambled that in place of what these musicians lacked in professional experience and technical skill would emerge a captivating, if rough, musical individuality.

More than most record producers, Phillips made records for himself; making records was a way of asserting his aesthetic and moral sensibility in the public square. His often-stated aim to "to draw out a person's innate, possibly unknown talents" was in the service of a musical ethic demanding a commitment he thought lacking in the world of professional show business.[58] Phillips was a radio announcer and engineer at Memphis station WREC from 1945 until 1952, where his duties included remote broadcasts of touring big band shows at the Hotel Peabody Skyway. Although he professed to "love the forties bands," he was convinced they lacked what he called "that instinctive intuitional thing." It seemed to him amazing that the musicians "might have played the damned song 4000 times and they were *still* turning the pages."[59] By contrast, Howlin' Wolf, his favorite singer, "was one of those raw people. Dedicated. Natural." When Wolf sang, Phillips, said, it was with "fervor" and "command of every word he spoke." Wolf had "*nothing* on his mind but that song, He sang with his damn soul."[60] These were the qualities Phillips wanted to get into a record's grooves.

Like Norman Petty, Phillips was unconcerned with studio time. "You didn't have no special time to get there," said Little Milton Campbell, "and no special time to leave. . . . I had all the freedom in the world there."[61] The sessions were long, all night, as long as it took. "Don't try to make a hit record," Phillips advised Rosco Gordon, "try to make a good one." The Bihari brothers, Gordon recalled, "just wanted Rosco . . . good, bad, indifferent." Phillips, on the other hand, "was demanding. He wanted you to record to his satisfaction. . . . I believe that Sam knew what he wanted, and knew what he wanted out of me, so he would keep me there until he got that out of me."[62] Phillips had a sense for the soul of a record. He understood that a great live performance and a great studio performance were not necessarily the same thing. Whether or not a studio performance had translated into a living record could only be judged after it had passed through the mediating electronic process and reappeared at the loudspeaker. He fixed his critical ear less on the performance than its recorded traces.

Phillips was convinced that the recording studio was a place of discovery. He knew the recording process could effect musical transformation, and he fostered an atmosphere from which recordings might emerge whose like had never before existed. He had no forethought of what a perfect take should sound like; it had to reveal itself. Carl Perkins told a story about working with Phillips that captured some of the flavor.

> You got to remember that Elvis, Cash, none of us had anything. We were very poor, came from poor people, and it was Sam—I know he did for me—bought me the first clothes I ever had to wear on stage. Well, you see, he really had the knack, he just seemed to know—when we'd be making a record, he'd step out from behind that little old glass window, and he'd say, "All right, boys, we just about on it now." He'd say, "Do it again. Do it one time for Sam." Oh yeah, he did me that way all the time. It was just that type of thing, you just forgot about making a record and tried to show him. It was things like that that'd cause me—I'd walk out on a limb, I'd try things I knew I couldn't do, and I'd get in a corner trying to do it and then have to work my way out of it. I'd say, "Mr. Phillips, that's terrible." He said, "That's original." I said, "But it's just a big original mistake." And he said, *"That's what Sun Records is.* That's what we are."[63]

Phillips's aesthetic idealism, however, was tempered with pragmatism. He was attracted to the earthy sounds around him, but he was no folklorist. If his label were to stay afloat, he needed to produce hits, and like other record men of the day he cast widely for potential profit. Among his early successes were Rufus Thomas's recording of "Bear Cat," a novelty blues Phillips wrote as an answer to Big Mama Thornton's "Hound Dog"; Little Junior Parker's "Feelin' Good," a free-form driving blues shuffle; and the Prisonaires "Just Walkin' in the Rain," a sweet, pop-styled vocal group recording by five black inmates at the Tennessee State Penitentiary in Nashville. He also released records by white performers—the Ripley Cotton Choppers, Harmonica Frank, Doug Poindexter, Hardrock Gunter—which sold poorly but showed that Phillips's idea of a country record was somewhere far to the left of Nashville. In the big picture, Phillips was after something he could articulate only as a vague notion: a young white performer possessed of a black-and-tan musical spirit. Malcolm Yelvington told a story about asking Phillips to audition his band, the Star Rhythm Boys. Phillips asked what kind of music they played. "Country," Yelvington answered. Phillips said he was not interested, and when Yelvington asked what Phillips wanted, he said, "I don't know, but I'll know when I hear it." Rhythm Boys guitarist Gordon Mashburn said that meant Phillips would "have to listen to every single person who comes in off the street," to which he responded, "I intend to."[64]

· 5 ·

Sun had no impact on the pop charts until Carl Perkins's "Blue Suede Shoes" rose to number two in 1956, followed by hits from Jerry Lee Lewis, Johnny Cash, Bill Justis, Charlie Rich, and Carl Mann. Yet well before he achieved mainstream success, Phillips's iconic status as a record producer was cemented by his work with Elvis Presley. Seeking to capture the musical values he cherished in a form that might sell like a pop record—which meant downplaying features too rough for broad appeal while retaining the soul and energy that made the music worth recording in the first place—Phillips was on the lookout for a synthesis of black and white styles and sensibilities. As longtime Memphis-based record producer Jim Dickinson explained it, Phillips was pursuing "an idea" as much as a sound.[65] The elements of the thing were familiar: he was attracted to raw emotion, spontaneous expression, unconventional sounds. But how these came together to make a good record was always mysterious; how they might produce a pop star was even more so. As it happened, when he came across what he was looking for, the meeting produced not an epiphany but only a sense that perhaps, eventually, the young man might amount to something. Exactly what that might be was, for some time, beyond Phillips's imagining.

Presley walked into the Memphis Recording Service one summer day in 1953. He was eighteen, just graduated from high school and working full time at a machinist's shop. He paid $3.98 to record a two-sided acetate, perhaps for his mother's birthday, as he said later, but more likely with the hope of being discovered. He met Keisker in the outer office and in his shy, tentative way mentioned that if she knew "anyone that needs a singer" he was available. She asked the young man what kind of music he sang and who he sounded like. "I don't sound like nobody," he said, although he claimed to "sing all kinds of music." Keisker pressed him. "We went through all the categories, and he insisted that he didn't sound like anybody else," she recalled. If it seemed a youthful boast, it no doubt also reflected an inability to explain the abundance of his influences. Over time, as Keisker heard Presley's mutable vocal persona render stylized ballads and blues and country and gospel, she decided "he was telling the truth"; he appeared not to "fit into existing types of music."[66]

Phillips thought the young man an "interesting" singer, but it would be close to a year before he invited him to record for Sun. The songs Presley recorded for his vanity disc —the pop ballads "My Happiness" and "That's When Your Heartache Begins"—were simply not the kind of material Phillips was looking for. The following summer, however, he was given a demo of a song called "Without You," a ballad but with an amateur roughness about it that made him think of Presley. He set up a session for the young singer in the early summer of 1954, but it was a disappointment. Whatever he was looking for, he did not hear it in Presley's performances of "Without You." Still he heard something. He stopped recording and had Presley sing whatever he knew, "pop stuff, spirituals, just a few words of [anything] I remembered," Presley later said.[67] Phillips listened deeply, his imagination scanning for the key to unlock the potential he sensed. There was nothing in any of it to keep, but still Phillips was intrigued by *something*.

Phillips's perplexed fascination was no doubt a response to Presley's remarkably idiosyncratic style, which borrowed liberally from a wide range of influences. Everything Presley had heard seemed to have left some kind of a mark in his memory, and the traces ran together when he sang, melding disparate stylistic residue. Yet in claiming to sound like no one else, Presley described not only himself but a musical zeitgeist. The composite mixture that Phillips sought was a looming cultural presence by the time Presley showed up at his studio. Revisions and recombinations of performance practices drawn from diverse idioms were ongoing throughout the indie universe. The electronic media exposed young performers to an astonishing range of music from which they formed a musical worldview with little regard for traditional borders. Presley drew in influences almost indiscriminately from the blues, country, pop, and gospel songs he had heard and loved to sing. "He had the most intuitive ability to hear songs without ever having to classify them, or *himself*," Phillips recalled, and "it seemed like he had a photographic memory for every damn song he ever heard."[68]

Phillips decided to put Presley with a couple of more experienced country musicians, Scotty Moore and Bill Black. He hoped the guitarist and bassist could help to give some shape to his intuition and help him figure out what it was he was hearing and whether it was something that could be captured and sold. The two professed to be not much impressed with the singer, but Phillips had the three in for a Monday night session on July 5, 1954. It was intended as little more than a rehearsal session to familiarize the young man with the studio and make him feel comfortable. The trio made several takes of two ballads: "Harbor Lights," a song from the 1930s revived with seven hit versions in 1950, one by Crosby; and Leon Payne's "I Love You Because," a country hit in 1949 with subsequent hit versions in 1950 from Ernest Tubb and Clyde Moody. None of the takes struck Phillips as the record he was after, but he remained fascinated with Presley's delivery. It was intensely emotional and stylistically strange. In Presley biographer Peter Guralnick's description, "[I]t was as if, Sam thought, [Presley] wanted to put everything he had ever known or heard into one song."[69] The performances were implicit dialogues among the musical characters that had left an impression, most via radio and records, on Presley's young life—his eclectic, personal cast of disembodied mentors and heroes.

The rest of the story of that night became one of rock and roll's most cherished founding myths, its details varying somewhat from one storyteller to another but its essential resonant truth captured by the recording machine. During a break, the musicians, starting with Presley, began playing spontaneously, thoughtlessly, just messing around as musicians often do. Although everything Phillips had heard from Presley was some species of heartfelt ballad singing, now the music was up-tempo, exuding a nervous energy that shot through the studio like quicksilver. Phillips's ears perked up. As Moore recalled it, "He stuck his head out [from the control room] and said, 'What are you doing?' And we said, 'We don't know.' 'Well, back up,' he said, 'and try to find a place to start, and do it again.'"[70] He had not supposed that the young singer even knew such a song let alone could carry it off. But it struck the chord in his imagination that had both driven and eluded him. Exactly what was happening was not clear to anyone involved, but it seemed to Phillips that whatever it was, this was the thing he had been looking for.

The song was "That's All Right," a blues-flavored song written and recorded originally by Arthur "Big Boy" Crudup in Chicago for RCA Victor in 1946. The song's fatalistic protagonist reckoned that women would be his doom, but "that's all right," he sang to a lightly swinging accompaniment of electric guitar, drums, and eight-to-the-bar bass line. Presley's version changed the rhythmic feel to a hillbilly groove, the bass holding solidly to the strong beats and acoustic guitar supplying light backbeat accents. In keeping with contemporary country styles, there were no drums. Presley's vocal performance, however, was not idiomatic country; nor was it blues, although he largely followed the phrasing of the original. His aggressive, driving rhythm was leavened with a timbral sweetness, evoking not Crudup's carefree libertine but a boy caught in the ambivalent moment between childhood and adulthood, wanting not "women" but a single "gal." Crudup sang, "Well my mama she done told me / Papa told me too / The life you're living son now / Women be the death of you," and his "That's all right" refrain came back relaxed, proudly defiant of the risk.

By contrast, Presley sounded torn: "Mama she done told me / Papa done told me too / Son that gal you're fooling with / She ain't no good for you." The unfailingly polite young man, ever mindful of his parents' wisdom, struggled to square that respect with his own consuming desire. In Presley's rendition, "That's All Right" was changed from a song of experience to one of innocence, its refrain less confident assertion than nervous chatter. The record was an unrefined pop confection imagined and created in the place where, only a short time before, the musicians had struggled to come up with a plausible version of "I Love You Because." The famous story of how "That's All Right" emerged in the midst of recording not only a different song but a completely different genre reminds us how unexpected the whole thing was. When the recording was finished, Sam Phillips's adrenaline fed both excitement and worry. "It's not black, it's not white, it's not pop, it's not country," he realized, and wondered where on earth "do we go from here."[71]

The other famous Phillips in Memphis was Dewey Phillips, a lord of the airwaves whose own eclectic musical sensibilities and ungovernable persona entertained the city nightly on his *Red Hot and Blue* radio show on WHBQ. He was the first to play "That's All Right" and to realize, observing his overloaded telephone switchboard, that it would be a hit, at least in Memphis. But the record could not be released. It had no B-side. It was a one-off stylistic fluke. In the uncertain search for another song, Sam, Elvis, Scotty, and Bill went through their collective repertory, feeling their way, trying to find another song that would somehow complement what they had done with "That's All Right." In Scotty Moore's memory, "there was nothing like a direction, there was just a certain . . . feel" they were searching for.[72] Finally, and again quite by accident, they hit on Bill Monroe's "Blue Moon of Kentucky," a bluegrass waltz. The transformation this time involved turning the waltz's rhythmic lilt into a rocking four/four. Presley reinterpreted Monroe's high-lonesome vocal melody as an edgy sprint, rushing ahead of the beat and veering between stylized huskiness and near baby talk as his voice moved from chest to head. For his part, Phillips set an electronic echo bouncing through the track's recesses, creating a textural backdrop of persistent rhythmic rowdiness.

And then, there it was: Presley's first Sun single—Sun 209—one side a blues song, the other a country song, neither side really blues or country.

Like the vocal groups and so many other contemporary young musicians, Presley got the chance to make records without serving the traditional apprenticeship—years of gigs and rehearsals, learning the ropes and habits of show business. In stepping overnight from the amateur ranks into the world of the professional with an unfamiliar hybrid style, Presley thrust on the industry yet another confusing image. No one called his records rock and roll at first. That was Alan Freed's term for black R&B, and whatever Presley was, he wasn't black, and the music wasn't rhythm and blues. Most observers thought it some sort of up-tempo country (Jerry Wexler called it "non-Nashville country"), which was confirmed by the chart history of the Sun recordings, whose only showing was on the country charts.[73] According to conventional understanding, there was no other category for a white, southern singer whose style was clearly something other than mainstream pop. But while legions of young southerners who could care less what the music was called became enthralled with this new star, many traditional country fans were skeptical. The country music scholar Bill C. Malone recalled his annoyance at a 1955 concert in Austin where his "hero" Hank Snow's portion of a joint appearance with Presley was cut to "an abbreviated medley" in order to accommodate a second Presley show for "the large throng clamoring outside to get in." To Malone, "a rock-ribbed country traditionalist," Presley was "neither fish nor fowl." Moreover, "he was not good and, more significantly, was not country."[74]

If he was not strictly country, it was because Presley partook of a legacy that included all the music he had ever heard. The industry's tendency to categorize styles according to geographic origin, ethnicity, manner of vocal expression, instrumentation, and song type was becoming increasingly arbitrary and problematic, obscuring developing trends and adding to the general confusion. If in 1954 no one had a word that really fit Presley's musical oddities, it was because no one knew exactly what was happening, only that the ground was shifting. In time, many of the emblems of change would be placed under the "rock and roll" rubric, but by then the term would have an altogether different meaning. At the moment, what stood out to the industry's establishment was that, for some reason, amateur or at least unschooled performers, songwriters, and record producers, partnering with a gaggle of rough-and-tumble entrepreneurial hustlers, were making records that had no business being as popular as they were.

As the 1950s wore on, amateurs and outsiders carved an ever-larger place in the market as their improbable encroachments on the pop mainstream mounted. Presley, after leaving Sun to sign with RCA Victor, would become the greatest star since Crosby, the center of the pop universe, the king of rock and roll. But while such outsized icons were key to crystallizing public awareness of the new idiom, the inexorable reshaping of the public soundscape was driven by a rising tide of myriad musical sounds flooding into the mainstream. Alongside the biggest hit records were hundreds of smaller ones, oftentimes one-shot outings by groups or individuals quickly forgotten. Yet the traces of their voices remained indelible and would return again and again, stubbornly persistent in their electronic incarnations. As their records accumulated they formed a store of memories bound up with a sense of identity and, finally, an aesthetic language and tradition whose enduring significance would become apparent with the next generation of musicians. The swing style, which had defined American popular music throughout the country's epochal economic depression and the world war, was growing distant beyond its historical years. The music of the 1930s and early 1940s, many of whose stars were neither old nor lacking in vitality, was being supplanted permanently.

FOUR

Crossing Over

Take our tune "Do You Love Me?" by the Contours. . . .
It was recorded r.&b. but by the time it reached the half-
million mark, it was considered pop. And if we hadn't
recorded it with a Negro artist, it would have been
considered rock and roll.
— BERRY GORDY

· 1 ·

As a young man, the sociologist Philip Ennis joined a team of researchers at Columbia University's Bureau of Applied Social Research charged with mapping the decision-making process for airing popular records on radio. Directed by the mass media scholar Paul Lazarsfeld, the project was initiated in 1953 by BMI director Sidney Kaye in response to a $150-million antitrust suit brought by thirty-three individual ASCAP members, led by songwriter Arthur Schwartz, on behalf of some three thousand other ASCAP composers and authors. The plaintiffs alleged a conspiracy on the part of BMI and its codefendants (which included several radio and television networks, as well as Columbia Records and Columbia Music Publishing) to give "preference to the performance of BMI controlled music" in order "to fix and reduce the price to be paid by the defendant networks and their co-conspirators in the broadcasting industry for the use of music on their programs."[1]

The suit was the latest skirmish in the ASCAP-BMI war that had shadowed the industry since BMI's creation in 1939. It would work its way through the courts over the course of the next eighteen years to an inconclusive outcome, dismissed with prejudice in 1971 long after its relevance had waned. The pair of studies undertaken by Lazarsfeld's team were concluded by 1955 (both exonerated BMI), ending the bureau's involvement in the matter. Yet Ennis was left with a nagging sense that something unearthed in the investigation was being overlooked and in fact the work had only begun. The upshot of the research, which was based, in part, on "a close examination of *Billboard*'s music popularity charts," was a paradox that failed to reconcile two opposing conclusions: (1) disc jockeys "were the key figures in making the hits of the day"; but (2) the rising commercial success of rhythm and blues records seemed to have a life of its own, with jockeys tending "to follow rather than lead popular taste."[2] The puzzling result set Ennis on a decades-long social and industrial history project, culminating in his 1992 book *The Seventh Stream: The Emergence of Rocknroll in American Popular Music*. In it, he set forth a theoretical frame describing the U.S. popular music economy in terms of "streams" running side by side, each representing "an artistic system, an economic framework, and a social movement."[3]

The six streams flowing in the late 1940s—pop, black pop, country pop, folk, gospel, and jazz—had been developing their market presence since the record business's first heyday in the 1920s. The seventh stream, which emerged in the mid-1950s, Ennis labeled "rocknroll," a new hybrid music that borrowed elements from all the others. Its birth was facilitated by the dilution of the main pop stream with elements of the other streams, especially black pop and country pop. The diversity challenged the music industry's status quo, a shakeup *Billboard* characterized with headlines such as "R.&B. Music Invades Pop Market," "Bursting Old Barriers," and "Pop—C.&W.—R.&B.: Demarcation Lines Are Growing Hazy." In the early years of the 1950s, music markets percolated with enough unexpected happenings to signal that restless audiences were blithely mixing and matching their musical selections.[4]

The industry's structure was based historically on the assumption of a segmented arena of public taste whose contours were definable and predictable. Years of market experience had produced ample evidence of particular customers' preferences correlating musical styles with social groups and geographic regions. There had long been individual cases of artists or single records that appealed to more than one market but never so many as to upset basic market principles. Now, however, markets began behaving capriciously often enough to put the industry on alert as songs crossed among the three pop streams with surprising ease. "Goodnight Irene," for instance, a pop hit for the Weavers and Gordon Jenkins in 1950 (as well as Frank Sinatra, Jo Stafford, and Dennis Day), was also popular with R&B audiences in a version by Paul Gayten (Regal) and with country fans in versions by Moon Mullican (King) and the duo of Ernest Tubb and Red Foley (Decca). That same year, "My Heart Cries For You," one of Mitch Miller's quasi-folk productions in Guy Mitchell's original recording, served as R&B material for Dinah Washington (Mercury) and country material for Jimmy Wakely (Capitol). Wakely's disc made both the country and pop charts, as did the country/pop duet version by Red Foley and Evelyn Knight (Decca).

When songs or records appealed across market categories, they were said to "cross over" in the sense that they transcended boundaries—between markets, of course, but also between the social and cultural worlds those markets reflected. The crossover phenomenon, as it gained steam, commingled cultural markers so that different social groups found themselves sharing and enjoying elements of a common aesthetic experience, which upset record men's long-standing commercial expectations. The unruly mixture of musical sounds enlivened the musical economy but also threw it into uncertainty. With the general order of things in dynamic flux, with hustlers and amateurs loose in the music business and young audiences registering an ever-greater voice, the market took on an ungovernable life of its own. The reason Ennis faced a paradox, he later realized, was that the country, at the time of the bureau project, was in the midst not simply of a temporary industry fad but of a fundamental realignment no one had any way of gauging let alone naming. In retrospect, he wrote, it would become "obvious" what had occurred, but only after the consequences of crossover had time to sink in. As it stood in the early 1950s, "rocknroll was simply not a word in the vocabulary of the people in the music business I dealt with."[5]

The term was certainly in the air. Alan Freed had begun using it prior to 1954 when he decided to name his show on WINS the *Rock 'n' Roll Party*. But as Freed himself made clear, the term "named the program, not the music."[6] It was a clever handle borrowed from black slang, with variants found in dozens of songs dating at least to the 1920s. It was a marketing slogan highlighting Freed's R&B format and hipster image. It was not, however, a specific industry category; in Freed's early usage, it conveyed no awareness of the emerging musical stream it would come to identify. In 1954, rock and roll was just another name for rhythm and blues.

In the 1940s, *Billboard* tracked the business activities of record companies, publishers, radio stations, jukebox operators, and retail outlets with charts based on surveys taken in various markets around the country. On March 24, 1945, the publication inaugurated its most comprehensive chart to date: a ten-song Honor Roll of Hits, "an authenticated tab of music popularity based upon weekly surveys of every known practical indication of public tune yens."[7] The chart's composite structure was based on the most thorough research *Billboard* had ever undertaken. Thousands of hours had been spent, the editors claimed, and "after consultation with leading research authorities as well as leaders in the [sheet] music and record industries" a weighted system had been devised to factor together six key indicators of a song's popularity.[8] Appearances on "screen, on network radio shows, and on indie radio station platter sessions" were considered "passive indicators" while "active proof of the public's acceptance" was registered in retail sales of sheet music and records and in "the nickeling of disks in juke boxes."[9] Although songs—not records—would remain the Honor Roll's unit of currency for some years to come, separate charts provided the details of each subcategory and three were devoted to analysis of pop record activity (Records Most-Played on the Air, Most-Played Juke Box Records, and Best Selling Retail Records), which increasingly outpaced sheet music sales and live radio performances in market volume.

While the Honor Roll and its subcharts tracked the mainstream pop market, *Billboard* also surveyed the smaller black pop and country pop markets. In October 1942, the Harlem Hit Parade chart began tracking the ten top-selling records in a few stores with largely African American clienteles. For the first few years, sales reports were garnered only from outlets east of the Mississippi (missing the music's surging popularity on the West Coast, especially in Los Angeles), most in New York City but also in such cities as Chicago, Atlanta, Newark, Cincinnati, Birmingham, and Richmond. In 1945, the survey area was expanded to present a broader national account of a record's activity. The new chart, however, tracked not retail sales but jukebox play. Following long-standing industry terminology, the chart was labeled Most-Played Juke Box Race Records. In 1948 *Billboard* began running concurrent national charts for jukebox and retail (Best Selling Retail Race Records). Both charts were rechristened Rhythm & Blues in 1949, and in 1955 a third chart was added tracking R&B airplay (Most Played by Jockeys).

The year 1942 also saw the beginning of a weekly *Billboard* column called "American Folk Records" "designed to help [jukebox] operators select money-making recordings" of "cowboy songs, hillbilly tunes, spirituals, etc."[10] In 1944, the column evolved into the Most Played Juke Box Folk Records chart, which was joined in 1948 by a second tabulating Best Selling Retail Folk Records. In 1949, these charts were renamed Country and Western and joined by a Country and Western Records Most Played by Folk Disk Jockeys chart. As with the R&B charts, the country charts augmented the national data with regional charts reporting activity in selected markets.

By the mid-1940s, then, all three of the largest popular music markets had at least some tracking measures in place to keep tabs on audience responses. The categories and rankings were meant to help those in the industry get a sense of which discs were attracting attention and where it was coming from—what kind of outlet, what geographic region, and what social demographic. Each category was something of a catchall; black music of all sorts tended to fall under R&B and white southern music under country. But if these tendencies overlooked important distinctions within a category, the charts were specific enough to account for broad differences between categories whose style features included dialect and vocal mannerisms, habits of rhythmic phrasing, types of melodic contour, instrumentation, song topic, instrumental and vocal texture, and a host of performance particulars. A white string band backing a "rustic warbler" singing a story in "the tragic vein," for example, described hundreds of records that appealed primarily to whites in the South and Southwest.[11] "A fine jump blues, engagingly shouted and backed crisply and swingingly by combo," was likewise a typical characterization of music favored by black audiences.[12]

Even allowing for variations, there was enough consistency to make the blunt descriptions workable, lending a certain order to the market and providing a rough guide for deciding which records to program or purchase for retail store or jukebox based on what one knew of the audience. Everyone involved, from songwriter to rack jobber, understood the broad stylistic outlines—exemplified vividly by the star performers in each market—and knew that audiences could be exclusive in their preferences. In Atlantic's early years, the company "never cared about a white market," recalled, Jerry Wexler. "We never looked for it."[13] Chuck Berry, not one to sit still for such constraints, was nevertheless aware that his performances of country songs for the black clientele at Huff's Garden in Saint Louis were deliberately inappropriate, having "no business in the repertoire of a soul-music-loving audience."[14] And Henry Glover, songwriter and producer at King in the late 1940s, recalled that "you couldn't sell Wynonie Harris to [white] country folk, and black folk weren't buying Hank Penny."[15]

There were two types of crossover—song and record—each of which represented a particular type of market response. Crossover *songs* originated within the industry as record men sought to capitalize on a song's appeal by recording new versions for separate markets. Crossover *records,* on the other hand, resulted from consumers' whims, alerting an often unsuspecting record firm that it had an intermarket hit on its hands. Songs traveled more readily among the streams than records because they carried with them fewer specific style markings. Their surfaces could easily be tailored to any market, retaining words and melody but changing performance style, arrangement, and sonic signature. And although songwriting conventions varied among idioms, all audiences accepted a fairly wide range of songs as long as the particular rendition was in a familiar vein. In a world of burgeoning record sales, proven song material was in hot demand, and it became increasingly common for songs released initially in one market to be recorded—covered—by a performer in another. The practice was simply an extension of what occurred routinely within markets.

The reasons for the multiple cuts were systemic in the industry, encouraged by copyright law, performance rights practices, and marketing strategies. Publishers—indeed any copyright holder—sought as many recorded versions as possible because they made money on every record sold. Record companies released cover versions because in an always uncertain marketplace, following the tried and tested mitigated some of the risk associated with releasing a new recording. Vitacoustic rolled the dice with the novelty "Peg O' My Heart," and its unlikely success caught other labels' attention, especially the majors, which had the resources to rush after a share of what was now a known hit. Covers by Buddy Clark (Columbia), the Three Suns (RCA Victor), Art Lund (MGM), Ted Weems (Mercury), and Clark Dennis (Capitol) were all top-ten hits in the same year as the Harmonicats' version. The majors would do the same thing a few years later with covers of R&B songs, "waiting for the tunes to break through on the indie labels" and then rushing out their own covers.[16] While each company had its own stars with their own fans and access to innumerable songs, riding a proven winner was just a sensible business practice.

While they translated songs from one idiom to another, cross-market covers still bore traces of their origins, which meant that an element of cultural fusion was practically unavoidable. Bull Moose Jackson's cover of Wayne Raney's "Why Don't You Haul Off and Love Me" and Wynonie Harris's version of Hank Penny's "Bloodshot Eyes," for example, were unmistakably R&B, although the songs were steeped in a country ethos. By the same token, Jimmy Ballard's version of Jackson's "I Want a Bowlegged Woman" or the York Brothers' recording of the Dominoes' "Sixty Minute Man" adapted the black originals to a country milieu. All of these performers were on King/Federal, which like many indies carried both R&B and country rosters, often releasing songs nearly simultaneously in versions for each market. The idea was simply to get as much mileage from a song as possible, especially since label owners held many of the copyrights. But as they served the record men's commercial pragmatism, the shape-shifted covers, in merging different aesthetic sensibilities, also played the part of cultural trickster.

Records, unlike songs, were immutable; their form, clearly aimed at a particular audience, remained the same wherever they turned up. It was extremely rare for a record to cross over directly between the country and R&B charts. The idioms' style features were rarely palatable to one another's core audiences, and if a record showed up on both the country and R&B charts it was likely in a performance by a well-known pop star that happened to blanket all markets—Bing Crosby's "Pistol Packin' Mama," for example, or Nat Cole's "Straighten Up and Fly Right." But it became increasingly common for country or R&B records to make a showing in the pop market. With each crossover, the pop stream grew wider, deeper, richer, and more difficult to control, as a large cross section of listeners in effect told the record men their tastes were growing more varied and unpredictable. It was not especially remarkable that such African American performers as the Mills Brothers, Ink Spots, Ella Fitzgerald, and Nat Cole routinely charted pop hits; in their polished performances and sophisticated arrangements, their records were perfect pop exemplars. But when the Orioles' "It's Too Soon to Know" crossed over to the pop charts in 1948, it brought with it an approach to singing and record production that challenged market assumptions. Its success in the R&B market, where expressive delivery and ethnic identity trumped pop refinement, was of little note to the mainstream industry. But when the record began unexpectedly doing business in markets of much broader social and geographic scope—when it showed up on the same chart and in the same year as the likes of records by Dick Haymes, Frank Sinatra, and Margaret Whiting—it not only introduced a new audience to new sounds but also raised eyebrows among the established powers in the business.

The *Billboard* charts from which we track market history are valuable yet problematic sources, part eyewitness report and part self-fulfilling construct. With the chief aim of providing subscribers with the most accurate and up-to-date information about the markets, the tabulations largely removed aesthetic preference from consideration. Both *Billboard* and its subscribers had money riding on accurate tracking of consumer activities, and editors urged that "personal whims or likes" be set aside in favor of letting "the public be the guide" as they made "their choices known at the juke box coin slot, the radio dial and the retail cash registers." In a free market, they reminded readers, the "buyer's always right."[17] (*Billboard* did offer opinion as well as reporting; a separate section in each issue was devoted to reviews of new releases, advising the trade of reviewers' estimation of a disc's business potential.) But inevitably and in spite of all principled intentions, reports of sales, airplay, and jukebox activity drew more attention to a disc, which might, in turn, increase its momentum. That is, chart reporting could not but become itself part of the story. Even so, the charts provide the best data we have about the market connections between audiences and generic musical types and how these connections evolved during the 1950s.[18] They offer a useful overview of the broad changes in the musical culture of the time, which were reflected first as anomalous chart activity and then, gradually, as a permanent shift in the nation's pop soundscape summarized in the evolution of "rock and roll" from a marketing term to a musical idiom.

The emergence of the new idiom, as Ennis learned, would become apparent only in hindsight, once the trappings of faddism had receded, leaving enduring musical residue. Moreover, it was not a thing accomplished by producers alone, be they songwriters, performers, or record men. It took a complicit audience to add fuel to the process, sanctioning new or aberrant artistic behavior, urging the producers on, and at times even pointing the way. In short, the crossover phenomenon was a measure of audience engagement. American musicians had for centuries borrowed from one another, creating a musical fabric of rich cultural mixture. But in the era of musical commodity and mass media, audiences' voices registered as never before. It turned out that they, too, could influence the process. Music fans could vote their preferences by buying records or selecting tunes on jukeboxes. They could register a more private vote by tuning in whatever radio station they chose without fear of social scrutiny. As the nation entered the 1950s, audiences made it increasingly clear that boundaries between musical styles and the cultural values they embodied were more porous than ever. The streams and their stylistic features remained distinct, but growing numbers of people chose to wade in more than one. Among these listeners was a generation of artists raised on an unprecedented access to the nation's musical abundance.

· 2 ·

In 1943, a *Time* magazine article titled "Bull Market in Corn" noted that songs "fragrant with hillbilly spirit" were growing popular with mainstream audiences. It was, the report claimed, "the biggest revolution in U.S. popular musical taste since the 'swing' craze began in the middle '30s." The analysis was overblown, but if it was overstatement to assert that "the dominant popular music of the U.S. today is hillbilly," it was certainly increasingly common to find a country artist on the mainstream pop charts and for pop performers to cover country hits. The timing of the article was probably influenced by the enormous crossover success of Al Dexter's "Pistol Packin' Mama," which had reached number one and sold at least a million copies earlier in the year. Bing Crosby and the Andrews Sisters soon followed with a pop version. The *Time* reporter flaunted many contemporary stereotypes in characterizing country music's lowbrow status. It was "homely," "foursquare," and formulaic, saturated with "Appalachian accents of the geetar and the country fiddle." It was a "much simpler (and often monotonous) musical idiom" than the swing music of the 1930s and "was old when nostalgic '49ers were singing Clementine." It was the descendant of antique tunes from the British Isles "preserved in the U.S. by generations of hard-bitten country folk."

In contrast to Tin Pan Alley songcraft, the reporter asserted, country songs were practically artless. "The songs get their quality, if any, from their words—long narrative poems evolved by generations of backwoods minstrels. . . . Any simple soul might write hillbilly words and the composition of music has always been regarded by Tin Pan Alley as a variety of unskilled labor." In the condescending conflation of factual description and aesthetic opinion, the reporter echoed a regional prejudice common in an entertainment industry dismissive of the cultural territory between New York and Los Angeles. The story ended with a last word from Jimmie Davis—soon to be governor of Louisiana, all-around character, and writer of "You Are My Sunshine," one of country music's most enduring evergreens.

> His wife is the touchstone by which Jimmie (who cannot read music) judges his songs. Says he: "When I have thought up a song, I run through it with my wife who's a graduate in piano from Centenary College. If she doesn't like it, it's going to be a smash hit."[19]

While the national press looked on bemusedly, however, the music demonstrated its appeal nationwide. As large numbers of fans voiced approval, it grew ever clearer through the 1940s that country music had left its rural roots and invaded cities.[20] Such factors as the wartime and postwar migrations of rural southerners, the broad exposure of troops to country records broadcast on Armed Forces Radio, and country music's regular presence on powerful radio stations (especially the *National Barn Dance* on WLS in Chicago and the *Grand Ole Opry* on WSM in Nashville) raised general awareness of the idiom throughout the United States. In 1947, for instance, country was the driving force behind a boom in record label startups in Philadelphia. With their distribution limited to eastern Pennsylvania and southern New Jersey, small firms were nevertheless finding plenty of customers. And at large amusement park venues throughout the region, country stars routinely drew bigger crowds than the top dance orchestras.[21] Later that year *Billboard* reported that the slackening band business was leading such top talent agencies as William Morris and General Artists Corporation to "move into the folk-music talent mart." Demand was such that venues on the "West Coast, the Dallas region in Texas, the Pennsylvania and Ohio territory, Detroit and its environs, and even the sedate New England territory" had all shown solid box office response.[22]

The year 1947 also saw what *Billboard* called "the first hill country invasion of New York's musical literati," with a Carnegie Hall concert featuring Ernest Tubb, Minnie Pearl, and various other stars of the *Grand Ole Opry*.[23] The front-page review a week later reported an unqualified success. "New York is sold on hillbilly music," it read. "These weren't just curious onlookers, out for a night of novelty. They were serious, devoted fans, almost rabid in their wild enthusiasm." It was the most screaming and applause the town had seen, the reporter reckoned, since legions of bobby-soxers had mobbed Sinatra's Paramount Theatre appearances during the war. The important distinction was that "instead of juveniles vocal-hopping all over the place, these were people beyond their teens."[24]

By 1951, with Patti Page's recording of "Tennessee Waltz" having sold in the millions, it seemed fair to claim that there was afoot "a revolution brewing in the music business," as a *New York Times* feature put it.[25] The song had been a country hit in 1948 with three successful recordings by Pee Wee King and His Golden West Cowboys (RCA Victor), Cowboy Copas (King), and Roy Acuff (Columbia); King's had even grazed the pop chart with a one-week showing at number thirty. (He would storm the pop market in 1951 with "Slow Poke," which claimed the top spot and remained on the chart for twenty-four weeks.) When *Billboard* noted the initial breakout of Page's version in the Philadelphia market, it reported that the song was a last-minute choice for the B-side of "Boogie Woogie Santa Claus" and that it came to Mercury A&R man Joe Carlton's attention by way of bandleader Erskine Hawkins's 1950 cover version.[26] Not surprisingly, then, although the specific musical parts differed, the records shared two key elements of instrumentation and arrangement: muted trumpet solos and piano responses to the melodic phrases of both voice and trumpet. Despite its serendipitous origins and convoluted lineage, Page's "Tennessee Waltz," a pop version of a country song filtered through an R&B cover, became the "bellwether song of the folk music trend," threatening, the *Times* reporter wrote, to "unseat the Alley's own favorite—Irving Berlin's 'White Christmas'—as the top popular tune of our time."[27]

Two years later, when conservative estimates put the country music take at 70 million dollars in appearance fees, record sales (30 million singles), and publishing royalties, the music had proven over the course of a decade that it was "anything but the step-child of the music, record, or talent industries." Rather, its fans had announced on a broad front that it was "an integral and major part of the entertainment world."[28] Indeed, it had integrated itself into the mainstream to such an extent that the two streams freely shared stylistic resources. Country star Rex Allen, riding the wave of his 1953 country/pop crossover, "Crying in the Chapel," reckoned that "the line between well-done country music and popular is very thin now."[29] "Well-done" implied the production standards of major-label pop, which augmented the string-band basics with "conventional instrumentation and arrangements . . . plus echo chamber and a choral group."[30] The closeness of the idioms was further underscored by such country/pop duos as Tennessee Ernie Ford and Kay Starr ("I'll Never Be Free," Capitol) and Red Foley and Evelyn Knight ("My Heart Cries For You," Decca).

As pop and country records increasingly rubbed shoulders in the mainstream, country songwriters became more frequent sources for pop cover material. The songs were durable, easily withstanding translation into thoroughly uncountry versions. Yet even dressed in big city glitz, they retained an essence unlike any Tin Pan Alley fare. One important difference was that country songs were often written by the person who sang them, which was often noted as a sign of authentic personal experience. The songs appeared to come "from the heart rather than the head," a *Billboard* reporter opined; they were more concerned with "authenticity and sincerity . . . than the slickness or cleverness needed in pop tunes."[31] Country music was "born of a people . . . who reject any attempt to be flossy or to appear out of their normal character," another *Billboard* writer enthused. "Unlike Tin Pan Alley writers who create music solely as a means of earning a living, country music is . . . bred by years of living and feeling a situation."[32] Such songs of "honest emotion" with "basic and sincere qualities" joined "contrived and artificial" mainstream pop songs as alternate choices on a rapidly expanding menu.[33] In the process, of course, these supposed opposites came to share a common aesthetic context.

Mitch Miller was quick to recognize both the broad appeal and malleability of country songs. Their direct, everyman quality meshed with his pop aesthetic, which held that "self-identification," "simplicity," and "universality" were the keys to success in an ever uncertain pop singles market.[34] "Keep it sexy, keep it simple, keep it sad," he advised. Entice listeners with a sense of personal involvement, leading them to feel "this could be me. If I could write words or music to express myself, this is how I'd say it."[35] When Jerry Wexler introduced him to the music of Hank Williams, Miller became a fan and a regular buyer. He forged a close relationship with Williams's publisher, Wesley Rose, forming a Nashville–New York connection that would loom large in the changing pop soundscape.

Williams had only six modest pop hits, none of which cracked the top twenty. (He had thirty-eight country hits during his lifetime.) But as a songwriter he made a deep impression on the pop mainstream. Convinced that cover versions of Williams's songs would appeal to the pop audience, Rose, in a maneuver he described as "a little fifth columnish," sought out pop A&R men and record producers and tried to persuade them to record the songs in mainstream garb.[36] At first, he found it tough going in a New York music scene deeply invested in Tin Pan Alley. But Miller heard right away that these were songs he could work with—straightforward songcraft with heartfelt lyrics that he could set in any way he pleased. He bought two at their first meeting, and more would follow. He arranged an exclusive deal to release pop versions of Williams's hits at a respectful distance of some months so as not to impinge on sales of the original. Among the songs he covered were "Jambalaya" (Jo Stafford), "Settin' the Woods on Fire" and "Hey Good Lookin'" (Stafford and Frankie Laine), and "Cold, Cold Heart," one of Tony Bennett's career-making hits of 1951.

Bennett was no kind of country singer. According to Miller, his response to the idea of recording a "cowboy song" was similar to Frankie Laine's when Miller suggested "Mule Train": "Tony didn't want to have anything to do with that one."[37] But in Miller's treatment, with Percy Faith's arrangement, the song's words and music were unmoored from their original context; any implication of rural southern sensibility was a residual association. The record was not unlike any number of other Miller productions in which plainspoken songs were spun into pop confections—songs like "My Truly, Truly Fair" (Guy Mitchell), "I Believe" (Frankie Laine), "This Ole House" (Rosemary Clooney), and "The Yellow Rose of Texas" (Mitch Miller with His Orchestra and Chorus). It was simply another novelty record blending unlike elements: a lush, string-rich pop arrangement underpinned by a faint country two-step rhythm and a vocal performance not much different from "Because of You," Bennett's other big hit of the summer. In this guise, strange to say,

"Cold, Cold Heart" appeared to exemplify the Italian American crooner genre widely popular at the time.

While pop covers of country songs largely masked the originals' regional flavor, crossover country records added to the mainstream a new range of performance styles and distinctive voices. In a 1957 feature extolling the music's virtues, Goddard Lieberson, by then president of Columbia Records, noted that what would have been considered shortcomings in a conventional pop performance were, in the country context, a source of expressive depth and poignancy. Sometimes the country singer's "vowels are incomprehensibly attenuated, his roulades piercingly nasal, sometimes he strays off pitch, but always his singing is intense and pervaded with compelling emotion."[38] The music had "a palpable country 'sound,'" Lieberson wrote, by which discerning fans would "recognize the true artist." But the larger effect of the country sound on the general pop music audience was practically the opposite of such exclusive connoisseurship. Rather, it meant a wider range of acceptable pop styles in the mainstream marketplace. The crossover audience cared little for idiomatic purity; their thrill came from the smorgasbord of sonic delights proffered in the ever-broadening pop marketplace.

Actually, by the time Lieberson wrote his encomium it described a style—epitomized by Hank Williams—that was passing into history. A foundation of rootsy flavor would remain, but country producers, no less than their pop counterparts, were interested in new sounds. As much as traditional country stylings had leeched into pop, a reverse process had also taken place. The biggest country/pop crossover hit of 1955–56 was Tennessee Ernie Ford's recording of "Sixteen Tons," which reached number one on both charts though bearing no trace of slide guitar, fiddle, or two-step meter. The lyrics are country in their working-man sensibility, and Ford's delivery is familiar. But the arrangement is hued in cool jazz colors—bass clarinet, muted trumpet, brushes on the snare drum—miles from Merle Travis's original recording. By the late fifties, country music's flirtation with pop would give rise to the so-called Nashville Sound, a smooth blend orchestrated in large part by the efforts of such producers as Chet Atkins and Owen Bradley.

Mixing idioms had long been a country music hallmark. Elements of blues, jazz, gospel, and pop were evident on some of the earliest country records, and the heteroglot impulse was on full display in its first great star, Jimmie Rodgers, who himself would have been exposed to a range of recorded music in the industry's first flush of success in the 1920s. Bob Wills and his Texas Playboys incorporated both contemporary dance rhythms and old-time song material into their eclectic "western swing," a style Bill C. Malone has aptly characterized as an outgrowth of "the diverse mingling of musical cultures (Cajun, Tex-Mex, German, Bohemian, black, cowboy, Anglo) that prevailed in the Southwest."[39] Trumpet lines in what was referred to in the 1940s as the Dixieland jazz style turned up on Al Dexter's "Pistol Packin' Mama" and Merle Travis's "Divorce Me C.O.D." (1946). And such discs as Johnny Barfield's "Boogie Woogie" (1939), the Delmore Brothers' "Hillbilly Boogie" (1945), and Moon Mullican's "Cherokee Boogie" (1951) pointed up yet another strand in country music's style complex.[40]

The intermingling of pop and R&B with country in the midfifties, then, was merely the most recent and high-profile stage in a thoroughly American cultural process. While country audiences continued to enjoy a purer honky-tonk strain, its marked hillbilly flavor confined it to the country stream. The idiom's most popular performer in 1955 was Webb Pierce, who, along with such stars as Faron Young and Ray Price, kept the honky-tonk sound alive and well. But none of Pierce's three number-one country hits that year crossed over either as records or songs. Instead, in country/pop records such as "Sixteen Tons" and in R&B-inflected country from young unknowns—Presley, Carl Perkins, Gene Vincent—the industry noted a more or less continual hybrid country presence on the national soundscape.

Rex Allen's "Crying in the Chapel" was only one of several versions to appear on the charts in 1953. The song was written by Artie Glenn, a country songwriter living in Fort Worth, Texas, and first recorded by his seventeen-year-old son Darrell for the Valley label based in Knoxville, Tennessee. Darrell Glenn's record reached well into both the pop (number six) and country (number four) charts in July, followed by pop versions from *Your Hit Parade*'s June Valli (RCA Victor) and then Ella Fitzgerald (Decca) and Art Lund (Coral). There was also a number-one R&B recording by the Orioles (Jubilee), which itself crossed over to pop (number eleven). As the music public became more difficult to predict, cross-market covering of successful songs, whatever their origin, was a matter of prudence for record men trying to wring all they could from whatever fleeting trend came along. Yet, while it was becoming common to find multiple recordings of a song aimed at different markets, the broad crossover success of "Crying in the Chapel," and a few others, showed, too, that the pop mainstream was becoming ever more permeable to *sounds* from other streams. As the song's pop, country, and R&B renderings all made top-twenty showings on the pop charts, the confluence told of tidal movements well under way but yet to be grasped.

The following year, R&B crossovers gained a full head of steam as the music "once limited in sales appeal to the relatively small Negro market . . . blossomed into one of the fastest growing areas of the entire record business."[41] It was a phenomenon the industry had witnessed before: "The rhythm and blues market, formerly restricted wholly to a Negro audience," a report read, "has repeated the move in the pop field, as did country and western music several years ago."[42] And as the music "caught the ear of the nation," *Billboard* welcomed the idiom to the mainstream with the same epithet its writers had used for country music: R&B was "no longer the stepchild of the record business." It had, over the previous five years, become "a stalwart member of the record industry," enjoying a "healthy following among all people, regardless of race or color."[43] The acknowledgment that both stepchildren had become full members of the pop market simply corroborated accelerating trends. In 1954, R&B would follow country in crossing not only songs but increasing numbers of records into pop waters.

· 3 ·

In 1949, *Billboard*'s "Race" chart was without fanfare renamed "Rhythm and Blues." To Jerry Wexler, a *Billboard* reporter at the time he suggested the change, it was "more appropriate to more enlightened times."[44] It was also a pithy description of the blues-laced dance music that had emerged in the late 1940s as the soundtrack of urban African American life and whose commercial impact by 1954 merited a special "Spotlight on Rhythm and Blues" section in *Billboard*. Through the early 1950s, the magazine's reporters had noted on several occasions a growing demand for R&B records, and some reports highlighted a new demographic trend. "White Fans Hyping R&B Platter Sales," a headline announced in May of 1952. The article explained that the normal early summer decline in record sales in Southern California was having less effect that year thanks to "a brand-new clientele which has taken up the jazz-blues buying and listening habit." The expanded audience—identified as "Spanish," "mixed-nationality," and "pop audiences"—was attributed to "the work of a group of leading d.j.'s, mostly on indie outlets" in and around Los Angeles. John Dolphin, owner of the Dolphin's of Hollywood record shop, capitalized on the radio-retail connection with midnight to 3:00 a.m. broadcasts from his store hosted by some of the hippest local spinners: Ray Robinson, Hunter Hancock, and Dick "Huggy Boy" Hugg. (The store was not actually located in Hollywood, a place forbidden to African Americans at the time, but on the corner of Vernon and Central Avenues in South Central Los Angeles.) Customer demand—primarily for instrumental discs by such bandleaders as Earl Bostic, Lynn Hope, and Jimmy Forrest—had the store running twenty-four hours a day seven days a week, and Dolphin reckoned that "about forty percent of his retail business now comes from white buyers, where previously his trade was almost entirely Negro buyers."[45]

Billboard's 1954 "Spotlight" section identified the new R&B audience more specifically. "Teen-Agers Demand Music with a Beat, Spur Rhythm and Blues," read a front-page headline. "Teen-agers have spearheaded the current swing to r.&b.," the report claimed, and were "largely responsible for keeping its sales mounting." The "teenage tide" had "swept down the old barriers which kept this music restricted to a segment of the population." The demographic implication was clear, confirmed by the report that "many disk jockeys who once restricted their programming only to popular records are following the change in listener tastes by including rhythm and blues selections with their regular popular offerings." Moreover, the phenomenon had become widespread. If Dolphin noticed white customers venturing to a black section of Los Angeles to get their hands on R&B records, the discs themselves were also turning up in places far from their traditional outlets. With their machines dotted throughout the nation's cities and towns, jukebox operators were "credited with being among the first to sense the teenager swing to r.&b."[46] Operators received requests to put R&B records into locations that "previously detested the low-down, noisy, but exciting numbers," particularly "teen-age spots, transient places, and late-closing taverns."[47] Increased supply of R&B on jukeboxes led, in turn, to "requests to disk jockeys and at record stores."[48] Retail, stores that had never carried R&B discs began not only selling them but featuring them in displays. Dealers, too, attributed the music's popularity in these new markets to "a word-of-mouth interest among the teen-agers."[49]

There was nothing new, of course, about black musicians showing up on the pop charts. Of the ten records listed on the first Harlem Hit Parade chart in 1942, six made the pop chart, as did most of the top-selling R&B discs from 1942 through 1947. In 1948, however, crossovers became scarce and would remain so for the next five years. The change reflected the rising popularity among African American audiences of urban blues. Crossover records during and immediately after the war had a couple of things in common that facilitated their pop success and distinguished them from the new crop of R&B hits: first, they were almost always on major labels, hence relatively hi-fi and backed by national promotion and distribution; and, second, their styles bore integral connections to mainstream pop, primarily swing jazz and sentimental ballads. The 1940s' most consistent two-chart artists were Louis Jordan (Decca), the Ink Spots (Decca), Ella Fitzgerald (Decca), Billy Eckstine (MGM), the Mills Brothers (Decca), Nat Cole (Capitol), Lionel Hampton (Decca), Duke Ellington (RCA Victor), and Erskine Hawkins (Bluebird, a Victor subsidiary). In addition to their pop success, these nine acts were among the decade's top-ten record sellers in the R&B market.

The one act missing from the list—Johnny Moore's Three Blazers, recording for the independent Philo and Exclusive labels—exemplified the club blues sound emerging in Los Angeles in the late 1940s, a style both earthy and world-weary, rooted in rural southern blues but inflected with an urban melancholy and a modern edge. The group included the Texan blues singer and pianist Charles Brown whose "gentle voice"—in Arnold Shaw's apt description—"had a hollowness that made it sound almost like an echo of itself."[50] The instrumentation was the same as the Nat Cole trio—guitar, piano, bass—and Brown's voice was a bluesman's croon. But Cole's jazz roots linked him to the 1930s pop mainstream in both style and attitude. The Blazers' repertory, performance style, and lo-fi records put them in a different arena. They, too, epitomized a sophisticated, adult musical sensibility, but theirs was rooted in lowdown traditions.

The R&B chart itself grew turbulent in 1948, producing nearly three times as many number-one hits as in 1946 and 1947. Of the nineteen records that topped the chart, only six crossed over, and just one in the year's second half, not a blues number but the Orioles' ballad "It's Too Soon to Know." Among the top-ten R&B records of 1949, only two made brief top-thirty showings in pop. The next year, it was one. Of the fifty top-ten R&B records released from 1949 through 1953, most of them varieties of urban blues, a total of nine crossed over. Such contemporary R&B favorites as Wynonie Harris, Roy Brown, and Amos Milburn never made pop showings.[51] Charles Brown, who left the Blazers for a solo career, had a stunning success with his 1949 recording of "Trouble Blues," which stayed at number 1 for fifteen weeks. It did not, however, make the pop chart.

The resurgence of crossover that began in 1954 included a few blues records, such as Guitar Slim's "The Things That I Used to Do" and Joe Turner's "Shake, Rattle and Roll," but the larger trend was toward the young African American vocal groups sprouting in cities across the country. This "newer-type r.&b. material," Paul Ackerman reported, "monopolized" the R&B chart and was beginning to make "a tremendous stir thruout the entire music business."[52] From New York City, the

Chords ("Sh-Boom"), Crows ("Gee"), and Drifters ("Honey Love"); from Los Angeles, the Penguins ("Earth Angel"); from Chicago, the Spaniels ("Goodnite Sweetheart, Goodnite") and Moonglows ("Sincerely"); and from Detroit, the Midnighters ("Work With Me, Annie") all had records that made both the R&B and pop charts in 1954.

In contrast to blues, these were kids' records. The blues was adult in tone and sensibility, expressing a complexity of soul whose sound might titillate an adventurous white teenager tuning it in on the radio but whose meaning most could hardly grasp. This was the music Jerry Wexler referred to when he said, recalling Atlantic's early years, "Our notion was to make black records, in a sense, by black artists for black grownups. There were no teenagers in those days."[53] This was the idiom that encompassed Ray Charles's early records, which he himself considered "more adult" and "more difficult for teenagers to relate to." It was "more serious, filled with more despair than anything you'd associate with rock 'n' roll."[54] The doo-wop sound, on the other hand, was innocent enchantment, its young performers exuding anything but despair.

Arnold Shaw, then A&R chief for the publishing powerhouse Hill and Range, was struck in particular by the "curious sound and appeal" of the Chords' "Sh-Boom."[55] The record was released on the new Atlantic subsidiary, Cat, a label launched, *Billboard* reported, "in order to cash in on the tremendous expansion of r.&b. disks over the past year into pop markets."[56] Shaw found the record "irresistible" in its "appealing dance vitality and a beguiling horniness in the lead singer," but he was not surprised that it "baffled even the Atlantic execs." He learned of the disc from arranger and independent record producer Morty Craft, who relayed the strange news that the fastest-selling pop record in Los Angeles in the spring of 1954 was by a previously unknown African American vocal group on a new independent label. Shaw called one of his friends in Hollywood and asked him to check the veracity of what he considered a "tall tale."[57] The story, it turned out, was true, confirmed by sales at Glenn Wallichs's record store on the corner of Sunset and Vine where "Sh-Boom" was outselling Perry Como, Kitty Kallen, and other pop performers with current hits. Armed with this information, Shaw determined to make a deal with Atlantic, securing half of the record's publishing rights for six thousand dollars, a princely sum for an unknown group.

Atlantic executives were as surprised as anyone at the record's success. Label boss Ahmet Ertegun admitted that when it was played at a sales meeting after its unsuspected hit potential had become apparent the consensus was bewilderment; the record "had something, but what?"[58]

The company was a standout in the R&B field, with a stable of such reliable hit makers as Ruth Brown, the Clovers, the Drifters, and Joe Turner, as well as songwriters, arrangers, and producers whose feel for the music and its audience translated regularly into successful records. But the emergent sounds of youth music were another matter. It had been barely four years since Atlantic had begun to figure out the rocking blues music that fueled indie labels in Los Angeles and Chicago. Ertegun and co-owner Herb Abramson, with staff writer and arranger Jesse Stone in tow, had set out on musical safaris to the South, studying the unfamiliar sounds to see if somehow they could be brought back to New York. Stone, a consummate music professional with many decades of experience, recalled that he "had to learn rock 'n' roll," which he found "backward, musically." Of course, at the time he and his Atlantic cohort "didn't call it rock 'n' roll," but whatever it was, he found the music surprisingly difficult to render in musical notation. It had a relaxed spontaneity about it that resisted capture.[59] Eventually, however, he was able to come up with songs and arrangements that were in themselves only loosely prescriptive, emulating the blues stomp and expressive vitality that raised the roofs of the sweaty southern roadhouses he had visited, songs such as "Money Honey" and "Shake, Rattle and Roll." But now came yet another kind of music, not southern and not blues, a funky sort of urban pop novelty whose appeal was both undeniable and inscrutable.

The Chords were five African American men in their early twenties from the Morissania section of the South Bronx. They were three tenors (Jimmy Keyes, Carl Feaster, and Floyd "Buddy" McRae), one baritone (Claude Feaster), and one bass (William "Ricky" Edwards). All had been members of other groups before coming together as the Chords, yet despite their experience they retained the raw energy of their street corner roots. Stone coached the group and developed the arrangements in preparation for their debut recording session, at which they were joined by session musicians on piano, bass, drums, guitar, and tenor saxophone. The record's A-side was to be "Cross Over the Bridge," a current hit for Patti Page, whose lyric and music—by Bennie Benjamin and George David Weiss—bore the sturdy and familiar earmarks of professional songcraft: artful manipulation of the title metaphor and expert handling of contemporary musical conventions. "Sh-Boom," on the other hand, written by the group's members, had but a few lyrics amounting to a zany come-on ("Life could be a dream / If I could take you up in paradise up above") punctuated by extended phrases of nonsense syllables. And its music, though somehow infectious, was repetitive nearly to the point of minimalism. Who would pick such a childish ditty to be a hit? Certainly not the grown-ups at Atlantic. Packaging the song with "Cross Over the Bridge" would garner some publishing royalties for the Chords and their record company as it rode the coattails of the A-side, but to send it into the marketplace as a contender in its own right would be foolhardy.

Disc jockeys heard it differently. When the record was distributed to radio stations, "Cross Over the Bridge" was deemed unremarkable, but "Sh-Boom" received repeated spins. Beginning in California, and in particular through airplay on Dick "Huggy Boy" Hugg's show on Los Angeles station KRKD, "Sh-Boom" began to attract listeners and orders flooded in to distributors. Shaw's expensive deal with Atlantic looked shrewd as the Los Angeles experience was repeated throughout the spring in markets across the country. Since Atlantic had no publishing stake in "Cross Over the Bridge" and the song had little part in selling the record, the company pulled it, made "Sh-Boom" the record's A-side, and added a new B-side, a song called "The Little Maiden" in which the company owned a significant publishing interest. Thus, with a helpful nudge from deejays and assurance from record buyers, Atlantic stumbled into the new crossover vortex.

Blues of a sort would eventually cross into the mainstream, but it was a simplified, if spunky, hybrid: Little Richard's "Tutti Frutti," Chuck Berry's "Maybellene," Bill Haley's "Crazy Man, Crazy." The genre's twelve-bar harmonic and phrase structure remained intact, but the sound and spirit departed markedly from grown-up R&B. If an adult blues song crossed over in a young pop star's rendition—say, Pat Boone's version of Ivory Joe Hunter's "I Almost Lost My Mind"—it was in a context that hardly resembled its soulful origins. By 1957, when Paul Ackerman and Ren Grevatt toasted "a great day for the blues," the work of bluesmen hardly figured in the statistic claiming a 25 percent blues share of the pop market. The records cited included Presley's "Jailhouse Rock," Danny and the Juniors' "At the Hop," Jerry Lee Lewis's "Great Balls of Fire," Buddy Holly's "Peggy Sue," and Little Richard's "Keep a' Knockin'." The reporters acknowledged that by "blues" they were referring "primarily to song structure and only secondarily to song material."[60] Like doo-wop ballads, rock and roll blues absorbed its influences—often merely superficial elements—in random, piecemeal ways and quickly turned them around in a different, usually simplified form. The deeper emotional and topical aspects of blues were absent. The blues of tradition was deconstructed and remade as a fledgling music bearing only fragments of its lineage.

· 4 ·

"Sh-Boom" had barely begun climbing the charts when the song appeared in another version by a Canadian vocal group, the Crew Cuts, on Mercury. Throughout most of the summer of 1954, both versions were on the radio, the jukeboxes, and the pop charts, although the Crew Cuts ultimately outpaced the Chords, holding the number-one spot for nine weeks. (The Chords made it as high as number two on the R&B chart and number five in pop.) The Canadian quartet, which was formed in 1952 as the Canadaires, featured John Perkins (lead tenor), Ray Perkins (bass), Pat Barrett (tenor), and Rudi Maugeri (baritone). The four had been students at the Saint Michael's Cathedral Choir School in Toronto where they had studied voice and music theory, developing the foundations of a refined style of harmonizing not unlike fellow Saint Michael's alumni the Four Lads.

The Crew Cuts' meticulous style must have owed a debt to choir director Monsignor John Ronan, who was a composer (a former student of Nadia Boulanger) and a Gregorian chant scholar. The classical training would have taught the young Canadians an approach very unlike that of the Chords, whose sidewalk rehearsals included occasional dousing with water thrown from an upstairs tenement. The frisky verve of the Chords' "Sh-Boom," which often bordered on shouting, was confined in the Crew Cuts' version to a stylized declamation rendering the song but not the attitude of the original recording. If the Chords brought to the song a feeling of raw enthusiasm betokening pop music's new wave, the Crew Cuts displayed a strong connection to pop traditionalism, with tightly structured vocal arrangements, controlled emotional expression, large instrumental forces heavy on brass and woodwinds, and high-fidelity production techniques. The cover version pushed the song farther in the direction of musical curio, adding its own corny-zany touch in the form of a couple of mock-dramatic pauses followed by timpani glissandi and further uncoupling the lyrics from any sensible meaning. The Chords sang the song's title with a swinging hipness that reflected its connection to a local street slang expression—"boom." The Crew Cuts' collegiate glee club style erased any culturally implied meaning, leaving only pure sonic thrill.

Jerry Wexler, an R&B advocate whose interest was both aesthetic and financial, reckoned that the Crew Cuts "buried" the song.[61] But the young audience heard it differently, and it was teenage record buyers, as inexperienced at critical reception as their pop idols were at making records, whose judgment record men were heeding as never before. The two recordings represented not an either/or choice but a spectrum of possibility for pop fans grown restive and assertive. Industry veterans could no longer rely on recognized aesthetic principles or stylistic practices because the young audience's tastes were diffuse and changeable. Crossovers, covers, and novelties made for an eclectic, ever-changing musical bazaar. Two facts of "Sh-Boom"'s reception history illustrated the uncertainty. Although the Crew Cuts outdid the Chords in the pop market overall, many operators with jukeboxes in venues catering to white teenagers reported more spins for the Chords' version. And, although the Crew Cuts' record did not make the national R&B charts, it was popular with some black audiences, showing up on regional R&B charts in Chicago and Charlotte, North Carolina.

Covers of R&B songs by major label pop singers had a midfifties vogue. Following the trend of country covers in prior years, when "almost any good c&w tune was jumped upon by big label pop A&R men," producers in 1954 were "looking for more tunes like 'Shake, Rattle and Roll,' 'Sh-Boom' and 'Oh, Baby Mine' [by the Four Knights]."[62] But, while country music was by now well integrated into the industry establishment, with most of the biggest country stars sharing the same labels as their pop colleagues, in R&B, despite numerous reports throughout the late forties and early fifties of major labels developing R&B rosters of their own, the indies had "virtually complete control of the field."[63] To be sure, the majors had their share of black artists, but the cutting edge eluded them. Their successful performers were, for the most part, mature professionals like Chuck Willis at Okeh, Dinah Washington at Mercury, Piano Red at RCA Victor, and Ivory Joe Hunter at MGM. Decca, of course, had a wealth of black talent, including the Mills Brothers, Ink Spots, Ella Fitzgerald, Louis Jordan, Lionel Hampton, and Sister Rosetta Tharpe. But where the majors were caught flatfooted was in the area of young performers plucked from outside the music business. It was not that they did not try; but with little knowledge of the rapidly moving African American youth market, the always risky job of selling records became all the more so. The A&R men were unaccustomed to tapping high schools and street corners as talent pools. They found it difficult "to crack the R&B formula," a *Variety* reporter wrote, not least because "most of the artists & repertoire chiefs frankly can't recognize a potential r&b hit when they hear one."[64] It was "no secret," Ackerman concurred, "that some of the larger publishers and various a.&r. men have trouble latching on to the idiom."[65]

The independent labels were closer to the new R&B sources. They had a better sense of the style, the repertory, and the potential of untested talent. Using "expensive, exhaustive research," the majors gained occasional successes, but indie record men and producers were, in one way or another, immersed in black culture.[66] Their research was firsthand. Jules Bihari's (Modern) decision to enter the record business stemmed from his frustration over the difficulty of acquiring R&B records for the jukeboxes he operated in "all-black locations."[67] Art Rupe (Specialty) "grew up in what you might call a ghetto area" in Pittsburgh. He recalled a school picture in which he stood out "like a sugar cube in a coal bin," and with his young black friends, he said, "the music I heard was black."[68] Don Robey (Duke/Peacock), one of the few African American label owners of the early fifties, started in the music business as proprietor of the Bronze Peacock Dinner Club in Houston's bustling Fifth Ward, for which he booked the talent—Louis Jordan, Ruth Brown, T-Bone Walker. Johnny Otis, an R&B bandleader and record producer, went so far as to adopt a black identity. His heritage was Greek, but he later wrote in his memoir that as a child he had "reacted to the way of life, the special vitality, the atmosphere of the black community" and decided that "if our society dictated that one had to be either black or white, I would be black."[69]

In addition to their feel for the music, the independent record men were more enterprising than their major label counterparts, willing to go out and find performers well off the beaten paths of show business. Ralph Bass, a prolific R&B producer for Savoy and Federal, among others, sought talent at its roots. "My thing for finding talent was to get out on the road down in the deep South," he said, "and we'd find raw talent. They never sang professionally."[70] Jerry Wexler recalled that in the early days:

> There were just literally hundreds, maybe thousands of young people who could play and sing this music and who had no outlet, because the major record companies were very limited in their exploitation of this. They sort of waited for it to come over the transom. So, the new breed of independent record makers were now going to look for them. They went into the boondocks. They went into the cities.[71]

Most covers of country songs owed little to the original recordings in terms of performance style or arrangement. The songs were simply taken as vehicles for pop performers to render in their own ways. Crosby's 1941 waxing of "New San Antonio Rose" with Woody Herman's orchestra, for instance, shared little with the Bob Wills original other than the lead sheet. Many R&B covers, on the other hand, became notorious for imitating specific details of the original recordings. Instead of creating new settings for the essential song elements contained in lead sheets—words, melody, and chords—producers often copied a record's instrumentation and arrangement, and performers borrowed at least some of the stylistic features of the original performance. In part, the copying reflected ignorance of what made this music tick. Pop producers found particular aspects of its appeal difficult to identify, so, to cover themselves, they opted for the whole. Furthermore, because R&B was not a scripted music, records were its primary source documents. Establishment publishers complained that R&B's success hurt their sheet business because it was "strictly a sound phenomenon" focused on record rather than sheet music sales.[72] Sheets for R&B songs gave producers little to work with because so much of the musical substance resulted from the collaborative interaction among musicians captured on recordings.

Tom Dowd, who as Atlantic's chief engineer had recorded and mixed LaVern Baker's "Tweedle Dee," claimed that Mercury, on the eve of Georgia Gibbs's cover session, asked him to join the production team to ensure a reasonably accurate sonic emulation for their near-duplicate arrangement. They "said that they were going to cut the songs again with Georgia Gibbs, and that they had the same musicians, the same arranger, and they wanted the same engineer."[73] (A loyal Atlantic man throughout his career, Dowd demurred.) The majors were not particularly happy with the situation, which was never as lucrative as being first to market with new material. But they were repeatedly caught clueless, forced to play catchup as the nimble indies produced hits with material the majors would not have picked as winners.

Interestingly enough, making roughly accurate copies—what, in a different climate, might have been considered faithful renderings—provoked a backlash. The poet Langston Hughes labeled the practice "highway robbery across the color line."[74] Alan Freed, who as a publishing stakeholder in the Moonglows' "Sincerely" profited handsomely from the McGuire Sisters' million-selling version, nevertheless decried the practice as "anti-negro" and refused to play pop versions of R&B songs on his WINS radio show in New York.[75] In 1955, the station instituted a policy prohibiting broadcast of what it called "copy" as opposed to "cover" records. Copies were records that imitated "often note for note the arrangement and stylistic phrasing of the singer." Cover records, on the other hand, were considered "an integral part of the disk business and . . . regarded as completely ethical by all."[76] The policy, drafted by station manager Bob Smith, applied to all the station's deejays and included "all fields—pop, country and western and rhythm and blues."

The issue, Smith explained, was one of fairness to both the original artist and the record label. But the policy also had an important conceptual dimension, for it implicitly conferred on original recordings a unique, authoritative value.

The WINS ban highlighted two issues that had been simmering throughout the early years of the decade. One was a question of unfair competition caused by cross-market covers; the second was an implicit recognition that a record's particular combination of elements amounted to a musical work in itself. Responding to Gibbs's successful cover of "Tweedle Dee," LaVern Baker had written a letter earlier in the year to Representative Charles Diggs Jr. of Michigan urging movement on the long-stalled revision of the Copyright Act. Alleging that Gibbs had "duplicated [Baker's] arrangement note for note on records," she declared the law "outmoded" and suggested that there might be "some wisdom in introducing a law to make it illegal for one singer to duplicate another's work." She made a similar distinction to Smith's, declaring that she did not mind another performer recording a song she wrote or had written for her but that she "bitterly resent[ed] their arrogance in thefting my music note for note."[77] There was in all this, of course, a fear that cover versions diluted sales of the original. That potential, however, existed for all varieties of covers and had long been considered simply one of the industry's competitive challenges. In fact, as regards indie releases, many record men believed the major label covers actually served to promote sales of the originals. There was something different about the R&B cover flap that transcended concerns about market share. A principle was emerging: a record's contents—its performances, arrangements, sounds—were owed the same protection as any other artwork.

· 5 ·

Along with concerns about fairness and the nature of recorded musical works, the cover debate involved a conception of qualitative authenticity not unlike Sinatra's views on high-class pop. In a 1950 *Saturday Review* piece, Jerry Wexler—not yet an Atlantic record man but a lifelong record collector weighing in as a critic—aimed "to post the reader on trends and fashions and what is worth his attention," to separate "the hot . . . from the hoke." The R&B field, he wrote, had "more and more been vitiated by the prurience, fatuity, and lack of pulse of the bad Tin-Pan Alley products." R&B records "were once almost unfailingly stamped with the honest sensuality, social identification, and strong, steady beat of the unadulterated Southern blues," but while the market continued to see "a core of honest blues records," there was a growing presence of records "infected" with the "pseudo-sophistication, sentimentality, and commercial tinge of our poorer pop records." He laid the "shift in emphasis" at the feet of major label black stars—Nat Cole, Billy Eckstine, Sarah Vaughan, the Ink Spots—and argued that the best work was to be found on indie labels, which were "more sensitive to changes in the world of rhythm and blues than the bigger, less flexible major diskeries."[78] Wexler's idealized aesthetic preference, like Sinatra's, insisted on a degree of stylistic purity that resisted the taint of pop gimmickry. Such principled stances helped to ensure that amid the fantastic swirl of style mixture and the vacating of time honored aesthetic criteria, each of the established streams would leave a strong imprint of its fundamental features on the emerging rock and roll idiom. But with stylistic overlap growing by the day, the connoisseur's argument would fall ever further out of step with public tastes.

A *Variety* report on the R&B cover craze of 1954 focused attention on the authenticity question from a market perspective, although its contradictory findings pointed up inherent problems with the whole idea. Despite successful covers by Georgia Gibbs, Perry Como, the McGuire Sisters, the Fontane Sisters, and the Crew Cuts, the reporter found that "several covers of r&b tunes by pop names have not been able to gain ground because they lacked that authentic low-down quality accented on the indie labels."[79] The article went on to say that "kids not only are going for the tunes and the beat, but they seem to be going for the original interpretations as well." The apparent paradox (which went unremarked in the story) described a wide-open market where authenticity might or might not be a key to success. While it was true that audiences seemed to identify songs increasingly with specific renditions, that in itself would favor not necessarily the original recording but the record with which a fan was most familiar. With pop radio stations far outnumbering R&B formats (recall that *Billboard* did not even begin tracking R&B radio play until 1955) and given the majors' superior promotion and distribution, many listeners might only hear the pop versions. For these listeners the covers were, in effect, the "originals." Also many pop fans simply preferred the more familiar sound of the slickly packaged pop style, as well as its easier social acceptability, a concern impossible to overstate in the world of teenagers. As R&B grew in popularity, so did its public condemnation, and, as one writer has put it, for whites in the early days of crossover "becoming an R&B fan required a certain amount of enterprise and individualism, and generally, rebelliousness as well."[80] As white teenagers became interested in R&B originals, the change represented not only a broader spectrum of musical familiarity but a loosening of social strictures among the young.

With industry insiders and observers alike scrambling to make sense of the dizzying pace of change, the authenticity angle was one way to try to keep some order in the midst of what was becoming a consuming aesthetic mess. Like anything else in the all's-fair music business, it could also be a marketing tool. When Patti Page's 1954 cover of Ruth Brown's "Oh, What a Dream" made a top-ten pop showing, Brown's label, Atlantic, took out a full-page ad in *Billboard*, claiming that her version was the authentic hit "because it has the style . . . because it has the feeling . . . because it can't be duplicated . . . because it's the *original*."[81] (Brown's record was a top R&B hit but failed to make the pop chart.) The argument was not new and not limited to the defense of R&B authenticity. When Francis Craig's "Near You" began taking off in the summer of 1947, covers had inevitably followed. The record company began running a large ad in *Billboard* that read, "The Tune Was Made by the Way It Was Played." The Craig recording was the "one and only," the ad insisted, and it urged buyers not to "settle for a substitute. Get the original."[82]

In 1956, despite the pop covers and the rockabilly launch of Presley, Carl Perkins, and Gene Vincent, longtime industry observer Bill Simon reckoned that the "most numerous invasion force" of the pop stream "came right out of the pure area of rhythm and blues." According to Simon, "as the adulterated product known as rock and roll caught on, the deejays led the kids in the appreciation of the true, original article. This led to the pop success of such performers as Little Richard, the Teen-Agers and many more."[83] If Simon's analysis was overly simplified and idealized, it nevertheless reflected accurately a continuing resistance from many quarters of the industry to the stylistic crosstalk that appeared to threaten the very idea of idiomatic integrity. A similar ethic pertained among some country music deejays, although it did not involve covers but the growing pop and R&B influence on country itself. Many refused "to play anything even faintly tinged with a pop or rhythm and blues flavor, even when recorded by a c.&w. artist." There was growing demand from young listeners for such hybrid records as Presley's "I Forgot to Remember to Forget" (Sun) or Eddy Arnold's "The Cattle Call" (RCA Victor), a collaboration with arranger Hugo Winterhalter, Gordon Jenkins's counterpart at RCA Victor. But one deejay cautioned that as far as country traditionalists were concerned the lush orchestration on Arnold's record was "about as far up town as we want to go."[84] Paul Ackerman recalled music executives from Nashville calling his *Billboard* office, insisting that he "remove Presley from the best-selling country chart on the ground—so they said—he was not truly representative of the country field."[85]

Pop covers of R&B songs had a similar status in the evolving market. They were generally regarded as hokum by purists, and that is the position they have been relegated to in rock historiography. But in 1955, as far as the young audience was concerned, they were simply part of the pop panorama, which was a thing not of exclusivity or connoisseurship but random diversity. The central reality of the pop mainstream's evolution was that it was changing from a market dominated by Tin Pan Alley principles and practices to one where musics of differing provenance shared the same stage and audiences' preferences followed no set patterns. Among the many covers of the Gene and Eunice recording of "Ko Ko Mo" (Aladdin), for example, the most successful was not the Crew Cuts' but Perry Como's. The Crew Cuts was a young group with a budding rock and roll reputation; Como was a 1940s crooner. A record man could be forgiven for wondering "What gives?" as he faced a young pop audience less discriminating than curious and heady with its newfound independence.

If 1954 was the dawning of a crossover movement, it was also a year in which teenage girls swooned over Eddie Fisher singing "Oh! My Papa."[86] And if teenagers embraced Georgia Gibbs, her broader constituency included the "sophisticated Monte Carlo night club habitué."[87] All of which is to say that the cultural forces afield in the midfifties had little to do with authenticity or idiomatic correctness. As the three streams mingled indiscriminately, some records floated freely across market boundaries while others, fitting none of the established categories, found an enthusiastic young audience open to anything. As one bedazzled *Billboard* reporter put it after the rock and roll explosion of 1955–56, "[H]its can come from anywhere," and this applied to "all taste categories." By the end of 1956, the Elvis year, the industry had become accustomed to "a steady criss-crossing of lines" that "show[ed] no sign of let-up."[88] What was left in the way of conventional wisdom regarding record markets was fast fading amid a rambunctious aesthetic free-for-all where novelty, however odd by existing pop standards, repeatedly met with success.

The WINS ban itself had a central contradiction: instead of determining on an individual basis whether recordings were covers or copies, the station simply listed protected records of which no other versions would be broadcast. It claimed there was a distinction to be drawn, yet it failed to act on its own rule. The upshot was that songs were, in effect, inextricable from their original recordings, a notion unprecedented in the industry. The integrity of the original was not to be violated either by stylistic incursions from other streams or even by new versions from performers in the same idiom, wishful purism that ran counter to events unfolding in all three markets. For even as R&B records infused the pop stream as never before, many R&B performers turned to vintage Tin Pan Alley material: the Dominoes' "Harbor Lights," the Five Keys' "Glory of Love," the Platters' "Smoke Gets in Your Eyes," Fats Domino's "Blueberry Hill" and "My Blue Heaven." And if country records had become common pop fare, their arrangements, like the "uptown" setting of Arnold's "The Cattle Call" or Ford's urbane "Sixteen Tons," achieved their pop success at the expense of their down-home twang.

The fact is that no covers were exact replicas of the originals, and because degrees of difference varied widely, covers further enriched the clamor reverberating across the musical soundscape of 1954–55. At the very least, the vocal styling of pop singers was markedly different from the black originals, usually trading nuances of pitch, rhythm, and phrasing for a more simplified melodic presentation with which it was easier to sing along. And arrangements were played with a characteristic precision that distinguished pop performances from R&B's looser grooves. Gibbs's "Tweedle Dee" largely copied Baker's arrangement, right down to the cowbell part, but her delivery was that of a seasoned pop trouper, a pro since her own teenage years in the 1930s, with a solid grounding in pop standards. Baker's lusty growl became, in Gibbs's version, a light, cheerful bounce. Baker made "tweedly-dee" sound suggestive; Gibbs made it sound like a birdcall. Both versions shared a lively feel, but their grain of voice pointed them at different markets. Other covers, like Como's "Ko Ko Mo," were bizarre transformations emphasizing the novelty element to the point of Spike Jonesish parody. Still others, like the Crew Cuts' "Earth Angel," with its strangely clipped delivery of the title phrase, simply lacked the expressive grace of the original. But if the Crew Cuts' cover was perhaps an inept emulation of black doo-wop style or, more precisely, of the Penguins' recording, it was nonetheless a unique musical artifact that found a place of its own in the hit parade.

While midfifties pop cover records of R&B songs did not, as a rule, involve the kind of wholesale revisions typical of country covers, they accomplished much the same effect. They absorbed the originals in a gathering atmosphere of pop artifice. They introduced R&B songs to the mainstream and, in many cases, capitalized on the popularity of established pop stars. They matched proven songs with proven performers, each from different musical worlds, and drew the stars' fans into a disparate crossover audience. Moreover, both in their attempts to replicate aspects of specific recordings and in the backlash they created, the cover versions helped to reinforce the idea that songs and recordings were interdependent in their effect on the listener.

In the summer of 1955, by which time imitative covers were on the wane, Ruth Cage, *Down Beat*'s "Rhythm and Blues" columnist, commented, "Although there is no longer the blatant imitation and out-and-out theft of r&b arrangements by pop personalities, the latter's styles have absorbed some techniques and ideas from the experience."[89] Her assessment was no doubt true, but whatever individual performers had absorbed, the greatest cultural effect of R&B-to-pop covers lay in their cumulative impact on the mainstream. As they joined a growing tide of hit records representing a variety of music that omnivorously consumed its sources and influences, they promoted the contemporary notion that merging contrasting musical markers was entirely appropriate. As commercial vehicles, pop covers of R&B songs were nothing new. They simply followed a long-standing industry practice in which record firms tried to mitigate their risk by reusing songs that had already proven their public appeal. But as music they were aberrant curios. The strange sounds of mainstream pop stars dabbling in styles for which they had no real affinity were yet another indication of the decade's aesthetic uncertainty and the major record companies' sometimes desperate attempts to keep up with the indies.

· 6 ·

In the fall of 1957, *Billboard* reporters admitted having a difficult time sorting out market activities in the discrete terms they had relied on in earlier years. Crossover between pop and R&B charts had become so common that the very notion of boundary crossing seemed a thing of the past.

> You can't tell the best-selling pop charts from the rhythm and blues listings these days without a caption. All but one of the top-15 best-selling r.&b. disks this week also appear on the pop list, and the sole exception—Jimmy Reed's "Honest I Do"—is just off the pop chart.
>
> The first five platters on both charts appear in identical order—Presley, the Everly Brothers, Sam Cooke, the Rays, and Ricky Nelson—while Jimmie Rodgers' "Honeycomb" is No. 6 on both listings.
>
> Presley's "Jailhouse Rock" and the Everlys' "Wake Up Little Susie" are No. 1 and 2 respectively this week on all three charts—pop, r.&b., and country.[90]

Adding to the confusion, an article two months later reported that six of fifteen discs on the R&B charts were by "country artists," as *Billboard* identified them. In addition to Presley and the Everlys, these included Buddy Holly ("Peggy Sue," "Oh Boy"), Jerry Lee Lewis ("Great Balls of Fire"), Jimmie Rodgers ("Kisses Sweeter Than Wine"), Bill Justis ("Raunchy"), and Bobby Helms ("My Special Angel"). The "wholesale upheaval" in the market was causing "not a little consternation in deeply-rooted, authentic r.&b. circles, not unlike the furor that attended certain quarters of the traditional country field when Elvis Presley made his weight felt in the rural charts."[91]

Presley's "Jailhouse Rock" was his thirteenth record in eighteen months to make all sales, airplay, and jukebox charts. It was also the latest (after "Don't Be Cruel," "Hound Dog," "All Shook Up," and "[Let Me Be Your] Teddy Bear") in a series of Presley discs to claim the top spot in all markets. The three-way crossover had been an elusive rarity, but by the fall of 1958 Presley would pull it off twenty-one times. This kind of alignment in this kind of quantity was unprecedented. It was sudden and spectacular and defied all attempts at explanation according to historical industry trends and practices. It was a resounding sign of the times indicative not only of Presley's personal appeal, but of an extraordinary moment in pop history when a vast, diverse audience embraced the same set of style features embodied in the same performer.

Presley's success with such a broad public was a vivid illustration of the crossover effect, both on artist and audience. Many young rock and roll performers wrote their own songs but not Presley. He was—like most of his pop elders—a stylist who personalized songs with unique interpretations. Throughout the 1950s, along with those he premiered, he recorded songs learned from records by Chuck Berry, Little Richard, Joe Turner, Fats Domino, Ray Charles, Dean Martin, Bing Crosby, Wynonie Harris, LaVern Baker, Lloyd Price, Hardrock Gunter, Clyde McPhatter, Frankie Laine, and many more. He crooned ballads with a soft tenderness and blasted through up-tempo numbers with impulsive abandon. He recorded country songs, R&B songs, pop songs, blues songs, gospel songs, and Christmas songs. Rather than pencil and paper, he used his voice and recording tape to fashion "compositions"—not of words and melody but of vocal gestures and stylistic collage reflecting his spongelike musical experience.

To many in the entertainment establishment, the records were musical nonsense, neither very original nor very good exemplars of any specific style. They were odd assemblages of musical junk. This "rage of the squealing teen-agers" whose records were "a top item in the never-never land of juke box operators and disk jockeys" had "no discernible singing ability," according to *New York Times* critic Jack Gould. His singing was "an undistinguished whine; his phrasing if it can be called that, consist[ed] of the stereotyped variations that go with a beginner's aria in a bathtub." He was an "unutterable bore, not nearly so talented as Frankie Sinatra" and lacking the "emotional fury of Johnnie Ray."[92] Yet more than any of his mainstream elders, Presley typified the era's crossover consciousness. As a historiographic symbol, his stature was established not only by his massive commercial success and undeniable musical and personal charisma but by his personification of the music industry's drift toward stylistic amalgam.

With crossover impelling a "desegregation of the charts," as a *Billboard* headline phrased it, the music industry faced a series of challenges.[93] The stylistic pluralism made once reliable indicators difficult to read. Was music that showed up repeatedly on multiple charts simply an illustration of broader audience taste? Or was the music itself somehow different from anything the categories had known historically, ill fitting the stylistic frames? Unfortunately for those seeking clear direction, the evidence pointed to yes on both counts. To the first, consider Fats Domino, who changed nothing about his style as he moved from his first period of success in 1950–55—when he had seventeen R&B chartings, of which only three went pop—to his years as a rock and roll star, from 1956 to 1964, when all but three of his eighty-two R&B hits appeared on the pop charts as well. The second question was answered by a new breed of performers, songwriters, and record producers who had absorbed influences from across the spectrum of American music and for whom nothing in the way of mixture was off-limits. In Chuck Berry's country-pop revisions of R&B, Presley's R&B-pop revisions of country, the neoballadry of the Platters, and the western jump of Bill Haley and the Comets were records that not only appealed to multiple markets but evinced in themselves a crossover fusion.

It was a central paradox of rock and roll that the more it invoked its sources—blues, country, R&B, gospel, pop—the more it became a thing in itself; its distinct identity arose from a willingness freely to incorporate stylistic elements associated with other popular idioms. There was never a rock and roll chart. There was, rather, a sea change in the content of the pop charts, which overturned old certainties. "Where Do You List R 'n' R?" jukebox operators wanted to know by 1957. Songs had always been grouped in the machines according to the industry's familiar style/market categories. But with so much "overlapping between traditional categories of pop tunes" the old distinctions were of diminishing use.[94] A "one world philosophy" had come to the music business, a *Variety* reporter concluded, meaning that "neither disk classifications nor geographic boundaries" were sufficient guides in the "new definition of a 'pop.'" Because "hits quickly cross[ed] chart lines to show up on pop lists despite their originations as rock 'n' roll or country music," pop music was now defined less by style than by sales. The reporter put the matter to Imperial's Lew Chudd for comment. Chudd was another of the Los Angeles–based record men who had started out in the forties and ridden the crossover wave to mainstream success due primarily to Fats Domino. "There is no longer any point to arbitrary distinctions," said Chudd. "When an artist sells 1,000,000 or more records, he's a pop artist, regardless of the type of material he's using."[95]

Mitch Miller on the job. (Photograph by William "PoPsie" Randolph, www.popsiephotos.com, copyright 2010 Michael Randolph.)

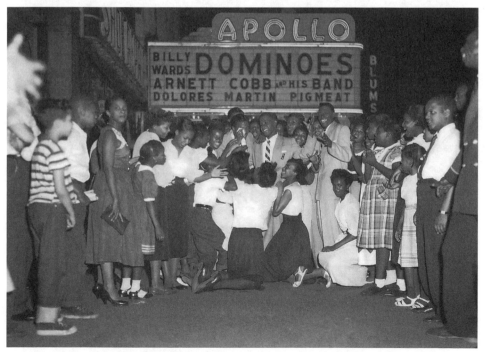

The Dominoes (with Clyde McPhatter) in 1952 outside the Apollo with adoring fans. (Photograph by William "PoPsie" Randolph, www.popsiephotos.com, copyright 2010 Michael Randolph.)

Frank Sinatra holding forth at WINS before the arrival of rock and roll.
(Photograph by William "PoPsie" Randolph, www.popsiephotos.com,
copyright 2010 Michael Randolph.)

Johnnie Ray gives his all. (Photograph by William "PoPsie" Randolph, www.popsiephotos.com, copyright 2010 Michael Randolph.)

Elvis Presley runs it down with Bill Black, Scotty Moore, and the Jordanaires. (Photograph by William "PoPsie" Randolph, www.popsiephotos.com, copyright 2010 Michael Randolph.)

Bill Haley and the Comets rock the joint. (Photograph by William "PoPsie" Randolph, www.popsiephotos.com, copyright 2010 Michael Randolph.)

Sam Phillips at his "instrument." (© Colin Escott.)

The Ronettes putting passion on tape. (Photograph by William "PoPsie" Randolph, www.popsiephotos.com, copyright 2010 Michael Randolph.)

The Marcels check their work. (Photograph by William "PoPsie" Randolph, www.popsiephotos.com, copyright 2010 Michael Randolph.)

By 1959, when this record was released, rock and roll already had a sense of its own history. (Photo by Mark Schmidt.)

FIVE

Surface Noise

We had a sound *baby, I mean a* sound.

—SAM PHILLIPS

· 1 ·

In the fall of 1948 a small, short-lived Los Angeles record company re-leased a record called "A Little Bird Told Me" by singer and pianist Paula Watson, her first for the company. The record became an R&B hit despite a *Billboard* review characterizing the disc as a "staccato rhythm novelty cleverly written and performed, but too pop flavored for the race lists."[1] The record's pop appeal, however, was confirmed by the crossover suc-cess that eventually pushed it past a million in sales. The record label, Supreme, was owned by an African American man named Al Patrick, who was also a dentist. He acquired the song from Harvey O. Brooks, a professional songwriter and pianist who had also written the score and theme song for Mae West's *I'm No Angel* (1933). Brooks had come up with the ditty some ten years earlier but thought little of it and set it aside until, in 1947, he decided to offer it to bandleader Woody Herman. When Herman declined, Brooks took the song to Patrick, whom he knew was looking for some "catchy novelties." The song was light as air— "nothin'," Brooks called it—with a perky melody, a bouncy beat, and an uncomplicated romantic lyric.[2] According to Arnold Shaw, the success of such novelty material relied "almost entirely on the whims of the young."[3] It fit easily alongside such lighthearted fare as Dinah Shore's "Buttons and Bows" or Doris Day and Buddy Clark's "Love Somebody," two of the year's top hits. It was just the kind of song to appeal to the "teen-age and collegiate market" that consensus held was "reawaken-ing," returning to its "prewar status as a key influence factor and a large-sized merchandising mart for the produce of the industry."[4]

Within weeks the song was covered for Decca by Evelyn Knight, one of the company's stable of fine and experienced pop singers, in an arrangement substantially similar to Watson's. Introductory a cappella humming was followed by a groove featuring heavy downbeat accents with prominent hand claps on the backbeat. Male backing vocals answered each lead phrase in a call-and-response pattern and took the lead melody through the song's middle section. Each track's outro featured similar harmonic phrases from the backing singers and a final "And now I know it's true" from the lead. Knight even mimicked Watson's chirpy bird sounds, and, since both women had sweet, light voices, the overall effect was quite similar. The Decca release became one of the most popular records of 1949. For Brooks, it was all unexpectedly good news, as were the two other covers by Blue Lu Barker (Capitol) and Janette Davis and Jerry Wayne (Columbia). It was, he said, "just like finding $100,000."[5]

Patrick, on the other hand, was furious. Although Watson's disc was the rare indie million seller, he felt certain that Knight's recording had robbed his company of even greater potential sales. In a surprise move, attorneys for Supreme filed a $400,000 lawsuit against Decca, claiming what amounted to plagiarism of its arrangement. It was the same complaint LaVern Baker would make against Georgia Gibbs four years later. While the assertion had musical merit, the legal case ran up against by now familiar problems concerning the nature of property rights in the technological age. After a three-day trial, federal judge Leon Yankwich ruled for the defendant. Only the songwriter (the "author") was afforded a right of ownership under current law. There was no such protection for arrangements or recordings because, the judge wrote, "[N]o recognition of the right of arrangement is given to anyone except the author," an interpretation he drew from a Patent Office rule.

In making his ruling, Yankwich cited many precedents—in intellectual property, trademark, copyright, antitrust, and trade regulation cases—including a nod to Judge Learned Hand's decision in the *RCA Mfg. Co. v. Whiteman* case from 1940. But no precedent addressed the implicit conceptual issues before the court. Nor did the argument put forward by Supreme's lawyers, which was limited to a claim of unfair competition: the Knight recording's substantial similarity to Watson's had "the object of misleading, confusing and deceiving phonograph record dealers and the public into the belief that the product of the plaintiffs was being sold."[6] Their evidence, however, failed to support the case's central point, for it was based not on the sound of the records but on the arrangement they shared. The object of deception, then, was not the Decca record itself but what it contained.

The more fundamental issue, the one Yankwich had to think through for himself, was one of ontology: did a recording have a distinctive identity (and was therefore a type of property in its own right) or was it merely a representation of its contents? As in the battles of the 1930s, sound recording's unforeseen ramifications were put before a court ill-equipped to measure their significance. The various copyright bills proposed since the war, each aimed in some way at addressing the new technological reality in the music business, had never made it past committee hearings. Without statutory guidance and faced with two records sharing almost identical arrangements but very different sounds, the judge relied on his own perception. The Decca recording would not mislead the public, he ruled, because its "full, meaty, polished" sound made an "entirely different" impression.[7] He expressed his opinion not in terms of clear-cut description but of subjective taste, with Decca "boasting a much better product."[8] It was a curious tack since the records were sufficiently distinct to support his ruling on factual grounds alone. The voices, obviously, were different, as was their phrasing. Watson danced across the heavy beat in a nimble syncopated flow that escaped Knight, a fine ballad singer but here uncertain and somewhat heavy handed in her rhythm. And musical features aside, it took no aesthetic judgment to notice that the Decca disk projected a sharper sound.

But Yankwich warmed to the role of musicologist and critic. He thought the Supreme recording "mechanical, lacking inspiration, containing just the usual accompaniments and the usual intonations which one would find in any common recording," and favored Decca's "popular" approach to Supreme's "race or blues and rhythm" style. The Decca recording had the "more precise, complex and better organized orchestral background, the fuller harmonization of the responses, the clearer intonation and expression, and the more musical entrances." It also had a better ending than the Supreme record, which, to the judge, was "an anticlimax."[9] Reaching even farther beyond his expertise, Yankwich went on to weigh the creative contribution of the arrangement's elements. He speculated that, while there was no precedent for granting a common law property right for an arrangement, if one were to entertain the idea (which he did repeatedly in his written opinion) the arrangement would have to exhibit "creative ability of a distinct kind."[10] The features of the Supreme recording—the introduction, the choral responses, the hand claps—were "of a type which would occur to any arranger, a kind of musique a faire."[11]

Of course, in considering each element of the arrangement as a separate generic musical topic, the judge was not addressing the specific aggregate of elements constituting the arrangement at hand. His analysis was based on a deconstructed abstraction. He suggested, "for the sake of argument," that a common law property claim would have merit only if the arrangement "consist[ed] of unique elements which combine to produce a finished product which has a being or distinctive existence of its own."[12] Incorporating an aesthetic component into the legal test, assuming a causal connection between an arrangement's "distinctive existence" and the uniqueness of its elements, Yankwich wandered into a non sequitur. While he argued, perhaps rightly, that the original recording's ingredients were generic, in failing to consider the arrangement as something more than the sum of its parts he made it impossible to acknowledge the obvious: that its uniqueness lay in its particular *combination* of elements.

Adding to the confusion, when it came to the actual recordings, Yankwich adopted the holistic perspective lacking in his analysis of the arrangement. The arrangement for the Watson recording existed in no written form; an expert witness for the plaintiff acknowledged that the only way to compare the two was by listening. Playing the records in the courtroom, Yankwich judged correctly that "the entire impression of the two recordings is different." Hearing the records as irreducible musical works, he could not conclude otherwise. Basing his ruling on "the impression to the ear" meant that all of the recordings' sonic features became part of the deliberation, which meant that Supreme's claim of exact replication had opened the way to its own defeat.[13] Seeking protection for the arrangement, the Supreme lawyers were inviting the court to speculate on the rights inherent in specific musical renderings of songs. But why stop at the arrangement? What could be more specific than a recording, especially if the arrangement had no other fixed existence? For all its amateur dabbling in musical criticism, Yankwich's ruling made one thing abundantly clear: any plaintiff claiming a record as intellectual property had better be ready and willing to go all the way.

The "Little Bird" case, though lightly reported, was seen as a "precedent-setting suit" on which "Decca put its big legal guns to work to prepare an ironclad defense."[14] It crystallized a point of tension in the industry that had been stewing for years. The song sheet had always been the central currency of the music commodity market. The entire apparatus of song plugging existed to sell songs—to performers who might showcase them, to retailers who might stock them, and ultimately to a public that bought them for its own music-making pleasure. In this system, records were latecomers and were widely viewed as promotional items. Any copyright owner whose song was recorded received a small return on record sales, but the real payoff was the sheet sales the records could help generate. Throughout the 1940s, however, music publishers had watched sheet music sales decline as record sales picked up steadily. The shift precipitated new ways of doing business for both publishers and record firms, but, more important, it fostered a conceptual change whose practical effects went to the heart of the nation's musical life.

Copyright law reflected the cultural primacy of written texts, which, for music, accorded with the established principle that a work's enduring identity was preserved in its written form. This idea took shape in the context of nineteenth-century European art music, but its implications trickled into conventional wisdom and formed a tacit assumption that underlay copyright provisions. The revised 1909 Copyright Act, for example, acknowledged mechanical reproduction as a source of royalties based not on the reproduction itself but on the musical piece it contained. Musical works were subject to copyright only in written form, which for popular songs meant words, melody, and chords. The other elements represented on a record—arrangement and performance—were not recognized as integral components of the original artwork. Whatever creative work went into them, arrangements were merely adaptations of an existing work, and performances were ephemeral renditions of works that recordings simply preserved. In the Whiteman case of 1940, Judge Hand had virtually scoffed at the notion that an engineer's contribution was anything other than hired labor. But as records formed a newly independent category of musical culture, they stipulated an obvious truth that was slow to be acknowledged. In presenting song, arrangement, and performance in a web of fixed relationships, they represented a new kind of work. Here, too, was a text and a commodity, one of even greater market value than that protected by law. But its features were invisible, both literally and legally. They could only be apprehended as sound. It was sound that was being made and sold, and that now dominated America's musical economy. The nature of that sound—what and who it represented—was the subject of ongoing contest and creative evolution throughout the postwar period, the latest phase in the struggle to come to grips with the machine that captured music.

· 2 ·

Publications devoted to the recording industry circulated from the beginning of the twentieth century, most notably the early flagship trade journal *Talking Machine World,* established in 1905. In 1923, a British publication, *The Gramophone,* came on the market with a new sort of format, a forum devoted to the aesthetics of recorded music. It was founded by the Scottish novelist Compton Mackenzie to provide an outlet for thoughtful record reviews, essays, and editorials. It was Mackenzie's hope that the periodical "might serve as a concentration point for intelligent opinion."[15] In that pursuit, *The Gramophone*'s critical commentary interwove issues of musical performance and sound reproduction, considering "every point of view, the artistic no less than the mechanical and technical," as one of the journal's longtime critics, Herman Klein, phrased it.[16]

When electrical recording (using microphones rather than acoustic horns) was introduced in 1925, *The Gramophone*'s writers expressed an initial skepticism about the new technology, which treated sound in a markedly different way than had the earlier mechanical method. Rather than cutting a groove using the direct force of sound waves, the electrical method turned the waves into electric current, which was then controlled by an amplifier. This meant that the strength of the signal arriving at the recording medium might bear little resemblance to that of its source, for it was the electrical process, not necessarily the musician's effort, that determined the signal's power. To Klein, the microphone was an "unconscious medium," imperfect but in itself not necessarily offensive.[17] The amplifier, on the other hand, which could "affect and alter volume, quality, carrying power, purity, verisimilitude, etc.," interfered perniciously with musical expression.[18] He returned many times to a problem he described as "over-amplification" and its distorting effect on its source, which he viewed as "a deliberate act of deception."[19] Representing the sound of a musical performance in a form shaped by electronic gadgetry, as Klein had observed, was liable to lead listeners to "commit the . . . fatal error of mistaking the doctored article for the real thing."[20]

Mackenzie, a dedicated collector and advocate, continued to prefer acoustic recordings even as the electrical method steadily improved and became the industry standard. In 1935, he wrote, "Of one thing only am I completely certain at this moment, which is that the really passionate devotee of the gramophone for a long time to come will get more pleasure out of his instrument if it is acoustical . . . than if it is electrical." The reason was elemental; the acoustic method was, in his mind and ear, the best one "to capture the spirit of the music," reflected in the genuine, unmediated effort of the performer.[21] In later years, Mackenzie remained of the opinion that "the horn did put the performer on his mettle and draw from him or her reserves of vitality which the microphone does not exact; and it was that extra vitality which made the stars of the record once upon a time."[22] In other words, if a performer had a big voice, so did the record. If he or she did not, there was no disguising the fact. What *The Gramophone*'s critics objected to in electrical recording was the notion that the medium would have a hand in the musical result. When electronic manipulation intruded into music making, as with exaggerated amplification, the result was a kind of artifice unacceptable to conventional notions of musical worth. Addressing the subject, Klein borrowed language from one of Mackenzie's editorials, expressing the concern that there was "serious danger of the public taste being 'irreparably spoilt' should the average vocal disc continue to be 'but little removed from an infernal row.' "[23]

Such debates were richly problematic and reflected in ideological ways the legal struggles over sound recording's influence on musical expression and perception. On the one hand, it was undeniable that electrical recording made for greater sonic clarity. Yet that clarity was achieved through a process utterly foreign to music making. The musical outcome was now a result not simply of a composer's ideas and a performer's physical effort, but of a collaboration with sound engineers in control of a mediating electronic interface. For a listener of Mackenzie's turn of mind, the issue was a matter not only of faithful phonography but of a deeper fidelity to the "spirit of the music," an aggregate of historical traditions, including performance practices, habits of perception, and aesthetic conviction.

The aesthetics of recorded music was born heavily freighted with attitudes rooted in the past, which begged a central question: could a recording claim a presence of its own independent of its origins? Or was its proper role restricted to faithful witness and representative? For such institutions as the AFM and ASCAP, and individual skeptics such as Igor Stravinsky, it was clearly the latter.[24] Records were useful for preservation and promotional marketing but held in themselves no real musical value. Advocates such as Mackenzie and Klein had a more nuanced attitude, but in the end they, too, were ambivalent toward the machine. They viewed the medium as a servant of tradition. Their conceptions of the recording machine's usefulness were deeply informed by the past, and their arguments were framed in terms of established practice. Yet the machine itself was bounding toward the future. Technical improvement and innovation were forward looking, driven by commercial competition and unceasing technological evolution. The project of representing musical sound thus became another contested area in postwar musical life as modern reality clashed with traditional attitudes.

Sonic representation under the "high-fidelity" banner became a hot topic in the United States in the early 1950s, with numerous articles appearing in newspapers and magazines. "High fidelity," Howard Taubman wrote in the *New York Times,* had "become the growing rage . . . a big industry, a fad, a mania . . . a way of life."[25] In the summer of 1951 a publication was launched devoted entirely to the subject. *High Fidelity* was "a magazine for audio-philes" featuring articles ranging from foundational topics, such as principles of acoustics and electronic design, to reviews of sound reproduction equipment and recordings.[26] The magazine addressed the emerging market for sophisticated home audio, which had recently seen the introduction of such advanced technologies as the 33 1/3 rpm long-playing microgroove disc and magnetic tape machines. Like *The Gramophone, High Fidelity* had a specific aesthetic stance that espoused preferences in both musical repertory and standards of sonic representation. There were no longer any reservations, however, about electrical recording. It was a settled matter that all the marvels of modern phonography and sound reproduction should be brought to bear in rendering accurately the sounds of musical performances in the natural sound world.

The project, though still essentially governed by opinion, now took on something of a scientific veneer, its aesthetic dimensions married to electronic specifications. Because, it was thought, recordings should provide listeners a transparent aural window on the music, artifacts of electronic mediation should be as muted as possible. A full frequency response, a wide dynamic range, and avoidance of distortion and extraneous noise were imperative technical standards for achieving a first-rate listening experience. These were among the criteria Capitol, for instance, used to rate its records, with each critical category defined as specifically as possible. Electrical distortion was the sort "attributable to electrical causes such as clipping of modulation peaks and/or slow recovery, leaving 'holes' in modulation or 'buzz' on certain types of modulation, usually on peaks." Acoustic distortion originated "in studio pickup, caused by undesirable intermodulation effects heard as unusual tones of instruments or sections; or confused sounds having unnatural resonances from the reverberation characteristics of the studio." Each category was rated on a point system to determine where the record stood with regard to Capitol's "Full Dimensional Sound" criteria.[27]

Classical music was *High Fidelity*'s preferred idiom, claiming the overwhelming majority of review space. Classical recordings were the exclusive province of the major labels, whose best production efforts went toward their classical catalogs. Musical and technological values were intertwined in the same aesthetic project, with the art music of the past both feeding and guiding the aspiration to high fidelity. Honoring and faithfully transmitting the music's hallowed tradition was high fidelity's noble purpose and technical challenge, and because classical music had already attained its perfect sounding form in a pre-electric, natural sound world, it gave the project of recorded representation something to aim for. In the pursuit, the recording engineer was "to be a truly transparent entity" said master Capitol recordist Carson Taylor.[28] No effort, in other words, was to be spared in crafting an illusion of musical presence bearing no trace of the process that produced it.

If the aim of classical recordings was transparency, the listener's proximity to any actual music making was nevertheless imaginary; however fine the illusion, the recording was not a performance but a rendering. Yet an ideological debate divided classical recordists in the early fifties, which a *Newsweek* feature summed up in the question "What is a record supposed to represent?" While some clung to the idea that a recording was simply a "captured concert," others saw it as a "different medium," something other than a "concert reproduction." Al Pulley, an RCA engineer, framed the issue pragmatically. "Electrical equipment cannot hear what the ear hears," he explained. "As things are, you must approximate."[29] Pulley's straightforward analysis cut to the heart of the matter: turning musical performance into durable artifact required electronic sleight of hand, which was bound to be shot through with aesthetic decision making. If the alchemy was to be practically inaudible, as the doctrine of hi-fi had it, this only heightened the sophistication of the artifice. "You had to know how to use your equipment," said Columbia engineer Frank Laico about his use of electronic compression. "I enjoyed using it, and yet it never sounded like I was using it. And that's the secret."[30] Transferring ephemeral expression into tangible form required a nuanced translation. In the end, to paraphrase Mackenzie, it was not only the truthful documentary account that moved the listener but also, and more important, the disc's ability to impart an impression of aesthetic experience. The recording had to capture and later convey the aesthetic impact of the performance. The translator was the recording engineer, and, although his skills were those of a craftsman, he was inevitably called on to function, too, as an artistic collaborator in the representation project.

As *High Fidelity*'s publisher, Milton B. Sleeper, acknowledged in an introduction to the first issue, "One of the most intriguing aspects of undertaking to publish *High Fidelity* is the number of widely divergent opinions held by the devotees of the field this magazine will serve."[31] *New York Times* writer John Briggs noted similarly that the whole matter was so subjective that it amounted to "a compound of acoustical science and sheer mysticism."[32] In 1954, *Billboard* began running a section called "High Fidelity" in each issue in response to the concept's market buzz. But a cautionary editorial acknowledged that there were "no accepted standards for 'hi-fi' recordings" and it would be foolish for an industry whose success relied on mass public consensus to allow criteria to be defined by a few "self-appointed arbiters."[33] *Down Beat,* too, chimed in with a piece by *High Fidelity*'s editor, Charles Fowler, an excerpt from his liner notes to a Capitol album called *Full Dimensional Sound: A Study in High Fidelity.* The very notion, Fowler wrote, required a feat of imagination. "'High fidelity' is a qualitative expression, and because there is no precise measure of it, it has many definitions." Still, its ultimate goal was to "create as nearly as possible the *illusion* of the live performance."[34]

The matter was further complicated by the developing notion in the pop field that records were not merely representations of distant musical events but realities in themselves, belonging to the time and place whenever and wherever they happened to be heard. A record's etched groove forced performance, composition, musical timbre, extraneous noise, aesthetic principle, historical circumstance, and stylistic sensibility into a fixed coexistence. It was the specific configuration of these elements that gave the recording its unique sonic persona. If fidelity was the goal—and it was as persistent a marketing theme for pop as for other idioms—a fair question was "fidelity to what?"

Thinking seriously about recorded representation should have accelerated awareness that different idioms and historical eras defined the project in different ways. Pop records had acquired a kind of acoustic autonomy unbefitting classical records and largely foreign to *all* record production in earlier decades. Before the overt artifice of producers such as Mitch Miller and Les Paul, records had stood for things other than themselves—a song or a symphony, a performance or a star performer—but by the early fifties many had taken on lives of their own. The concept was wholly contrary to the historical essence of musical performance and listening, and, while it was readily accepted by pop fans, critics remained perplexed. In a rare article on pop recordings, a *High Fidelity* writer recounted his and his listening companions' disappointment at hearing such current hits as Nat Cole's "Too Young" (Capitol), Guy Mitchell's "My Truly, Truly Fair" (Columbia), Stan Kenton's "Laura" (Capitol), and Perry Como's "Cara Cara Bella Bella" (RCA Victor) on hi-fi equipment. The sounds were "falsely brilliant and lacking in depth . . . sadly devoid in clarity of tone." Cymbal crashes seemed "to simulate an empty garbage can rolling down the cellar stairs," and "forte passages involving brass or strings were completely 'mashed.'"[35] The listeners were repeatedly let down by sounds that impinged on their suspension of disbelief, their illusion of being in the presence of actual music making. Interestingly, the only records singled out as exceptions were three high-artifice efforts whose intention was anything but sonic realism: Les Paul and Mary Ford's "How High the Moon," Paul's "Josephine," and Jane Turzy's "Good Morning, Mr. Echo," all of which were permeated with special electronic effects. These records' only real advantage, however, was not acoustical but psychological. Since they made no attempt at transparency, they freed listeners from the subliminal distraction of constant comparison with a referent.

Despite their deficiencies, the writer admitted that all the records sounded good on such non-hi-fi reproduction equipment as jukeboxes and low-end record players. This curious double negative—poor recording combined with poor reproduction equipment produces a positive result—spoke to the complementary nature of sound recording and reproduction, but it also held an unexplored implication: removing the goal of hi-fi realism also removed an aesthetic impediment. Again the change was psychological, attitudinal, but in this case no special effects were required. Surrendering to the medium's terms, pleasure could be taken in the sound of the record itself without the triangulating interference of comparative expectation. As records became the most common everyday mode of musical perception—spinning on radio, jukebox, and lo-fi record players—this kind of direct apprehension gradually changed the public's sense of recorded sound. Disembodied, electronically mediated pop sounds accumulated as members of a new sonic lexicon supporting a developing system of musical rhetoric. In the new world of pop record production, making a record meant making an aesthetic argument framed in terms not only of the natural sound world but of other records.

· 3 ·

In their lack of any real world counterpart and their frank artifice, pop records of the early fifties rendered the goal of real life sonic depiction meaningless. With ad hoc ensembles electronically balanced, exaggerated reverb, and overdubbed voices and instruments, they integrated music making and studio craft as never before. Pop records made the freest, boldest, and for many the most tasteless but ultimately most creative uses of technology, for their only purpose was to make an immediate impact. If their gimmicks wore thin and success proved fleeting, it mattered little once the money had been made. Yet in their preoccupation with commercial success lay also their aesthetic liberation. Despite a lowly mandate of attention-grabbing sensationalism, postswing recordists and producers worked the interface between music and gadgetry with an inventive, often visionary mind-set.

Among the vanguard to emerge in the late forties was Bill Putnam, who upon his discharge from the Army Signal Corps following the war went into the recording business in Chicago. His aim, he said, was "to concentrate on two prime areas: the development of new recording techniques and the development of new technical equipment, which was more specialized and suitable for the specific needs of the recording studio."[36] Putnam saw the recording studio as a unique site for music making, distinct from live venues and radio stations and requiring its own tools and techniques to realize its musical potential. It followed that records were not mere reflections of the natural sound world but works of aural craft and imagination. A sound engineer, he wrote some years later, required not only technical know-how and musical sensitivity: "He must be creatively artistic, imaginative, have a flair for showmanship, be willing to try the impossible."[37] His 1948 production of the Harmonicats' "Peg O' My Heart," which presented to an approving public a singular performance of an old song in the form of a sound narrative, illustrated what he had in mind. The story, however, was carried not by the foley artist's sound effects—gunshots, thunderclaps, horses' hooves—but by the sound of architectural space, that is, reverberation, what Mitch Miller called the "sonic halo."[38]

Reverb, or ambience, is the warming patina that enriches sounds as they bounce off surfaces in an enclosed space, producing innumerable, variously timed echoes that merge into a single composite impression. The farther a microphone is placed from a sound source the more reverb it will capture, which affects such listener impressions as proximity, timbre, focus, and clarity. Before any music recording gets under way, decisions about mic placement introduce an aesthetic component to the project as recordists deliberately shape relationships between source sounds and their ambient images. Also, as a practical matter of low-frequency control, studios were often forced to limit reverberation, resulting in a relatively lifeless sound. To counter the dry effect, a second, "live" space (the so-called echo chamber) was outfitted with a loudspeaker and a microphone. Sound from the studio was fed to the speaker, and the microphone collected the reverberant room sound, which was fed back to the mixing console and combined with the dry studio sound. The technique added several more aesthetic decisions: how much signal to feed to the speaker, where to place the speaker in the room, where to place the mic, how much of the added reverb to mix with the original sound. And in Putnam's case there was a further question of how not simply to enhance the recorded sound but how to call attention to the ambience as an element of the musical narrative.

On "Peg O' My Heart" Putnam created a montage, changing scenes, as it were, through the course of the track. The sonic theme was introduced at the outset when the introduction's single chord cut off abruptly, revealing the residual sound of a large, reverberant space. Listeners' expectations were immediately subverted when the reverb died away and the track continued with a much drier sound, close now and intimate. At the end of the verse, at the turnaround, the music again took on a momentary reverberant aura, a fragmentary reminiscence of the track's opening. The second verse was once again dry. These first ambient shifts were so brief that little could be made of them. The real surprise came after the second verse when the musical pulse was suspended for a modulating transition that was suddenly bathed in a cavernous ambience. A third iteration of the tune followed, and now the reverb remained, its prefigurement fulfilled in a broad canopy of airy sound that swept the music into an altogether different place. There was no particular meaning in all this. As the music appeared to move from place to place, it simply arrested attention, called forth wonder; the trick itself was the hook. It was, recalled engineer Bruce Swedien, who would become a Putnam apprentice, "the first time that anyone used reverb *artistically*. . . . Up 'til then, people used reverb only to re-create the sound of the studio, tried to use it in a 'natural' manner. Bill changed all that. That record sounded unlike anything on the radio at that time."[39]

Putnam's thematic concept was novel, but reverb's general affective power was recognized by recordists early on. Peter Doyle, who has devoted an entire monograph to the topic of echo and reverb, notes that country singer Jimmie Rodgers's "Blue Yodel No. 1 (T for Texas)," from 1927, "might be pinpointed as a landmark moment in the history of popular recording practice" precisely because, in contrast to contemporary habit, the record highlighted the ambience of RCA Victor's Camden, New Jersey, studio (a former Baptist church).[40] Whatever one makes of reverb's symbolic implications (Doyle's study engages reverb as a topic of critical inquiry), there is no question it added to a record's distinctive sonic personality. It made the record sound full, assertive, lifelike. In the 1930s and 1940s, such storied New York recording venues as Liederkranz Hall (former home to a German singing society), the Pythian Temple, and Columbia's Thirtieth Street studio (a former Greek Orthodox church) all provided pop recordists with a richly reverberant " 'open' sound," as Putnam characterized it, a welcome contrast to "the 'pinched' sound of the conventional studio recordings."[41]

Moreover, while many studios produced makeshift reverb in stairwells and bathrooms, others began building their own dedicated reverberant chambers, experimenting with size, shape, and materials. "Nobody knew too much about how it should be shaped or anything," recalled engineer John Palladino of the chamber built on the roof of Radio Recorders in Hollywood, recording base for Capitol in the 1940s. "But you just worked with it a little bit," he said, "and put the hardest plaster you could get on there and put a good mic and a good speaker."[42] No two chambers were alike, and their unique sounds often factored in a studio's appeal. Capitol engineer Irv Joel recalled that many clients chose Capitol's New York studio on Forty-sixth Street "specifically because they liked the sound of the chamber."[43] Phil Spector fell in love with the chambers Dave Gold built at Gold Star Studios in Hollywood and made them a fixture of his "wall of sound" production style.

Added reverb provided an imaginary "setting" for recorded music. It created the appropriate illusion for the Orioles' "Crying in the Chapel"; it drew listeners into the imaginary realm of the Cadillacs' wistful "Gloria"; and it made Duane Eddy's guitar appear to call forth the sound of vastness. But as reverb became a fundamental constant in record construction it sometimes lost its spatial associations altogether and functioned simply as a timbral artifact. A good example is Buddy Holly's "Peggy Sue," which alternated dry and ambient drum sounds in a way that made no acoustic sense. It is impossible to imagine what would make reverb in the natural world behave in this way. The ambient shifts are simply the result of creative whim applied to a denatured acoustic phenomenon.

Putnam produced another novelty ditty in 1951, Jane Turzy's "Good Morning, Mr. Echo," for which he and his wife Belinda wrote the music and lyrics. Although the record featured several types of electronic manipulation, its central hook was indicated by its title. In the natural sound world, echoes are particles of reverberant sound that mass together in a dense cloud. But in record production echo is a separate category of effect. Whereas reverb has its own sonic character, an echo simply replicates its source; it is a discrete, exact reiteration of a sound. Reverb, even if contrived, is a naturally occurring phenomenon. The ear may be fooled by artifice, but the sonic impression is rooted in real world experience. Echo, on the other hand—the kind heard on records—is an electronic product. Because sounds must be recorded before they can be repeated, echo asserts a specific linkage between musical affect and electronic craft.

The echo effect on "Good Morning, Mr. Echo" was a metaphor for loneliness, an aural image of a person talking to herself. Turzy addressed Mr. Echo in the aftermath of a love affair, confident that, unlike her former lover, Mr. Echo would always answer. The electronically produced echo had something of an inhuman quality, giving the track a sort of sci-fi feel befitting its novelty status. (The record was credited to the Jane Turzy Trio, highlighting its other novelty aspect, the fact that there were three Turzy voices generated by overdubbing.) The record was not the hit "Peg O' My Heart" was, but it charted for several weeks, peaking at number twelve. Of greater interest than the record's modest appeal, however, was the fact that both Mercury (Georgia Gibbs) and Capitol (Margaret Whiting) had hits of their own with cover versions that, though different in most other aspects of their arrangements, both included the electronic character of Mr. Echo. Among them, the three records kept echo in the public ear through most of the summer.

"Good Morning, Mr. Echo" used the effect in an obvious, literal way; it was a gag. Several echoes were simply added to the voice at the ends of phrases in an electronic embodiment of the song's subject. The echoes were timed to fit the tempo of the music: "Good morning, Mr. Echo (echo, echo, echo) / How are you today (today, today, today)." But far more extensive and subtle applications were beginning to permeate pop record production, and none were more creative and innovative than those of Les Paul. In his home studio, first with disc recording technology and then magnetic tape, he devoted himself to exploring the musical possibilities of electronic sound manipulation, and over time his studio tricks developed from experimental curiosity to compositional technique. He came to recognize echo as not only a mimetic device but a versatile sonic resource. He learned its effectiveness in subtly thickening a solo line (especially for a voice) and animating an arrangement's rhythmic texture. In Paul's hands, echo became an element of musical substance and form. On his 1951 recording with Mary Ford of "Mockin' Bird Hill," for example, rhythmically synchronized echoes alternated with strummed tremolo in the guitar accompaniment. The echoes, heard in the instrumental sections, were muted and timed as triplets; the tremolo, which underlay the vocal sections, was unmuted and strummed beat subdivisions of four. The contrast marked a formal plan mirroring the arrangement's overall layout.

On the duo's "Falling in Love with Love," a similar rhythmic application enhanced the effect of the rippling guitar obbligato. Here, however, the echo shimmered continuously throughout the track, its timbre by turns muffled (during the vocal phrases) and glittering. The echoes gave the track a watery feel, while the alternating timbral contrast, together with Paul's darting guitar lines in between vocal phrases, provided a sense of narrative montage. In the introduction to one of Paul and Ford's biggest hits, "Vaya Con Dios," quiet echoes shadowed the opening guitar phrase. As they disappeared into the background, they called the listener's attention to the track's textural depth, a reflection of the song's introspective tone. The answering phrase, in a lower register, was dry (echoless). The contrast was suggested by the song's melody, which set the lines "Vaya con Dios my darling / Vaya con Dios my love" as a pair of phrases suggesting first a plea and then resignation. In the merging of electronic trick with musical phrase structure and affect, the trick was transformed—no longer a trivial gag or novel adornment but an integral element of the musical arrangement.

A musical world away, another production pioneer, Sam Phillips, whose spartan studio had no reverberant chamber, invested in a second tape recorder—an echo machine—to beef up his recordings. Phillips's echoes only occasionally lined up with the beat; instead, the effect enriched the texture of small musical groups with electronic clutter or timbral exotica. The results depended on tempo, phrasing, sound source, and balance. On Presley's "Blue Moon of Kentucky" or "Baby Let's Play House," the voice's echoes prominently mirrored Presley's aggressive performance, injecting a nervous rhythmic disturbance into the texture. These are classic examples of the so-called slapback effect. Toned down, the technique translated into a fullness of the vocal presence on "Mystery Train," which also featured a pronounced echo on the electric guitar produced not by the studio's echo machine but a small device built into Moore's amplifier. The tempo determined a near-sixteenth-note relationship between the guitar and its echoes, creating persistent afterbeats that pushed the rhythmic drive. On slow ballads such as "Blue Moon" or "Tomorrow Night," the effect was less rhythmic than timbral and atmospheric, an electronic buzz on the voice rendering it strangely spectral.

Like Paul, Phillips discovered in echo a range of sonic possibility and musical uses that would become common production techniques. The slapback mode in particular became a standard feature of rockabilly style, a first in popular music history—electronic effect as generic hallmark. It was an enduring acknowledgment of the music-machine synthesis. In the wake of Presley's growing fame, slapback was featured prominently on Gene Vincent's "Be Bop A Lula," for example, and Eddie Cochran's "Sittin' in the Balcony." Hardrock Gunter, a rockabilly cat long before the term was coined, recut his 1950 recording of "Birmingham Bounce" in 1958. In the interim, echo had become a rockabilly staple, which Gunter acknowledged by substituting a prominent slapback for the driving boogie rhythms of the original.

While manipulating reverb and capturing echoes distinguished records from acoustic reality, the height of artifice—the thing that most clearly and unabashedly declared a record's independence from any specific performance—was the musical double created by overdubbing. Overdubbing—which required mixing live performance with a prerecorded track—was first accomplished using a disc-to-disc method, then sound-on-sound tape recording, and finally multitrack tape. The practice rendered transparency irrelevant, for it meant instead to dazzle listeners with impossible feats of contrivance: a single musician singing or playing multiple parts simultaneously. While the ambient shifts of "Peg O' My Heart" were unusual, improbable except perhaps for a marching band or strolling bistro musicians, the mind could nevertheless conjure a plausible image of what was taking place. But what image came to mind at the sound of a person singing along with herself? Vocal twins? Astral projection? Magic? It was too disorienting or comical to contemplate for long. Easier simply to accept it as an aural image without a real world analogy, to suspend disbelief and become aurally transported into a fantastical sound world. From a traditionalist perspective, any such post facto meddling was widely seen as musical buffoonery, for it violated the integrity of the musical moment. Indeed, it ensured that a recording could claim to represent no particular performance at all. The "performance" was in fact a construction project. For classical and jazz recordings, such trickery rendered the result false, worthless. But pop music, whose lowly artistic rank obviated such concerns, eagerly embraced the trick. Rather than disguising the overdub, it was highlighted. It was not stupid; it was clever. It caught the fancy.

Overdubbing was among the aural curiosities the public found so enticing in the years following the war, its novelty appeal confirmed by several famous examples. Patti Page sang two overlapping parts of an antiphonal call-and-response on her first hit, "Confess," recorded under Miller's supervision in December of 1947. Although the lyrics for both parts were quite similar, the melodies differed and the lead voice was more or less dry while the answers were treated with added reverb. ("She answered her own singing via an echo chamber," *Newsweek* told a curious public.)[44] The differences between the two parts implied separate characters, but because they both shared the same voice, their dialogic positions were conveyed not by the singer's enactment but by sound, melody, and, above all, temporal situation. In real world terms, the voices' overlap meant they could not represent the same person. And yet they were identical. The answering voice implied a reflexive introspection, a musing shadow, or, as one writer has suggested, "an inner thought."[45] Whatever the perceived association, the technique created a narrative structure and dramatic conceit unique to the record.

According to Page's manager, Jack Rael, the overdubbing on "Confess" was a result of financial constraints. Mercury had seen the twenty-year-old singer's ten previous sides fail to make a dent in the market and had restricted her recording budget accordingly. The song called for a second singer—as in the version by Doris Day and Buddy Clark—but there were funds enough only for the accompanying George Barnes Trio. With the record's breakthrough success, however, overdubbing became something of a Page hallmark, turning up on such hits as "Money, Marbles and Chalk," "Mockin' Bird Hill," "Mister and Mississippi," and the blockbuster "Tennessee Waltz," which made Page's overdubbed voice a national fixture unknown to "only the deaf and the dead," as *Time* magazine put it. Two particularly ambitious efforts, "With My Eyes Wide Open I'm Dreaming" and "And So to Sleep Again," featured the singer as a one-woman quartet.

Les Paul pushed overdubbing to the point of virtuosity beginning with his 1948 recording of "Lover," a piece of multilayered guitar high jinks (no vocal) that reveled in its clever, unprecedented artifice as it climbed the pop chart. Paul was obsessed with what seemed to most an odd idea: playing music by himself with only prerecorded parts (prerecorded by him, that is) for a "band." The project, especially with the disc-to-disc method, was daunting, both musically and technically. Even with flawless musical execution, each successive layer meant more noise and less clarity in the final result. Paul, however, was a tireless experimenter, and in the course of hundreds of failed tries he devised ingenious solutions that allowed far more overdubs than anyone had imagined possible. To limit room noise, he recorded his electric guitar without a microphone. He recorded parts in reverse order of importance so the inevitable sonic degradation was largely confined to background parts. He modified his equipment in pursuit of ever greater overdubbing capacity. In short, he created a process for building records based on electronic and musical procedures specific to record production. Putnam reckoned that the number and quality of Paul's overdubs were "impossible" for the time.[46]

With the success of "Lover," and Bing Crosby's gift of an Ampex tape machine, which allowed even more layers of clean sound, overdubbing became the foundation of Paul's record production style. From 1948 to 1954, he landed thirty-seven such sides on the *Billboard* pop charts. Some were guitar only, but most included vocal performances by Mary Ford, who, as Colleen Summers, had made a name for herself as a country singer and rhythm guitarist with regular engagements on Cliffie Stone's *Dinner Bell Roundup*, the *Hollywood Barn Dance*, and Gene Autry's *Melody Ranch*. Paul and Ford began recording together in 1948 and were married a year later. Her warm voice and cool delivery made an appealing contrast to his hyperactive guitar work, but she was clearly his equal in overdubbing skill, singing multiple parts in perfectly fabricated unison ("In the Good Old Summertime"), harmony ("How High the Moon"), or contrapuntal riffs ("Don'cha Hear Them Bells"). She, too, recorded the least prominent parts first, crafting a precisely blended ensemble that started in her imagination and emerged gradually as material sound. The duo's first hit came at the beginning of 1951, a version of "Tennessee Waltz" that outdid Patti Page's recording in overdubs if not sales. Three months later their "How High the Moon" claimed the number-one spot, where it remained for two months, much of that time in the company of "Mockin' Bird Hill" at number two. Both sides remained on the charts for almost six months, joined later in the year by "I Wish I Had Never Seen Sunshine," "The World Is Waiting for the Sunrise," and "Just One More Chance." With sales surpassing four million by August, the pair was "establishing a record at Capitol for consistency in hits," as the public registered its unqualified enthusiasm for the "new sound."[47]

Amid the ephemera of rapidly changing 1950s popular music trends, echo, reverb, and overdubbing joined novelty songs, eccentric arrangements, and unrefined performance styles in drawing critics' ire. But the integration of electronic processing and music making would prove revolutionary. By the early 1960s, the gimmicks had become fundamental production techniques; they made records *sound* like records. Moreover, while the audible evidence of electronic manipulation signaled the recording engineer's presence in a frankly collaborative creative project, artifice pervaded the process in far more subtle ways as well. The sounds of performances were increasingly fabricated in ways of which listeners were rarely aware. "Recording techniques have become so ingenious that almost anyone can seem to be a singer," wrote *New York Times* critic John S. Wilson in 1959. He offered these examples.

> A small, flat voice can be souped up by emphasizing the low frequencies and piping the result through an echo chamber. A slight speeding up of the recording tape can bring a brighter, happier sound to a naturally drab singer or clean the weariness out of a tired voice. Wrong notes can be snipped out of the tape and replaced by notes taken from other parts of the tape.

Wilson reckoned that "the bulk" of contemporary pop discs were "propped up by some form of gimmick or engineering acrobatics," indeed that a singer "may actually be nothing more than the product of a recording engineer's creative ingenuity." In contrast, of course, were the "'singing' singers," pop traditionalists such as "Perry Como, Frank Sinatra, Patti Page, Nat 'King' Cole or such more recent arrivals as Pat Boone and Johnny Mathis," who made successful discs "without resorting to non-musical crutches."[48]

In fact, however, unmediated performances were becoming scarce as the pursuit of distinctive recordings led to new ways of thinking about recorded sound. Columbia engineer Frank Laico, who worked extensively with Mitch Miller, recalled spending at least two hours at the beginning of a Mathis session "just developing a sound on his voice."[49] Part of the process involved crafting a unique reverberant image, as Laico did for many singers at Columbia's Thirtieth Street studio. The room's own yawning ambience was often reduced with absorption and then supplemented with the sound of a twelve-by-fifteen-foot concrete storeroom in the basement. In addition to the usual tailoring techniques of mic placement and loudspeaker volume, Laico sometimes delayed signals before they reached the chamber—which further separated the reverb from its source sound and effectively lengthened its decay time—and altered the reverb's timbre. This palette of techniques allowed the engineer to create for each singer a unique aural image, which became part of their sonic identity. "Once we'd honed Mathis's vocal sound—i.e., the amount of echo, shades of EQ [timbral control], where the mic was situated in the chamber, etc.—we'd mark it down, and presto, that would be the formula for him," said Laico.[50] Crafting such signature sounds intrinsic to a record's character, the engineer became an artistic partner. Recalling his own work with Laico, Tony Bennett recalled, "It just would not have been the same without him. He worked that studio like an artist."[51]

By the late forties, the record groove was no longer simply a container for musical performances but a musical line in itself produced through a new mode of musical composition. It became a site of musical and sonic interaction with a distinct identity and, through mass exposure, the power to shape the public soundscape as never before. The record groove did not discriminate; it welcomed all music and all sound. The gatekeepers were the recording team members who worked the groove like a blank canvas. As record production evolved through the fifties, the result was not only new music but a new way of making music. It was perhaps the most enduring musical concept to emerge from the postwar period: records were no longer simply aural snapshots but deliberately crafted musical texts. Despite much initial criticism and resistance, the idea has stood the test of time, developed and refined by each succeeding generation of record producers from Mitch Miller to Timbaland.

· 4 ·

As the large record companies rolled out their hi-fi campaigns, the surging sales of the independents filled the music marketplace with sounds of another sort altogether. Fidelity was usually unattainable in the makeshift studios that sprang up across America in the late forties and early fifties. Generally speaking, technical resources were rudimentary, studios were often makeshift, and recordists were largely self-taught. Not only was fidelity a long-shot outcome, it was not even necessarily desirable. Like the electronic tricks animating pop records, scuffed sounds and uniquely peculiar musical balances gave indie records an identity apart from real world music making. Their roughness translated into expressive energy; it was part of their charm.

In general, the indies allowed more noise into a record's grooves than the majors would tolerate. Engineers at the big companies, for example, strove to prevent electronic distortion by carefully controlling input levels for microphone preamplifiers and tape machines. Many R&B and rock and roll records, on the other hand, drove levels past the breaking point. Although the resulting noise was a mistake according to hi-fi precepts, the records were released anyway, and whether through indifference or by design, the sound of electronic distortion gradually became an accepted element of the recorded music lexicon. Distortion lent records not simply a timbral roughness but often a brash, vital loudness that the record's grooves seemed barely able to contain. There is hardly a better example than Howlin' Wolf's "Moanin' at Midnight," recorded by Sam Phillips at his Memphis studio in 1951. The visceral intensity of the musical expression is perfectly matched by its electronic representation. The sound of the medium struggling to contain the electronic signal only intensified the effect on the listener created by the Wolf's own struggle with formidable unnamed demons. Cleaning up the sound would have rendered the musical performance more transparently but at a cost to the record's aura.

Legitimizing lo-fi sound would turn out to be a significant achievement that further expanded the record groove's aesthetic scope. But like so much else in the musical fifties, the sounds of indie records often resulted less from conscious planning than casual circumstance. Los Angeles record man Dootsie Williams, for example, had no idea he was making one of doo-wop's classic records when he took the Penguins to Ted Brinson's garage studio to record "Earth Angel" in the summer of 1954. He intended it as a demo and a B-side at that; the record's A-side was to be an up-tempo rhythm number called "Hey Senorita." The arrangement for "Earth Angel" was spare, the recording left unfinished, for it was only an initial attempt. As Williams recalled the recording session,

> Ted would turn on his recorder and then pick up his bass. He played in that steady, fundamental style from the big bands. We muffled the drums with pillows because we didn't want the lower register to drown out the voices. Every time the dog barked next door, I'd have to go out and shut him up and then we'd do another take. I was planning to put an electric guitar and saxophone on the song later on, but first I wanted to get the recordings down to John Dolphin and get his opinion on them.

When Williams took the record to Dolphin's record shop, Dolphin had Huggy Boy Hugg air both sides on his remote broadcast for KRKD. The positive public response led Williams to forgo any further refinements and release the record as it stood. Convinced it was "Hey Senorita" that was causing the stir, he stuck with his initial plan for the record's A- and B-sides, but again the market returned its own verdict. It was "Earth Angel" that became the hit, and its crude, lo-fi expression of fragile innocence and head-over-heels longing remains a doo-wop archetype.

If high fidelity was a remote prospect for indies, it was also beside the point. The audience that bought Johnny Ace's "My Song," a piece of sonic junk by audiophile standards, was clearly responding to something else, something in the voice, a sense of pathos that was only heightened by the ragged sound of the recording. If anything, the sound seemed to make the singer's emotion all the more genuine. The record was clearly not of the kind that issued from the majors' unapproachable electronic wonderland, accessible only to a select elite; rather, it gave the impression of something overheard, a piece of everyday life captured in a grainy verismo. Like the performers whose voices they conveyed, the lo-fi records that succeeded in the market took their places as equals among the polished offerings from the majors and, in time, as emblems of cultural memory.

The Five Satins' "In the Still of the Nite" is another good example. The song was written by lead singer Fred Parris, a nineteen-year-old draftee, reportedly during a night of guard duty. In the world of doo-wop, Parris was a relatively old hand. At James Hillhouse High School in New Haven, Connecticut, he led a group called the Scarlets that went on to record a few sides for the Red Robin label in New York. The group split up when its members were drafted into the army in 1955, but occasionally Parris was able to travel from his Philadelphia post back to New

Haven, where he formed the Satins. In 1956, on one of his trips home, the group began recording for the Standord label, a firm owned by New Haven teenager Marty Kugell and his partner Tom Sokira. The young entrepreneurs' only resource of significance was a bare-bones recording rig, which they carried from place to place. The Satins' first record, the beautiful a cappella ballad "All Mine," was recorded at the local VFW hall. For "In the Still of the Nite," the group was joined by a band of musicians at the Saint Bernadette Parish Hall in East Haven.

The recording was sonically bizarre, its odd balance sounding less like a blended musical ensemble than a sonic collage whose elements were set in strange juxtaposition. The only instrument heard clearly through most of the track was a loud snare drum pulsing on each backbeat. The piano appeared distant. While it shared the same temporal frame as the rest of the music, its prominent billowing reverb cast it into a separate, parallel dimension. The balance of the harmony voices, a fairly even blend on "All Mine," here highlighted the middle voice throughout the course of the track, its minimalist two-note part protruding insistently just behind Parris's lead. A slight haze of muffled distortion permeated the overall texture.

Although by a certain measure it was preposterously rough-hewn, the record had a respectable chart run (top five on the R&B chart and top thirty on pop). Its success in 1956, however, was only the beginning of its influence. It resurfaced in 1959 on Los Angeles deejay Art Laboe's first *Oldies but Goodies* collection, an album retrospective of rock and roll hits. "In the Still of the Nite" now became a staple of the emergent oldies radio format, as well as a reliable retail item whose sales continue to the present. Its primitive sonic patina, suggesting a faded yet cherished past, only enhanced its nostalgic power. Its enduring popularity was one of many similar signs that for the rock and roll audience records were not about transparency but character. Rock and roll records *were* high fidelity in the only sense that mattered: they were true to themselves. The full title of Laboe's collection (which to audiophiles must have appeared an absurdity) said as much—*Oldies but Goodies in Hi-Fi.*

The coarsely crafted records that accumulated in the public ear during the first ten years after the war were almost all the rough-and-ready products of indie firms. But in 1956 from the pinnacle of the pop establishment came a record that proved that clamorous sounds might also result from deliberate, painstaking craft. On July 2, 1956, Elvis Presley spent the day recording at a New York studio owned by his new label, RCA Victor—Studio A on East Twenty-fourth Street. He and his band, joined by the Jordanaires on backing vocals, cut three songs—"Hound Dog," "Don't

Be Cruel," and "Any Way You Want Me (That's How I Will Be)." The most difficult of the three was "Hound Dog." It took thirty-one takes, some partial, before Presley was satisfied. The final result was a strident racket, a blast of irrational and barely controlled rock and roll fury that went to number one on the pop, R&B, and country charts. It was astonishing evidence that the mainstream of recorded popular music, already a promiscuous hotbed of style mixture, was intentionally tilting toward cacophony. The sonic edge that lent a low-tech patina to so many indie records now emanated from a high-tech New York studio owned by one of the world's premier record labels—home to Arthur Rubinstein, Arturo Toscanini, Dizzy Gillespie, and Duke Ellington—with a history of technical innovation and high-quality recording dating back to the industry's earliest days.

By the time of the July session, Presley was in full control of his studio process. In Memphis, Phillips had steered the young singer and shown him the creative potential inherent in record making. When Presley moved to RCA Victor, his first sessions, held in Nashville in early January of 1956, were nominally supervised by Chet Atkins and Steve Sholes, head of A&R for RCA's country division. But although Sholes selected songs and Atkins oversaw the recording, Presley's talent was so unusual for a country singer that the results were largely self-determined. He began to take on the rarest of roles: a self-produced recording artist. According to songwriter Jerry Leiber, who observed many subsequent Presley sessions, "Steve Sholes had very little to say. . . . Presley was so far removed from anything that the old guard had been accustomed to hearing in studios that they really couldn't identify with it and they couldn't judge it." Engineer Bones Howe, who assisted on many of Presley's Los Angeles sessions, had the same impression, recalling, "Elvis produced his own recordings in those days—there's no mistaking it. . . . [Sholes] made no creative contribution."[52] At the Nashville sessions, guided by intuition and his memory of Phillips's tutelage, Presley exuded confident authority. "It was just so damn exciting," recalled Atkins.[53] One of the tracks recorded, "Heartbreak Hotel," would become Presley's first pop hit and a massive one at that.

His next sessions were in New York at the end of the month, his first visit to Studio A. Eight sides were recorded, mostly up-tempo rockabilly versions of rhythm and blues songs. None was released as a single, but the sound pointed in a new direction both for Presley and for RCA Victor—loud and bright, a brash, big-city version of the Memphis sides. On track after track, the band struggled to keep up with Presley's breathless momentum as he rushed ahead, impatient and barely able to contain a restless energy. Despite their major label provenance, the recordings had a low-tech, raucous punch with mix balances featuring an aggressive vocal presence, a crackshot snare, pumping bass, and Scotty Moore's incisive electric guitar. As it turned out, the sonic images from these sessions were preliminary sketches for "Hound Dog."[54]

Five months later, in the midst of a series of TV appearances that were increasing his visibility by the week, Presley was back in Studio A recording "Hound Dog." In six months at RCA Victor, during which he produced five top-forty hits, Presley established a working style that ignored entirely the standard three-hour recording session format. Nor could Sholes expect the normal four sides to emerge from a session, however long it went. Presley followed the routine he had learned at Sun. No clock, no boundaries. Pour yourself into the microphone with every take and then listen hard to the playback. Only when the record had a sense of the extraordinary about it was the work done. Photojournalist Alfred Wertheimer, who followed Presley through 1956, took photos at the session that show the singer listening to playbacks with a look of deep concentration, his critical ear searching for a telltale spark. Wertheimer later wrote an account of what he witnessed as engineer Ernie Ulrich played back various takes for Presley's consideration. At a certain point:

> Elvis left his chair and crouched on the floor, as if listening in a different position was like looking at a subject from a different angle. Again, he went into deep concentration, absorbed and motionless. At the end of the song he slowly rose from his crouch and turned to us with a wide grin, and said, "This is the one."[55]

The result of Presley's perfectionism revealed little of the intense work that produced it. The record made a blunt impact. The lyrics bore little resemblance to the original song, a blues number written by Jerry Leiber and Mike Stoller and recorded in 1953 by Willie Mae Thornton for Don Robey's Peacock label in Houston. Presley, an avid R&B fan, would not have thought to cover the song because its lyrics were so clearly in a woman's voice. But during a week of shows in Las Vegas, he heard a version of "Hound Dog" by Freddie Bell and the Bellboys that did away with most of the lyrics and added the "never caught a rabbit" line, turning the song's metaphoric sexuality into a literal rebuke of a lazy or inept pooch. The Bellboys' animated, nonsensical novelty delighted him, and when he added it to his live show it delighted audiences as well. The very meaninglessness of the words (and in their repeated iteration they became ever more so) gave the revised song a willful quality, more tantrum than tune yet undeniably exuberant.[56]

The sound of the record—which emerged over the course of the many takes—was willful as well. Presley attacked the title phrase in a one-bar solo anacrusis that launched the record on its headlong two-minute, seventeen-second romp. The rest of the texture dropped in on the downbeat, a reverberant haze of sound from which only a bright snare drum and loosely coordinated hand claps stood out. The Jordanaires' sustained harmonies, part of the haze during the vocal sections but emerging into clearer audibility behind the guitar solos, wheezed away like an oblivious harmonium caught at the wrong recording date. Moore's lead guitar, far from his usually reliable riffing, was in a state of spasmodic eruption—"ancient psychedelia" he would call it later—each response to the voice a sharp, noisy fragment, the solos careening at the brink of a musical train wreck.[57] The arrangement was punctuated by a yammering set of triplets on the snare at the end of each verse. In the midst of the ruckus, Presley sang in an aggressive yet joyful holler, presiding over the whole mess with a star's command.

The record's spectacular success was among the shocks produced by what the New York Times termed "the overwhelming nature of the arrival of Elvis Presley as a national figure."[58] In Melody Maker, English critic Steve Race addressed the record head on, writing, "My particular interest in Presley's 'Hound Dog' does not lie simply in the fact that I don't like it. The point about the whole thing is that, by all and any standards, it is a thoroughly bad record."[59] Race's judgment was at once defensible and irrelevant for, "bad" or not, the record was the most popular in America, a potent anti-hi-fi assertion of principle. Its crudeness was not a matter of inferior resources or skill but a wholly intentional aesthetic choice. The record's contrasting flip side, Otis Blackwell's "Don't Be Cruel," underlined the point. It was a well-crafted pop song recorded in an altogether more presentable form, not so far from a record Mitch Miller might have made with Johnnie Ray. "Don't Be Cruel," in other words, leaned toward professional polish while "Hound Dog" legitimized apparently amateur noise making. The difference in production values proclaimed that general criteria for fidelity were now solidly trumped by the pursuit of specific dramatic effect. Presley had learned from Phillips that making a record meant doing whatever was necessary to breathe life into it. The natural sound world, which provided a model for realistic representation, was of little help in this new sonic realm where the project was no longer capturing reality but creating it. The only sure guide was an intuitive sense of the disembodied aura—its authenticity, its truthfulness, its life.

The emergence of rock and roll, the decade's most disruptive development, was directly related to the record groove. In fact, it might be said that the groove gave birth to the idiom, which, in turn, liberated recording from the stricture of replication. Few would have thought to say so at the time, but rock and roll was at the cutting edge of a musical culture reshaped by recording consciousness. For an older pop generation the irony would have been too bitter to acknowledge: in the music's din lay crude confirmation that record making had become an art form. Rock and roll records declared the groove a noisy place—loud, gritty, loose, chaotic—prone to all manner of interference, which was, in turn, incorporated into the musical utterance. With no aspiration to high fidelity, the records asserted instead an irreducible musical line; everything in the groove was part of the music. In the willful guitar distortion of Link Wray's "Rumble," the buzzing phase shift of Toni Fisher's "The Big Hurt," the ever-changing ambient images of Buddy Holly's "Peggy Sue," sound took its place with song, performance, and arrangement as an integral component of musical expression and language.

In addition to the sonic complexity of the groove, it likely contained a stylistic unruliness fusing heterogeneous musical bits in a state of permanent cohabitation. It was such stylistic noise that pervaded doo-wop records like "Gee" and "Sh-Boom," where young a cappella groups were paired with seasoned instrumentalists, the pros' swing-inflected accompaniment joined with the singers' simpler rhythmic phrasing. The musical standoff was awkward. Early rock and roll saw triplets regularly banging into straight eighth notes in a contest that charged the record groove with messy tension. Since rock and roll had yet to establish any normative conventions, such mismatches were simply provisional, probing gambits. Whether a particular sound or stylistic amalgam made sense was determined by audience response. If a record gained the public's approval, it shed its provisional status and became one more item of concrete evidence in a developing case for the new music, stipulating an individual authenticity defined by whatever happened to be in its grooves.

SIX

"Hail! Hail! Rock and Roll"

*It was a kind of teen code, almost a sign language, that
would make rock entirely incomprehensible to adults. . . .
You either had to accept its noise at face value or you had
to drop out completely.*

—NIK COHN

*I couldn't write rock 'n' roll if I tried. The kids would
detect it as imitative right away.*

—HOAGY CARMICHAEL

· 1 ·

Kay Starr's "Rock and Roll Waltz" (RCA Victor), a novelty record whose
central irony is a mismatch between its playful narrative and its supporting musical arrangement, was a number-one hit in January of 1956. At
year's end, it was reported to be the year's "most played pop record in
juke boxes."[1] The waltz meter and instrumentation, which included a full
orchestra of brass, strings, winds, and percussion, offered no musical cor-
roboration of the song's nominal topic. Even its triplets, an ostensible
rock and roll feature, were satirical rather than idiomatic. The only clues
to what rock and roll might have sounded like were in the song's lyrics.
The teenage protagonist expressed bemusement at the scene she encountered upon returning home from a date: her "cute" but confused parents
waltzing to one of her rock and roll records. Presumably, then, the music
was not intended for waltzing. The lyrics gave some general idea that
rock and roll was a music of the young and that it marked a collective
identity distinct from the adult world. Listeners learned that the music
had a "jump" feel and that it was at home on a young person's "record
machine." Starr's performance suggested one further hint: rock and roll
evidently had some sort of lowdown feel because her light pop voice
turned to a lusty growl when belting the chorus, "One, two, and three
rock! One, two, and three roll!" The musical arrangement, however, gave
away nothing; if anything, it was a musical portrait of the waltzing parents, oblivious to the new sounds of the time. With no specific musical

references to rock and roll, the song's comic novelty relied entirely on an audience's ability to fill in the musical blanks with a tacit understanding of the disparity between rock and roll and Tin Pan Alley waltz. The record's success was a telling sign that a broad audience got the joke—they knew, by the end of 1955, what rock and roll was.

But whatever anyone thought rock and roll was in early 1956 was not what it would be by the end of the year, or the next, or the one after that. The stylistic contours of the pop chart remained in flux through the rest of the decade as new performers and new records continued the trends toward novelty and crossover. The trickle of music from the margins into the mainstream had become a steady flow, with musical styles merging recklessly and record production standards varying wildly. What it all meant was beyond knowing. The old guard of songwriters and publishers resident in New York's Brill Building, as lyricist Hal David remembered it, "thought rock 'n' roll was a fad, and they were just gonna wait it out."[2] They "assumed," *Variety* reported, "a 'this too shall pass' attitude" while the major record firms, in the winter of 1955, thought R&B, both crossover and cover, was "due for a pop fadeout before the summer."[3]

Things were moving so quickly, and the era had already seen so much change, that simply ignoring the hype seemed a reasonable bet. The numbers in record sales and concert attendance were impressive, but the idea that so many poorly produced records of such primitive music might have any lasting effect was surely absurd. Rock and roll was probably (hopefully) just another novelty gag writ large. Anyway, even if a Tin Pan Alley traditionalist wanted to try rock and roll, it was difficult to get a handle on it. Its far-flung stylistic features were a muddle of musical scraps strung together or superimposed in what the pros thought a nonsense doggerel. And the lyrics were little more than inane juvenilia or offensive gutter speak. Yet for some reason teenagers had adopted the music with a fervor. *Variety* sought to assure readers with a report that even the heralded high-pop bandleader Woody Herman had once had to endure his teenage daughters' "fondness for rock 'n' roll." As they grew older, however, they lost their "love for 'rock'" and developed "musical selectivity and discrimination."[4] Rock and roll, it could be safely assumed, was simply a phase of teenage experience and would no doubt fade as the current generation moved on to young adulthood.

Initial press accounts, seeking to describe the music to an adult readership, focused on the roughness of timbre in honking saxophones and shouted vocals, the pounding backbeat and simplistic lyrics, the sheer loudness of the records and the riotous scenes of teenagers dancing. In

1955, *Life* magazine explained the "frenzied teen-age music craze" as a combination of "both music and dance."

> The music has a rhythm often heavily accented on the second and fourth beat. The dance combines the Lindy and Charleston, and almost anything else. In performing it, hollering helps and a boot banging the floor makes it even better. The over-all result frequently is frenzy.

The songs also included "frequently suggestive and occasionally lewd" lyrics.[5]

The following year, *Time* summed up the rock and roll sound this way.

> Characteristics: an unrelenting, socking syncopation that sounds like a bull whip; a choleric saxophone honking mating-call sounds; an electric guitar turned up so loud that its sound shatters and splits; a vocal group that shudders and exercises violently to the beat while roughly chanting either a near-nonsense phrase or a moronic lyric in hillbilly idiom. . . . Only the obsessive beat pounds through, stimulating the crowd to such rhythmical movements as clapping in tempo and jumping and dancing in the aisles. Sometimes the place vibrates with the beat of music and stamping feet.[6]

John S. Wilson, surveying the 1956 rise of Elvis Presley in the *New York Times,* concluded that the problem with rock and roll was its lack of tasteful idiomatic proportion, rendering the music dull and brutish. "Essentially," he wrote, "rock 'n' roll is a grotesque extension of the blues." Setting aside the "sociological furor" to reflect on the music, Wilson found that elements of Presley's recorded output not only drew "effectively on some valid aspects of American folk music" but also demonstrated "an impressive, if sometimes distorted talent." Presley was "imbued with the spirit and style of those Negro country blues singers represented . . . by Big Bill Broonzy" and had "absorbed the straight-forward, unhokumed part of country singing that runs from Jimmie Rodgers to Eddy Arnold." By contrast, however, his "outright rock 'n' roll efforts" were "based on exaggeration of his blues roots . . . combined with further exaggerations of the less-palatable elements of his country influences, all amplified to brain-shattering proportions by doom-filled echo chambers."[7] One of Wilson's *Times* colleagues, reporting not on the records but on the street-level view of rock and roll activity around New York City, formed a similar impression. Focusing on her respondents' attraction to the music's beat, she informed readers that rock and roll took

R&B's stressed backbeat and made it "heavier, lustier and transform[ed] it into what has become known as The Big Beat. It is a tense, monotonous beat that often gives rock 'n' roll music a jungle-like persistence."[8]

Teenagers were indeed excited, and much of the music certainly projected a primal quality, but most popular press accounts glossed over some fundamental tensions that made defining rock and roll a tricky prospect. In *Billboard*'s 1956 "Spotlight on Rhythm and Blues," Bill Simon pointed out that "the term 'rhythm and blues' barely begins to describe the myriad material that today is grouped in that particular category." Performers such as Little Walter and Jimmy Reed were upholding the blues wing of R&B, but they were overshadowed commercially by the young black singers who in recent years had won public acclaim with "pop-influenced 'blues-ballads' and lively rhythm novelties in what has come to be known as the 'rock and roll' idiom."[9] In the late summer of 1956, the weekly U.K. music publication *Melody Maker,* noting that "no one knew what kind of music qualified for inclusion under the R-and-B heading," conflated R&B with rock and roll and based distinctions on aesthetic opinion. Wynonie Harris and Jimmy Witherspoon were "good R-and-B singers," while Bill Haley "set out a formula for the commercialized R-and-B product . . . watered down jump blues with hillbilly overtones and a hand-clapping type of off-beat." Although it was too often "intentionally cheapened to appeal to mass taste," R&B/rock and roll, "at its best," was "simply hot jazz," which had "put a beat into the popular picture."[10]

Three years earlier, Jerry Wexler had written the same thing. "Called upon to explain rhythm and blues to people who 'confuse' it with jazz," his unequivocal answer was "there is no definable difference and there never has been." Wexler went on to argue that R&B was simply a designation for African American popular music and much of what eventually became "enshrined in [jazz] discographies the world over" was, in its own time, simply "typical popular Negro music of the day."[11] But if a Kid Ory or Bessie Smith, two of Wexler's examples, had clear heirs in the adult R&B of the early fifties, the young vocal groups complicated the picture. Jazz was among the least of their formative influences. Wexler could steer around this snag in 1953 because doo-wop was still an upstart music without proven staying power. But by the time *Melody Maker* weighed in, there was no denying that a new generation had come to dominate the R&B charts and accounted for most of the crossover records. That "hot jazz" remained the British writers' frame of reference pointed up the challenge rock and roll's inconvenient untidiness posed to critical perspectives tinted with a nostalgia for the musical past.

"Few people—outside the music business—have a true understanding of what this musical genre, loosely termed Rock-and-Roll really *is*," Paul Ackerman wrote in 1958, addressing not his customary *Billboard* audience but the readers of *High Fidelity*.[12] In fact, few people inside the music business understood it either. *Life,* having acknowledged by 1958 that rock and roll was "more than a flash in the piano," quoted one record man complaining, "Anyone who thinks he can pick what kids'll want next, his orientation is in Cloudsville."[13] As a marketing slogan, "rock and roll" was a winner, but could it really denote a single stylistic category given the wide range of musical contrivance linked to it? Were Patti Page and Ella Mae Morse really rock and roll performers, as record company ads proclaimed? Did Alan Freed's claim that rock and roll was "just a variation of the 4-by-4 tempo that was used by singers of the Al Jolson–Harry Richman–Eddie Cantor era" make any sense apart from its self-serving attempt at legitimation?[14]

Ackerman himself was none too precise in his usage; like many at the time, he often used the terms *rock and roll* and *rhythm and blues* interchangeably. On the one hand, "so-called rock and roll" was simply the teenager's term for R&B; on the other, he used the term as a more specific designation for the " 'back shack' sound" of the rocking country music exemplified by Sam Phillips's Sun recordings of Presley, Carl Perkins, and Warren Smith—what he called "rock and roll–c.&w." Drawing in yet another stylistic strand, Ackerman reported that Bill Haley's "(We're Gonna) Rock around the Clock" was among 1955's "big rock and roll hits." And in a 1957 summary of the broad stylistic changes sweeping pop music, he stated that "so-called rock and roll" was a "pop adaptation of r.&b."[15]

These pronouncements represent a rough chronology of Ackerman's developing notion that rock and roll was somehow distinct from its sources. But his persistent use of the "so-called" qualifier suggested that even for this open-minded reporter, always in the forefront of championing the changes in the industry, which he took as a sign of progressive thinking, the music was a conundrum. He repeatedly lauded country and R&B music as "strongly rooted in the traditions of the people," infusing the pop mainstream with welcome drafts of "authentic musical Americana."[16] But rock and roll had no tradition; it was a nascent thing and difficult to pin down. It drew on many traditions, lovingly but without respect for their normative habits. Strangely, its idiomatic authenticity lay in its blithe artifice. The music seemed unconcerned, comfortable even, with contradiction, paradox, and absurdity, all of which gave observers, Ackerman included, understandable difficulty.

Another 1956 *Billboard* article, attempting to describe market events in terms of musical style, placed Presley, the Platters, Sanford Clark, Bill Doggett, and Gene Vincent in the "rock and roll groove," while records by Fats Domino, the Clefs, and Bill Haley were "primarily rhythm and blues." With Doggett in rock and roll and Haley in R&B, the categories made little sense, and the reporter's fuzzy summary admitted as much; the teenagers who were "calling the shots" in singles sales went for "rock and roll and/or rhythm and blues. In brief, The Big Beat."[17] Because all of these performers stood side by side in the teenage market, distinctions became increasingly tenuous. Reporters trying to make sense of new realities in terms of established convention confronted the same perplexity as the industry at large. Perhaps the most honest assessment of the situation came from a recording engineer, Stan Ross, who, as co-owner of Gold Star in Los Angeles, worked daily to craft records that might have a chance in the utterly unpredictable market. "Every time engineers went into the studio," he said, "we were feeling our way, trying to find out what rock and roll was."[18]

The confusion over just what rock and roll *was* stemmed from something no one could know at the time: throughout the early years, rock and roll was more a process transforming the pop mainstream than a concrete musical type. It was part crossover, part appropriation, part revision, part accident, and part market dynamics. It was born of the transitional turbulence that had roiled the pop scene ever since it began throwing off the conventions of the swing era. The novel admixture that made rock and roll so difficult to pinpoint had been brewing for years until, by 1955, as *Variety* reported, there seemed to be "no trends to guide A&R men."

> There's no masterminding the record business any more. In the past few months, tunes that have hit have been so diversified that the artists & repertoire men don't know which trend to follow. In fact there is no discernible trend.

In recent weeks, the report continued, "the spread on hit wax has included ballads, marching songs, religiosos, hillbilly, rhythm & blues and instrumental."[19] The pop mainstream was now open to musical essays of almost any kind, many of which hailed from environs utterly foreign to the industry establishment.

Wilson saw rock and roll as a further extension of the gimmick pop of the first half decade, which was "stepped up when the gimmick searchers picked up the basic beat and lightheartedly bawdy lyrics of Rhythm and

Blues, a specialized channel of popular music aimed primarily at the Negro market." The transformative appropriation was easily described: "Stripped down to its simplest form and driven home with power-hammer intensity, this music became rock 'n' roll."[20] The statement was true enough as far as it went. The beat was amply evident both on record and in the live performances that were electrifying teenagers. As Johnny Otis summed it up, rock and roll "took over all the things that made R&B different from big band swing: the after-beat on a steady four; the influence of boogie woogie; the triplets on piano; eight-to-the-bar on the top-hat cymbal; and the shuffle pattern of dotted eighth and sixteenth notes."[21]

But young people's fascination was not limited to the big beat or R&B and country borrowings. What the first descriptions of rock and roll usually omitted was how much it also owed to mainstream pop. Commentators failed to grasp that what made the new music so unpredictable, for many unbearable, yet ultimately revolutionary was its indiscriminate merging of all existing idioms regardless of provenance or aesthetic tradition. It remained in a continuous state of novelty, an evolutionary process in which repertory and stylistic habits were intermingled freely. When, for example, Clyde McPhatter sang "Harbor Lights," the 1937 ballad by Jimmy Kennedy and Hugh Williams, he reworked the melody thoroughly in a highly ornamented, mannered vocalise. His performance consisted of a series of disjointed phrases delivered with an overwrought passion at odds with the song's performance history. As gospel, his testifying fervor would have been typical, but as pop it was strange, uncharacteristic. In the existing order of things, combining gospel, R&B, and pop made little sense. Only an extraordinarily inclusive musical frame could admit such a mixture.

The young audience, moreover, was not as easily pegged as reports claimed. While they reveled in the big beat's energetic stomp, they were also fond of older pop styles. A 1956 survey of ten thousand high school students in the New York metropolitan area found that while Presley was the kids' "favorite male singer," such stars as Doris Day and Joni James were also very popular. And in the "favorite music" category, "which listed pop vocals, rock and roll, semi-classical, jazz, show tunes, instrumentals, ballads, etc.," rock and roll was preferred only by the boys. The girls' (who were the more reliable record buyers) preferred category was pop vocals.[22]

Amid all the market turmoil and critical puzzlement, there was one element of rock and roll for which there was universal consensus: whatever else it might be, rock and roll was without doubt a cherished essential of teenage life, "a teen-age must" that radio programmers timed to the clock of the teenager's day. "Soon as three o'clock rolls around," as Chuck Berry sang in "School Day," teenagers headed for the jukebox, radio, or record player, and "the typical management attitude" at radio stations was that rock and roll programming "timed for peak teen-age listening hours" was "obligatory." Stations often struggled to balance rock and roll with more adult pop programming, trying to retain as broad a listenership as possible. The minority of stations unconcerned with teenage commerce, those "aiming at a specialized audience (the daytime female group, older people in general, foreign language listeners, a college town audience, etc.)," programmed no rock and roll at all. Most, however, "had to concede" by late 1956 that the music was "no 'fad' that will vanish with the wave of a wand."[23]

In 1954 it was already apparent that, aside from a few celebrities, individual deejays were less of a factor in record promotion than in the recent past; they were "following rather than leading the hit parade."[24] As the rock and roll phenomenon gained steam, it emerged that "a very big percentage of the currently employed deejays do not play the disks that they themselves prefer" and that there was "considerable straining on the part of jocks to free themselves from 'the rock and roll strait-jacket.'" The average deejay, having grown up on "ballads, slick instrumentals, dance bands and jazz" would have had little more sense of what moved a teenager's heart, mind, and money than the major label A&R men.[25] They were guided by the requests that poured in to stations, by the industry popularity charts, and by the emerging top-forty format, which prescribed a list of records to play based on a chart formula. In an informal survey conducted in 1956, in the wake of the Presley eruption, publisher Wesley Rose discovered that country deejays were playing rockabilly records not by their own choice but "chiefly because they feel it necessary to go along with listeners' preferences."[26]

Early in 1957, *Billboard* changed the name of its long-running "Rhythm-Blues Notes" column to "On the Beat: Rhythm & Blues–Rock & Roll." Pointing out that the "unusually wide acceptance of the r.&b. idiom" had led to the development of new "musical areas," most notably "'rock and roll' and what has come to be called 'rockabilly,'" columnist Gary Kramer suggested that the industry "revise and perhaps abandon some of its old boundary lines." In the current market, he argued, "no abstract categories prevent the teen-ager . . . from buying records by Fats Domino, Elvis Presley, Bill Haley, Carl Perkins, or Little Richard at one and the same time."[27] As teenagers expressed their whims and passions in the music market, they steadily, if unwittingly, accomplished what the industry found unfathomable: they defined rock and roll. If they bought a record in sufficient numbers, its performers became instant stars regardless of their sketchy showbiz credentials. Reviewers often deplored the young stars' poor live performances, but these were relative afterthoughts and, in any case, fleeting. It was records that made the initial impact and whose sounds lingered in the public mind. In short order, the accumulation of diversely styled records began to resemble a de facto canon, although few would have thought to call it that at the time.

The power of teenagers' market influence took the industry by surprise. As early as 1952, the success of one record in particular, "Oh, Happy Day," showed how thoroughly their enthusiasm could trump the pros' collective wisdom. *Billboard* accurately described the performance, despite the song's lyric, as "a melancholy lament."[28] The record left "many record men . . . somewhat aghast and puzzled."[29] Was it irony or stupidity, the industry wondered. The "rudimentary little piece," as *Time* called it, was recorded by a seventeen-year-old Cleveland Heights High School student named Don Howard Koplow (going by Don Howard), reportedly in the family garage.[30] He claimed to have written it, but a legal settlement appended the name of "a young housewife, Nancy Binns Reed, of Washington," who appeared to have originated the song in some form, although she had never written it down or recorded it.[31] Koplow sang in a voice that was tentative and entirely lacking in resonance, as though dulled by a psychotropic sedative. He began his performance with a hesitating rhythm, as if it were his first time singing the song or perhaps singing at all. As *Time* described the performance, "Donnie himself moos his happy tune with the hoarse lilt of a fogbound ferry whistle."[32] The accompaniment consisted of only an acoustic guitar strumming once on each beat.

Yet in the record's utterly unadorned, halting expression was a poignancy that spoke to the young record buyer. Although it "kicked off a shocked reaction in the business," *Billboard*'s review read, "the chanter's odd style produces a definite sound and where the record has been well exposed has resulted in definite sales."[33] A small local label, Triple-A, released the record initially, and then Dave Miller's Essex (Bill Haley's label) leased it for wider distribution. Despite "the shouting and the tumult . . . the sundry lamentations, the initial alarm" erupting from industry veterans, the record sold some four hundred thousand copies, and once the majors saw that "it was indisputable that kids were actually buying Don Howard records," the song was covered by Dick Todd (Decca), the Four Knights (Capitol), and Lawrence Welk (Coral). It also prompted a parody answer by Homer and Jethro called "Unhappy Day" (RCA Victor). All sold well, and sheet music sales were above two hundred thousand.[34] Koplow would be all but forgotten after his sole moment of pop success, but the fluke of "Oh, Happy Day" served notice that the youth market had the power to override the judgment and taste of even the most established industry powers.

· **2** ·

Rock and roll gained its first ubiquitous symbol in 1955 when Bill Haley's "(We're Gonna) Rock Around the Clock" was placed in the film *Blackboard Jungle* after languishing for a year on the B-side of Decca single number 29124. (The A-side was the post-nuclear-attack fantasy number "Thirteen Women [And Only One Man in Town].") Although the record and the film had initially had nothing to do with one another, the combination of high-energy sound and the film's theme of restive teenage rebellion produced a bombshell whose influence spread rapidly around the world. As it claimed the number-one spot on the pop chart, where it perched for eight weeks, the record crystallized in the public mind a particular musical aggregate. It blended familiar elements of country, jump blues, and novelty in a loud burst of youthful enthusiasm. The rhythm was sharp, the riffs full, and the sound big. Haley was never more than a competent vocalist and, in contrast to Presley, Little Richard, or Chuck Berry, he was a mild presence as a front man. But the Comets were not about a single iconic figure. They were a group presence whose overall sound was far greater than any of its parts, a prototypical rock and roll *band*.

Haley's prior experience in blending idioms made him the right man for the job, but it also cast him in an odd role. The teenager's new rock and roll hero was nearly thirty years old when *Blackboard Jungle* was released, a journeyman trouper with many recordings to his credit. For years, he had led a country band based outside Philadelphia called first the Four Aces of Western Swing and then the Saddlemen. (Haley was an accomplished yodeler.) He made his first recording, a cover of Hank Williams's "Too Many Parties and Too Many Pals" backed with "Four Leaf Clover Blues," in 1948 for Jack Howard's Cowboy label, one of the Philadelphia-based country startups *Billboard* trumpeted in 1947. The band moved on to other labels in the city, changed its name one more time (to the Comets), and scored a top-twenty hit in the spring of 1953 with "Crazy Man, Crazy," a record with the same rim shot crack, slapped bass, and frantically pastiched electric guitar solo as "Rock Around the Clock."

How the Saddlemen became the Comets and arrived at "Crazy Man,

Crazy" is another of the era's improbable tales illustrating how musical events of key significance were often driven by random circumstance and chance opportunity. In 1951, Dave Miller approached Haley about recording a cover version of Jackie Brenston's "Rocket 88." Miller thought a hillbilly version held potential appeal, and he knew that whenever the band played a version of Jimmy Preston's 1949 R&B hit, "Rock the Joint," on their club dates it invariably made a great hit with audiences. At WPWA in Chester, Pennsylvania, Haley hosted a country music show, which followed *Judge Rhythm's Court,* an R&B program featuring "Rock the Joint" as its theme song. "I used to listen to this show while I was getting ready," Haley recalled, "and that probably influenced me a lot too."[35] Miller offered the group a deal, and they recorded "Rocket 88" at the WPWA studio.

Following "Rocket 88," over the course of the next four singles the group recorded a few more boogie-flavored numbers as a novelty contrast to the honky-tonk fare that was their core repertoire. In 1952, "Rock the Joint" became the B-side for a recording of Haley's own "Icy Heart," a country weeper with a gimmick reverb treatment released on Miller's new Essex label. Haley hoped the record, its song no doubt influenced by his idol Hank Williams's "Cold, Cold Heart," would land him an appearance on the *Grand Ole Opry.* (According to Haley, Williams, who Haley had known for several years, congratulated him on his potential breakthrough shortly before Williams's death.[36]) But with the band on the road promoting their new record, Miller telephoned Haley to say that it was not "Icy Heart" but "Rock the Joint" that was getting local radio and retail attention. Haley faced a problem: "I had never in years thought that this would happen. What was I going to do? Here I was with the sideburns, cowboy boots and almost ten years of promoting myself as a country and western singer."[37] The R&B material was effective as a novelty item, but Haley knew from years on the bandstand that his country audience would not countenance a steady stream of cowboy blues numbers. And early bookings into R&B clubs, whose audiences did not know in advance that the band members were white, proved disastrous. ("People would come in for one song and just get up and leave.")[38] If the band was to embrace the buzz "Rock the Joint" was generating, they would be traveling unknown territory in pursuit of an uncertain audience.

The Saddlemen billed themselves as a frankly heterogeneous outfit: "The Cowboy Jive Band" that was "rockin' the show world with a modern cowboy swing and jive." Playing "cowboy," "jive," "popular," and "hillbilly," they were "The Most Versatile Band in the Land."[39] This promotional poster sought to explain the group's sound to their public,

and perhaps to themselves, but meanwhile a new fan base was material-
izing beyond the familiar reaches of the Pennsylvania, New Jersey, and
Delaware hillbilly circuit. According to then bassist Marshall Lytle, the
radio exposure for "Rock the Joint" brought fan mail from high school-
ers throughout the area; the Saddlemen were breaking through not as a
live act but as a sound. The rhythm was infectious and the lyrics appeal-
ingly anarchic: "We're going to tear down the mailbox, rip out the floor /
Smash out the windows and knock down the door / We're gonna rock,
rock this joint." The guitar solo, which would end up replicated on
"Rock Around the Clock," was frenetic, and the steel guitar solo added
a slightly manic hillbilly touch. A new manager sought to book the group
into a broader range of venues, which required a change of costume from
western garb to dinner jackets. As Lytle put it, "We took our cowboy
clothes off and put suits on and became a rock and roll band."[40] The
change of image also included the name change. A fellow deejay at
WPWA, Bix Reichner, who was also a songwriter, suggested Bill Haley
and His Comets, and provided a song, "Stop Beatin' Round the Mulberry Bush," for the "new" group's debut recording. (The song had been
a hit in several band versions in the late thirties.)

Along with the change of image came an important change in sound.
Like other honky-tonk groups, the Saddlemen had not used drums. The
groove was a collective texture with the bass and rhythm guitar providing a foundation while steel guitar, lead guitar, and piano alternated between rhythmic riffing and melodic fills. But on "Stop Beatin' Round
the Mulberry Bush" and its B-side, "Real Rock Drive," the Comets
brought drums into the group, focusing on the wallop of rim shot accents. The insistent rhythm of the slapped bass, which had characterized the group's up-tempo blues records since "Rocket 88," remained
the driving force, the drums erupting occasionally at surprise moments
with fills or responses that sent bracing jolts of energy through the
record. The new sound was a prototype that propelled the band toward
rock and roll. The next record, "Crazy Man, Crazy," developed the
concept further. The record had more drum action, including a solo introduction and a continuous whacking backbeat during the guitar and
steel guitar solos. The drums shot an electricity through the track that
permeated the overall texture and seemed to incite the shouted group
exhortations "Go, Go, Go everybody." It was an exciting sound they
would cultivate when the Comets moved on to Decca in 1954 after five
more Essex singles.

Upon signing with Decca, and under the supervision of Milt Gabler,
the Comets' first recording session included "Rock Around the Clock," by

songwriting veteran Max Freedman and Philadelphia publisher James Myers, who also helped the group land the Decca deal. The collaboration with Gabler connected emergent rock and roll with pop's venerable past. The Comets were now working with one of the industry's most experienced producers and an expert, through his long association with Louis Jordan, in the techniques of riff-based jump blues, an important element of the Comets' developing sound. Even the recording venue, Decca's studio in the third-floor auditorium of the Pythian Temple, a building at 135 West Seventieth Street designed in the 1920s by the architect Thomas Lamb as a meeting place for the Knights of Pythias, connected the Comets to the reverberant sonic aura of innumerable earlier recordings. As it happened, the record that would garner so much attention a year later only grazed the chart for a week at number twenty-three in the spring of 1954. A far bigger hit would come later in the summer with a cover of Joe Turner's "Shake, Rattle, and Roll," which provided a good example of how R&B source material might be transmuted into rock and roll.

Entering the postwar pop mainstream usually involved a trade of some kind: things needed to be simplified, expressed directly, shorn of ambiguity and nuance, and sonically hyped in some way. The Comets' revision of "Shake Rattle and Roll" had little of Turner's sly, earthy humor or easygoing feel. With the industry facing widespread public condemnation of what were termed "lewd" lyrics, or "leer-ics," in R&B, Gabler was in no mood to trifle with censors and so removed most of the song's delicious double entendres. The original track began with a lightly twittering piano riff, a boogie bass pattern, and a big snare backbeat, followed by Turner's customary blues shout, a powerful yet relaxed rhythmic presence. The saxophones answered the vocal phrases with understated riffing, leaving room for the arrangement to develop gradually as the song took its time coming to its "shake, rattle and roll" hook, which finally appeared after the third verse. The sound was spare in texture yet rich in expression. The Comets' track, by contrast, was a straightforward blast of sonic energy from start to finish. The saxophone riff that kicked off the introduction erupted with a sudden rhythmic crispness and an arresting loudness. It was reinforced in rhythmic unison by guitar and pedal steel, as were all subsequent riffs, creating a punchy composite texture. Instead of the loose-jointed ensemble groove of the Atlantic disc, the Comets' ensemble playing was tightly rehearsed and calibrated for maximum sonic impact. The track's opening riff, which Gabler claimed to have devised, was itself based on the chorus, and the sung chorus appeared after only one verse. In a rush to seize the listener's attention, no time was lost in getting to the point and hammering it home.

To achieve the Decca sound, the Comets themselves made a trade, removing much of the interplay that characterized their Essex recordings. They largely eliminated Billy Williamson's swinging, humorous, and often exhilarating steel guitar solos, opting to stick with guitar or saxophone solos. Williamson was largely confined to what Gabler called "lightning flashes"—short, sharp stabs that further heightened the rhythmic effect even as they disguised the band's country roots.[41] The freer call-and-response interplay among instruments and voice of the earlier years was replaced with rehearsed figures doubled in rhythmic unison. It added up to a simpler yet bolder texture that struck with an immediate force.

Its status as an international teenage anthem made "Rock Around the Clock" exhibit A for rock and roll. The currents gathering through the early years of the decade—the widespread popularity of rhythm and blues, the various mergings of country and pop, the crossover records by young black performers, the evidence of teenage buying power—were reflected in the Comets' breakout stardom. For several years, hundreds of records from Chicago, Memphis, New Orleans, Houston, New York, and Los Angeles featuring an insistent, heavy beat had thumped away among pop's byways. The big beat had become a rhetorical fundamental that the Comets' record invoked with the full sonic splendor of major label recording resources. The rhythmic dynamism fueled a spirited performance that teenagers found irresistible. And in the Comets' stage antics—it was not unusual for the bass player to lie atop his bass while the saxophone player, Rudy Pompilli, sat astride him, the band wailing all the while—the audience could see as well as hear the glorious abandon that seemed to mirror their own adolescent yearning for liberation.

On the heels of "Rock Around the Clock" came a wave of rock and roll hits from a host of newcomers. Among them was Richard Penniman, Little Richard, a performer of unsurpassed manic intensity dubbed by his principal biographer "the quasar of rock." Only twenty-two when "Tutti Frutti"—his first release on Art Rupe's Specialty label—began climbing the charts in the fall of 1955, Richard was already an experienced trouper. From his early teenage years, he had performed with several professional bands, and in 1951, with the help of Billy Wright (Atlanta's flamboyant "Prince of the Blues") and deejay Zenas Sears, he secured a recording deal with RCA Victor, which yielded eight sides of urban blues. In 1953, he moved on to Don Robey's Peacock label where he remained unhappily under contract until he sent an audition tape to Specialty's Los Angeles office in February 1955. ("He was so possessive," Richard said of Robey. "He would control the very breath you breathed.")[42] On the audition tape, Richard was accompanied by his touring band, the Upsetters, on two of his own songs, "Baby" and "All Night Long," a couple of midtempo blues sung in a high, sweet voice with an expressive edginess but little hint of the strident belter who would erupt on the national scene later in the year. Robert "Bumps" Blackwell, a conservatory-trained musician and composer working A&R for Specialty, was impressed with the voice, and Rupe loaned Richard the six hundred dollars he needed to buy out his contract with Robey. Neither Rupe nor Blackwell had any premonition about Richard's rock and roll future; they were simply looking for a distinctive blues stylist.

Richard told Rupe that he admired Fats Domino's records, and Rupe was immediately reminded of Specialty's greatest R&B success to date, Lloyd Price's "Lawdy Miss Clawdy," recorded, like Domino's tracks, at Cosimo Matassa's J&M studio in New Orleans. Rupe often used Bunny Robyn's Hollywood Recorders, a hotbed of gospel and R&B recording in Los Angeles. But mindful of the ineffable chemistry involved in producing a record, he elected to have Blackwell and Richard meet in New Orleans to record with the J&M session players, men like Lee Allen (saxophone), Frank Fields (bass), and Earl Palmer (drums).

The first New Orleans sessions produced nine sides over the course of two days in September of 1955. Eight sides had been scheduled, but during a break Richard began playing his "Tutti Frutti" and Blackwell insisted they record it in the little time remaining. While he was aware that Richard had a reputation for wild showmanship, Blackwell had heard little evidence of it in the studio performances. Now, finally, he heard a sound he knew would stand out. "There was a definite trend toward a more basic and simple music in which the feeling was the most important thing," Blackwell recalled. "People were buying feel," and "Tutti Frutti" was little else, a distilled manic essence.[43] Richard's bawdy lyrics were quickly rewritten by local songwriter Dorothy La Bostrie, on hand because Richard was recording her "I'm Just a Lonely Guy" that same day. (Interestingly, although this song is a slow blues, it came closest of all the other tracks from these sessions to the fervency of "Tutti Frutti.") From its opening "Awop-bop-a-loo-mop, Alop-bom-bom," "Tutti Frutti" unleashed an expressive eruption in the pop mainstream. Its crossover was perhaps the year's most spectacular single piece of evidence that pop tastes had moved into uncharted territory.

The famous story of "Tutti Frutti" is reminiscent of Presley's "That's All Right": a seminal sound discovered accidentally by a producer who overheard something surprising. In both cases, the performers had been relatively restrained during sessions in which they tried to deliver with earnest discipline what they imagined the producers were after, an effort that would somehow fit conventional stylistic expectations. As it turned out, it was the utterly unexpected that caught the producer's ear, something the performer had harbored yet perhaps assumed was too idiosyncratic for pop consumption. "Tutti Frutti" made the pop chart in January 1956, followed by eight more top-forty hits running through the summer of 1958, by which time Little Richard was out of show business, having renounced rock and roll in late 1957 while on tour in Australia, a nervous wreck in need, he felt, of spiritual renewal. In addition to his records, Richard appeared several times on television and in films, confirming his ultravivid performance style. Again there was a parallel with the Presley story. In 1956, both performers had strings of hit records supported by mass media appearances in which they appeared to be at the edge of control. It was all somewhat reminiscent of Johnnie Ray's histrionics, but the music was much more aggressive—faster, louder, and unlikely to turn up at the Copa. Charged performances would become a rock and roll fundamental. It would become a tenet—exemplified by future generations of performers in various states of apparent emotional and psychic transport—that the music held an almost supernatural potency that promised rhapsodic transcendence. There was, however, another side to the story.

· 3 ·

In the film *Rock Around the Clock,* the Comets starred alongside the Platters, a mixed-gender vocal group as silken as the Comets and Little Richard were brash. The Platters' 1955 hit, "Only You (And You Alone)," was the first in a series of twenty top-forty hits they scored over the course of six years, almost all of which were ballads. The song was written by Buck Ram, who also managed the group, along with several others in Los Angeles, including the Penguins. Ram had worked as a songwriter and arranger since the 1930s and was in his late forties as rock and roll began to dawn. Yet, unlike so many of his peers who resisted the new music, he was able to write songs with a feel for the musical present using a craft steeped in the past. In the songs he wrote for the Platters, which included "The Great Pretender," "(You've Got) The Magic Touch," "Heaven on Earth," and "My Dream," he managed to marry a straightforward harmonic-phrase design with a melodic elegance and lyrics that appealed to an all-ages romantic sensibility. The songs had a classy refinement about them, yet they sounded perfectly idiomatic set to the requisite triplet rhythm and backbeat accent of rock and roll.

The Platters emerged from the Watts high schools in Los Angeles and the amateur nights at Club Alabam on Central Avenue, a scene that produced dozens of vocal groups. It was a "close-knit community of singers," Al Frazier of the Rivingtons recalled, a hotbed of musical interaction among amateur musicians who were only one record away from being pros.[44] By the time the Platters were signed to a recording contract with Syd Nathan's Federal label, all were out of school and only Herbert Reed and Alex Hodge remained from the original group. The two were joined by David Lynch and Tony Williams, who was newly arrived from Elizabeth, New Jersey, and then, in an unusual move suggested by Ram, by a young woman named Zola Taylor.

The original version of "Only You" was produced by Ralph Bass, who was working at the time for Syd Nathan as an A&R man. Bass started the amateur night contests at Club Alabam with deejay Hunter Hancock and backing from the Johnny Otis band "specifically to find new talent," and it was there that he first heard Williams, not a winner that night but a stunning voice nonetheless.[45] Noting that vocal groups, more than soloists, were the current vogue, Bass introduced Williams to Ram, who was both managing and coaching the still raw Platters in preparation for recording. Over the course of some months rehearsing in Ram's garage, and with the addition of Taylor, the Platters began developing the sound that would make them, by the end of 1956, the "hottest and highest paid popular vocal group in the U.S."[46]

Nathan's labels had some of the highest production standards among the indies, and Bass was one of the great pioneering R&B producers, the man who convinced a doubtful Nathan to sign the young James Brown. But his production of "Only You" was in most respects an indifferent record. The backing vocals were barely audible until they chimed in with the coda phrase, "one and only you," drawn out in a lugubrious bleat at an absurdly slow tempo that only heightened the effect of the wobbly intonation. The accompaniment from piano, bass, and drums was both minimal and mechanical, the ensemble barely ticking over with one bass note to the bar, a heavy piano triplet figure on alternate beats, and brush-snare ticktocking continuously, none of which was very well coordinated. The record's only bright spot was Tony Williams's spectacular tenor. In the manner of such contemporary virtuoso pop vocalists as Jackie Wilson and Sam Cooke, Williams melded a seemingly effortless lyricism with gospel-tinged passion.

When Mercury wanted to sign the Penguins following the success of "Earth Angel," Ram made the deal conditional on signing the Platters as well. He insisted that the group re-record "Only You," and this time he got what he was after, a gorgeous performance supported by a polished production, which claimed the upper reaches of the R&B and pop charts in the fall of 1955. The backing voices and the instrumental ensemble, augmented with guitar and saxophone, were blended smoothly in a balanced texture supporting the lead voice. The slow tempo was animated by piano triplets, which, unlike the earlier recording, pulsed continuously in a soft shimmer, along with a bass line tracing a slow two-bar boogie pattern and a drum part that lightly but firmly articulated the backbeat. The key was lowered from G-flat to E-flat, which allowed Williams freer play in alternating between chest voice and falsetto. The overall sound had the high-tech polish that was a consistent Mercury hallmark. In short, "Only You" was a record that bore both conventional rock and roll features and the controlled sonic and expressive refinement of mainstream pop. "To me," Bass recalled, "Williams was a modern day Bill Kenny."[47] Indeed, within a year the Platters would have a number-one hit, their fourth consecutive in the top five, with a remake of "My Prayer," the Ink Spots' 1939 classic.

In the summer of 1957, the *New York Times* ran an editorial calling attention to what the editors termed "an encouraging new trend." The presence of sweet records alongside rockers indicated that "a crack already has appeared in the wailing wall of rock and roll," offering a hope that its "alleged tunes" would before long "be elbowed aside" and a measure of "sanity" restored to pop music. "The sounds known as rock and roll . . . will soon become faint, to be replaced by more melodious fare," went the prediction, offering a familiar prescription of "slow-tempo tunes containing an element current 'pops' so sorely lack—romance, accompanied by lyrics that are sung and not shouted."[48]

Billboard, however, cautioned readers that "altho the consumer press has been loudly proclaiming the comeback of sweet music in the pop field and simultaneously rejoicing over the 'demise' of rock and roll," a look at the charts for the first eight months of the year proved that the "jubilation" was "largely wishful thinking."[49] By fall, it was clear that the year's "most significant and best selling records were those in the 'music with a beat' category—the rockabilly and the rocker."[50] Presley led the way with "All Shook Up," "Jailhouse Rock," "(Let Me Be) Your Teddy Bear," and "Too Much." Buddy Holly's "That'll Be the Day" and "Peggy Sue," Chuck Berry's "School Day," Jerry Lee Lewis's "Whole Lot of Shakin' Going On," the Everly Brothers' "Wake Up Little Susie" and "Bye Bye Love," and Fats Domino's "Blueberry Hill" were also among the year's overall top-forty hits. If Patti Page was still able to hold her own among the youngsters' rhythm tracks, engaging a large public with "Old Cape Cod," that only illustrated the diversity of the new mainstream.

Yet at year's end, amplifying his paper's prognosis on rock and roll's future, Wilson speculated that "for the shattered ears of oppressed American parents, surcease may be at hand."

> Teenage taste, which determines the immediate twists and turns of our popular music, may just be moving away from the strident, frenetic sounds which have blared out of radios, phonographs and jukeboxes with increasingly cacophonic violence over the past decade. The new sound that lures the young ear is one familiar and even nostalgic to captive parental audiences: a simple, straightforward melodic ballad.[51]

He cited as evidence such covers as the Dominoes' "Star Dust" and Pat Boone's "Love Letters in the Sand," songs that had first caught the public fancy in 1931.

In truth, ballads had never gone out of fashion; they were part of rock and roll, complementing the revelrous shout with the dreamy sublime. Presley's "Love Me Tender" spent five weeks at number one in the fall of 1956. The Platters had three of 1956's biggest hits, all ballads. Boone also had three of the year's top hits with his earnest, deliberate versions of Ivory Joe Hunter's "I Almost Lost My Mind" and the Flamingos' "I'll Be Home," and the string-laden "Friendly Persuasion (Thee I Love)," repertory that suited him far better than the Fats Domino and Little Richard songs he covered so clumsily. And through the heart of the emergent rock and roll idiom ran a stream of doo-wop ballads stretching back to 1948 and the Orioles' "It's Too Soon to Know." If one tried, as many did, to read 1957 as the end of rock and roll, ballads, or, more generally, sweet music, offered scant evidence to support the idea. There was no such suggestion, for instance, in the fact that Debbie Reynolds's "Tammy" was one of the year's biggest records or that Johnny Mathis broke out with a series of five hits. The youth market had always shown a fondness for sentiment, and slow dancing to romantic ballads meant touching, to which few teenagers of any era would object.

Moreover, Tin Pan Alley songs did not disappear with the rock and roll surge; they simply took their place in a far richer mosaic, often transformed by the company they were now forced to keep. The second-biggest-selling record in 1958 was Tommy Edwards's "It's All in the Game," which was a remake of a hit he had in 1951. The original was performed with the rubato phrasing and deemphasized pulse characteristic of many contemporary discs. The instrumental accompaniment featured an orchestral palette of strings and winds. In the 1958 version, Edwards sang with more emphatic, beat-directed accents while piano triplets pulsed continuously and a snare backbeat kept steady time. The production simply assumed some of the stylistic trappings of rock and roll. It was persuasive evidence of Ackerman's contention that rock and roll had become "so firmly integrated with the pop medium that backings on even so-called quality songs are scored with distinctive rock and roll figures," a practice that had become "so common as to go completely unnoticed."[52]

Many vocal groups featured covers of pop standards in their shows and on records. In 1950, on their Sunday morning radio show on WVEC in Hampton, Virginia, the Five Keys performed Billy Hill's "The Glory of Love," a 1936 hit for Benny Goodman, as their opening and closing theme song. In between they sang a mix of R&B, gospel, and pop.[53] The next year they recorded the song for Aladdin, scoring a number-one hit with R&B audiences. Billy Ward and his Dominoes, famous for landing the risqué "Sixty Minute Man" briefly on the pop chart in 1951, also recorded a number of pop covers with a series of lead tenors, including Clyde McPhatter on "Harbor Lights" (1950), "These Foolish Things Remind Me of You" (1951), and "When the Swallows Come Back to Capistrano" (1952); Jackie Wilson on "Rags to Riches" (1953); and Gene Mumford on "Star Dust" and "Deep Purple" (1957). The Platters would follow their successful revival of "My Prayer" with recordings of "Smoke Gets in Your Eyes," "Harbor Lights," "Red Sails in the Sunset," "To Each His Own," "If I Didn't Care," and "I'll Never Smile Again," all top-forty hits.

Solo performers, too, tapped into the traditional vein. A 1956 *Billboard* article trumpeted the windfall for publishers, anticipating that "some rock and roll versions of standards . . . figure to bring in a lot more performance loot on the oldies than the pubbers could have ever expected from most other sources."[54] Fats Domino had hits that year with "Blueberry Hill," "When My Dreamboat Comes Home," and "My Blue Heaven," first popularized by Glenn Miller (1940), Guy Lombardo (1937), and Paul Whiteman (1927). Mindful of the successful Fats Domino connection, Art Rupe had Little Richard reach even farther back in the song bag to record "Baby Face" (1926) and "By the Light of the Silvery Moon" (1910), which were included on his second album "especially for his fans' parents," the liner notes said, "who still may not 'dig the beat.'"[55] Presley recorded "Harbor Lights" and "Blue Moon" during his time at Sun. Sam Phillips, believing that young tastes were turning away from such material, decided not to issue the recordings, but Presley was plainly at home with the songs, delivering them, as he did the blues and country songs, with an innocent panache and utter conviction.

In the revisionist rock and roll covers of pop standards, the music showed a reach both audacious and poignant. For a music of limited scope and amateur execution aimed at the nation's youngest pop audience, purveyed in the hope of quick and temporary profit, what could such dabblings mean? Clearly, the new music, in the minds of its performers, was not a thing apart from pop tradition; it was the playful, exuberant expression of a new generation filtering its pop legacy through an unconstrained musical adolescence. The recordings remade the songs of Tin Pan Alley, no less than R&B and country songs, as rock and roll. On records such as the Flamingos' curiously modernist adaptation of "I Only Have Eyes for You," a song from the 1934 Busby Berkeley musical *Dames*, or the Marcels' zany overhaul of "Blue Moon," the creative revisions of the old songs were so thorough that they were absorbed into a new existence. The songs became components of larger entities—records—which were in themselves a new kind of artwork. As it developed its own distinct language, rock and roll steadily reinterpreted the expanse of American popular music for all to hear.

· 4 ·

In 1972, the composer and songwriter Alec Wilder published a loving paean to Tin Pan Alley songwriting—*American Popular Song: The Great Innovators, 1900–1955*.[56] The cutoff year coincided pointedly with the rise of rock and roll, and Wilder intended no second volume for, in his mind, "after that the amateurs took over."[57] While the book contained no mention of Wilder's own music, it was something of an aesthetic testament. On one hand, it was a serious appraisal of the sort of popular music that Wilder had always felt should be accorded the same prestige as the classical canon. He wrote about the songs of Gershwin, Kern, and Rodgers "as if they were Schubert lieder," one reviewer wrote.[58] But the book was also a statement of Wilder's resistance to a transformed pop landscape devoid, he thought, of the "old virtues" of "work, excellence, self-discipline, perspective, wit, fun, joy, wonderment." As far as he was concerned, songwriting exemplifying such traits had been missing from the hit parade since the mid-1950s and the chief reason was a lack of professionalism. "My particular complaint about rock," he wrote soon after his book's publication, "is its continuing amateur point of view."[59]

A different perspective might easily have seen analogous evidence of Wilder's "old virtues" in the new songs, but in matters of style and execution they clearly represented a different set of aesthetic principles. With few exceptions, hit songs of the late fifties were far less sophisticated than those of Tin Pan Alley. The lyrics rarely dabbled in the nuanced word-play, clever rhymes, and layered meaning of the finest high-pop standards. (Chuck Berry was the conspicuous exception proving the rule.) Melodic design and harmonic texture were often stripped to the bone. In practically every dimension, a song's content was spare. If their first public appearance had been in the form of sheet music, as in previous decades, the songs may have offered little enticement. But the situation had become reversed. Songs were now released initially as records, and only with a record's success would a sheet music version come to market. "The thing to remember," Jerry Leiber stressed, "is you're not writing a song but a record," which is why Leiber and Stoller took up record production as a natural extension of their writing.[60] When they wrote for Presley, Leiber recalled, they "had the sound of his voice in mind."[61] In this new era of pop music, a song was akin to a film's screenplay; it was a starting point for record production.

More than ever before, audiences identified songs with particular recorded versions—the records *were* the songs. The fact that an enormous amount of rock and roll song material used one of two basic harmonic patterns—blues variants and the doo-wop sequence I–vi–IV(or ii)–V—without losing the audience's interest indicated the degree to which the recording as a whole was the object of listeners' delight. If the songs in themselves lacked substance in comparison with those of the Tin Pan Alley masters, the records presented a total experience more complex than any song sheet ever could. In doo-wop, as the critic Greil Marcus has phrased it, "the feeling put into the words overwhelmed the words themselves, until the highest moments were often those when the soaring, breaking voices cut loose from words altogether."[62] Similarly, if the chorus of Little Richard's "Tutti Frutti" was nothing more than nonsense set to a common twelve-bar blues pattern, his manic rant made the song appear thrillingly transgressive, a sense entirely lost, for example, in Pat Boone's straightlaced cover version. A twelve-bar blues pattern and a few words were all Richard and his collaborators needed to craft some canonic classics—"Good Golly Miss Molly," "Lucille," "Long Tall Sally"—because his recorded vocal persona completed the songs.

The composite nature of songs as recordings brought a change not only in songwriting principles and techniques but in the industry's production and marketing structure as record companies surpassed publishers in the business of bringing music to the public. "In the old days," said Tin Pan Alley veteran Johnny Green, writer of such standards as "Body and Soul," "I Cover the Waterfront," and "Out of Nowhere," "the impetus for making a successful popular song came first from the composer and lyricist, through the publisher, and finally to the performer. . . . Nowadays, it's the performing artist who makes or breaks a song and who is the initiator of all activity, the funnel through which the song reaches the public."[63]

Yet if the words and music package was less autonomous than before, the new songwriting was not a repudiation of the old. Nor was it a matter of exclusion or reaction. Rock and roll songs happily bore vestigial features of their source influences—R&B, country, pop ballad, novelty, blues, and so forth—but in the hands of rock and roll songwriters the sources were deconstructed and their elements recycled as pastiches of found objects. If stylistic integrity was sacrificed, vitality and freshness were at the fore, as was an implicit understanding that a song need only suggest an expressive direction. For ultimately a rock and roll song's spirit and sense relied on the material form of a sound recording. Rock and roll songwriting was a reimagining of pop song style that recognized the transformative effects of both crossover and recording technology. That such songs as Chuck Berry's "Maybellene," "Thirty Days," and "You Can't Catch Me," for example, were amalgams of country and R&B became apparent only in the form of their recordings. Records conveyed emotion, style, sound, and persona, all of which enhanced the songs. A lead sheet reduction, formerly the standard unit of pop song commerce, could not possibly represent all that the songs truly were.

Tin Pan Alley's division of labor often pertained to rock and roll as well, with songwriters and performers playing distinct roles. Such songwriters as Jerry Leiber and Mike Stoller, Otis Blackwell, Buck Ram, Felice and Boudleaux Bryant, Willie Dixon, and Jesse Stone worked behind the scenes providing performers a wealth of song material in the new style. But there was also a trend toward the writer-performer commonly found in country and R&B, songwriters whose songs were tailored to their own performance style. These included Little Richard, Buddy Holly, Eddie Cochran, Carl Perkins, and the most prolific hit maker of the early writer/performers, Chuck Berry. Among Berry's songwriting strengths were his timely lyric wit, which spoke directly to the new audience, a knack for reinventing blues as pop, and an awareness that the sense of a song lay, ultimately, in its manifest expression. Before he made his first record, he already understood the effect of singing songs "in their customary tongues": "sentimental songs with distinct diction," "downhome blues in the language they came from, Negro dialect," and country songs with a "stressed . . . diction so that it was harder and whiter."[64] This sense of aural language infused his songwriting with a sonic dimension perfectly in accord with a "songs as records" mentality. Berry grasped intuitively that rock and roll songs contained four interrelated dimensions: words, music, performance, and sound. Sound recording was a medium not only for turning music into a commodity but for implementing a new conception of songwriting.

Most of Berry's hits used some sort of blues variant in their harmonic sequence, yet their sound was nothing like his deep blues label-mates at Chess—men such as Howlin' Wolf, Muddy Waters, or John Lee Hooker. Berry mixed in melodic and rhythmic elements from pop and country to leaven the blues effect, which gave the songs a broader base of appeal. Songs such as "Maybellene," "Carol," and "Rock and Roll Music" used a blues chorus as a recurring refrain, periodically punctuating the song's narrative. Each song, however, employed the technique in a different way. "Maybellene" used the conventional blues lyric structure (AAB), as well as the twelve-bar harmonic progression, juxtaposing the chorus with verses that unfolded over a prolonged tonic chord. "Carol" used a blues progression for the verses, as well as the chorus (although the verses were elongated from twelve to twenty-four bars), but dispensed with the AAB lyric structure. "Rock and Roll Music" also omitted the AAB configuration, but, in contrast to the other two songs, the verses deviated into a more lyrical pop style, abandoning the blues altogether and creating a stylistic juxtaposition that sharpened the song's message. Even where the blues affinities occurred in all three songs, however, the melodies so avoided the flatted third over the tonic chord in favor of the major third that the blues effect was light-handed, as it was on "Roll Over Beethoven," "Sweet Little Rock and Roller," "Reelin' and Rockin'," and all the rest of Berry's transformations of blues into rock and roll.[65] (Contrast these songs with Berry's more traditional club-blues style on "Wee Wee Hours.") For Berry, the blues was an endlessly flexible trope to be shaped according to the songwriter's whim.

Although he was a thirty-year-old father and husband when he became a rock and roll star, Berry's lyrics, which dipped into memories of his own high school years, engaged central themes of youth culture with cleverness, metaphor, and wry humor. In such songs as "School Day," "Roll Over Beethoven," "Sweet Little Sixteen," and "Rock and Roll Music," he described features of teenage identity in rock and roll terms. "School Day" traced the teenager's day from the drudgery of the classroom to rock and roll transcendence before the jukebox. "Roll Over Beethoven" celebrated the thrill of irreverent iconoclasm and the power of the new to throw over the hallowed past. "Rock and Roll Music" was an anthemic rallying cry. It shouted that in the musical universe rock and roll was the fundamental reality.

But Berry's songwriting went beyond teenage life. Drawing his images from the nation's places, stories, and customs, he crafted songs with an encompassing American resonance. "Did I miss the skyscrapers, did I miss the long freeway / From the coast of California to the coast of the Delaware Bay," he sang in "Back in the USA," interweaving symbols of American modernity with place-names spanning the continent. In "Promised Land," he sang of a coast-to-coast odyssey using city names to pace the narrative—Norfolk, Raleigh, Charlotte, Rock Hill, Atlanta, Birmingham, New Orleans, Houston, Albuquerque, Los Angeles. Traveling by bus, train, and jet plane, he headed for the promised land of California, picking up a silk suit and some money and dining on "T-bone steak a-la-carte-y," along the way. One of Berry's best satirical tunes, "Too Much Monkey Business," expressed the "botheration" of everyday working folk by presenting a series of deft sketches of daily indignities beyond the protagonist's control. The only relief from the monkey business was music, the blues refrain that answered each vignette. "They're really rocking in Boston," he sang in "Sweet Little Sixteen," as well as Pittsburgh, Texas, San Francisco, Saint Louis, New Orleans, and Philadelphia. Berry invented a rock and roll mythology that drew in the entire nation, a prescient assertion that rock and roll was not only here to stay but was on its way to claiming a central place in the American psyche.

Perhaps Berry's most enduring classic is "Johnny B. Goode," in which he imagined a founding myth for the new music with a guitar player as its rustic hero. Johnny was "a country boy" from the deep woods of Louisiana. His home—rock and roll's primeval home—was at once remote yet close to America's musical crucible, New Orleans. Without much schooling but with a magnetic musical gift and a blue-collar work ethic, Johnny practiced down "by the railroad track," where passersby stopped and commented "oh my but that little country boy could play." His mother forecast his fate: when he grew up, she told him, he would lead a band and draw people "from miles around." Stardom was not guaranteed—"*maybe*" his name would "be in lights," she said—but the mere possibility fueled an incandescent desire and ambition. The song, wrote Ed Ward, one of the first generation of rock historians, was "the story of rock and roll Everykid" and, of course, a fictionalized autobiography.[66] In casting the electric guitar in a starring role, Berry not only identified himself as Johnny but also enshrined the instrument as rock and roll's enduring symbol of individual expression. More than most early rock and roll, Berry's songs had a depth of narrative that gave them a strong presence independent of their original recordings, which is why they became core rock and roll repertory covered by bar bands and star performers alike. Still it was the records that the students learned from. And on Chuck Berry records, the guitar—its sound and its riffs—was as integral to the songs as the words and melodies.

Another type of rock and roll song presented a marked contrast with up-tempo rhythm numbers like Berry's and signaled that the boundaries of rock and roll would not be easily inscribed. The emergent genre known as the "rockaballad," which *Billboard* reported as "one of the most recorded types of pop tunes" in 1958, showcased the music's quieter side with a melodic lyricism and ethereal introspection that made strong impressions on both the pop and R&B charts.[67] Records such as the Teddy Bears' "To Know Him Is to Love Him," the Fleetwoods' "Come Softly to Me," Ritchie Valens's "Donna," and the Everly Brothers' "All I Have to Do Is Dream" emanated a teenaged pathos whose wide appeal effectively established a subgenre of record production as well as a song type. Such records varied widely in many of their features but had in common a hushed quality, an all-permeating softness of diction, phrasing, and vocal timbre. The recordings effectively enhanced the intimacy of the performances, placing the singer at the ear of the listener. The textural settings complemented the emotional tone set by the vocals with an enveloping sonic aura that enriched the records' impressionistic quality.

"To Know Him Is to Love Him" expressed ardent, unrequited longing in the cadences of a nursery rhyme ("To know, know, know him / Is to love, love, love him"). Eighteen-year-old Phil Spector wrote the song and produced the record, his first. The artful use of reverb imparted both a sense of airiness and an indistinct haze to the instrumental texture, itself a gentle, soft-focus murmur punctuated by a prominent snare—precisely the concept Spector would eventually develop into his "wall of sound." The Fleetwoods' song, written by group members Gary Troxel, Gretchen Christopher, and Barbara Ellis, was shot through with nonsense syllables, a sort of baby talk set in counterpoint to the come-hither lyrics. Male and female voices took turns at the lead, each with a passionless, inscrutable cool. The textural interplay, which contrasted doubled women's voices with a solo male voice, was suggestive, though of what was entirely up to the listener. Accompanied by a nylon-string (i.e., classical) guitar obbligato, the voices' understated erotic plea held a mix of eeriness and poignancy.

"Donna" was seventeen-year-old Ritchie Valens's mournful tale of heartbreak and loss, whose inward focus was reinforced by the record's subdued, murky texture. There was a strange contrast between the deep background with its submerged piano triplets and the foreground electric guitar fragments. Valens's lead guitar was the only instrumental part that stood out clearly, and its too jaunty replies to the voice's sad phrases seem out of place yet touching for failing to realize it. Like the song's protagonist, the guitar (Valens's other "voice") seems a bit lost.

The Everlys' "All I Have to Do Is Dream," was written by Boudleaux Bryant who, usually in collaboration with his wife Felice, wrote many of their early hits. The Bryants were successful country songwriters who had written a string of hits, beginning with Little Jimmy Dickens's "Country Boy" in 1949. Crossover versions of their songs were also recorded in the early fifties by such pop performers as Frankie Laine ("Hey Joe!") and Tony Bennett ("Have a Good Time"). With such a background, they were an unlikely pair to contribute substantially to the early rock and roll canon, but, like Leiber and Stoller, they learned to write songs with records in mind. They wrote "song after song," Boudleaux recalled, "which was tailored directly for the Everlys' harmony," the brothers' unique vocal blend cultivated since childhood. "The song had to have certain ingredients like the harmonies, Don's guitar intro and of course the words of the song had to be aimed at the young record buyers."[68] On "All I Have to Do Is Dream," the song's mix of erotic yearning and wistful fantasy was evoked in the brothers' hushed harmonies and watery guitar tremolo. The tone was, once again, reflective and introspective, and the record's soft moodiness proved hugely popular with a diverse young audience; it was the number-one record on the pop, country, and R&B charts in the spring of 1958.

Each of the songs on these records spoke of some aspect of romantic love in all its uncertainty, tenuousness, and vulnerability, classic themes of the sentimental love ballad. The rockaballad was another of rock and roll's revisionist appropriations, tapping a traditional pop genre to produce a novel result. With their performances and sonic treatment complementing lyrics and music as elements of "song," these records showed that such a conception of songwriting could transform virtually any genre or stylistic tradition. Merely by incorporating sound recording in the creative process, writing in sound rather than notation, songwriters could turn almost anything into rock and roll.

Buddy Holly adopted this new songwriting mode to produce the most stylistically varied body of original recordings of any late-fifties writer/performer, with up-tempo rockers such as "That'll Be the Day" and "Not Fade Away" contrasting with such sweet pop numbers as "Everyday" and "Words of Love." Some were sonically brash, others subdued. Some featured energetic performances, others were gentle, caressing. Some were paradigm examples of rock and roll instrumentation, others used such unlikely rock and roll sounds as celesta and harp. Holly made most of his records at Norman Petty's studio in Clovis, New Mexico, over an eighteen-month span beginning in February 1957, an environment perfectly suited to creative record production. Mindful that "creativity does not come by the hour," Petty ran a flexible shop. "We would just work as inspiration hit all of us," he recalled, which suited Holly's inclination toward intuitive experimentation.[69]

On August 15, 1958, six months before his death, Holly married Maria Elena Santiago, and the two took up residence in New York, her home city. The rockabilly pop star from West Texas now made New York his creative base, recording at Decca's Pythian Temple. The change of scene could hardly have been more pronounced, but it suited Holly's expanding aspirations. "I'd prefer singing . . . something a little more quieter," he had told Canadian deejay Red Robinson in the fall of 1957, speculating on the future of rock and roll and his own plans.[70] On October 21, 1958, under the direction of Brunswick-Coral A&R head Dick Jacobs, Holly joined a group of studio musicians to record Paul Anka's "It Doesn't Matter Anymore," Petty's "Moondreams," the Bryants' "Raining in My Heart," and his own rockaballad, "True Love Ways," written for his bride. The collaboration between Holly and Jacobs—like Ram and the Platters or Gabler and the Comets—merged the sensibilities and techniques of old hand and newcomer. The recordings, which would be Holly's last in a commercial studio, featured Jacobs's arrangements scored for an eighteen-piece studio orchestra laden with exotica—strings, harp, and Abraham "Boomie" Richman's buttery tenor saxophone. (Earlier, Richman had played in both Tommy Dorsey's and Benny Goodman's bands.) The only apparent rock and roll connection was Holly's voice and his characteristic, though here considerably less mannered, performance style.

"True Love Ways," which like so many rockaballads would soon see revival with the groups of the British invasion, had an especially lush, schmaltzy treatment redolent of adult easy listening. Its harp glissandi and sighing strings were reminiscent of Doris Day's "Secret Love," a number-one hit in 1954. The strings answered Holly's phrases in a tender commentary, which turned faintly exotic at the song's chromatic bridge, a *Scheherazade* moment in rockabilly history. In the song's second A-section, the strings fell to a hushed tremolo as the saxophone took up the responses in gentle, dreamy jazz phrases perfectly suited to the rockaballad aesthetic but stylistically distant from rock and roll saxology. There was a steady beat articulated by an acoustic guitar but no drums. With no big beat and no exuberant shouts, no piano triplets or boogie bass line or electric guitar or honking saxophone, the record seemed to lack the rock and roll basics. Yet in Holly's voice were the rocking echoes of "Peggy Sue," "Oh Boy," and "Rave On." His rock and roll persona was well established in the popular consciousness, and wherever his voice turned up its sound, married with the public's associations, called forth a sonic history.

Because the music was so new, and its audience so unpredictable, there was no telling whether such a record was rock and roll or a harbinger of the much awaited return to good music. But in fact the record was simply another example of the music's indiscriminate cast and, for future historians, a case study of rock and roll as process. As his stylistic horizon broadened, Holly turned to the sounds of pop's grand tradition as a matter of curiosity and fascination. In this way, he was like rock and roll itself, expanding his musical universe by absorbing influences not to achieve fluency in other idioms but, rather, with the conviction that everything was in play. Every sound might be acquired in some form and used to make something new. He bought a used Ampex tape recorder from Petty and took it to New York, where it sat in the living room of the couple's Greenwich Village apartment. Holly used the machine like a sketchbook, a rock and roll singer-songwriter composing his songs as sound. According to biographer Philip Norman, Holly's aspirations in the last months of his life included recording jazz and classical music, idioms he was only beginning to absorb. He also envisioned collaborations with Ray Charles and Mahalia Jackson, a Cajun project, and an album of songs from South America that he would sing in Spanish. It is unlikely that Holly imagined any of these plans to involve years of learning new techniques and rhetorics. As with "True Love Ways," he would simply filter the influences through his own musical consciousness and instinctively meld them in his own creative imagination.

· 5 ·

The irony of "Rock and Roll Waltz" turned out to be historical as well as musical. For, although the record bore no trace of rock and roll, it kicked off the music's watershed year. Rock and roll, *Billboard* reported, was "the most important artist and repertoire trend during 1956." Despite "numerous wishful predictions and reports of its 'grossly exaggerated' importance and early demise," both from within the industry and from adult society at large, the music had in fact flourished and developed an imposing presence in the pop mainstream.[71] *Melody Maker* concurred, reporting that, although it was "one of the most terrifying things ever to have happened to popular music," rock and roll was the "influence of the year."[72] Among the evidence for such claims was the emergence of new stars with staying power. Early in the year, *Billboard*'s Ren Grevatt had pointed out that while young R&B stars had often proven to be one-hit wonders, there was a growing tendency to multihit longevity. "The awareness of the vast and constantly growing teen-age market for rhythm and blues material," he wrote, "has made artist and repertoire men sit up and take notice via the exercising of great care in marrying good material to good artists. The result is a growing group of individual artists and groups who have clicked again and again with hit disks," including the Platters, Chuck Berry, and Fats Domino, all continuing their successes from 1955.[73] Along with the new R&B stars, the Comets, Crew Cuts, and Pat Boone also made return trips to the chart's upper reaches.

The most powerful indication of a new trend, however, was the year's relentless stream of records by both R&B and country newcomers that made the pop charts, weekly proof, wrote Ackerman, that "hard and fast cleavages between the country and western, pop and rhythm and blues fields are rapidly breaking down."[74] Johnny Cash, Little Willie John, Clyde McPhatter (solo for the first time), the Cadillacs, and the Five Satins all had top-thirty hits. Frankie Lymon and the Teenagers, Gene Vincent and His Blue Caps, Bill Doggett, Sanford Clark, Little Richard, and Carl Perkins made the top ten. Most came into the instant limelight as if from nowhere. At the center of it all was Presley, whose spectacular record sales and "outstanding example of the growing trend toward 'integration' of chart categories" amounted to "something of a trend all by himself."[75] His first pop hit, "Heartbreak Hotel," entered the top forty in March on its way to number one. By year's end, with nine further top-forty singles, four of which reached number one, he had sold at least ten million records, appeared on national television thirteen times, and starred in a feature film. All in all, it was a stunning and widely decried assault on the pop market. The rock and roll naysayers got a bit of a boost as the short-lived calypso craze gained momentum at year's end, but as 1957 unfolded it became clear that instead of waning the new music was exerting an influence that threatened to alter the mainstream permanently.

The explosion of rock and roll, however, was only part of the story in 1956. It was also "a sock 'comeback' year, with such veteran artists as Bing Crosby, Vic Damone, Johnnie Ray, Guy Mitchell and . . . Frankie Laine showing up among the most-played platter fraternity for the first time in several years." Deejays preferring such fare had shown a resurgent influence, promoting the records through "concentrated spinning." Again Mitch Miller was in the thick of things: Damone, Ray, Mitchell, and Laine were all Columbia artists under Miller's direction, as were Doris Day, the Four Lads, and Don Cherry, also among the year's top sellers.[76] Other pop hit makers to continue their long-running success were Patti Page (Mercury), Perry Como (RCA Victor), Dean Martin (Capitol), and Theresa Brewer (Coral). Throw in the instrumental hits of Nelson Riddle ("Lisbon Antigua"), Les Baxter ("The Poor People of Paris"), Hugo Winterhalter ("Canadian Sunset"), and Morris Stoloff ("Moonglow and Theme from *Picnic*") and such curiosities as Jim Lowe's "The Green Door," Gogi Grant's "The Wayward Wind," and Lonnie Donegan's "Rock Island Line" skiffle record and the picture was mixed indeed. The year showed not only that record sales seemed to have no upward limit, with "more good records . . . being turned out by more labels than ever," but that the "public's taste" had further "broadened in scope."[77]

Bill Simon, who had written on the American pop and jazz scene for many years, gave a roundup of the year's hit records that broke the mainstream pop chart into categories of the kind that usually merited charts of their own. There was "rockabilly," which referred to "country talent in the pop play area" (Presley, Perkins), the "pure area of rhythm and blues" (Little Richard, Frankie Lymon and the Teenagers), and "rock and roll, which now is identified virtually as a distinct idiom." The latter referred to such cover acts as the Diamonds, as well as original songs with arrangements tinged with traces of R&B; Simon's examples were Gloria Mann's "Teen Age Prayer" and Bobby Scott's "Chain Gang."[78] The Mann disc featured a lyric of teenage erotic longing set to an overstuffed arrangement: heavy pulsing triplets played by a brass and reed section, occasional solo French horn, piano triplets, a bit of electric guitar, and tubular bells ringing out the I–vi–ii–V progression—a Milleresque concoction of genre-bending artifice. Finally, Simon included pop singers of the old guard, songs from films, and "the occasional instrumental," which ranged from Winterhalter to Bill Doggett. It added up, in Simon's estimation, to a "fresh, vital, interesting and unpredictable" record business.[79]

In the spring of 1957, Ackerman wrote a summary overview of the churning pop scene proceeding from a heady assessment that "the diversity of current domestic repertoire far exceeds any other period within the memory of the disk and music publishing business." Commercial popular music had "never been . . . so quick to reflect grass roots influences" nor "so free of control by any one group." It had "burst all bounds of geography," and its "varied repertoire" represented several "broad streams" of musical practice.

(1) Pop material of the traditional Brill Building type; (2) pop material as affected by rhythm and blues and its modification, rock and roll; (3) pop

as affected by country and western. (4) Country music in its various forms, including so-called traditional country, country in its rockabilly manifestations, as indicated by the throbbing country blues of material with typical guitar and bass backing, country as influenced by pop, noticeable in addition of choral groups to string backgrounds; (5) folk and folk-flavored material, of varying degrees of authenticity, and much of it originally derived from non-American roots, such as the present calypso trend.

Yet, while Ackerman's lucid musicological analysis painted a picture of near rampant hybridity, the idea, he cautioned, "that the musical categories of pop, country and rhythm and blues are merging" and that "once-clear boundaries are disappearing" was a "bromidic observation," a distorting "oversimplification." While he himself had several times noted such a blurring of boundaries, he now sought to refine his analysis. Despite pop music's drift to the polyglot, he pointed out that the established idioms had "not yet lost their identity" but, rather, contributed a wealth of characteristic sounds to the pop arena. In trying to reconcile the idiomatic and the hybrid, Ackerman was attempting to get his mind around the musical economy's complex crosswinds, to account for the syncretic influence of consumers as well as producers. Heterogeneity in the pop mainstream, he observed, was not simply a matter of hybrid production. Even records bearing no trace of style mixture might participate in the reshaping of the mainstream if consumers so decided: "The pop buyer purchases country records, therefore c.&w. has become pop. Ditto rhythm and blues."[80]

Ackerman articulated one of the era's persistent themes, which amounted to an ongoing puzzle for record men. Because musical style was tied increasingly to market whims, producers and consumers responded to one another in a continuous push and pull that made for unremitting volatility. The uncertainty, *Variety* reported, had led to an "outpouring of pop tunes of all categories," which in 1957 was "reaching avalanche proportions." A "flood of new names" had become "an integral facet of the current music biz in which anything and anyone can hit it big." Record firms employed a " 'buckshot method' of releases where a lot of disks are thrown on the market with the hope that one or a couple may hit."[81] *Billboard,* too, found the "buckshot" metaphor useful, for it "mirror[ed] the fact that so many pop best sellers continue[d] to come out of left field."[82]

If in 1955 there was "no masterminding the music business," as *Variety* phrased it, by the end of 1958 the field was more volatile than ever, although rock and roll was by then a grudgingly accepted fact. ("For two years," *Time* reported, "lovers of peace, quiet and a less epileptic kind of minstrelsy have waited for Elvis Presley and the adenoidal art form, rock 'n' roll, to fade. But knowledgeable disk jockeys and trade bulletins offer such purists little hope.")[83] In response to a potential musicians' strike, there was talk of stockpiling recordings for future release, as record firms had done during previous work stoppages. As it turned out, there was no strike, but the prospect moved Ren Grevatt to speculate on how one might predict even the immediate future in audience taste. "How do you know what today's market is going to be buying next week, let alone next month?" he asked. To make the case, he ticked off some of the year's top hits: "'Volare,' a strictly Italian tune by Domenico Modugno . . . the interesting and offbeat Civil War period folk song, 'Tom Dooley,' by the Kingston Trio, a group which has a strongly Hawaiian background . . . Cozy Cole, veteran swing era drummer . . . with his first number one hit 'Topsy II,' . . . the Teddy Bears' recording of 'To Know Him Is to Love Him,' a rockaballad . . . the cha cha influence, with Perez Prado's 'Patricia,'" and finally Tommy Edwards's "It's All in the Game," a remake of his own 1951 hit, "a fact which in itself brought about a trend."

If the list were longer, it would also have included four novelties—"The Purple People Eater," "The Chipmunk Song," "Witch Doctor," and "Short Shorts"—and records by Andy Williams, Frank Sinatra, and Perry Como, alongside Elvis Presley, the Platters, the Everly Brothers, Ricky Nelson, the Coasters, and Chuck Berry. The only thread that seemed to link most popular tunes of the day was the presence of a steady beat, which produced oddities like the "rock-a-cha cha, rock-calypso, and some rock-a-hula." "It is possible in this crazy business," Grevatt concluded, tongue-in-cheek yet genuinely baffled, "that we will see such things as rock-a-folkas, rock-a-polkas, rock-a-sambas and maybe even rock-a-Indian war dances. Who knows?"[84]

At midyear, another *Billboard* reporter noted that "the fickleness of the American record buyer" and the "constant shifting of tastes" had opened the way for dozens of performers to make the pop charts for the first time, many with their first records. Some, like Danny and the Juniors' "At the Hop" and the Champs' "Tequila," went straight to number one on their maiden outing. There was also a new wave of one-hit performers and a series of trends that rose rapidly and faded just as quickly.[85] And amid the flood of weekly record releases there appeared what to Grevatt seemed a "curious paradox": "more new labels . . . introducing more new artists performing more new tunes than ever before" vying for top chart positions with "old line artists and even older songs."[86]

Adding to the uncertainty was the question of who was buying the records. Conventional wisdom in the industry held that teenagers accounted for anywhere from 75 to 90 percent of singles sales. But in 1958 *Billboard* teamed up with the New York University School of Retailing to study the question and tallied only 54 percent, with most of the rest purchased by fans between the ages of eighteen and thirty. The groups showed different preferences, with the younger group going for the likes of Jerry Lee Lewis's "High School Confidential" and Link Wray's "Rumble" while the older set preferred such discs as the Platters' "Twilight Time" and Dean Martin's "Return to Me."[87]

The picture painted by these reports was of an accommodating pop mainstream whose broadening style spectrum and varied audience demographic reflected the totality of American popular music as never before. If some establishment pros bemoaned a loss of market share, the news for the industry as a whole was good. "American musical tastes are expanding all the time," *Billboard* reported in the fall of 1957, "and the growth of recorded music . . . is assured."[88] Rock and roll was the quintessential recorded music; its genesis and development were inseparable from records. The pop mainstream had set the stage perfectly for the rise of such a music. It was already in a state of ferment generated by a steady drift away from the swing ethos. Pop records already tended toward fanciful concoction. The boom in record sales had put significant power into the hands of consumers. "The record business has turned America into a musical democracy," marveled the folk song collector Alan Lomax in 1959.[89] During the decade's latter years, thousands of records were released on the nation's soundscape, sending reverberant tremors through a musical economy whose eclectic tone had become its only constant.

SEVEN

New Traditions

He puts them through hours and days of recording to get the two or three minutes he wants. Two or three minutes out of the whole struggle.

—TOM WOLFE ON PHIL SPECTOR

Who knew those songs would live on?

—ELLIE GREENWICH

· 1 ·

On February 3, 1959, Buddy Holly boarded a plane at Mason City Municipal Airport near Clear Lake, Iowa, bound for Fargo, North Dakota, the closest airport to the next night's show in Moorhead, Minnesota. He was in the midst of a three-week package tour billed as the Winter Dance Party, which also included the seventeen-year-old Mexican American Ritchie Valens; nineteen-year-old Italian American Dion DiMucci and his doo-wop group, the Belmonts; and J. P. Richardson, the Chantilly lace–loving Big Bopper, a deejay at KTRM in Beaumont, Texas, on a rock and roll sabbatical. The tour was hectic, twenty-four cities in twenty-three days. The weather was arctic, and the heating system on the tour bus worked only sporadically. Tired and fed up, Holly chartered a single-engine, four-seat, Beech Bonanza aircraft from the Dwyer Flying Service. He and two others would have a warm and relatively quick trip, arrive early, rest up, and do some laundry before the next show.

Waylon Jennings, Holly's bass player, gave up his seat to Richardson, who was running a fever. Valens pestered Tommy Allsup, another member of Holly's band, to give him the remaining seat. After refusing repeatedly, Allsup finally agreed to flip a coin for it. Valens won. The three young stars boarded the plane with the pilot, twenty-one-year-old Roger Peterson, and the plane took off shortly after 1:00 a.m. in light snow. Soon after takeoff, Jim Dwyer, the plane's owner, watched its taillight descend gradually and disappear from view. Attempts to contact the pilot failed, and at 9:35 the next morning the plane's wreckage and the bodies of its occupants were found in a field five miles from the airport. The

Civil Aeronautics Board concluded that the pilot, unfamiliar with the kind of instrument flying the weather conditions demanded, had unwittingly flown the plane into the ground.[1]

Coming in the midst of other turbulent events in the lives of rock and roll's first generation of stars, the accident would become a symbol for the denouement of the music's genesis story. With many of its brightest lights fading from the scene, rock and roll seemed a spent force. Little Richard had abdicated first, in 1957. Then, almost a year before the Clear Lake crash, on March 25, 1958, draftee Elvis Presley was sworn in to the U.S. Army for a two-year tour of service. While RCA Victor still managed to cut some records when Presley was on leave, his meteoric rise was at its apex, and it was unknown how his public would weather his relative absence from the spotlight. By late spring of 1958, Jerry Lee Lewis's "stormy" life—as he called it in his full-page "open letter to the industry" ad in *Billboard*—caught up with him.[2] In May, upon discovery of his marriage to his thirteen-year-old cousin Myra, the British Rank Organization, which owned the theaters on Lewis's twenty-seven-stop U.K. tour, abruptly canceled all his appearances. "He was met by boos and catcalls . . . and British newspapers called him a cradle-snatcher," the Associated Press reported.[3] He returned to Memphis, hoping, he said, to "straighten things out," but, although he charted one more top-thirty hit three years later with a recording of Ray Charles's "What'd I Say," his rock star run was effectively over, his career awaiting rebirth in the country music sphere.[4]

In the summer of 1958, Chuck Berry began a series of run-ins with the police involving young women, which ended with indictments in 1960 on three counts of violating the Mann Act, also known as the White-Slave Traffic Act, and one weapons charge. Berry was acquitted of most of the charges and even in the midst of his legal troubles continued to record. But one of the charges led finally—after trial, successful appeal, and retrial—to a conviction and three-year prison term beginning in 1961. In 1960, Eddie Cochran, another gifted rock and roll singer-songwriter whose records sparkled with freshness even as they invoked a rock and roll pantheon—Berry, Presley, Little Richard, the Coasters, Carl Perkins—was killed in a car accident during a concert tour of the United Kingdom. He was thrown from the car and never regained consciousness. His tour partner, Gene Vincent, suffered injuries in the crash that would afflict him the rest of his life.

On November 21, 1959, New York radio station WABC fired Alan Freed for refusing to file a signed affidavit providing information concerning "acceptance of gratuities in connection with music promotion."[5]

The payola hysteria, spawned by the news that several popular television game shows were rigged, had spread to the music industry, setting off a scramble to avoid the taint of bribery and the resulting legal and commercial sanctions. Freed was still among the biggest names in rock and roll media, with radio, television, movies, and concert promotion all keeping his name before the public. He was also a lightning rod. The previous year he had lost his job at WINS and been indicted for street disturbances attributed (with little evidence) to his Big Beat concert at the Boston Arena on May 3, 1958; the running fracas was described in press accounts as a riot.[6] Freed had long been one of the music's chief apologists and promoters, and he repented neither of rock and roll nor his business dealings. In short, he was the perfect scapegoat.

There were in fact few clean hands in the payola affair. Although ASCAP, for example, tried to use the issue against its long-standing enemy, BMI, it represented publishers that made cozy pay-and-play deals with television producers. Arkansas congressman Oren Harris, who chaired the payola hearings in the House Subcommittee on Legislative Oversight, was found by his own investigator to have a serious conflict of interest given his part ownership of a television station that had received favorable consideration from the FCC. And FCC chairman John C. Doerfer was forced to resign when he was charged with accepting the gift of a Caribbean cruise from a broadcaster who had a matter before the commission. As for the low-level, everyday workings of the music business, making promotional payments of one sort or another was an age-old practice. There was a periodic outcry in the industry, but it was mostly an argument over ethical business practices. There were no federal and very few state laws prohibiting it, and never before had the issues risen to such a level of government involvement. Unluckily for Freed, New York was one of the few states with a law treating such gratuities as commercial bribery.[7] He was indicted in February 1960 and in April faced a grilling from Harris's subcommittee. But for his many young fans the damage had been done the previous fall when, just after his firing from WABC, Freed lost his WNEW television show. After the final airing "his worshipers were awash in bitter tears . . . teen-agers weeping uncontrollably," reported *Life*. "Wailed one, 'Now they're trying to take our father away.'"[8]

With so many key figures out of action by 1960, the charged musical, cultural, and commercial energy unleashed by the big-beat sounds and charismatic stars appeared to be waning. A *Variety* reporter described a "classy comeback" for the music industry, with "the wheel . . . starting to turn in favor of the pro songwriter" and record companies "in full flight from the rock, the roll, the big beat and the teen tunes."[9] In 1961, Freed's original New York platform, WINS, began switching to "the so-called 'good music' format," which the *New York Times* took to be further evidence of "the decline in rock 'n' roll that has been going on for some time."[10] The change was gradual, "with more and more 'pretty' disks worked in between rockers," but by February 1962 it was complete, marked with a sixty-six-hour Sinatra marathon that broadcast over five hundred consecutive Sinatra recordings.[11] The station joined others in New York "switching to 'pretty music' formats," briefly stoking hopes that rock and roll was finally fading from the scene.[12]

The turn of the decade, which a young Peter Guralnick called "the treacle period of the late fifties and early sixties," became the butt of a historiographic cliché that Guralnick admitted had already "grown stale from repetition" when he invoked it in 1971 in his first book, *Feel Like Going Home*.[13] "Elvis in the Army, Buddy Holly dead, Little Richard in the ministry, Jerry Lee Lewis in disgrace and Chuck Berry in jail," he wrote. "[R]ock 'n' roll died. It was over." The idea that rock and roll was over had been circulating from the beginning. In the early spring of 1955, *Variety*, always eager to promote the idea, reported on a poll of teenagers, suggesting that "the popularity of the rock 'n' roll beat in the New York area is slipping."[14] And in the fall of 1956, despite Presley's incandescent arrival, ASCAP president Paul Cunningham expressed a belief that "from this point on, we can expect a revival of good music in the style of the Gershwins, the Kerns and the Rombergs."[15] Yet despite periodic hints that it was just a short-lived fad, rock and roll proved stubbornly durable, mixing it up with the likes of calypso and cha cha, a resurgent Sinatra, and an ever-successful Mitch Miller and ending the decade in a commanding market position.

Guralnick, however, was talking not about commercial success but spirit. The first rock critics and historians were devoted to a particular construct of rock and roll authenticity, by which measure they concluded that rock and roll's essence had in fact died by 1960. What they meant was that the music no longer satisfied their aesthetic needs. "The burst of creation that exploded in the fifties was drying up," Greil Marcus lamented in a 1969 essay. In its place was "the clean, sugary rock 'n' roll of Bobby Vinton and Annette Funicello."[16] Langdon Winner, again invoking the straw figure of Funicello as malign symbol, complained that "all of the elements in the life-support system of rock and roll—rhythm, lyric, melody, instrumentation, spirit, and authenticity—withered and disappeared."[17]

These young writers' assessments represented articles of faith from which grew a body of advocacy criticism that helped to cement rock music's central place in latter-twentieth-century culture. A romantic quest for authentic, even mythic origins set the tone for rock's deeply polemic historiography, typified by Marcus's midseventies landmark *Mystery Train: Images of America in Rock 'n' Roll Music*. But a nonpartisan hearing of the musical evidence reveals the degree to which their opinions were based on an aesthetic exclusivity and a litmus test for authenticity wholly at odds with the musical climate that brought about rock and roll in the first place. It was the decade's messy unpredictability that had unleashed and driven the tides of change. The notion that there was some sort of movement with an authentic core of ideal exemplars was wishful, and the attachment to iconic figures (almost exclusively male) obscured much of the grassroots upheaval.

Worse, conventional wisdom neatened up historical reality to the point of simply ignoring important figures and events, a willful historiographic silencing given that the recorded evidence remained in circulation. In James Miller's otherwise insightful *Flowers in the Dustbin: The Rise of Rock and Roll, 1947–1977*, for example, American music of the early sixties is omitted entirely. Miller, too, was among the first generation of rock critics; he published his first record review in *Rolling Stone* in 1967 and in the late seventies edited the *Rolling Stone Illustrated History of Rock & Roll*. In *Flowers in the Dustbin,* he develops a "tacit critique" of what he calls rock's "essentially romantic narrative" by identifying and exploring the "broader implications" of key historical moments and actors.[18] In the early sixties, his sense of historical significance points Miller across the Atlantic to the Beatles, and the implicit reason is epitomized by his assessment of Presley's style after his release from the army: "If 'Are You Lonesome Tonight' and 'It's Now or Never' were now regarded as rock and roll, one might well wonder what, if anything, distinguished Presley's new music from old-fashioned pop."[19]

Why such an apparent retreat from rock and roll's clamorous side should so circumscribe the historical narrative was summarized in another *Rolling Stone* publication, an ambitious history called *Rock of Ages* published in 1986. In a chapter titled "The Dark Ages," Ed Ward wrote:

> As America sailed into a new decade, rock and roll, the music of hooligans and streetcorner singers, the music of hillbillies who'd listened to too many R&B records, the music of misfits and oddballs, was dead. . . . [R]ock and roll had passed into the mainstream, fast becoming the

province of established corporate interests rather than the renegade visionaries of the past. For a while at least, the music would be in the hands of professionals, who knew what teens wanted and how to sell it to them. These developments might have outraged older rockers, who would hardly recognize the fruits of their creative vision.[20]

Ward insists on a rock and roll bohemianism apart from the music's essentially commercial aspiration, a sort of purity bestowed through an imagined transcendence of music industry lust. But hits, mass sales, are what had always mattered most. Record companies could not survive without hits. Performers had no shot at national exposure and influence without hits. The principle of crossover is based on hits in multiple markets; if a crossover alerts us to a larger set of issues, our first tip comes from sales figures. The very notion of rock and roll—an emergent mass idiom—is unthinkable without hit records. "We lusted for hits," wrote Jerry Wexler. "Hits were the cash flow, the lifeblood, the heavenly ichor—the wherewithal of survival."[21] Nothing in these fundamentals had changed by decade's end. The difference was that the pursuit of hits now meant an ever-evolving musical exploration with few boundaries of style, taste, ethnicity, or class. Pop record making was an improvisation, a day-to-day pursuit of novelty and distinctive sounds. Young record buyers had long bedeviled the record men with quirky, unpredictable tastes that proved consistently broader and more peculiar than most could calculate. But if the promiscuous cohabitation of sublime expression and complete junk on the pop charts was hard to fathom, it was precisely such indiscriminate musical thrill seeking that had injected so much chaotic vitality into fifties pop culture. Still, like Mitch Miller's critics in the early fifties, the young rock critics—struggling to craft an aesthetic narrative whose grandeur might match their deep emotional involvement with the music—relied on an aesthetic value system that disdained pop kitsch and electronic artifice, in effect limiting what counted as true rock and roll.

A couple of key issues, however, were overlooked. First of all, by the standards of transparent sonic representation and stylistic authenticity, *all* rock and roll records were contrivances. They flaunted a bargain with the recording machine and a disregard for boundaries of style or idiom. A certain number of appalling hit records was simply a sign that the process was working properly. And second, nothing had been settled during the years of rock and roll's ascendance. The new music had not yet established a new order. The records forced all of American society to take note, but they were among a range of styles jostling in what remained a fractious musical economy. Rock and roll had not displaced older forms of pop but, rather, had dramatically increased the pace of tendencies afoot since the war. The effects of the postwar volatility, year by year, were exponential; rock and roll was a radical intensification of gathering forces in the music industry and listening public. But no tipping point had yet been reached. It was clear to no one in the late fifties or early sixties that a new era of pop music was dawning, only that things remained in flux. And if some of rock and roll's most important early figures were out of the picture, there were plenty of new faces to carry on.

In their own ways, the styles and sounds of the early sixties were as essential to the foundation of what would follow as Chuck Berry, Elvis Presley, Little Richard, or Fats Domino had been. As the blues and rock historian Robert Palmer put it in his midnineties "unruly history" of the music, "[T]he late fifties/early sixties was in many ways a uniquely rich time for rock and roll, and one that found the music growing in fresh and unexpected directions."[22] True, the traces of blues and country that early critics saw as rock and roll's crucial connections to authentic roots were nearly indiscernible in much early sixties pop. The music was, in a sense, further assimilated into the commercial pop universe, further removed from an identifiable cultural home and an attendant set of style features. But that, too, was evidence of the rock and roll process and ethos at work, embedding influences deeply in contrived creations and showing off a spectacular ability to absorb and transform almost anything musical. The honky-tonk soul of Roy Orbison's "Only the Lonely" was not its most apparent surface feature, yet it haunted the track's deepest reaches. And even when Sam Cooke tossed off a lighthearted confection— "Twistin' the Night Away," say—it had a gospel truth about it. This melding was among the chief fruits of the 1950s musical revolution. If the process produced a good deal of rubbish, it also allowed for constant reinvention and an aesthetic openness that would soon blossom into the century's second great pop music era.

Still, while the decade's general trends—novelty, diversity, artful record production—went forward, there was something about the early sixties that distinguished the period from rock and roll's first flowering. It had the feel of a second act. Many of the new pop performers and producers had either grown up on rock and roll or adopted it as their entry into the music business. Whereas the first generation of rockers was revising long-standing musical traditions, the newer stars revised the revisions; the fads became foundations. The musical trends of the early sixties included the stirrings of Motown, surf music (both instrumental and vocal), girl groups, and a new generation of black male singers who would help to define a new genre, soul: Chuck Jackson, Otis Redding, Solomon Burke, and, most prolifically, James Brown. One trend drew on the Weavers' legacy: the commercial breakthrough of a new wave of folk acts that included Joan Baez; Peter, Paul and Mary; the Limelighters; the Kingston Trio; the Chad Mitchell Trio; and the Village Stompers. The vibrant folk scene would nurture the young musicians who formed many of the post–British invasion American rock bands: the Byrds, Jefferson Airplane, Grateful Dead, Mamas and the Papas, and Lovin' Spoonful.

By 1960, many record men simply accepted a scattershot experimental approach, "latching on to virtually any idea they [could] get their tapes on and turning out a record," which often produced a surprising hit.[23] A "crazy fluidity" pervaded the music business of the late fifties, shown in rapid chart turnover, stylistic diversity, and an ever-growing number of labels accounting for the top hits. In 1958, for example, seventy-two labels placed at least one disc in the top fifty.[24] Most early critical accounts of rock and roll engaged only favored subsets of a broad, sweeping pop music phenomenon. Yet identifying too closely with any particular subset—practically unavoidable for a critic who was also an ardent fan—rendered the whole inscrutable. Much about the pop music scene certainly felt different in 1959 than it had in 1955, but it had been changing all the while, which simply accorded with pop's market dynamics since the war; rapid turnover had become the way of things.

Billboard's Bob Rolontz who, like many of the publication's writers, moved back and forth between working in the record business and reporting on it, reckoned at the end of 1958 that "the great rock and roll wave" that had engulfed the industry over the previous three years was "slowly receding." He cautioned, however, that this did not mean the music was "dead or even dying" but, rather, "moving closer to pop in style and content." At the same time, pop was "absorbing the rock and roll beat," with rock and roll "fallout . . . permeating almost all pop hits."[25] It was a concise description of a radically changed soundscape, whose idioms overlapped routinely in a cluttered marketplace denoting aesthetic randomness.

· 2 ·

In 1956, Sam Phillips had steered Roy Orbison away from ballads. "We're at the wrong stage of rock 'n' roll to come out and start croonin' like Dean Martin," he said. "If I put you out singin' some damn ballad, the world will never hear of Roy Orbison again. That's not the tenor of what is going on in the United States of America as far as music and rock 'n' roll are concerned."[26] But by 1959 Phillips's comments on the music industry led *Billboard* to report that even he now believed that the pop singles market was "moving into a period of greater variety in taste," which in his mind meant a reconciliation with the past. The rock and roll beat had brought young people back to dancing after too much unswinging pop balladry in the early fifties, and its impact on pop music, he predicted, would prove permanent. But going forward he foresaw a return of the big dance bands. Rock and roll had served as the catalyst to jump-start a swing resurgence.[27]

If Phillips's swing band prediction was clichéd, an industry fixture since the late forties, it was also an acknowledgment that one of rock and roll's original oracles had no idea where things were headed. (Interestingly, neither of the two radio stations he now owned programmed any rock and roll at all.) At the beginning of 1960, Mitch Miller, following record-breaking sales at Columbia in 1959, predicted that the year "would see more emphasis on quality and professionalism" of the sort exemplified by the records he had produced throughout the decade.[28] While he himself had once been "considered by many recording executives and music publishers to be an arch-revolutionary, destroying the business with wild sounds, French horns, swinging harpsichords, 'bad' songs and singers who couldn't sing," he always maintained that his records provided the public a level of durable, quality pop entertainment that insipid, flash-in-the-pan rock and roll records could not match.[29] Insisting that "there is no conflict between profit and good taste," Miller saw the industry "return[ing] more and more to great performers and great songs."[30]

As it turned out, Columbia had the number-one record of 1960 in Percy Faith's "The Theme from *A Summer Place*," as good a confirmation of Miller's prediction as could be imagined. But the rest of the year's top-selling records loudly displayed the residual effects of the latter half of the 1950s. Presley was out of the army and back to excellent chart form with three number-one singles, "Are You Lonesome Tonight," "Stuck On You," and "It's Now or Never," all far slicker and more controlled than his earlier rockabilly ruckus yet a potent reminder of his market power and further evidence of his ability to absorb and integrate all kinds of America's popular genres. There were many black voices. Ray Charles had finally made a strong impression on the pop chart in 1959 with "What'd I Say," and with 1960's number-one "Georgia on My Mind" he unleashed a run of hits that would span the new decade. He was joined by the Drifters, Chubby Checker, Sam Cooke, Maurice Williams and the Zodiacs, Jimmy Jones, Joe Jones, and Jackie Wilson. Country flavors included Marty Robbins, Johnny Horton, Jim Reeves, and Hank Locklin. Two instrumental hits featured, in marked contrast to "*Summer Place,*" the electric guitar: the Ventures' "Walk Don't Run" and Duane Eddy's "Because They're Young" (which paired the king of twang with a violin section). There were many records by young stars aimed at teenagers, including the Everly Brothers' "Cathy's Clown," Johnny Preston's "Running Bear," Mark Dinning's "Teen Angel," Paul Anka's "Puppy Love," and Kathy Young and the Innocents' "A Thousand Stars." Fifteen-year-old Brenda Lee had two of the year's biggest records in "I'm Sorry" and "I Want to Be Wanted." And there was Roy Orbison's breakout record "Only the Lonely," a strange and wonderful disc whose gestation began years before in Clovis sessions with Norman Petty.[31] All in all, it was as colorfully mixed a chart as any in the previous five years. Not only was rock and roll not gone, but its eclectic influence was widely apparent. Faith himself reckoned that despite his big year it was now clear that "there'll always be rock 'n' roll."[32]

With single releases more prolific than ever and dramatic growth in album sales, the first years of the 1960s were at least as tumultuous as the latter fifties.[33] Indeed, Paul Ackerman, who began his reporting in 1938, wrote in his 1961 year-end summary, "If one were forced to describe the American record business in a phrase . . . one would have to state that it is currently more fiercely competitive than ever in its history."[34] The contours of the story had grown familiar. A report from 1958—claiming the "road to hitville still wide open," with "numbers of vastly different nature and origin" populating the upper reaches of the Hot 100—was simply rephrased in 1961 to explain that "the wildest scramble of artists, labels and styles of repertoire" proved, once again, that "practically anything goes."[35] The album market was dominated by the majors, but the singles chart saw "24 separate labels occupy[ing] the top 25 spots" and "38 different labels . . . in the top 50." In fact, the "four top majors and their subsidiaries occup[ied] only 18 of the top 100 slots."[36] Eighteen months later, in the fall of 1962, another report noted that "among the first 25 big sides this week . . . 21 labels have a piece of the action," with Capitol and three indies—Imperial, Vee-Jay, and Dimension—the only companies to place two discs among the top twenty-five. With hits by a raft of newcomers (about 25 percent of the top one hundred were first-timers) mingled with a "resurgence of standard, old-line talent," it appeared that "every kind of tune, artist and label" was in the running for popular success.[37]

With the industry splintered and fiercely competitive, marketing conviction shifted with the wind. There was no better example than WINS, which after dumping its rock and roll format for "good" music reversed course almost immediately. Four months after its Sinatra marathon, the station claimed the New York market's highest ratings thanks to a three-part programming strategy with the "softest" music played during the morning hours—"housewife time"—picking up in the afternoon with "teen-oriented jockey," Bob Lewis, and finally kicking into high rocking gear with Murray (the K) Kaufman's evening show, which was "aimed solidly at teen-agers."[38] A similar story was part of *Billboard*'s year-end roundup of general happenings around the country, which noted, "Many radio stations in the U.S. switched from rock and roll to sweet music at the start of the year and quietly swung back to more rock and roll by the end of the year."[39]

Amid the ambivalence, the industry's happiest news of 1962 was the resurgence of singles sales, which, by helping "the indie dealer and the old fashioned mama and papa store maintain some sort of equilibrium," assured more diverse grassroots retail action than the album market.[40] The upbeat retail story, however, only further complicated the musical one. With Acker Bilk's sentimental clarinet solo on "Stranger On the Shore" and the Tornados' sci-fi electronic clavioline on "Telstar" both producing top selling instrumentals (and both British at that), and with Nat Cole ("Ramblin' Rose"), Sinatra ("Pocketful of Miracles"), Johnny Mathis ("Gina"), and Patti Page ("Most People Get Married") turning in top-forty hits alongside Gene Chandler ("Duke of Earl"), Dee Dee Sharp ("Mashed Potato Time"), and the Contours ("Do You Love Me"), many were forced to take a new view of the singles market. "The idea that singles are only for kids has largely evaporated," the reporting went, "and manufacturers are no longer concerned about issuing pretty music, jazz or anything else on singles."[41] Side by side in the pop market "sweet records and rocking records jumped into breakout contention."[42] On one hand, the pop mainstream seemed confoundingly capricious. Yet the fact that Ray Charles's "I Can't Stop Loving You"—a balanced blend of pop schmaltz, R&B expression, and country pathos—was among the year's top sellers indicated that perhaps the market was not so much a picture of aimless conflict among opposing stylistic sensibilities as an eclectic mosaic reflecting a new normal.

Although it did not look or sound like what Miller envisioned, there was a new wave of professionalism about the industry in the early sixties as a new generation of successful rock and roll entrepreneurs challenged the oldest corporate institutions. In Los Angeles, twenty-one-year-old Phil Spector was not only a very young record producer but also a successful and hard-nosed label owner. In Detroit, Berry Gordy founded what would grow into an entertainment empire—management, publishing, records—as did Dick Clark in Philadelphia. In New York, Don Kirshner put together an operation manned by young songwriters whose tunes, often performed by the writers themselves, he hawked to a variety of record companies. Songwriters in Gordy's and Kirshner's organizations put in a regular workday, much like the old Tin Pan Alley routine. There was also evidence of an old-school showbiz discipline among some rock and roll performers. While the overnight recording star was now a fixture in the music business, such virtuoso vocalists as Sam Cooke, Jackie Wilson, and Roy Orbison came to pop stardom only after years spent honing their craft.

Unlike their indie predecessors, these newcomers did not happen accidentally into the mainstream. They built new institutions based on assumptions of pop style and market fundamentals reflecting the transformations that had taken place since the war. For them, the turbulence of the 1950s represented not an anomaly but a new reality. Crossover was now routine. A record's power to launch an unknown performer to instant stardom was taken for granted. So, too, was the conception of a record as an integrated artwork—a fusion of song, performance, and recorded sound. There was no doubt about who the audience was or how much buying power it possessed. And the playing field, while not level, remained open to newcomers. Young amateur performers landed atop the charts alongside experienced pros, and small, budding businesses competed effectively with established firms.

In New York City, a group of young songwriters and producers took up residence in the heart of the old-time music business in and around the Brill Building at 1619 Broadway. The Brill had been the center of Tin Pan Alley activity since the thirties, housing a cast of characters that included publishers, songwriters, arrangers, and musicians, while the ground floor held at one end the upscale Jack Dempsey's Restaurant and Bar and at the other the more down-market Turf, where hustling writers conducted business out of phone booths. Also comparatively low rent, but buzzing with vitality, was the building across the street and a block north at 1650 Broadway where, in 1958, twenty-one-year-old Don Kirshner, without a marketable song property to his name, set up shop as a music publisher under the trade name Aldon Music. His partner and mentor was a semi-retired veteran, Al Nevins, longtime member of the Three Suns and co-composer of the 1944 hit "Twilight Time," for which Buck Ram later supplied lyrics for the Platters' hit version. Kirshner's small office contained two desks and a piano, which he could not play. He had written a few lyrics, but by his own admission he had no musical skill. He turned out, however, to have a keen ability to spot potential hit songs and a relentless drive as a song plugger.

Soon after launching Aldon, Kirshner was approached by songwriters Neil Sedaka and Howie Greenfield, who, having failed in their search for full-time employment as staff writers at the major New York publishers in the Brill Building, had heard about Kirshner from fellow songwriters Doc Pomus and Mort Shuman. They hiked over to 1650 to meet the would-be publisher. "I probably looked like an 18-year-old kid that was taking out the garbage," Kirshner recalled at the songwriters skepticism when informed that he was in fact the firm's co-owner. For his part, Kirshner could not believe these two young men had actually written the songs they pitched. "Where did you steal these songs," Sedaka recalled being asked, "because we were pistelehs—we were kids." Actually, Kirshner's suspicions were twofold. If the young men had in fact written the songs, he could not believe that no established publisher "would take that talent."[43] All agreed to a provisional arrangement; Aldon would have four months to produce a hit from one of Greenfield and Sedaka's songs. If the company could not deliver, the contract would be canceled. Kirshner went to work and in short order placed "Stupid Cupid" with a college friend, Connie Francis, whose MGM recording became her third top-forty hit of 1958.

With his first signing an immediate success, Kirshner went on to assemble a stable of writers—including two more of the era's most successful songwriting partnerships: Barry Mann and Cynthia Weil and Gerry Goffin and Carole King, whose songs appeared on hit records by such artists as the Drifters, Shirelles, Crystals, Righteous Brothers, Paris Sisters, Everly Brothers, Ronettes, Jay and the Americans, Chiffons, Cookies, Animals, Bobby Vee, Little Eva, Gene Pitney, Steve Lawrence, Skeeter Davis, and Maxine Brown. The firm worked much as the old Tin Pan Alley publishers had, its writers toiling away each day in small rooms with little more than a piano and a chair while Kirshner and other song pluggers pitched the songs to record company A&R men. An important difference, however, was that the songwriters had access to a primitive recording setup with which to sketch out their songs as demo recordings rather than lead sheets. In an industry now awash in recorded sound, demos had become an essential stage in preparing songs for presentation. Almost inevitably, the next step was for the songwriters themselves to become involved in production as an extension of their creative work. "I wanted them to learn to produce," said Kirshner of his writers, and they did.[44] Arranging, performing, and recording were all part of their "writing" process. As their skill increased, distinctions between demos and masters could sometimes blur. A famous example is Little Eva's demo of Goffin and King's "The Loco-Motion," which Kirshner decided to use as the initial release for his new record company, Dimension. The record hit number one in the summer of 1962.

The steady flow of pop from the New York writers (among whom were also the non-Aldon-affiliated teams of Pomus and Shuman, Burt Bacharach and Hal David, and Ellie Greenwich and Jeff Barry) reflected the new lay of the pop landscape. The songs and records drew on all manner of musical stuff to create one-off confections that transported listeners on brief journeys of escapist sonic fantasy made real by the fervency of fan devotion. Bits of Broadway, Latin touches, rock and roll, even classical traces turned up in the songs and arrangements. Many of the interactions between songwriters and performers combined the experiences and sensibilities of distinct cultural spheres: the Jewish kids, most of them from Brooklyn, who wrote the songs; and the black performers, many of whom were also kids, who recorded them. Carole King recalled the revelation of listening to Freed's radio show, captivated by the sound of "another culture that really we were not close to and we became close to it through the music."[45] The songs and sounds would become emblematic of the time: "Up On the Roof," "Will You Love Me Tomorrow," "Be My Baby," "Uptown," "Da Doo Ron Ron," "Save the Last Dance for Me," "This Magic Moment," "He's a Rebel," "On Broadway." With the exception of Doc Pomus, who had attempted a career as a blues singer, neither the writers nor the performers knew much about one another's social worlds, but they shared a musical language born of many tongues, drawn together now in the multihued pop mainstream.

Though only twenty-four, Jerry Leiber and Mike Stoller were already elder statesmen when they arrived in New York in 1957 from Los Angeles. They had been writing together since 1950 and by the time they were twenty had written the R&B classic "Kansas City" (originally titled "K. C. Loving") and Willie Mae Thornton's number-one R&B hit "Hound Dog." They partnered with Lester Sill, an old hand on the postwar Los Angeles indie record scene, to form Quintet Music, a publishing firm, and Spark, a record label. They produced song-plugging demos for songwriters, finished masters for lease to various record companies, and records of their own songs on their own label. During the year of their New York move, their songs were recorded by Elvis Presley, Ruth Brown, Eddie Fisher, Julius La Rosa, Clyde McPhatter, Jaye P. Morgan, Screamin' Jay Hawkins, LaVern Baker, Roy Hamilton, and Jack Jones. Having begun as aficionados of black culture—absorbing the language, sounds, and milieu to the point that Jerry Wexler, something of a purist, reckoned they made "great r&b records . . . very idiomatic"—they now moved easily among a range of pop styles.[46] They had become industry pros on their own terms.

Leiber and Stoller moved to New York in part to take A&R positions at RCA Victor, but they were free to continue working independently and continued to make most of their records for Atlantic and its subsidiary Atco. (The corporate culture was a poor fit; the pair lasted only months at Victor.) In 1959, they took a recently overhauled Drifters into the studio to record "There Goes My Baby," written by the group's new lead singer, Ben E. King.[47] The Drifters' name was still famous, but the original group—with Clyde McPhatter long gone—had become a faded presence on the R&B scene. Wexler's hunch that Leiber and Stoller, who had struck gold with another Atlantic vocal group, the Coasters, could help to launch the new Drifters proved correct. But while "There Goes My Baby" began a run of pop hits Leiber and Stoller would produce for the group over the next five years, it was a curious sonic oddity and not at all what Wexler had in mind.

"Whenever I heard it on the radio," Stoller recalled, " I kept thinking I was getting two different stations on the same wavelength."[48] His impression was based on what appeared to be an aural image of multiple sonic dimensions sharing the same two minutes of musical time. The vocal introduction spelled out a standard doo-wop chord sequence with the bass voice answered at each chord change by a riff from the higher voices, all treated to a cavernous reverb. The only instruments audible in the muffled mix were a distant timpani and a double bass playing a rhythm pattern Leiber and Stoller associated with the Brazilian *baião*. Because no competent timpanist was available, the timpani never moved from the tonic bass note, droning along as the harmonies changed from I to vi to IV to V. After one turn through the chord sequence, a group of violins ushered in the lead vocal as the backing voices dropped out, leaving a minimalist texture of muffled rhythm section, violin melody, and lead vocal, all sounding to be in different rooms or, as Stoller heard it, on different radio stations.

The strange sound was made more striking, on the one hand, by enlisting strings, an exotic first for the Drifters, and on the other by using them in such a lo-fi presentation and stark arrangement. Strings were nothing new on R&B records; in early 1957, *Billboard* had pointed out "how elegant some r&b records are these days."[49] Billy Ward and the Dominoes (formerly best known for "Sixty Minute Man" and "Have Mercy Baby"), in a deliberate turn to the pop market, had two respectable pop hits in 1956–57 with "St. Therese of the Roses" and "Star

Dust," both drenched in luscious schmaltz. But the generic role of strings in pop arrangements is to add high-class luster and aid in blending disparate sounds into a smooth textural whole. On "There Goes My Baby," grainy violin melodies provided a melodramatic commentary on the singer's emotional performance. There were no sustained harmonies and full-bodied string section to pull the texture together, only the violins' bare melody and the distant-sounding rhythm section. The overall effect left the lead voice isolated, intensifying its lonesome cry.

"I pronounced it dogmeat," wrote Wexler in his autobiography. "I hated the muddy swirling-string sound."[50] When it was eventually released, however, it rose to number two on the pop chart, and a stylistic habit was set. Leiber and Stoller would not return to the more or less unintentionally surreal sound—the track was recorded in a poor studio and Atlantic ace engineer Tom Dowd was assigned the mix as a salvage job—but they would develop the combination of soulful vocal and Latin rhythm/string accompaniment on numerous subsequent Drifters hits, including "This Magic Moment" and "Save the Last Dance for Me," by Pomus and Shuman, "Up On the Roof," by Goffin and King, and "On Broadway," which they cowrote with Mann and Weil.

Collaborating with other young songwriters in the New York scene, Leiber and Stoller were at the center of a creative hotbed. "We don't idolize many people, but we idolized them," Mann recalled of his and Weil's experience writing "On Broadway." "It was like going to songwriters' school," Weil agreed.[51] In Carole King's recollection, "they were definitely that one step ahead that we always looked at and went, 'Look at that. We should go that way.' They were really trailblazers."[52] Leiber and Stoller's innovations and mentoring went beyond songwriting and record production; they were among a new breed in the industry, independent contractors who handled creative work while leaving record companies to concentrate on marketing and distribution. Surrounded by gifted young writers and budding producers, they founded a company based on this new industry model. In the winter of 1961, Leiber and Stoller Enterprises opened shop as an umbrella organization involved with "producing disks, management of talent, publishing firms, development of new writers and development of new record producers." The move fit with "the ever-growing trend of production of records by outside a.&r. men or teams" that was "becoming more and more organized, so that they offer a whole production package, including the artist, the songs and the a.&r. know how." Leiber and Stoller had "no intention of starting their own record label" but would "take new writers under their wing and help them get started" in this newly independent field.[53]

In 1959, Berry Gordy, another young entrepreneur with an experienced grasp of the connection between songwriting and record production, launched his first record label, Tamla. Gordy was a songwriter who had written or cowritten songs for LaVern Baker ("Jim Dandy Got Married," "It's So Fine"), Etta James ("All I Could Do Was Cry"), and Jackie Wilson ("Reet Petite [The Finest Girl You Ever Want to Meet]," "Lonely Teardrops," "To Be Loved," "That's Why [I Love You So]," "I'll Be Satisfied"). As he learned the ways of the music business, Gordy came to long for the artistic and financial control only ownership could provide. Owning copyrights, publishing rights, artists' management contracts, record masters, and—if ambition and luck held—a record label or two was the best way to stay close to the money in the music business. The notion was perhaps outlandish (though no more so than Kirshner's) for a twenty-nine-year-old songwriter who, despite some success, had little to his name and, by his own admission, had already pursued "two rather unsuccessful careers" as a boxer and record store owner.[54] But with an eight-hundred-dollar loan from his family's Ber-Berry savings fund, which required the unanimous approval of his parents and siblings, he launched Tamla.

The company's first release was Marv Johnson's "Come to Me," which Gordy cowrote with Johnson and produced at United Sound Studios in Detroit with Joe Syracuse engineering. Gordy had definite, if intuitive, ideas about record production. He had been deeply impressed watching George Goldner and Dick Jacobs in recording sessions in New York, and he now put his observations into practice. At the Johnson session, finding the engineer's mix balanced "too smoothly," he insisted on building it up again from scratch. He called it out: "heavy on the bass and drums," "separate mike on the tambourine," balance the background singers but move the bass vocal "to his own mike and turn it way up," and finally pull the lead vocal "up over everything else." The mix was an early stage of what would become recognized the world over as the Motown sound, an infectious illusion of spontaneous expression carefully crafted at the recording console and developed in an often protracted creative process. The object was not to capture a clean image of the sound heard in the room but to use it as raw material. After ten takes, Gordy reckoned, "I got an even better sound than I had heard down in the studio."[55]

With contacts in local radio, Gordy secured airplay and the record began to take off in the regional market, at which point he learned the same hard lesson all indie record men confronted: a hit could bankrupt a young company. He had the savvy to move quickly on a lease arrangement, placing the record with United Artists, which handled nationwide distribution and promotion as the record became a top-thirty pop hit. Gordy continued to lease his masters even after he was able to scrape together enough money to buy the house at 2648 West Grand Boulevard that he named Hitsville U.S.A., the nerve center of what would become one of the most successful recording and publishing enterprises in the world. Hitsville handled artist development and management for its performers, as well as record promotion and sales. It also housed a recording studio. It was a music factory modeled, Gordy said, on the Chrysler auto plant in which he had once worked. In the summer of 1960, Tamla finally managed its first national release with the Miracles' "Way Over There," selling only sixty thousand records but proving that the fledgling firm was ready to deal directly with the nationwide network of independent record distributors and handle its own promotion. Gordy added a second label, Motown, followed by Gordy, V.I.P., Melody, and Soul. In addition to his record labels, he owned a publishing company, Jobete, and artist management firm, International Talent Management.

Hitsville's recording studio allowed Gordy the same freedom Sam Phillips and Norman Petty had enjoyed in their exploratory pursuit of novel sounds: creativity was off the clock. "I no longer had to worry about the cost of the studio," he wrote. "I owned it." Arrangements and performances could follow a course of developmental growth aimed specifically at a recording. The first national chart success to emerge from the new studio was Barrett Strong's "Money" (1959, leased to Anna), written by Gordy with an added verse by Hitsville receptionist Janie Bradford. Gordy produced it over the course of several days in the studio, developing the arrangement and sound in a workshop atmosphere in which musicians were both performers and collaborative composers. "It was like an in-house rehearsal," Gordy recalled, "a party."[56]

Like those of his New York counterparts, Gordy's staff included songwriters and record producers. In fact, they were often one and the same. A song written by the team of Lamont Dozier and Brian and Eddie Holland, for instance, would be recorded under their supervision (Dozier and Brian Holland, that is). Similarly for Norman Whitfield, Mickey Stevenson, and Smokey Robinson. The producers guided the process but relied on contributions from the entire recording team, particularly the group of musicians known informally as the Funk Brothers. "Motown didn't have any 'sound'—they had ideas, and when they brought the music to us it was all lead sheets," recalled saxophonist and arranger Thomas "Beans" Bowles. Since a song required sound to make its way as a record, the musicians' collaboration was essential. Their musical ideas emerged as performances, a sort of "out loud" musical thinking that, according to Bowles, might go something like this.

> The producer said: "Play something for me man!" "What do you want to hear?" "We don't know what we want to hear, ya'll just play!" And then they'd hear something: "Hey man, what's that you just played?" "You mean this?" "Yeah, let me hear that again, that's what I want, right there!" . . . We could be there all day to do one song.[57]

Gordy was a perfectionist in the studio, recutting tracks that he felt had not come off as well as they might. Unhappy with the sound of "Way Over There" when he heard it on the radio, he went in search of "that big New York sound," flying the Miracles to Chicago to recut the track with strings at Universal, still the city's finest studio even though its original owner, Bill Putnam, had moved to Los Angeles. Gordy learned two things from the experience: first, he loved the polished sound of the new version; and second, despite the trouble and expense, the remake was a pointless exercise. The record never sold. "Everyone loved it," Gordy wrote, "except the public." The original version, he now realized, "had an honesty and raw soul" that the remake lacked. An indifferent public confirmed that the track had "lost the magic," and the commercial failure caused Gordy "to better appreciate the sound produced by our own little studio." There was no point in changing what listeners had already approved.[58] Like record men before him, Gordy learned that the "Sound of Young America," the slogan Motown etched on its records, was something in which young America itself would have a say.

· 3 ·

In late 1957, riding high on the success of his previous find, Frankie Lymon and the Teenagers, Richard Barrett brought another vocal group to George Goldner. Like the Teenagers and countless other young harmonizers in the schools and streets of New York, the group's members were all in their early teens. There was, however, one significant difference: they were all girls, students at Saint Anthony of Padua High School in the Bronx who called themselves the Chantels. Records by black female groups were rare, and the few that broke through, like Shirley Gunter and the Queens' "Oop Shoop" (1954) or the Hearts' "Lonely Nights" (1955), were confined to the R&B charts. They also had a more mature emotional character—more experienced grit, less innocent fantasy—than the young singers Barrett now brought to Goldner's newest label venture,

End. There was, however, evidence of a potential mass audience in the recent top-ten pop showing of the Bobbettes' "Mr. Lee" on Atlantic, and once again Goldner made a successful roll of the dice. After working with Barrett, the quintet (Lois Harris, Sonia Goring, Jackie Landry, Rene Minus, and Arlene Smith) began recording, and with their second release— a song called "Maybe," written by lead singer Smith—they had a crossover hit. The record, a young woman's desperate, yearning plea for love presented in idiomatic doo-wop lo-fi, was a top-twenty hit in the winter of 1958, the first of four Chantels top-forty records over the next four years.

Three months later Florence Greenberg, in her words "a white woman who was in a black business and who couldn't carry a tune," released a record by a group of young women from Passaic High School, the Shirelles (Shirley Owens, Doris Coley, Addie Harris, and Beverly Lee).[59] A New Jersey housewife with teenage children who was "anxious to get out of the house," Greenberg had been making the trip to Manhattan for two years, hanging around the Brill Building and the Turf with a vague aspiration somehow to get into the business.[60] She started her own label, Tiara, and convinced the skeptical Shirelles, her daughter's classmates, to sign with her. The song, "I Met Him On a Sunday," which the girls wrote themselves, was a schoolyard chant, a cautionary tale celebrating a girl's power over a faithless boy. The story unfolded gradually, with each line's three-note phrase accompanied only by the girls' hand claps and finger snaps. In between the lead phrases, the rest of the group chimed in with wordless responses ("oo-oo-oo") imparting both empathy and fascination. At the punch line, "I said bye-bye baby," the group broke into catchy rhythmic syllables ("do-run-dey-run-dey-run-dey-papa") that sounded an insider's code as the girl gang tripped along lightly arm in arm.

"I Met Him On a Sunday" was picked up by Decca, and the proceeds allowed Greenberg to open an office of her own at 1674 Broadway, another in the Brill orbit. The record was a modest hit, managing to just graze the top fifty, but this new sound—essentially female doo-wop not only in its vocal character but in its poignant primitivism—was not something Decca, or any major, really knew how to develop. The group's two follow-up singles failed to chart, and not long after signing them the company released them. Greenberg seized the chance to re-sign the Shirelles, now to a new label she called Scepter. She and her son Stan produced the next single, a cover of the Five Royales' "Dedicated to the One I Love," which made the Hot 100 in the summer of 1959—barely.

With so much talent concentrated in so small an area in midtown

Manhattan, serendipitous chance meetings often led to relationships that, in turn, produced successful commercial ventures. In one such encounter, Greenberg was introduced to Luther Dixon, a songwriter and producer who had placed songs with several big-name artists—Pat Boone, the Four Aces, Perry Como, and Nat Cole—and had also cowritten and produced the Crests' "Sixteen Candles," a top-five hit in 1959. Greenberg saw record promotion as her chief strength and was keen to enlist a more experienced studio hand for the Shirelles. For his part, Dixon was impressed with the group's potential. He and Greenberg agreed to form a partnership whereby he would write, arrange, and produce while she ran the record company and promoted its products.

The first Dixon-produced Shirelles single was "Tonight's the Night," written by lead singer Shirley Owens with help from Dixon. His arrangement was somewhat similar to "There Goes My Baby" in its use of strings and what he called a "West Indian rhythm," another variant of the *baião*.[61] Desire and vulnerability mingled in Owens's performance, enacting the mix of expectancy and uncertainty expressed in the song's lyrics. The record spoke with a young woman's sensibility to a young woman's concerns, and fans responded. Despite a competing cover by the Chiffons that largely mimicked the original in arrangement and sound, the Shirelles' disc was a top-forty hit in the fall of 1960. Flush with new success, Scepter moved to bigger offices at 1650 Broadway, where, as it happened, Dixon found the song for the Shirelles' crucial follow-up single. Kirshner passed along a newly minted demo of a song he had pitched unsuccessfully to Mitch Miller for a Johnny Mathis recording. The song was called "Will You Love Me Tomorrow," written by eighteen-year-old Carole King and her twenty-one-year-old husband Gerry Goffin in their small Sheepshead Bay apartment between working full-time jobs and caring for their infant daughter. What Dixon heard in King's simple voice-and-piano homemade demo was a song whose protagonist's situation and emotional state provided a natural sequel for "Tonight's the Night."

Goffin and King had recently signed with Aldon and submitted many songs in quick succession. Some became records, but they made little impression. "They were derivative. They were novice. They weren't melodic, and the lyrics were poor," recalled Goffin of such songs as "Short Mort," a parody of Annette Funicello's "Tall Paul," and "Oh, Neil," an answer to Sedaka's "Oh! Carol," both performed by King herself.[62] But with "Will You Love Me Tomorrow" the couple raised their game considerably. The song was cast in a classic AABA form. The verse's third phrase introduced a piquant applied dominant chord, intensifying a brief move to the minor mode that underscored such lyrics as "tonight the light of love is in your eyes" and "can I believe the magic of your sigh." The bridge, twice as long as the conventional middle eight, raised the emotional urgency to a climactic peak. Throughout, the melody reflected the protagonist's emotion with expressive nonharmonic tones—appoggiaturas, suspensions, and anticipations. In all respects, the song was a youthful evocation of Tin Pan Alley songcraft.

The record, however, was rock and roll, its rhythmic groove once again a variation on the *baião* but with the snare drum pattern lending a distinct note of surf style similar to the Ventures' "Walk Don't Run," a recent hit. Along with its rock and roll beat and electric guitar, the record would again feature strings, and King wanted to write the parts. She had no experience, but with a fresh innocence and the help of an orchestration book she came up with an arrangement that Dixon agreed to use, a charming thing possessed of the same young ardor as the singers and the song. The cellos were given an incisive rhythm, doubling the snare drum's backbeat accents while filling in the harmonic texture. The violin flourishes provided what one writer has described as a "rapturous" quality whose "passion threatens to overwhelm reason."[63] Owens sang the song with unaffected honesty in a straightforward tone that left emotional heat to the violins. Her performance had a dignity about it, a strength that avoided sentimentality or pathos, as if to say that whatever the answer to the question in the song's title she would choose love every time. Again, the sensibility and sound spoke to a vast audience. The record reached number one on the pop charts in January of 1961, the first such accomplishment by an African American female vocal group. The Shirelles would follow it with another ten top-forty hits over the next three years, including a re-release of "Dedicated to the One I Love."

The spectacular success of "Will You Love Me Tomorrow" was followed by a torrent of records featuring women's voices by all-female groups, mixed groups, solo artists, and male-female duos. In 1961, girl group hits included the Marvelettes' "Please Mr. Postman" (also number one), the Angels' "'Til," the Crystals' "There's No Other Like My Baby," the Paris Sisters' "I Love How You Love Me," the Chantels' "Look In My Eyes" and "Well, I Told You," and four more Shirelles records. Over the next three years the charts registered hits by the Cookies ("Chains"), Ronettes ("Be My Baby"), Chiffons ("One Fine Day"), Jaynetts ("Sally, Go 'Round the Roses"), Little Eva ("The Loco-Motion"), Martha and the Vandellas ("Heat Wave"), Shangri-Las ("Leader of the Pack"), Dixie Cups ("Chapel of Love"), Exciters ("Tell Him"), Jelly-Beans ("I Wanna Love Him So Bad"), Betty Everett ("The Shoop Shoop Song [It's In His Kiss]"), Claudine Clark ("Party Lights"), Little Peggy March ("I Will

Follow Him," a kitchen-sink track with both male and female backing voices), Skeeter Davis ("I Can't Stay Mad at You"), Robin Ward ("Wonderful Summer"), Murmaids ("Popsicles and Icicles"), a mere sampling of girl group sounds.

Women soloists included Connie Francis, Brenda Lee, Mary Wells, Lesley Gore, Barbara Lewis, Dionne Warwick, Carla Thomas, Sue Thompson, Tina Turner, and Wanda Jackson; among the mixed-gender sounds were records by Paul and Paula, Dick and Dee Dee, Nino Tempo and April Stevens, Dean and Jean, Dale and Grace, Chubby Checker and Dee Dee Sharp, Chuck Jackson and Maxine Brown, Gladys Knight and the Pips, Ruby and the Romantics, the Essex (four men and a woman lead, all members of the Marine Corps), and, from the folk scene, Peter, Paul and Mary, the Rooftop Singers, and the New Christy Minstrels. If, as *Billboard*'s Ren Grevatt remembered, "during that earlier floodtide of rock and roll . . . the popularity of girl singers was at a nadir," things had clearly been reversed.[64]

The style and quality of girl group records varied widely. Grevatt made an informal distinction between "girl singers," who were either "straight, [or] of the more pallid and sickly variety," the latter a reference to what he had earlier identified as a subgenre labeled by "knowledgeable tradesters" as the "'sick' sound." With Kathy Young and the Innocents' "A Thousand Stars" and Rosie and the Originals' "Angel Baby" as prime examples, he wryly summarized the sound of "this interesting new kind of artist" as "not necessarily true to the pitch."[65] Kathy Young was fourteen; Rosie Hamlin, who also wrote her song, was sixteen. The vocals were indeed primitive, as was the rest of the production. These top sellers were the kinds of records that proved the amateur spirit in pop music continued to flourish; they were the legacy of Don Howard's "Oh, Happy Day" and Johnny Ace's "My Song." They spun alongside suave Dionne Warwick records, Connie Francis's major label pop, the soulful Tina Turner, and the frenetic rockabilly Wanda Jackson in a stylistic spectrum whose aesthetic range reflected its fifties heritage.

The vital and vast girl group repertory (there were hundreds of such records) was, of course, part of the interregnum era marginalized in rock's early historical narratives. The records' seductive charm, however, confused the issue. They clearly had a soulful expressiveness not found among the packaged teen idols—Frankie Avalon, Fabian, and, yes, Annette. "If you were looking for rock and roll between Elvis and the Beatles," wrote Greil Marcus in the *Rolling Stone Illustrated History of Rock & Roll,* "girl groups gave you the genuine article." Yet his two-page entry was one of the shortest in the book, half the space allotted to "Italo-

American Rock" and a quarter that of "Doo-Wop." A standard criticism was that this was "producer's music," that the production process swallowed up performers' individuality and cast them as a Svengali's marionettes. But rock and roll had always been "producer's music." Or, better, it was always a collaborative music. There were inevitable power relationships among members of a creative team, but the process was thoroughly interactive nevertheless. It is an irony that he would perhaps have disavowed, but rock and roll was in many ways heir to Mitch Miller's conception of record production: a creative team project similar to filmmaking. The romantic portrait of the musical artist as lone hero, an archetype in musical narratives of all sorts, has little place in a recording culture. Performers, songwriters, arrangers, engineers, and producers all had a hand in making rock and roll records. If some producers of girl group records managed to call more attention to themselves than had been customary, that was due in large part to their independent operator status, a break with the traditional model of the corporate A&R man.

In a complex and competitive market, independent producers added yet another layer to the system, allowing novel sounds to continue surfacing from almost anywhere. Some followed the familiar pattern of starting their own record companies. Frank Guida created a distinctive sound in Norfolk, Virginia, using an abundance of electronic compression and what he called "pure recording trickery."[66] He scored top national hits with such raucous, exhilarating records as Gary U.S. Bonds' "Quarter to Three" (1961) and Jimmy Soul's "If You Wanna Be Happy" (1963) released on his Legrand and S.P.Q.R. labels. Other regional releases found their way to national prominence through arrangements with larger indies or majors. Joe Jones's "You Talk Too Much" (1960) and Ernie K-Doe's "Mother-In-Law" (1961), for example, brought funky New Orleans novelty to the top of the national pop charts via local labels' affiliations with Roulette and Imperial, respectively.

Some producers, as we have seen, chose to freelance. Leiber and Stoller, Nevins and Kirshner, Bob Crewe and Frank Slay, and Lester Sill and Lee Hazelwood were identified in a *Billboard* report as being among a group of producers "who constantly work on disks for a quantity of labels as free-lance a.&r. men." Many such producers—whose ranks also included Allen Toussaint, Bert Berns, the Tokens, Shadow Morton, and Jerry Ragovoy—were also songwriters and artist managers, which, again, bound the writing, performing, and recording projects symbiotically. Publishers, too, were turning freelance "recording men for various and sundry labels."[67] Delivering "a goodly percentage of the country's hit singles," the "indie producer" acquired "a new status" in the industry, sought by record companies as an extension of their in-house A&R. No longer "fly-by-nights, working out of cubbyholes in the Brill Building," independent producers now had "plush offices of their own."[68] Moreover, in "one of the most interesting . . . recent trends" (because it was such a rarity historically), record companies were open "to the artist himself doing his own a.&.r. work."[69] Such was the case for the likes of Jackie Wilson, Bobby Darin, Ray Charles, Sam Cooke, and Lloyd Price—performers who selected or wrote their own material and supervised arrangements and recording sessions.

One of Leiber and Stoller Enterprises' first signings was Phil Spector, whose 1958 hit with the Teddy Bears had put the eighteen-year-old wunderkind on the map as a songwriter and producer. "To Know Him Is to Love Him" was recorded at Gold Star Studios in Los Angeles where, after an apprenticeship under the auspices of Lester Sill that included time spent in sessions with Lee Hazelwood in Phoenix and Leiber and Stoller in New York, Spector took up residence in 1961, by then a partner with Sill in Philles Records. Gold Star was built by Dave Gold and Stan Ross in the early fifties as a songwriters' demo studio, but it gradually became one of the city's respected record-making venues.[70] Gold and Ross designed the control and recording rooms, and much of the studio's equipment was custom built by Gold. The most famous Gold Star resource was its echo chamber, for which Gold devised a reflective wall coating that produced an attractive ambience. (He has, over the years, refused lucrative offers to divulge the coating's secret formula.) Spector, enthralled with reverb's ethereal quality, used the combination of Gold Star's studio A and the chamber to create what would become known as the "wall of sound," a production style that yielded a string of hit records marked by the sonic character of a specific place.[71]

The "wall of sound" was based on a thick, murky sonic texture created by putting too many instruments in too small a space, their individual characters obscured by a complex, blended resonance. The composite studio sound was fed to the echo chamber whose reverb was mixed in with the direct sound, further blurring timbral distinctions. This became the foundational canvas for arrangements that varied considerably from track to track but most of which featured girl group vocals: the Crystals, the Ronettes, Darlene Love, Bob B. Soxx and the Blue Jeans. Usually some instrument or instrumental combination emerged from the texture to provide a point of timbral clarity amid the haze, for example, the Spanish guitar and strings on "Uptown," the exuberant saxophone break on "He's Sure the Boy I Love" (doubled at the octave), the castanets and whopping snare drum doubled with hand claps on "Be My Baby," and the introductory guitar riff on "Then He Kissed Me" followed by the ecstatic string line in the bridge. Riding the deep cushion of sound were the voices, pushed to an urgent edginess—nearly shouting out the melody—by the vast sonic wave behind them. The effect was a riveting blast of emotional declamation surrounded by a mysterious sonic cloud pouring forth from the loudspeaker with a monophonic punch.

Philles had its first number-one hit within the year when the Crystals' "He's a Rebel" entered the chart in late summer of 1962, followed by another twenty-seven records that made *Billboard*'s Hot 100, ending with Ike and Tina Turner's "River Deep–Mountain High" in 1966. Spector became at least as famous as his performers. A Crystals record might feature Barbara Alston, Darlene Love, or La La Brooks, but it was always a Phil Spector record. Moreover, Spector's general style, a thickly layered, reverb-saturated arrangement fronted by declamatory vocals, became one of rock's archetypal sounds. His influence transcended his early sixties celebrity, most notably in his later work with George Harrison and John Lennon.

Yet, while Spector cut an outsized public figure, the most famous producer since Mitch Miller to come on the scene, he was only one of dozens of young record makers for whom the once radical notion that records were musical works unto themselves had become a commonplace. Despite their influence, however, most producers were still little known by the public. It was the records themselves that held the spotlight, and for most listeners a record was a song, a sound, a performer's name, and an associated image gleaned from magazines, television, or, for some, a live performance. In keeping with the era's dynamic, decentralized production process, the records launched into the market each week were of disparate provenance, style, and sonic color. The relative few releases that lodged in the public soundscape added their sounds to an ever-growing pop lexicon that supplied an evolving language with artistic resources and market guidance. On all counts, the evidence of the early sixties was that the rock and roll process continued unabated, now adding women in key creative roles and greatly expanding their numbers as star performers. If the industry's institutional sexism was little diminished from earlier times, despite the remarkable successes of Greenberg and Vivian Carter, cofounder of Vee-Jay records in Chicago, the turbulence of the market and the urgency of responding to any perceived audience whim continued to open new avenues. No one could argue with a hit record; it spoke for itself and, implicitly, for those who made it and bought it.

· 4 ·

The pop music economy of the early sixties appeared to be a hodgepodge of records vying for fleeting attention. Summarizing record sales in 1962, *Billboard* reported "a dazzling crop of newcomers . . . with the heftiest show of sales strength the record industry had witnessed in many a year," while at the same time "a number of vet record names either continued their longtime steady sales pattern or else came back with hot-breaking items that catapulted them again into the limelight."[72] The newcomers, a diverse group, included Bobby Vinton, the Four Seasons, Peter, Paul and Mary, Booker T. and the M.G.'s, Dee Dee Sharp, Mary Wells, the Crystals, and the Duprees. Holding steady or making comebacks were Presley, Sinatra, Miller, Lawrence Welk, Nat Cole, Johnny Mathis, Sam Cooke, Connie Francis, Ricky Nelson, Pat Boone, and Tony Bennett.

But amid the apparently haphazard assortment, something more or less coherent was in fact taking shape. The accumulating numbers of records aimed at teenagers were pushing things finally toward a tipping point. In 1961 and 1962, there was still room among the top hits for singles by Lawrence Welk and His Orchestra ("Calcutta"), Bert Kaempfert and His Orchestra ("Wonderland By Night"), David Rose and His Orchestra ("The Stripper"), Kenny Ball and His Jazzmen ("Midnight in Moscow"), and Mr. Acker Bilk ("Stranger On the Shore"). In 1963, however, there were no such easy-listening instrumentals among the year's overall top forty. Nor would there be another until 1968 with Paul Mauriat's "Love Is Blue."

The 1963 pop charts saw the greatest ever preponderance of rock and roll records; there was little question this was the new mainstream. Over the course of the year, the Beach Boys, Jan and Dean, the Chantays, the Surfaris, and the Trashmen produced thirteen top-forty hits as the surfing/hot rod trend spilled out of Southern California and swept the country. Motown acts had fifteen top-forty hits, including a number one in thirteen-year-old Little Stevie Wonder's "Fingertips—Part 2." The sounds of girl groups were a constant presence, and the Kingsmen's "Louie Louie," a classic specimen of garage-band primitivism, was one of the year's top singles. There were several folk groups among the top sellers (Peter, Paul and Mary, the Rooftop Singers, the Village Stompers, and Trini Lopez), but these, too, represented a scene—led now by its young prince, Bob Dylan—that would soon deliver a large new group of American rock stars. Only three of the year's biggest hits still carried something of the middle-of-the road "good" music banner, at least in their arrangements: Al Martino's "I Love You Because," Steve

Lawrence's "Go Away Little Girl," and Andy Williams's "Can't Get Used to Losing You." Martino's record was a country song from the forties (covered by Presley and Johnny Cash), while the other two were from the pens of rock and roll songwriters—Goffin and King and Pomus and Shuman. As Paul Ackerman, recently retired from *Billboard,* put it in a year-end editorial, "It would seem that the old, narrow concept of Tin Pan Alley as the . . . center of American music has gone by the board."[73]

The next year's annual top-forty chart summary was unlike anything the industry had ever seen: eight records (five at number one) by a single group, the Beatles; four more by other British groups (Animals, Zombies, Peter and Gordon [with yet another Lennon and McCartney song], and Manfred Mann); another three (all number one) by the Supremes along with two other Motown acts (Mary Wells and Martha and the Vandellas); several more female acts (Dixie Cups, Murmaids, Shangri-Las, Lesley Gore, Millie Small); two by the Four Seasons; and surf discs from the Beach Boys, Jan and Dean, and the Marketts. This was a picture of a record industry overwhelmed finally and for good with music by and for the young, though now in a guise that turned out to hold an appeal for many older listeners as well. (The surprising adult participation in the twist craze of 1962 and the pop appeal of the urban folk revival were harbingers of a blurring of generational divisions evinced in the Beatles' audience, which ranged from teenyboppers to the British royal family.) The Beatles' arrival in America was as astonishing a scenario as could be imagined. The country and the world had seen nothing like it since Presley in 1956–57; but this was even bigger, and imported at that, unheard of. Into America's seething pop life, for years a picture of more or less continuous mutation, came what turned out to be a stabilizing influence with enough market clout and genuine talent to argue forcefully and coherently that rock and roll, the music of the young, was also the music of the age.

On a chilly February day in 1964, a crowd of more than three thousand young people, mostly young women, stood on the upper arcade of the International Arrivals Building at New York's Kennedy Airport, awaiting the arrival of a Pan American Airways flight from London carrying the Beatles (and a small entourage that included Phil Spector) on their first trip across the Atlantic. As the plane approached the gate, the sounds of whistling, screaming, and singing arose from the crowd, and signs were held aloft that read "Beatles, we love you," and "WELCOME." "An official at Kennedy Airport," the *New York Times* reported, "shook his head and said, 'We've never seen anything like this here before. Never. Not even for kings and queens.'"[74] Along with the delirious fans, a press contingent of some two hundred reporters and photographers jostled for access at the press conference that introduced the band members to America. Two days later the Beatles would appear on the *Ed Sullivan Show,* and more than seventy-three million viewers would tune in. Beatlemania, already an established phenomenon in Britain and Europe, had landed in America with an improbable bang. No British group had ever generated so much excitement in the United States. The group members themselves were skeptical and apprehensive about the trip. "The thing is," recalled John Lennon, "in America it just seemed ridiculous—I mean the idea of having a hit record over there. It was just something you could never do."[75] During the flight, McCartney is reported to have wondered aloud, "They've got everything over there. What do they want *us* for?"[76]

Indeed, before the world had the Beatles, America had already had everything rock and roll offered—its artists, its characters, its hucksters, its songs, its sound, its entire history. The Beatles propelled themselves into the American pop consciousness with their deep grasp of that history. America wanted the Beatles because the band crystallized and validated the musical upheavals of the previous decade. From rock and roll, in all its variety, the Beatles had learned how to write songs and arrangements, how to play and sing, how to be artists. They acknowledged and celebrated their musical mentors both in their live sets and on their recordings. Newly penned Beatles songs fit right in next to their cover versions of Chuck Berry rockers, Little Richard rants, Carl Perkins rockabilly, and Motown and girl groups and even Meredith Wilson. And along with Wilson's "Till There Was You" were other such exemplars of earlier pop styles—"The Sheik of Araby," "Besame Mucho," and "Ain't She Sweet." The band astutely worked the rock and roll process, absorbing sources and making them anew. The Beatles brought not only infectious good humor and ebullient music making to a country saddened by the recent assassination of its popular young president but also a sense of tradition and the seeds of awareness that America's apparent musical meltdown in the 1950s was in fact a musical watershed, a transitional period that produced both a permanent stylistic break from the swing era and a fundamental ontological shift from written to recorded musical works.

The Beatles were not amateurs; they were seasoned veterans of countless hours on the bandstand. But their musical sensibility was permeated by the sounds of primitive records whose expressive core had redefined the aesthetics of recorded sound. For the Beatles, it was understood that a record could, should, be a rambunctious, unfettered noise; a good record shouted forth from loudspeakers, celebrating its vitality. The doubled lead vocal line, the overly bright guitars, the banging drums, the overall mix skirting the edge of distortion as the group pushed for the maximum the medium would allow—all of these were evidence of a rock and roll conception of record making, which was the Beatles' principal aim. "I always was a record man, I always liked the studio best," said John Lennon.[77] From their early days, recalled Paul McCartney, "records were the objective. That was what we bought, that was what we dealt in. It was the currency of music: records."[78] In time, they would give up live performance altogether to devote all their energy to making records. Along with their producer George Martin, the "fifth Beatle," and some adventurous and creative recording engineers, they would spend the latter years of their career in the recording studio "painting sound pictures" as Martin put it, using "an infinite palette of musical colours."[79]

"For better or worse, like it or loathe it, rock 'n' roll is the sound of the Sixties," *Time* announced in a 1965 cover story.[80] But it was not the rock and roll of the fifties; indeed, many felt compelled to adopt a distinguishing moniker: simply "rock." Several years of evolution had changed the music's surface. "Tradesters have . . . noted lately the virtual disappearance of the so-called 'honking' tenor sax chorus, a trademark of so many earlier rock-'n'-roll records," reported Ren Grevatt in Britain's *Melody Maker* in 1960.[81] The electric guitar was now the preferred instrument leading the solo breaks. And triplets, that crude vestige of swing so often cited as a sine qua non of fifties rock and roll, were replaced with a solid duple groove. (The shift is neatly encapsulated in Manfred Mann's cover of the Shirelles' "Sha La La.") Triplets, too, it turned out, were part of a transitional phase. When we hear Chuck Berry and his pianist, Johnnie Johnson, throw two and three against one another with abandon or Little Richard hammer out straight eighth notes against the shuffle of his backing band, we hear the sound of rock's archetypal groove being born. "The only reason I started playing what they come to call a rock-and-roll beat came from trying to match Richard's right hand. *Ding-ding-ding-ding!*" recalled session drummer Earl Palmer years later. "On 'Tutti Frutti' you can hear me playing a shuffle. Listening to it now, it's easy to hear I should have been playing that rock beat."[82] By the midsixties the matter was settled. Duple had become and would remain rock's essential rhythmic foundation. Triplets henceforth would invoke an earlier time.[83]

But if some aspects of the stylistic surface had changed, a durable core of conventions had been established. The new rock styles that emerged in the sixties—soft and hard rock, blues and pop rock, psychedelic and country rock—all had common elements distinguishing them from pre–

rock and roll styles. Most important, they shared a concept of musical culture—stylistically inclusive, aesthetically pliable, intrinsically electronic, and fundamentally democratic—reflecting the deeper significance of the fifties revolution. The cast of iconic characters, too, was a fifties portrait. The pre–rock and roll pop exemplars—Crosby, Page, Stafford, Clooney, Bennett, Paul and Ford, Starr, Gibbs, Fisher, Damone, Laine—all of whom held on bravely through the fifties, were now clearly in an emeritus position. The great Andrews Sisters were not among the girl groups on the pop charts in the early sixties, although they continued to perform. They and the others represented something bygone. The relevant elders now dated only to the midfifties: the likes of Presley, Berry, Little Richard, Bill Haley, Clyde McPhatter, Jerry Lee Lewis, Bo Diddley, Sam Cooke, Buddy Holly. The standard repertory included "Hound Dog," "Rock and Roll Music," "Lucille," and "Great Balls of Fire"—records marking the genesis of the new age.

While the British invasion featured an international cast of characters, it was fueled by American rock and roll. Excepting the Beatles, the first wave of British groups to arrive in America relied heavily on covers of American songs for their hits. Consider some of the top-forty singles charted by British bands in 1964 and 1965, followed by their writers and original recordings.

Animals

"House of the Rising Sun" (traditional), many earlier versions, including one by Joan Baez and one by Bob Dylan

"We Gotta Get Out of This Place" (Barry Mann and Cynthia Weil), demo by Mann and Weil

"Bring It On Home to Me" (Sam Cooke), Sam Cooke

Dave Clark Five

"Do You Love Me" (Berry Gordy), Contours

"Reelin' and Rockin'" (Chuck Berry), Chuck Berry

"I Like It Like That" (Chris Kenner and Allen Toussaint), Chris Kenner

Herman's Hermits

"I'm Into Something Good" (Gerry Goffin and Carole King), "Earl-Jean" McCrea

"Silhouettes" (Bob Crewe and Frank Slay), Rays

"Wonderful World" (Sam Cooke), Sam Cooke

Manfred Mann

> "Do Wah Diddy Diddy" (Jeff Barry and Ellie Greenwich), Exciters
> b/w "Sha La La" (Robert Taylor, Robert Mosely, Luther Dixon,
> and Curtis Ousley), Shirelles

Peter and Gordon

> "I Go to Pieces" (Del Shannon)

> "True Love Ways" (Buddy Holly), Buddy Holly

> "To Know You [Him] Is to Love You [Him]" (Phil Spector), Teddy
> Bears

Rolling Stones

> "Time Is on My Side" (Jerry Ragovoy), Irma Thomas

> "It's All Over Now" (Bobby Womack and Shirley Womack),
> Valentinos

Searchers

> "Needles and Pins" (Jack Nitzsche and Sonny Bono), Jackie
> DeShannon

> "Love Potion Number Nine" (Jerry Leiber and Mike Stoller), Clovers

Of course, there were many more British covers of American rock and roll—B-sides and album tracks. By my rough count, the Beatles released twenty-four such covers before 1965, which does not include recordings of their live performances on the BBC or at Hamburg's Star-Club.[84] In showcasing their influences, the British bands acknowledged their debts and their inspiration. Their sources included the earliest rock icons, the latest Motown and Brill Building pop, sounds of New Orleans, rocka-ballads, and blues records that had rarely managed to crack the pop charts. The covers continued the fifties rock and roll process of absorption and stylistic evolution. But while fifties music had often reached far back into the Tin Pan Alley catalog, the new records' historical sources were concentrated in a more recent past.

A sense of history, or at least a backward-looking nostalgia, was already apparent in rock and roll culture by the time the British invasion began. Actually, the latter half of 1959 saw record buyers seeking out older recordings of all sorts. Companies cashed in with reissues of singles from their catalogs dating back to the 1930s, newly packaged as album collections. RCA Victor had success with *60 Years of Music America Loves Best,* a four-sided album that interspersed classics and pop—Enrico Caruso to Perry Como, Arthur Rubinstein to Perez Prado. Decca released a series of six albums filled with former hits by such stars as Bing Crosby, the Andrews Sisters, the Mills Brothers, and Glen Gray and the Casa Loma Orchestra. While the majors had in their vaults decades' worth of recordings to cull for such projects, many indies had also amassed large holdings of recordings that retained a steady popularity even though their chart runs had passed.

At decade's end it was apparent that "many old (circa 1952–'57) rhythm and blues hits—and some that were only near-hits—[were] still consistent sellers."[85] Surveying record retailers, jukebox operators, and radio deejays nationwide, *Billboard* found that "old waxings by Fats Domino, the Platters, the Moonglows, Little Richard, Clyde McPhatter, Chuck Berry, and the Nutmegs are among the prime r.&b. 'standards.'" The Penguins' "Earth Angel" had "sold an additional 4,000,000 copies since its initial click as an r.&b.-pop hit in 1955," and the Five Satins' "In the Still of the Nite" (1956) had posted "an even more impressive sales record." One Brooklyn record store owner reckoned that in "slack seasons," sales of oldies were "the margin between profit and loss."[86] Among his top-ten sellers he named "Earth Angel," "In the Still of the Nite," the Three Friends' "Blanche" (1956), and the Mello Kings' "Tonite Tonite" (1957). The latter two had been local hits in a few cities but only grazed the lower reaches of *Billboard*'s national charts at the time of their initial release.

Radio stations, too, found that listeners responded enthusiastically to the older recordings, and some stations devoted as much as half their programming to oldies. "Stations across the country are programming more and more hits of the past on a regular basis," June Bundy reported in *Billboard,* "and aging rock and roll fans are proving particularly avid audiences for shows made up of r.&r. oldies."[87] Stations ran such promotional features as "24 hours of all-time hits," and "300 top song hits of the past 10 years" determined by audience vote.

The retrospective cast of the oldies phenomenon also swept up many records that had never made the pop charts but would prove influential going forward. Chess and its subsidiaries, for example, issued album collections of former R&B hits—*Remember the Oldies, Love Those Goodies, Bunch of Goodies, Oldies in Hi-Fi*—that kept in circulation recordings by such stars as Jimmy Witherspoon, Bo Diddley, Little Walter, Clarence Henry, Paul Gayten, Willie Mabon, Lowell Fulson, and Jackie Brenston. The stylistic residue, if not the records themselves, would figure prominently in sixties rock as blues took on a central mainstream presence through such bands as the Yardbirds, Rolling Stones, Cream, and Jimi Hendrix Experience. The popularity of older records signaled a staying power, an aesthetic durability, that went beyond pop's weekly sales tabulations. The collections of past hits and, more tellingly, misses were in effect miniarchives, repositories of music and memory.

As sixties rock took center stage—the soundtrack for social upheaval, war, political dissent, and rites of passage, as well as everyday life—it refined the rude shocks of fifties rock and roll simply by virtue of its self-consciousness. It grew more ambitious, more artful. Now in command of the pop mainstream, its dazzling revenues conferred a cloak of institutional power. Yet from the big beat to the electric guitar to the vocal harmonies to the self-penned songs, and, most of all, to its consensus that sound was the irreducible medium of musical meaning, what would become known as classic rock was deeply infused with 1950s musical DNA. The random stylistic churning in the postwar pop mainstream had roughly coalesced in a new musical idiom. The thousands of records issued in the fifties had left imprints that reverberated through the pop soundscape. Rock and roll now had its own history and the makings of a distinct language. It had, in other words, all that was necessary to sustain future generations of artists and fans for many years to come.

Epilogue

At the dawn of the 1950s, *Billboard* ran a piece paraphrasing Sinatra's "pioneering thoughts on LP pop tune production." The singer was "thinking in terms of the 10-inch 15-minute record," rather than the 78 rpm single, a move that called for "an entirely new approach to recording." He saw the new format as "opening new production vistas . . . call[ing] for much more of a production package."[1] With his 1946 album *The Voice of Frank Sinatra* (a collection of four 78s), he had showcased his ambitious vision for pop recording. Now, he was eager to exploit the new avenues of creative possibility he sensed in the LP. As the decade unfolded, with his move to Capitol and career rebirth, Sinatra approached album projects with a focused sense of purpose, settling on an overall mood and then selecting a complementary set of songs. The album titles—*Songs for Young Lovers, In the Wee Small Hours, Only the Lonely, Come Dance with Me*—set the tone for each collection.

Nineteen years later, in 1965, the Beatles released *Rubber Soul,* their sixth album in less than three years. According to producer George Martin, the fourteen-song collection represented a first for the group. "For the first time," he said, "we began to think of albums as art on their own, as complete entities."[2] The record was a world away from Sinatra in style and attitude, but along with Bob Dylan's *Highway 61 Revisited,* released earlier that year, it showed a similar aspiration to transcend the limitations of pop singles with a coherent extended work. Although rock and roll album sales had seen a steady increase in the first half of the sixties, the LPs were mostly collections of previously released singles and other miscellaneous tracks. After 1965, however, the rock album became a full-fledged musical genre evinced in a spectacular series of groundbreaking releases: the Beach Boys' *Pet Sounds,* the Beatles' *Revolver* and *Sgt. Pepper's Lonely Hearts Club Band,* Simon and Garfunkel's *Bookends,* Jimi Hendrix's *Electric Ladyland,* the Doors' and Led Zeppelin's eponymous debuts, the Rolling Stones' *Let It Bleed,* Dylan's *Blonde on Blonde*—album after album of music conceived as incorporated musical works brought to life in recording studios.

In 1966, the Beatles took the extraordinary step of suspending live performances. The shows were more Beatlemania rituals than concerts. The recording studio was where the band thrived and where they would spend their remaining time together. Before embarking on their final, controversy-ridden tour, the group had released *Revolver,* the follow-up to *Rubber Soul.* The record was a masterpiece of artifice, its imaginary soundscapes replete with timbral distortion, backward tape effects, unusual stereo treatments, and tape loops of found sounds. Its unlikely pop song topics ranged from tax protest ("Tax Man") to psychedelic experience ("Tomorrow Never Knows") to the sad, curious story of Eleanor Rigby. The palette of instrumental timbres included sitar, tabla, brass, and strings along with the conventional rock and roll instruments. The "Eleanor Rigby" arrangement used only a double string quartet—no drums, no bass, no guitars. *Revolver* was rock's most ambitious effort to date, and the record's creative exhilaration represented the most dramatic rupture yet between studio recording and live performance. Whatever other misgivings the Beatles had about performing, as a practical matter *Revolver* was impossible to reproduce onstage.

In an odd twist of fate, Dylan also left the pop stage after 1966. He not only stopped touring, but he stopped releasing records as well. He did not, however, stop recording. As he took refuge in Woodstock, New York, he continued to play music regularly with the Hawks—his former touring bandmates—in the basement of a plain house in nearby West Saugerties affectionately dubbed Big Pink. The musicians played old songs and wrote new songs "in a peaceful, relaxed setting, in somebody's basement, with the windows open and a dog lying on the floor," as Dylan described it.[3] "We were having a really good time writing music, hanging out" recalled guitarist and songwriter Robbie Robertson.[4] The sessions had no particular goal, certainly not any specific commercial outcome. And yet the musicians took the trouble to record their efforts. The recording rig was primitive, to be sure, just a portable reel-to-reel operated by organist Garth Hudson and no more than three mics. The performances were rough; the songs were often in formative stages. But the musicians were clearly keen to "write" down the proceedings of their informal sessions. All told, and with a few more demos made in professional studios, the take added up to some 150 songs. Several years later, 25 were released by Columbia on a two-record set called *The Basement Tapes,* offering fans an intimate, behind-the-scenes listen to what had been private creative musings.

By then, the Saugerties house had assumed a mythic iconicity. The Hawks—rechristened the Band—released their debut album in the summer of 1968, calling it *Music from Big Pink*. Everything about its packaging suggested that the record sprang from this rustic setting. The front of the gatefold sleeve featured a primitivist Dylan painting. Inside was a faux-daguerreotype black-and-white photograph of the members of the Band standing in a field with mountains and mist rising behind them, exuding in their garb and manner a nineteenth-century aura. On the facing panel was a large color photograph called "Next of Kin." In it, the group's members stood in what appeared to be a barnyard, mingling with a small crowd of people—old and young—all posing as if at a family reunion, for that's what it was. The picture imparted a sense of tradition, heritage, and community. On the back panel was a photograph of Big Pink. The only annotation was a brief statement to the effect that "Big Pink bore this music and these songs along its way. It's the first witness of this album that's been thought and composed right there inside its walls."[5] The suggestion, then, was that here was a homemade record, not an industrial commodity but a homespun artwork fashioned in the quiet sanctuary of an artist's retreat, a place where music was not only played but given durable form. The message was that the record's birthplace had somehow left its mark in the sound.

In truth, technical limitations precluded professional-quality record making in the house. The record was made at A&R Studios in Manhattan and Capitol in Los Angeles, with the Band striving to capture in these high-tech settings the feel of their upstate experience. The record sleeve, however, made no mention of these other places. Instead, it looked and felt like a window on the group's atelier, which in a sense it was. For, although the record was not actually made at Big Pink, its sonic atmosphere was all over the album. According to Robertson, when producer John Simon asked the group what the record should sound like they replied, "Just like it did in the basement."[6] The songs had been conceived as sounds; they were recorded as soon as they were written, sometimes before they were even finished. The basement—its acoustic limitations and sonic signature—indicated the record's stylistic direction just as surely as did the songs and arrangements.

Music from Big Pink was widely acclaimed, and the Band was hailed as a group of seasoned artists blazing a new path. The record "washes the ears," wrote Al Aronowitz in *Life*, "with a sound never heard before."[7] A 1970 *Time* magazine cover story distinguished the Band from its peers with typical high-low rhetoric. Instead of "harddriving, ear-numbing rock," the group produced an "intricate, syncopated modal sound that, unlike rock but like fine jazz demands close attention." In concert they "showed a no-nonsense absorption in music that would have done credit to the Budapest String Quartet," and Robbie Robertson cut a figure that suggested "pictures of James Joyce as a young man."[8] But *Music from Big Pink* was, from conception to completion, an exemplary reflection of the contemporary rock zeitgeist. It was, like the later Beatles records, a work of musical performance completely divorced from any public music making, a mode of musical creativity unthinkable a scant twenty years prior. (The Band recorded two full albums before the musicians stepped onstage as an independent unit.) If their album sounded like nothing else on the pop charts of 1968, neither did Dylan's *John Wesley Harding,* Hendrix's *Electric Ladyland, The Beatles* (White Album), Van Morrison's *Astral Weeks,* Sly and the Family Stone's *Dance to the Music,* or the Rolling Stones' *Beggar's Banquet.* And as much as the Band exuded an aura of pastness, their album of cover tunes (*Moondog Matinee*) plainly showcased their rock and roll roots—Chuck Berry, Sam Cooke, Clarence "Frogman" Henry, Bobby "Blue" Bland, the Platters, Junior Parker, Fats Domino, Lee Dorsey, LaVern Baker.

Yet these immediate musical influences were only part of a bigger story. Cutting-edge late-sixties rock also bore a conceptual link to the stars of the earlier postwar years—Sinatra, Mitch Miller, Les Paul, and all the rest who made records *as* records. Whatever the musical particulars, the shift from music writing to sound recording was the backstory to all the changes that led from swing to rock. The novelty pop of the early fifties would not stand the test of time, but it was a telling reflection of the changing climate, and many of its production techniques would endure and continue to evolve. Despite their aesthetic and stylistic differences, postwar pop musicians of all stripes participated in laying the foundation for a new way of making and experiencing music that remains fundamental to music culture worldwide. When Frankie Laine's concert audience demanded a public debut of his "Mule Train" disc in 1949 while the singer sat mute onstage, the scene surpassed mere curiosity. It was, rather, a sign that the public and the disembodied voice had fallen in love.

Notes

INTRODUCTION

1. Gunther Schuller, *The Swing Era* (New York: Oxford University Press, 1989), 6.

CHAPTER 1

1. Thomas Allen Greenfield, *Radio: A Reference Guide* (Westport, Conn.: Greenwood Press, 1989), 5.

2. Joe Carlton, "Columbia Profits Jumped 850% in 1946, Industry Dough Swirls for Majors," *Billboard* (29 March 1947), 16.

3. Arnold Passman, *The Deejays* (New York: Macmillan, 1971), 114.

4. Richard Schroeder, *Texas Signs On: The Early Days of Radio and Television* (College Station, Tex.: Texas A&M University Press, 1998), 4.

5. Bing Crosby and Pete Martin, *Call Me Lucky: Bing Crosby's Own Story* (New York: Da Capo Press, 2001), 150.

6. Ibid., 152.

7. "Radio Row: One Thing and Another," *New York Times* (25 August 1946), 55.

8. Philip K. Eberly, *Music in the Air: America's Changing Tastes in Popular Music, 1920–1980* (New York: Hastings House, 1982), 76.

9. David B. Carson, memo to Assistant Secretary Huston (27 January 1922), U.S. National Archives, Record Group 173, cited in Michael Biel, "The Making and Use of Recordings in Broadcasting before 1936," PhD diss., Northwestern University, 1977, 230–31.

10. Cited in Biel, "The Making and Use of Recordings," 232.

11. Federal Radio Commission, "Statement Made by the Commission on August 23, 1928, Relative to Public Interest, Convenience, or Necessity, 2 FRC Ann. Rep. 166 (1928)," cited in Biel, "The Making and Use of Recordings," 603–4.

12. Reported in *Broadcast Advertising* (December 1929), 41, cited in Biel, "The Making and Use of Recordings," 606.

13. Reported in *Broadcasting* (15 February 1932), 14, cited in Biel, "The Making and Use of Recordings," 617.

14. Reported in *Broadcasting* (1 June 1933), 6, cited in Biel, "The Making and Use of Recordings," 620.

15. Reported in *Broadcasting* (1 February 1936), 7, 58, cited in Biel, "The Making and Use of Recordings," 635.

16. These organizations are, respectively, the American Society for Composers, Authors and Publishers; National Association of Broadcasters; Music Publishers Protective Association; Songwriters Protective Association; National Association of Performing Artists; American Federation of Musicians; Major Markets Group; and Independent Radio Network Affiliates.

17. "The Pied Piper of Chi," *Time* (26 January 1948), 19.

18. E. T. Cunningham to David Sarnoff (10 October 1933), NBC, cited in Biel, "Making and Use of Recordings," 644.

19. The Statutes at Large of the United States of America, from December, 1895, to March, 1897 (Washington, D.C.: Government Printing Office, 1897), 481–82.

20. Cited in Lucia S. Schultz, "Performing-Rights Societies in the United States," *Notes* (March 1979), 513.

21. ASCAP Articles of Association, Article III: 2, cited in John Ryan, *The Production of Culture in the Music Industry: The ASCAP-BMI Controversy* (Lanham, Md.: University Press of America, 1985), 53.

22. Cited in Ryan, *The Production of Culture,* 63, 69.

23. Quoted in "Rock 'n' Roll Laid to B.M.I. Control," *New York Times* (19 September 1956), 75.

24. "An Editorial," *Billboard* (30 January 1961), 13.

25. "Buck Holds Radio Kills Songs Today," *New York Times* (9 September 1936), 30.

26. Quoted in Virginia Waring, *Fred Waring and the Pennsylvanians* (Urbana: University of Illinois Press, 1997), 138.

27. Ibid., 139 (emphasis in original).

28. *Waring v. WDAS Broadcasting Station,* 327 Pa. 433, 435, 194 A. 631, 632 (Pa. 1937).

29. *Waring v. WDAS Broadcasting Station,* 327 Pa. 433, 435, 194 A. 631, 632 (Pa. 1937).

30. *Waring v. WDAS Broadcasting Station,* 327 Pa. 433, 439–440, 194 A. 631, 634 (Pa. 1937).

31. *Waring v. WDAS Broadcasting Station,* 327 Pa. 433, 439–440, 194 A. 631, 634 (Pa. 1937).

32. *Waring v. WDAS Broadcasting Station,* 327 Pa. 433, 441, 194 A. 631, 635 (Pa. 1937).

33. *RCA Mfg. Co. v. Whiteman,* 114 F.2d 86, 90 (C.A.2 1940).

34. *RCA Mfg. Co. v. Whiteman,* 28 F.Supp. 787, 789 (D.C.N.Y. 1939).

35. Waring, *Fred Waring,* 141.

36. *RCA Mfg. Co. v. Whiteman,* 28 F.Supp. 787, 789 (D.C.N.Y. 1939); *RCA Mfg. Co. v. Whiteman* 28 F.Supp. 787, 791 (D.C.N.Y. 1939).

37. *RCA Mfg. Co. v. Whiteman,* 28 F.Supp. 787 (D.C.N.Y. 1939).

38. "Court Limits Rule of a Record's Use," *New York Times* (17 December 1940), 28.

39. *RCA Mfg. Co. v. Whiteman,* 114 F.2d 86 (C.A.2 1940).

40. *RCA Mfg. Co. v. Whiteman,* 114 F.2d 86, 88 (C.A.2 1940).

41. *RCA Mfg. Co. v. Whiteman,* 114 F.2d 86, 89 (C.A.2 1940).

42. Benjamin Kaplan, "Publication in Copyright Law: The Question of Phonograph Records," *University of Pennsylvania Law Review* (January 1955), 473, 488.

43. Quoted in Waring, *Fred Waring,* 140.

44. Paul Whiteman, *Records for the Millions,* ed. David A. Stein (New York: Hermitage Press, 1948), 48, 51, 52.

45. Jack Gould, "Portrait of the Unpredictable Petrillo," *New York Times* (28 December 1947), SM11.

46. Quoted in James P. Kraft, *Stage to Studio: Musicians and the Sound Revolution, 1890–1950* (Baltimore: Johns Hopkins University Press, 1996), 127.

47. Alexander Bremer, quoted in Kraft, *Stage to Studio,* 24.

48. Kraft, *Stage to Studio,* 24. The so-called Silk Hats and Prince Alberts earned the sarcastic epithets by their fancy dress and haughty attitudes.

49. "The Pied Piper of Chi," 20–21.

50. Quoted in Kraft, *Stage to Studio,* 160.

51. "Canned Crosby," *Newsweek* (26 August 1946), 56.

52. John K. Hutchens, "It Doesn't Have to Be 'Live,'" *New York Times* (25 July 1943), X7.

53. Carter Harman, "Records: Comedians–Radio Artists Form Company to Release Transcriptions of Their Shows," *New York Times* (13 July 1947), 54.

54. Carroll Carroll, *None of Your Business, or My Life with J. Walter Thompson (Confessions of a Renegade Radio Writer)* (New York: Cowles, 1970), 235.

55. John T. Mullin, "Creating the Craft of Tape Recording," *High Fidelity* (April 1976), 62, 67.

56. Carroll, *None of Your Business,* 234.

57. Ibid., 235.

58. Joe Carlton, "Waxer's Red Carpet Spreads as Decca Firm Capitulates to Wooing of Disk Jockeys," *Billboard* (26 April 1947), 4.

59. Joe Carlton, "Ork Air Thins in the West," *Billboard* (29 March 1947), 17.

60. Ted Husing, *Ten Years before the Mike* (New York: Farrar and Rinehart, 1935), 38.

61. Carlton, "Waxers's Red Carpet," 19.

62. "Victor and Col to Sink Mint in Air Bally," *Billboard* (13 December 1947), 3, 18.

63. Eberly, *Music in the Air,* 273.

64. John K. Hutchens, "Disk Jockey at Work," *New York Times* (30 January 1944), X9.

65. *Billboard,* "KFWB to Get Block Cuffo in Smart Mutual Network Deal: Disk Jockey's Fabulous Take" (31 May 1947), 7.

66. "Pitchman's Progress," *Time* (11 December 1939), 62.

67. Martin Block, "The Case for the Disk Jockey," *Billboard, Band Year Book* (26 September 1942), 46.

68. "A Salute and a Word of Caution," *Billboard* (22 October 1949), 19.

69. Howard Taubman, "Tonal Plethora: Music Is Omnipresent in Modern Life," *New York Times* (9 September 1956), X9.

70. Block, "The Case for the Disk Jockey," 46.

71. William Barlow, *Voice Over: The Making of Black Radio* (Philadelphia: Temple University Press, 1999), 31.

72. "Radio and Race: Cantor and Kaye Break Radio Rules to Star Negroes," *Ebony* (January 1946), 41–43.

73. "Cooper Is Highest Paid Negro in Radio," *Ebony* (December 1947), 47.

74. "Spinners Capture Big White Audience," *Ebony* (December 1947), 49.

75. Ibid.

76. "The Forgotten 15,000,000," *Sponsor* (10 October 1949), 24–25.

77. Quoted in Brian Ward, *Radio and the Struggle for Civil Rights in the South* (Gainesville: University Press of Florida, 2004), 188.

78. *Rock and Roll Invaders: The AM Radio Deejays,* DVD, Paul Eichgrun (Dramarama Productions, 1998).

79. Charles Gruenberg, "The Rock and Roll Story: Alan Freed," *New York Post* (5 October 1956), 64.

80. Quoted in Arnold Shaw, *The Rockin' '50s: The Decade That Transformed the Pop Music Scene* (New York: Hawthorn Books, 1974), 105.

81. Alan Freed, "Alan Freed Says: 'I Told You So . . .,'" *Down Beat* (19 September 1956), 44; John A. Jackson, *Big Beat Heat: Alan Freed and the Early Years of Rock and Roll* (New York: Schirmer Books, 1991), 33–36.

82. Quoted in Gruenberg, "The Rock and Roll Story," 64.

83. Bob Rolontz, "Alan Freed Attracts Mob in Newark," *Billboard* (15 May 1954), 37.

84. "Rock 'n' Roll Pied Piper Alan Freed," *New York Times* (20 May 1960), 62.

85. Paul Ackerman, "1957 Adds to DJ Responsibilities," *Billboard* (26 January 1957), 45.

86. *Rock and Roll Invaders.*

87. "Versatility Keynote for Disk Shows," *Billboard* (9 August 1947), 19.

88. Aunt Enna, "Bill Randle's Story: From Cool to Hot to Luke Warm," *Down Beat* (7 May 1952), 8.

89. Freed, "'I Told You So,'" 44.

CHAPTER 2

1. "Second Annual Disc Jockey Poll Shows Strong Recording Trends," *Down Beat* (23 March 1955), 4.

2. John S. Wilson, "Creative Jazz," *New York Times* (5 April 1953), X9.

3. "Youth Movement Sweeps Records," *Billboard* (29 September 1951), 16.

4. Bob Rolontz, "Lush Days Are Over; Oldtimers Give Young Pop Artists Rough Time," *Billboard* (29 May 1954), 31.

5. Paul Ackerman, "Pop Record Public Blesses New Faces with Ready Dollars," *Billboard* (27 May 1955), 1.

6. Wilson, "Creative Jazz," X9.

7. Cited in Robert Rice, "Profiles: The Fractured Oboist," *New Yorker* (6 June 1953), 43.

8. Quoted in Fox, *In the Groove: The People behind the Music* (New York: St. Martin's Press, 1986), 33.

9. Mitch Miller, "Mitch, the Bearded Hit-Maker, Slaps Musical Snobbishness," *Down Beat* (July 16 1952), 2.

10. Mitch Miller, "June, Moon, Swoon, and Ko Ko Mo," *New York Times* (24 April 1955), SM19, 69.

11. Quoted in Dean Jennings, "The Shaggy Genius of Pop Music," *Saturday Evening Post* (21 April 1956), 43.

12. Quoted in "New Pop Era Plotted by Col Records: Miller Post Sparks It," *Billboard* (11 February 1950), 3.

13. Quoted in Richard Grudens, *The Music Men: The Guys Who Sang with the Bands and Beyond* (Stony Brook, N.Y.: Celebrity Profiles Publishing, 1998), 90.

14. Nev Gehman, "Columbia Pop-Disk Primacy Apparent in Billboard Charts," *Billboard* (26 April 1952), 1, 18.

15. Jennings, "The Shaggy Genius of Pop Music," 43.

16. "Mitch Miller: The State of Records," *Metronome* (November 1952), 13, 32.

17. Quoted in Nat Hentoff, "Mitch, Hunting New Stars, Glues Ear to Sample Discs," *Down Beat* (18 November 1953), 4.

18. Quoted in Peter Guralnick, *Last Train to Memphis: The Rise of Elvis Presley* (Boston: Little, Brown, 1994), 93.

19. Quoted in Shaw, *The Rockin' '50s*, 46.

20. Frankie Laine and Joseph F. Laredo, *That Lucky Old Son: The Autobiography of Frankie Laine* (Ventura, Calif.: Pathfinder, 1993), 15.

21. Quoted in Shaw, *The Rockin' '50s,* 46–48 (emphasis in original).

22. Laine and Laredo, *That Lucky Old Son,* 95.

23. Quoted in Fox, *In the Groove,* 35.

24. Laine and Laredo, *That Lucky Old Son,* 95.

25. Ibid., 98.

26. Ibid., 100.

27. Ibid., 108.

28. Mercury Records advertisement, *Billboard* (4 February 1950), 20.

29. Fox, *In the Groove,* 34.

30. Laine and Laredo, *That Lucky Old Son,* 94; David Simons, *Studio Stories* (San Francisco: Backbeat, 2004), 34.

31. Fox, *In the Groove,* 38.

32. Miller, "The State of Records," 13.

33. Mack McCormick, "Dick Haymes Refuses to Sing 'Current Crud,'" *Down Beat* (4 April 1952), 6.

34. Rice, "Fractured Oboist," 43.

35. Quoted in Jonny Whiteside, *Cry: The Johnnie Ray Story* (New York: Barricade Books, 1994), 12.

36. Quoted in Shaw, *The Rockin' '50s,* 55.

37. LaVern Baker, who opened the show, described events at the Flame as "an opening act, a comedian second, then a dancer, and then the principal act, followed by a closing act" (Whiteside, *Cry,* 53).

38. Quoted in Arnold Shaw, *Honkers and Shouters: The Golden Years of Rhythm and Blues* (New York, Macmillan, 1978), 448.

39. Quoted in Whiteside, *Cry,* 59.

40. Quoted in ibid., 63.

41. Hy Gardner, "Prince of Wails," *Look* (June 1952); "Johnnie's Golden Rays Dazzle Music Business," *Down Beat* (18 April 1952), 1; Barry Ulanov, "Tears and Grace Notes," *Metronome* (April 1952), 34; Howard Taubman, "Crooners, Groaners, Shouters, and Bleeders," *New York Times* (21 November 1954), SM54.

42. Howard Taubman, "Cry with Johnnie Ray," *New York Times* (27 April 1952), X7.

43. "Johnnie's Golden Rays Dazzle Music Business," *Down Beat* (18 April 1952), 1.

44. Taubman, "Cry," X7.

45. Taubman, "Crooners, Groaners," SM26, 27, 54–56.

46. Miller, "June, Moon, Swoon," SM69.

47. Taubman, "Cry," X7.

48. George T. Simon, "Tony Bennett: A Hot Commercial Bet Likes Hot Jazz Better," *Metronome* (February 1952), 17.

49. Nat Hentoff, "Tony Bennett Happy but Wants to Make a Wail of an Album," *Down Beat* (16 June 1954), 3.

50. Pat Harris, "Can't Make Money as a Jazz Singer: Starr," *Down Beat* (15 December 1950), 6.

51. Nat Hentoff, "Patti Page Likes Simplicity: But Don't Get Her Wrong, She Still Digs Money," *Down Beat* (30 July 1952), 6.

52. Jerry Wexler and David Ritz, *Rhythm and the Blues: A Life in American Music* (New York: Knopf, 1993), 63.

53. Quoted in Fox, *In the Groove,* 73.

54. "Fancy and Flashy," *Time* (26 June 1950), 74.

55. Quoted in Bruce Jenkins, *Goodbye: In Search of Gordon Jenkins* (Berkeley, Calif.: Frog Books, 2005), 54.

56. Quoted in Leonard Feather, "The Blindfold Test: Jenkins Digs Goodman the Most," *Down Beat* (21 May 1952), 12.

57. Will Friedwald, *Sinatra! The Song Is You: A Singer's Art* (New York: Da Capo Press, 1997), 349.

58. Quoted in Jenkins, *Goodbye,* 19, 32.

59. Gordon Jenkins, "Armstrong's Alter Ego," *Metronome* (June 1952), 16.

60. John S. Wilson, "Now They're Reviving the Recorder," *Down Beat* (5 May 1950), 3.

61. Quoted in Jenkins, *Goodbye,* 230.

62. Quoted in Doris Willens, *Lonesome Traveler: The Life of Lee Hays* (New York: Norton, 1988), 125.

63. Wilson, "Reviving the Recorder," 3.

64. Carl Sandburg, *The American Songbag* (New York: Harcourt, Brace and World, 1927), viii.

65. *The Weavers at Carnegie Hall* (Vanguard VRS 9010-A, 1956), cited in Robert Cantwell, *When We Were Good: The Folk Revival* (Cambridge: Harvard University Press, 1996), 178.

66. Quoted in Willens, *Lonesome Traveler,* 126.

67. Quoted in Jenkins, *Goodbye,* 236.

68. Quoted in ibid., 236.

69. Lee claimed that the idea came from a film image of galloping horses, whose gathering momentum struck her as akin to musical key changes and whose hoofbeats called to mind the busy interaction of a Latin percussion section. Her account names a 1935 film by Jean Gabin, *La Bandera,* as the inspiration. That film, however, has no such scene.

70. Ella Mae Morse, "Terrible Thing Is Happening to Singers! Everybody Shouts," *Down Beat* (19 November 1952), 2. Mel Blanc was the voice of such famous cartoon characters as Bugs Bunny, Daffy Duck, and Porky Pig.

71. Fran Warren, "A Rebuttal to Ella Mae's Morse Code for Singers," *Down Beat* (17 December 1952), 2.

72. *The New Sound!* liner notes, Capitol H 226 (1950).

73. "Les Paul," *Down Beat* (10 March 1948), 22.

74. "Les Paul, Mary Ford," *Metronome* (July 1952), 31.

75. "The New Sound," *Time* (29 October 1951), 71.

76. Jack Tracy, "Les Paul," *Down Beat* (20 April 1951), 15.

77. Barry Ulanov, "All-Star Paul," *Metronome* (February 1952), 18.

78. Ibid., 31.

79. Rice, "Fractured Oboist," 46.

80. John S. Wilson, "What Makes 'Pop' Music Popular," *New York Times* (8 December 1957), SM28.

81. "Natural Sound," *New Yorker* (17 July 1954), 17.

82. Barry Ulanov, "Mitch the Goose Man," *Metronome* (July 1950), 34.

83. "Why the Slump in Dance Biz? 'Beat' Plans to Find Out," *Down Beat* (30 December 1949), 1; "Special Edition of 'Beat' to Feature Dance Biz Revival," *Down Beat* (21 April 1950), 1.

84. See, for example, Norman Weiser, "Upheaval in Remotes Threatens," *Billboard* (18 October 1947), 18, 47.

85. "Parks Nix High Ork Fees, Want Sweet with Show," *Billboard* (29 March 1947), 3, 102. "Ork" is *Billboard*'s idiosyncratic abbreviation for orchestra.

86. Hal Webman, "Campus Kids' Ork Squawks," *Billboard* (14 February 1948), 3, 19.

87. "Orks Resorting to Vaudeville Hambone to Give Biz Good Shot in the Old Soupbone," *Billboard* (10 January 1948), 4, 15.

88. "New Birth for Dance Bands," *Billboard* (18 February 1950), 1, 45.

89. Bill Simon, "Jocks Not Playing Disks They Prefer," *Billboard* (11 November 1957), 38.

90. Quoted in Friedwald, *Sinatra!* 188.

91. Murray Schumach, "Lady among Roisterers," *New York Times* (3 December 1950), X13.

92. Quoted in Mary Alice Shaughnessy, *Les Paul: An American Original* (New York: William Morrow, 1993), 224.

93. Mitch Miller, "To the Disc Jockeys, with Love," *Music Journal* (June–July 1958), 18, 39.

94. Miller, "June, Moon, Swoon," 69, 78.

95. Miller, "Disk Jockeys," 19.

96. "Bumper Crop of 45 Sold Million in '58," *Billboard* (5 January 1959), 4; Bob Rolontz, "72 Labels Landed on Chart in'58: A Feverish Year," *Billboard* (5 January 1959), 3.

97. Quoted in George Simon, "What's Wrong with Music!" *Metronome* (February 1948), 16.

98. Quoted in Abel Green, " 'New' Music Biz Faces the Crossroads," *Variety* (6 January 1954), 225.

99. Crosby and Martin, *Call Me Lucky*, 142–43.

100. Ibid., 140.

101. Ibid., 143.

CHAPTER 3

1. "Buddy Knox," Rockabilly Hall of Fame, http://www.rockabillyhall.com/BuddyKnox.html. All Buddy Knox quotes are collected from "BBC Radio London radio interviews with Charlie Gillett and Stuart Colman, and earlier interviews with *New Kommotion* editor Adam Komorowski."

2. Philip Norman, *Rave On: The Biography of Buddy Holly* (New York: Simon and Schuster, 1996), 90.

3. Jimmy D. Self, liner notes for *The Original Norman Petty Trio and Ensemble*, Ace 443 (1994). Self was a longtime acquaintance of Petty's and in 1954 was one of the first clients, along with his group, the Sunshine Playboys, at the West Seventh Street studio.

4. Bill Simon, "Indies' Surprise Survival: Small Labels' Ingenuity and Skill Pay Off," *Billboard* (3 December 1949), 1, 13.

5. June Bundy, "Swingin' Indies Still Tops on Billboard's Singles Chart," *Billboard* (30 September 1957), 18.

6. Quoted in Charlie Gillett, *Making Tracks: The Story of Atlantic Records* (London: Souvenir Press, 1988), 21.

7. Wexler and Ritz, *Rhythm and the Blues*, 20–21, 35.

8. Quoted in Colin Escott, *Tattooed on Their Tongues: A Journey through the Backrooms of American Music* (New York: Schirmer Books, 1996), 63–64, 67.

9. "Diskers' Drop-In Dragnet: Pre-planned Pub Plugs Way-Siding as Smaller Labels Hunt for 'Material' Firsts," *Billboard* (17 May 1947), 22.

10. Quoted in Todd Mouton, "BackTalk with Cosimo Matassa," Offbeat, http://www.offbeat.com/artman/publish/article_579.shtml (accessed January 2006). Interview appears in *Offbeat* (August 1997).

11. Quoted in "It's Tough to Find a Good, Really Bad Song," *Billboard* (20 May 1957), 20.

12. Simon, "Indies' Surprise Survival," 13.

13. "Indies in There Swinging," *Billboard* (20 April 1946), 112.

14. Quoted in Shaw, *Honkers and Shouters,* 182.

15. "Modern Woos Race Artists," *Billboard* (8 January 1949), 14.

16. "Indies in There Swinging," 20.

17. "Distrib Pitch for Race Wax Seen Cause of Bogus Disks," *Billboard* (22 May 1948), 26.

18. Bob Rolontz, "Mushrooming R.&B.'s: Labels Sprout New Labels, Even Subsids Have Subsids," *Billboard* (23 May 1953), 14, 18.

19. "Small Firms Tops in Blues," *Billboard* (24 April 1954), 1.

20. "'Peg' Zooms Indie into Million Class, Harmonicats into Big $," *Billboard* (19 July 1947), 21.

21. "Diskers' Drop-In Dragnet," 22.

22. Quoted in Martin Hawkins, *A Shot in the Dark: Making Records in Nashville, 1945–1955* (Nashville: Vanderbilt University Press, 2006), 1. Fowler later backed out of the deal and was replaced by Orville Zickler, an assistant cashier at the First American National Bank.

23. Quoted in ibid., 25.

24. Quoted in ibid., 61.

25. "Disk from Dixie," *Newsweek* (15 September 1947), 84.

26. Quoted in George Simon, "What's Wrong with Music!" *Metronome* (February 1948), 16 (emphasis in original).

27. "Novelties Hit High, Lead a Short Life," *Billboard* (8 April 1950), 14.

28. "Diskers' Drop-In Dragnet," 23.

29. Greil Marcus, "The Deborah Chessler Story," in Greil Marcus, *The Dustbin of History* (Cambridge: Harvard University Press, 1995), 236.

30. Ren Grevatt, "R&B Stars Develop Strong Stay Power," *Billboard* (4 February 1956), 54.

31. Quoted in Marv Goldberg, "The Orioles, Part 1: The Jubilee Years, 1948–1951," Marv Goldberg's Yesterday's Memories Rhythm and Blues Party, http://home.att.net/~marvy42/Orioles/orioles1.html.

32. "'Too Soon,' by Obscure Quintet, Latest Boom Disk," *Billboard* (4 September 1948), 17.

33. Hal Webman, "Night ClubVaude Reviews: Strand, New York," *Billboard* (12 May 1951), 38.

34. James A. McGowan, *Here Today, Here to Stay: A Personal History of Rhythm and Blues* (Amber, Pa.: Akashic Press, 1983), 9–10.

35. Ibid., 1.

36. Joel Friedman, "Rush on for Vocal Combos: Waxers Sign Flocks of Warblers Who Cut Disks in All Fields," *Billboard* (22 May 1954), 40.

37. Quoted in Steve Loza, *Tito Puente and the Making of Latin Music* (Urbana: University of Illinois Press, 1999), 32.

38. Quoted in Frederic Dannen, *Hit Men: Power Brokers and Fast Money Inside the Music Business* (New York: Times Books, 1990), 40.

39. See Art Peters, "Comeback of a Child Star," *Ebony* (January 1967), 42–50.

40. Ronnie Spector, with Vince Waldron, *Be My Baby: How I Survived Mascara, Miniskirts, and Madness, or My Life as a Fabulous Ronette* (New York: Harmony Books, 1990), 13.

41. Quoted in James Segrest and Mark Hoffman, *Moanin' at Midnight: The Life and Times of Howlin' Wolf* (New York: Pantheon Books, 2004), 71.

42. Quoted in James Dickerson, *Goin' Back to Memphis: A Century of Blues, Rock 'n' Roll, and Glorious Soul* (New York: Schirmer Books, 1996), 84.

43. Louis Cantor, *Wheelin' on Beale: How WDIA-Memphis Became the Nation's First All-Black Radio Station and Created the Sound That Changed America* (New York: Pharos Books, 1992), 2.

44. James M. Salem, *The Late Great Johnny Ace and the Transition from R&B to Rock 'n' Roll* (Urbana: University of Illinois Press, 1999), 69.

45. Quoted in ibid., 42–43.

46. "Rhythm and Blues," *Down Beat* (8 October 1952), 11.

47. "Talent Corner," *Billboard* (29 January 1955), 34.

48. "1955, the Year R.&B. Took over Pop Field," *Billboard* (12 November 1955), 126.

49. Quoted in Salem, *Johnny Ace,* 45.

50. Quoted in Cantor, *Wheelin' on Beale,* 184.

51. Quoted in Jimmy Guterman, *The Sun Records Collection,* Rhino R2 71780 (1994), 3.

52. Quoted in Colin Escott with Martin Hawkins, *Good Rockin' Tonight: Sun Records and the Birth of Rock 'n' Roll* (New York: St. Martin's Press, 1991), 10.

53. Quoted in ibid., 35.

54. Jerry Hopkins Archive, University of Memphis, Mississippi Valley Collection, tape 9/33.

55. Quoted in John Floyd, *Sun Records: An Oral History* (New York: Avon Books, 1998), 130.

56. Personal interview, 11 August 2003, Memphis, Tennessee.

57. *Good Rockin' Tonight: The Legacy of Sun Records,* Bruce Sinofsky, director/producer, Educational Broadcasting Corporation and SLM Productions (2001).

58. Quoted in Greil Marcus, *Mystery Train: Images of America in Rock 'n' Roll Music* (New York: E. P. Dutton, 1976), 168.

59. Quoted in Peter Guralnick, *Lost Highway: Journeys and Arrivals of American Musicians* (New York: Harper and Row, 1989), 329 (emphasis in original).

60. Quoted in Escott, *Good Rockin' Tonight,* 30–31 (emphasis in original).

61. Quoted in Floyd, *Sun Records,* 116.

62. Quoted in ibid., 117.

63. Quoted in Guralnick, *Lost Highway,* 334–35 (emphasis in original).

64. Quoted in Escott, *Good Rockin' Tonight,* 170.

65. Personal interview, 12 August 2003, Memphis, Tennessee.

66. Jerry Hopkins Archive, tape 9/33.

67. Quoted in Guralnick, *Last Train to Memphis,* 64, 85.

68. Quoted in ibid., 135 (emphasis in original).

69. Ibid., 94.

70. Quoted in ibid., 95.

71. Quoted in ibid., 99.

72. Quoted in ibid., 103.

73. Quoted in Shaw, *The Rockin' '50s,* 79.

74. Bill C. Malone, "Elvis, Country Music, and the South," *Southern Quarterly* (fall 1979), 123.

CHAPTER 4

1. *Schwartz v. Broadcast Music, Inc.,* 180 F.Supp. 322, 326 (D.C.N.Y. 1959).

2. Philip H. Ennis, *The Seventh Stream: The Emergence of Rocknroll in American Popular Music* (Hanover, N.H.: Wesleyan University Press and University Press of New England, 1992), 5.

3. Ibid., 21.

4. Steve Schickel, "A La Country and Western: R.&B. Music Invades Pop Market—Jukes, Disk Stores Feeling Trend," *Billboard* (14 August 1954), 13, 18; "Editorial: Bursting Old Barriers," *Billboard* (24 April 1954), 13; Bob Rolontz, "Pop–C.&W.–R.&B.: Demarcation Lines Are Growing Hazy," *Billboard* (12 September 1953), 15, 20.

5. Ennis, *The Seventh Stream,* 6.

6. Quoted in Jackson, *Big Beat Heat,* 82.

7. "Honor Roll of Hits Tabbed," *Billboard* (24 March 1945), 3.

8. "The Billboard Music Popularity Chart," *Billboard* (24 March 1945), 16.

9. "Honor Roll," 64.

10. "American Folk Records," *Billboard* (3 October 1942), 69.

11. Steve Schickel, "Acceptance of C.&W.: Jukes in Big Role for Passing Word," *Billboard* (22 May 1954), 28; Steve Sholes, "Developing Country Scene: Styles Change and Quality Improves Artists, Firms Increase in 10 Years," *Billboard* (22 May 1954), 18.

12. "Record Reviews," *Billboard* (11 March 1950), 124. The quote is from a review of Calvin Boze's "Waiting and Drinking" (Aladdin 3045).

13. Quoted in Shaw, *The Rockin' '50s,* 79.

14. Chuck Berry, *Chuck Berry: The Autobiography* (New York: Harmony Books, 1987), 89.

15. Quoted in Shaw, *Honkers and Shouters,* 278.

16. "Top Names Now Singing the Blues as Newcomers Roll on R&B Tide," *Variety* (23 February 1955), 1.

17. "Editorial: The Buyer's Always Right," *Billboard* (29 January 1955), 56.

18. Tracking charts were also compiled by publications such as *Cashbox, Peatman Report,* and *Variety.*

19. "Bull Market in Corn," *Time* (4 October 1943), 49–50.

20. For good accounts of the growth of the country music business, see Bill C. Malone, *Country Music, U.S.A.* (Austin: University of Texas Press, 1985); and William Kenney, *Recorded Music in American Life: The Phonograph and Popular Memory, 1890–1945* (New York: Oxford University Press, 1999).

21. "Down in Philly They Go Silly for Hillbilly—But Rilly, Rilly!" *Billboard* (5 July 1947), 22.

22. Hal Webman, "Gold in Them Hillbills!" *Billboard* (27 December 1947), 3, 18.

23. "Folk Festival Sept. 18–19 at Carnegie Hall," *Billboard* (13 September 1947), 20.

24. "Hillbilly Bash in Carnegie Perks Stem Interest," *Billboard* (27 September 1947), 3, 21.

25. Allen Churchill, "Tin Pan Alley's Git-tar Blues," *New York Times* (15 July 1951), SM5.

26. "'Tenn. Waltz' Cracks thru from Flip," *Billboard* (11 November 1950), 13.

Jerry Wexler expanded the story in his autobiography, claiming to have suggested the song to Page's manager, Jack Rael, after hearing the Hawkins version (with Ace Harris on vocal). Wexler was not aware at the time of the King original (Wexler and Ritz, *Rhythm and the Blues,* 66).

27. Churchill, "Git-tar Blues," SM5.

28. Joe Martin, "Country Music Field Full of Green Stuff—Folding Kind, That Is," *Billboard* (22 May 1954), 30.

29. Quoted in Leo Zabelin, "Line between Popular, C&W Growing Thinner: Rex Allen," *Down Beat* (18 November 1953), 6.

30. Ibid.

31. Bob Rolontz, "Close Pub-Artist-Disker Ties Result in Hits from the Heart," *Billboard* (22 May 1954), 18.

32. Joel Friedman, "'Genuine' Quality Sets Country Field Apart from Tin Pan Alley Music," *Billboard* (5 December 1953), 42.

33. Churchill, "Git-tar Blues," SM5; Sholes, "Developing Country Scene," 39.

34. Miller, "Moon, June, Swoon," SM19.

35. Quoted in Jennings, "The Shaggy Genius of Pop Music," 77.

36. Quoted in Roger M. Williams, *Sing a Sad Song: The Life of Hank Williams* (Urbana: University of Illinois Press, 1981), 116.

37. Quoted in David Simons, *Studio Stories* (San Francisco: Backbeat Books, 2004), 41.

38. Goddard Lieberson, "'Country' Sweeps the Country," *New York Times* (28 July 1957), 153.

39. Malone, *Country Music, U.S.A.,* 158.

40. This phenomenon is treated in colorful detail in Nick Tosches, *Country: The Twisted Roots of Rock 'n' Roll* (New York: Da Capo Press, 1996).

41. Bob Rolontz and Joel Friedman, "Teen-Agers Demand Music with a Beat, Spur Rhythm-Blues," *Billboard* (24 April 1954), 1.

42. Schickel, "A La Country and Western," 13.

43. "Editorial: Bursting Old Barriers," 13.

44. Wexler and Ritz, *Rhythm and the Blues,* 62.

45. "White Fans Hyping R&B Platter Sales," *Billboard* (31 May 1952), 20, 41. Dolphin said his shop's name was an assertion of pride in his own neighborhood and a symbolic gesture meant to "bring Hollywood to the blacks" (quoted in Tom Reed, *The Black Music History of Los Angeles: Its Roots* [Los Angeles: Black Accent on L.A. Press, 1992], 78).

46. Rolontz and Friedman, "Teen-Agers," 1.

47. Shickel, "A La Country and Western," 18.

48. Rolontz and Friedman, "Teen-Agers," 1.

49. Shickel, "A La Country and Western," 18.

50. Shaw, *Honkers and Shouters,* 93.

51. Brown would finally make the pop charts with a 1957 cover of "Party Doll."

52. Paul Ackerman, "Rhythm and Blues Notes," *Billboard* (5 March 1955), 16.

53. *The Hit Makers: The Teens Who Stole Pop Music,* DVD, Morgan Neville, Peter Jones Productions (1999).

54. Ray Charles and David Ritz, *Brother Ray: Ray Charles' Own Story* (New York: Da Capo Press, 2004), 177.

55. Shaw, *The Rockin' '50s,* 74.

56. "Atlantic to Start New R&B Firm," *Billboard* (10 April 1954), 22.

57. Shaw, *The Rockin' '50s,* 74.

58. Quoted in ibid., 74.

59. Quoted in Charlie Gillett, *Making Tracks: The Story of Atlantic Records* (London: Souvenir Press, 1974), 53.

60. Paul Ackerman and Ren Grevatt, "Biggest Wax Trend on March: A Great Day for the Blues," *Billboard* (18 November 1957), 1, 55.

61. Wexler and Ritz, *Rhythm and the Blues,* 85.

62. Schickel, "A La Country and Western," 13.

63. "Small Firms Tops in Blues," *Billboard* (24 April 1954), 1. On the larger firms' forays into R&B, see, for example, "Columbia Race Dept. Expands," *Billboard* (22 March 1947), 16; "Mercury Adds to Race Department," *Billboard* (1 January 1949), 12; "RCA Plans New 45 R&B Pitch," *Billboard* (21 March 1951), 16; "Col. Revives Okeh for Heavy R&B Bid," *Billboard* (26 May 1951), 10, 33; "M-G-M Readies Push into R&B Field," *Billboard* (20 December 1952), 27; and "Decca Speeds Up R&B Pace," *Billboard* (15 August 1953), 15.

64. "Top Names Now Singing the Blues as Newcomers Roll on R&B Tide," *Variety* (23 February 1955), 1.

65. Ackerman, "Rhythm and Blues Notes," 16.

66. "Majors, Indies Square Off in Competition over Disk Fields," *Billboard* (3 March 1951), 10.

67. Quoted in Shaw, *Honkers and Shouters,* 195.

68. Quoted in ibid., 181.

69. Johnny Otis, *Listen to the Lambs* (New York: Norton, 1968), 12.

70. *That Rhythm, Those Blues,* video, George T. Nierenberg and David McCullough, PBS Video (1989).

71. Ibid.

72. "Music Biz Now R&B Punchy: Even Hillbillies Are Doing It," *Variety* (9 February 1955), 51.

73. Quoted in Gillett, *Making Tracks,* 109.

74. Langston Hughes, "Highway Robbery across the Color Line in Rhythm and Blues," *Chicago Defender* (2 July 1955), 9.

75. Charles Gruenberg, "The Negro Issue in Rock and Roll," *New York Post* (9 October 1956), 50.

76. "WINS Issues Ban on Copy Records," *Billboard* (27 August 1955), 21.

77. "LaVern Baker Seeks Bill to Halt Arrangement 'Thefts,'" *Billboard* (5 March 1955), 13.

78. Jerry Wexler, "Rhythm and Blues in 1950," *Saturday Review* (24 June 1950), 49.

79. "Top Names," 1.

80. Jonathan Kamin, "The White R&B Audience and the Music Industry, 1952–1956," *Popular Music and Society* (6:1978), 152. R&B songs' often racy lyrics were a particular source of controversy. See, for example, "A Warning to the Music Industry," *Variety* (23 February 1955), 2; Bob Rolontz, "Rhythm and Blues Notes," *Billboard* (9 October 1954), 20; and "Indie Diskers back WDIA's R&B Bans," *Billboard* (30 October 1954), 16.

81. *Billboard* (21 August 1954), 35.

82. *Billboard* (30 August 1947), 28.

83. Bill Simon, "Who Juices the Spotlight?: Jock Showcasing of New Talent Keeps Wax Fresh," *Billboard* (26 January 1957), 45.

84. "Diskeries Score Anti-pop Bias of Some DJ's," *Billboard* (3 March 1956), 54.

85. Paul Ackerman, "What Has Happened to Popular Music," *High Fidelity* (June 1958), 37.

86. Paul Ackerman, "Eddie Fisher Rocks Kids at Carnegie Hall," *Billboard* (5 June 1954), 15.

87. Hannah Altbush, "Monte Carlo to U.S., Miss Gibbs Finds She Is Always Her Nibs," *Down Beat* (6 April 1955), 5.

88. Gary Kramer, "More Good Disks Make Spins Tougher," *Billboard* (26 January 1957), 48.

89. Ruth Cage, "Rhythm & Blues," *Down Beat* (27 July 1955), 15.

90. "Pop, R&B Just Won't Stay in Own Backyards," *Billboard* (4 November 1957), 20.

91. "C&W Artists Play HOB with R&B Charts," *Billboard* (6 January 1958), 16.

92. Jack Gould, "TV: New Phenomenon," *New York Times* (6 June 1956), 67.

93. June Bundy "DJ Plays Mold Trends: Desegregation of Chart Categories Earmarks '56," *Billboard* (26 January 1957), 48.

94. "Where Do You List R 'n' R?" *Billboard* (6 May 1957), 1.

95. Mike Kaplan, "New Definition of a 'Pop,'" *Variety* (27 March 1957), 51.

CHAPTER 5

1. "Record Reviews: Race," *Billboard* (16 October 1948), 112.

2. "Salady Days," *Time* (28 February 1949), 47–48.

3. Arnold Shaw, "The Music Goes Up and Down," *New York Times* (18 May 1947), SM18.

4. Hal Webman, "Bands Pin Faith in Teen-Agers," *Billboard* (31 December 1949), 3.

5. "Salady Days," 48.

6. *Supreme Records v. Decca Records,* 90 F.Supp. 904, 905 (D.C.Cal. 1950).

7. *Supreme Records v. Decca Records,* 90 F.Supp. 904, 912 (D.C.Cal. 1950).

8. "Supreme Loses Case for 400G against Decca," *Billboard* (13 May 1950), 12.

9. *Supreme Records v. Decca Records,* 90 F.Supp. 904, 912 (D.C.Cal. 1950).

10. *Supreme Records v. Decca Records,* 90 F.Supp. 904, 912–13 (D.C.Cal. 1950).

11. *Supreme Records v. Decca Records,* 90 F.Supp. 904, 911 (D.C.Cal. 1950).

12. *Supreme Records v. Decca Records,* 90 F.Supp. 904 (D.C.Cal. 1950).

13. *Supreme Records v. Decca Records,* 90 F.Supp. 904, 912 (D.C.Cal. 1950).

14. "Supreme Loses Case," 12.

15. Compton Mackenzie, "The Gramophone: Its Past; Its Present; Its Future," in *Proceedings of the Musical Association* (London: Musical Association, 1924–25), 106.

16. Herman Klein, "A Seven Years' Retrospect," in *Herman Klein and The Gramophone,* ed. William R. Moran (Portland, Ore.: Amadeus Press, 1990), 329. First published in September 1931.

17. Herman Klein, "The Distortions of Over-Amplification," in *Herman Klein and The Gramophone,* ed. William R. Moran (Portland, Ore.: Amadeus Press, 1990), 309. First published in December 1930.

18. Herman Klein, "The Singer and the Microphone," in *Herman Klein and The Gramophone,* ed. William R. Moran (Portland, Ore.: Amadeus Press, 1990), 372. First published in May 1933.

19. Klein, "The Distortions of Over-Amplification," 309.

20. Herman Klein, "The Penalties of Exaggeration," in *Herman Klein and The Gramophone,* ed. William R. Moran (Portland, Ore.: Amadeus Press, 1990), 377. First published in September 1933.

21. Quoted in Oliver Read and Walter L. Welch, *From Tin Foil to Stereo: Evolution of the Phonograph* (Indianapolis: H. W. Sams, 1959), 353.

22. Compton Mackenzie, "Recording in the Old Days," *New York Times* (21 July 1957), X12.

23. Klein, "The Distortions of Over-Amplification," 310.

24. Writing in the 1930s, Stravinsky was impressed with the medium's ability to capture "all my intentions with real exactitude." His recordings had "the importance of documents which can serve as guides to all executants of my music." Beyond this practical use, however, listeners must beware of "the musical deception arising from the substitution for the actual playing of a reproduction. . . . It is the same difference as that between the *ersatz* and the authentic." Igor Stravinsky, *An Autobiography* (New York: Norton, 1962), 150–54.

25. Howard Taubman, "High Fidelity in American Life," *New York Times* (22 November 1953), X39.

26. Charles Fowler, "As the Editor Sees It," *High Fidelity* (1:1, 1951), 8.

27. Milton B. Sleeper, "Rating Recorded Music," *High Fidelity* (2:2, 1952), 31.

28. Charles L. Granata, *Sessions with Sinatra: Frank Sinatra and the Art of Recording* (Chicago: A Cappella, 1999), 47.

29. "Men behind the Microphones: Makers of Music for Millions," *Newsweek* (8 September 1952), 56–57.

30. Quoted in Susan Schmidt Horning, "Chasing Sound: The Culture and Technology of Recording Studios in America, 1877–1977," PhD diss., Case Western Reserve University, 2002, 215.

31. Milton B. Sleeper, "By Way of Introduction," *High Fidelity* (1:1, 1951), 6.

32. John Briggs, "A Look at Commercial High Fidelity," *New York Times* (22 November 1953), X43.

33. "Stop Abusing 'Hi-Fi,' " *Billboard* (1 May 1954), 38.

34. Charles Fowler, "The Illusion of High Fidelity," *Down Beat* (24 February 1954), 7 (emphasis in original).

35. Carl Eton, "Tops . . . for the Juke Box," *High Fidelity* (1:2, 1951), 62, 74.

36. Quoted in Jim Cogan, "Bill Putnam," *Mix* (October 2003), http://mixonline.com/recording/interviews/audio_bill_putnam/index.html.

37. Quoted in "An Afternoon With: Bill Putnam," *Journal of the Audio Engineering Society* (September 1989), 730. The quote dates from 1962.

38. Quoted in Eric Olsen, Paul Verna, and Carlo Wolff, *The Encyclopedia of Record Producers* (New York: Watson-Guptill, 1999), 539.

39. Quoted in Cogan, "Bill Putnam" (emphasis in original).

40. Peter Doyle, *Echo and Reverb: Fabricating Space in Popular Music Recording, 1900–1960* (Middletown, Conn.: Wesleyan University Press, 2005), 69.

41. Milton T. Putnam, "A Thirty-Five-Year History and Evolution of the Recording Studio," Audio Engineering Society Reprints, no. 1661 (New York: Audio Engineering Society, 1980).

42. Quoted in Horning, "Chasing Sound," 172.

43. Ibid., 173.

44. "Patti's Voices," *Newsweek* (11 December 1950), 84.

45. Serge Lacasse, " 'Listen to My Voice': The Evocative Power of Vocal Staging in Recorded Rock Music and Other Forms of Vocal Expression," PhD diss., University of Liverpool, 2000, 21.

46. Quoted in Shaughnessy, *Les Paul,* 140.

47. "Disks by Duo Sell 4 Million," *Billboard* (25 August 1951), 1.

48. John S. Wilson, "How No-Talent Singers Get 'Talent,' " *New York Times* (21 June 1959), SM16.

49. Quoted in Simons, *Studio Stories,* 37.

50. Quoted in ibid., 30.

51. Quoted in ibid., 43.

52. Hopkins Archive, tape 9/28; Hopkins Archive, tape 9/20.

53. Quoted in Guralnick, *Last Train to Memphis,* 238.

54. For a comprehensive discussion of Presley's recording history, see Ernst Jorgensen, *Elvis Presley: A Life in Music* (New York: St. Martin's Press, 1998).

55. Alfred Wertheimer with Gregory Martinelli, *Elvis '56: In the Beginning* (New York: Collier Books, 1979).

56. Presley's version has only two stanzas, each repeated three times.

57. Quoted in Guralnick, *Last Train to Memphis,* 298.

58. John S. Wilson, "Elvis Presley: Rocking Blues Shouter," *New York Times* (13 January 1957), X16.

59. Quoted in Laurie Henshaw, "Rock-'n'-Roll Swamps '56 Music Scene," *Melody Maker* (15 December 1956), 21.

CHAPTER 6

1. Bill Simon, "Jock Showcasing of New Talent Keeps Wax Fresh," *Billboard* (26 January 1957), 45.

2. Quoted in David Kamp, "The Hit Factory," http://davidkamp.com/2006/09/the_hit_factory.php.

3. "Music Biz Now R&B Punchy," *Variety* (9 February 1955), 51.

4. "Inside Stuff: Music," *Variety* (4 December 1957), 58.

5. "Rock 'n' Roll: A Frenzied Teen-Age Music Craze Kicks Up a Big Fuss," *Life* (18 April 1955), 166, 168.

6. "Yeh-Heh-Heh-Hes, Baby," *Time* (18 June 1956), 54.

7. John S. Wilson, "Elvis Presley: Rocking Blues Shouter," *New York Times* (13 January 1957), X16.

8. Gertrude Samuels, "Why They Rock 'n' Roll, and Should They?" *New York Times* (12 January 1958), SM16.

9. Bill Simon, "Term R&B Hardly Covers Multi-material So Grouped," *Billboard* (4 February 1956), 55.

10. Max Jones and Sinclair Traill, "About Rock 'n' Roll," *Melody Maker* (8 September 1956), 6.

11. Jerry Wexler, "Mainstream of Jazz Is R and B: Wexler," *Down Beat* (15 July 1953), 15.

12. Paul Ackerman, "What Has Happened to Popular Music," *High Fidelity* (June 1958), 35.

13. "Rock 'n' Roll Rolls On 'n' On," *Life* (22 December 1958), 37–38.

14. Alan Freed, "One Thing's for Sure, R 'n' R Is Boffo B.O.," *Variety* (8 January 1958), 214.

15. "So-called rock and roll" and "big rock and roll hits" are quoted from Paul Ackerman, "Square Circles Peg Rock and Roll Idiom as a Beat to Stick," *Billboard* (4 February 1956), 1. "'Back shack' sound" and "rock and roll–c.&w." are quoted from Paul Ackerman, "Diskeries in Race for R&R Country Talent," *Billboard* (12 May 1956), 12, 14. "Pop adaptation" is quoted from Paul Ackerman, "C&W Booms as Vital Force in Music-Record Business," *Billboard* (23 March 1957), 79.

16. Ackerman, "C&W Booms," 79.

17. "Fall Blood, Sweat, and Tears Outlook for Brill Building," *Billboard* (15 September 1956), 15.

18. Quoted in Mark Ribowsky, *He's a Rebel* (New York: E. P. Dutton, 1989), 29.

19. "Anything Goes for a Pop Hit," *Variety* (9 November 1955), 39.

20. John S. Wilson, "What Makes 'Pop' Music Popular," *New York Times* (8 December 1957), SM28.

21. Quoted in Shaw, *Honkers and Shouters,* 165.

22. "Pops Tops with Teeners: Kids Dig Pop Vocal Most but Don't Always Buy Them," *Billboard* (15 December 1956), 31. See also June Bundy, "Gals Best Disk and Phono Buyers in Teen-Age Bracket," *Billboard* (25 August 1956), 15.

23. Gary Kramer, "R.&R. a Teen-Age Must," *Billboard* (10 November 1956), 21.

24. "D.J.: Hitmaker or Hitchhiker?" *Variety* (4 August 1954), 41.

25. Bill Simon, "Jocks Not Playing Disks They Prefer," *Billboard* (11 November 1957), 38.

26. Ackerman, "Diskeries in Race," 12.

27. Gary Kramer, "On the Beat: Rhythm and Blues–Rock and Roll," *Billboard* (16 February 1957), 27.

28. "'Happy' Hits Million: Sales Climb Despite Sundry Lamentations," *Billboard* (28 March 1953), 18.

29. "Few New Diskery Artists Able to Hit Big Time in '52," *Billboard* (13 January, 1953), 13.

30. "Mystery Hit," *Time* (9 February 1953), 49.

31. "'Happy' Hits Million," 46.

32. "Mystery Hit," 49.

33. "This Week's Best Buys," *Billboard* (29 November 1952), 34.

34. "'Happy' Hits Million," 18.

35. Quoted in John Swenson, *Bill Haley: The Daddy of Rock and Roll* (New York: Stein and Day, 1982), 37.

36. Shaw, *The Rockin' '50s,* 140.

37. Quoted in Swenson, *Bill Haley,* 37.

38. Quoted in ibid., 37–38.

39. Ibid., 28.

40. Quoted in Bill Dahl, liner notes for *The Best of Bill Haley and His Comets, 1951–1954,* Varèse Sarabande 302 066 549 2 (2004).

41. Fox, *In the Groove,* 92.

42. Quoted in Charles White, *The Life and Times of Little Richard: The Quasar of Rock* (New York: Da Capo Press, 1994), 38.

43. Ibid., 45.

44. Quoted in Harry Weinger, liner notes for *The Magic Touch: An Anthology,* Mercury 314 510 314-2 (1991), 7.

45. Quoted in Shaw, *Honkers and Shouters,* 241.

46. "The Platters: Four Boys and a Girl Form Highest Paid Vocal Group," *Ebony* (December 1956), 109.

47. Quoted in Shaw, *Honkers and Shouters,* 241.

48. "Topics of the Times," *New York Times* (17 June 1957), 22.

49. "Demise of R&R Just So Much Wishful Thinking," *Billboard* (9 September 1957), 18.

50. Howard Cook, "No Lack of New Talent on Disks," *Billboard* (11 November 1957), 31.

51. Wilson, "What Makes 'Pop' Music Popular," SM13.

52. Paul Ackerman, "Diversified Sphere of American Music at Peak Influence," *Billboard* (29 April 1957), 21.

53. Marv Goldberg, "The Five Keys," Marv Goldberg's Yesterday's Memories Rhythm & Blues Party, http://home.att.net/~marvy42/5Keys/5keys.html.

54. Ren Grevatt, "Rock and Rollers on Standard Kick Reap Fat Loot for Pubbers," *Billboard* (22 September 1956), 42.

55. Quoted in Peter Guralnick, *Feel Like Going Home: Portraits in Blues and Rock 'n' Roll* (New York: Outerbridge and Dienstfrey, 1971), 4.

56. Alec Wilder, *American Popular Song: The Great Innovators, 1900–1955* (New York: Oxford University Press, 1990). First published in 1972.

57. Quoted in Gene Lees, *Inventing Champagne: The Worlds of Lerner and Loewe* (New York: St. Martin's Press, 1990), 5.

58. Walter Clemons, "American Popular Song," *New York Times* (23 April 1972), BR6.

59. Alec Wilder, "In Rock, Amateurs May Make a Million, Then Disappear into Oblivion," *New York Times* (5 November 1972), D17–18.

60. Quoted in "Jailhouse Rock," *Time* (20 April 1959), 48.

61. Hopkins Archive, tape 9/27.

62. Greil Marcus, "The Deborah Chessler Story," in Greil Marcus, *The Dustbin of History* (Cambridge: Harvard University Press, 1995), 226.

63. Quoted in "Songwriter Johnny Green Likens R&R to Tarragon," *Down Beat* (19 September 1956), 44.

64. Berry, *Chuck Berry*, 90.

65. The flatted third of the scale occurs in these songs primarily as a harmonic component of the IV7 chord.

66. Ed Ward, "The Fifties and Before," in Ed Ward, Geoffrey Stokes, and Ken Tucker, *Rock of Ages: The Rolling Stone History of Rock and Roll* (New York: Summit Books, 1986), 180.

67. Howie Cook, "Road to Hitville Still Wide Open," *Billboard* (8 December 1958), 1.

68. Roger White, *Walk Right Back: The Story of the Everly Brothers* (London: Plexus, 1984), 55.

69. Quoted in John Beecher and Malcolm Jones, *The Buddy Holly Story*, MCA 6-80,000 (1979), notes for record 5.

70. Holly interview with Red Robinson backstage at the Georgia Auditorium, Vancouver, B.C., 23 October 1957; transcript at http://www.ritchievalens.org/buddyredrobinson1.html.

71. June Bundy, "DJ Plays Mold Trends: Desegregation of Chart Categories Earmarks '56," *Billboard* (26 January 1957), 48.

72. Henshaw, "Rock-'n'-Roll Swamps Music Scene," 21.

73. Ren Grevatt, "R&B Stars Develop Strong Stay Power," *Billboard* (4 February 1956), 54.

74. Paul Ackerman, "Barriers Being Swept Away in C&W, Pop, and R&B Fields," *Billboard* (3 March 1956), 54.

75. Bundy, "DJ Plays," 48.

76. Ibid.

77. Gary Kramer, "More Good Disks Make Spins Tougher," *Billboard* (26 January 1957), 48.

78. Simon, "Jock Showcasing," 45.

79. Ibid.

80. Ackerman, "Diversified Sphere," 1.

81. Herm Schoenfeld, "Platter Output Staggering," *Variety* (3 April 1957), 67.

82. June Bundy, "Diskeries' Talent Search Make for Artists Market," *Billboard* (20 May 1957), 20.

83. "The Rock Is Solid," *Time* (4 November 1957), 48.

84. Ren Grevatt, "On the Beat," *Billboard* (15 December 1958), 8.

85. Howard Cook, "One-Hit Artists Dominate Current Disk Landscape," *Billboard* (4 August 1958), 1.

86. Ren Grevatt, "Vet Artists, Old Tunes Bid for Lead in Chart Derby," *Billboard* (29 September 1958), 1. See also "Charts Point High Mortality Rate for Disk Artists," *Billboard* (24 March 1958), 1, 6.

87. "Who Buys Singles? Plenty Adult $$$," *Billboard* (22 September 1958), 4.

88. Ren Grevatt, "Expanding Tastes Assure Growth of U.S. Disk Features," *Billboard* (7 October 1957), 1.

89. Mike Gross, "U.S. Now a 'Musical Democracy' as Result of Disk Spread: Lomax," *Variety* (25 March 1959), 58.

CHAPTER 7

1. Civil Aeronautics Board Aircraft Accident Report (Beech Bonanza N 3794N; Mason City, Iowa; February 3 1959), adopted 15 September 1959.

2. Jerry Lee Lewis, "An Open Letter to the Industry from Jerry Lee Lewis," *Billboard* (9 June 1958), 11.

3. "Jerry Lee Lewis' Tour Off," *New York Times* (28 May 1958), 36.

4. "Jerry Lee Lewis Back," *New York Times* (29 May 1958), 23.

5. Payola affidavit, ABC, 13 November 1959, cited in Jackson, *Big Beat Heat,* 247.

6. See "Rock 'n' Roll Stabbing," *New York Times* (5 May 1958), 48; and "Rock 'n' Riot," *Time* (19 May 1958), 50.

7. New York State Penal Law of 1909, section 439.

8. "Payola Axes 'King' Freed," *Life* (7 December 1959), 30.

9. Herm Schoenfeld, "Music Biz's Classy Comeback," *Variety* (16 March 1960), 1, 78.

10. Jack Gould, "Radio: Format Changes," *New York Times* (5 March 1962), 47.

11. June Bundy "Sinatra Marathon Debs 'New' WINS," *Billboard* (24 February 1962), 4.

12. "WINS Completes Shift from R.&R. to 'Pretty,'" *Billboard* (27 January 1962), 5.

13. Guralnick, *Feel Like Going Home,* 4.

14. "R&B's Slip Is Now Showing," *Variety* (30 March 1955), 49.

15. "R&R Has 'Had It' Here," *Variety* (17 October 1956), 54.

16. Greil Marcus, "Who Put the Bomp in the Bomp De-Bomp De-Bomp?" in *Rock and Roll Will Stand,* ed. Greil Marcus (Boston: Beacon Press, 1969), 12.

17. Langdon Winner, "The Strange Death of Rock and Roll," in *Rock and Roll Will Stand,* ed. Greil Marcus (Boston: Beacon Press, 1969), 39.

18. James Miller, *Flowers in the Dustbin: The Rise of Rock and Roll, 1947–1977* (New York: Simon and Schuster, 2000), 18, 21.

19. Ibid., 173.

20. Ed Ward, Geoffrey Stokes, and Ken Tucker, *Rock of Ages: The Rolling Stone History of Rock and Roll* (New York: Summit Books, 1986), 224.

21. Wexler and Ritz, *Rhythm and the Blues,* 91.

22. Robert Palmer, *Rock and Roll: An Unruly History* (New York: Harmony Books, 1995), 35.

23. Ren Grevatt, "Is Big Beat Still on Singles Throne?" *Billboard* (12 September 1960), 58.

24. Bob Rolontz, "72 Labels Landed on Charts in '58—A Feverish Year," *Billboard* (5 January 1959), 3.

25. Bob Rolontz, "R&R Recedes Slowly; Still Packs Punch; Ballads Gain," *Billboard* (24 November 1958), 3.

26. Quoted in Ellis Amburn, *Dark Star: The Roy Orbison Story* (New York: Carol Publishing, 1990), 49.

27. Bernie Asbell, "Sam Phillips Notes R&R Fading but Imprint Permanent," *Billboard* (18 May 1959), 4, 21.

28. "Mitch Sees Quality, Know-How 1960 Keys," *Billboard* (11 January 1960), 6.

29. "Mitch Miller on March to Still More Victories," *Billboard* (30 January 1961), 4.

30. "Mitch Sees Quality," 6.

31. For a detailed style study of Orbison's early development on records, see Albin Zak, "Only the Lonely: Roy Orbison's Sweet West Texas Style," in *Sounding Out Pop: Analytical Essays in Popular Music*, ed. Mark Spicer and John Covach (Ann Arbor: University of Michigan Press, 2010).

32. John G. House, "Col's Percy Faith Sees 'Music Getting Better' but Big Beat Is Here to Stay," *Variety* (5 October 1960), 57.

33. See "50 Labels on Hot 100, Many Artists 'Unknown,'" *Billboard* (27 March 1961), 2.

34. Paul Ackerman, "Indie Labels Facing Critical Problems," *Billboard* (25 December 1961), 219.

35. Howie Cook, "Road to Hitsville Wide Open," *Billboard* (8 December 1958), 1; Ren Grevatt, "Diverse Artists, Styles, Labels Scramble 'Hot 100,'" *Billboard* (17 April 1961), 2.

36. Grevatt, "Diverse Artists," 2.

37. "Piece of the Action for All in Race for Singles Honors," *Billboard* (29 September 1962), 5.

38. "WINS Rocks to New York Top," *Billboard* (7 July 1962), 28.

39. Bob Rolontz, "The Profit Picture Still a Muddled One," *Billboard* (29 December 1962), 77.

40. Ibid, 76. The album market was subject to control by large chain stores (through deep discounts) and major label record clubs. Singles markets remained the most decentralized and hence the best barometer of grassroots demand.

41. "Singles Records Build Phenomenal Following," *Billboard* (29 December 1962), 77.

42. "Sweet and Swing Vie for Nation's Dollar," *Billboard* (24 March 1962), 1.

43. Quoted in David Kamp, "The Hit Factory," http://davidkamp.com/2006/09/the_hit_factory.php.

44. Quoted in Ken Emerson, *Always Magic in the Air: The Bomp and Brilliance of the Brill Building Era* (New York: Viking, 2005), 106.

45. *The Hit Makers: The Teens Who Stole Pop Music*, DVD, Morgan Neville (Peter Jones Productions, 1999).

46. Robert Palmer, *Baby That Was Rock and Roll: The Legendary Leiber and Stoller* (New York: Harcourt Brace Jovanovich, 1978), 23, 26.

47. This version of the Drifters bore no resemblance to the earlier hit-making incarnation featuring Clyde McPhatter. With McPhatter pursuing a solo career, the other original Drifters carried on until 1958 when, with sagging record sales and mounting personal problems, the entire group was fired by its manager, George Treadwell. He hired as stand-in Drifters a journeyman group called the 5 Crowns, which

had worked the margins of the business for several years. The new group had a run of sixteen top-forty hits from 1959 to 1964.

48. Quoted in Gillett, *Making Tracks,* 162.

49. Gary Kramer, "On the Beat," *Billboard* (2 March 1957), 61.

50. Wexler and Ritz, *Rhythm and the Blues,* 136.

51. Quoted in Emerson, *Always Magic in the Air,* 137–38.

52. *The Hit Makers.*

53. "Leiber, Stoller Form Own Production Co., Serving All," *Billboard* (30 January 1961), 2, 66.

54. Berry Gordy, "What Makes an Entrepreneur?" *New York Times* (14 January 1979), F7.

55. Berry Gordy, *To Be Loved: The Music, the Magic, the Memories of Motown* (New York: Warner Books, 1994), 110–11.

56. Ibid., 122.

57. Quoted in Lars Bjorn and Jim Gallert, *Before Motown: A History of Jazz in Detroit, 1920–1960* (Ann Arbor: University of Michigan Press, 2001), 200–201.

58. Gordy, *To Be Loved,* 132–33.

59. Robert McG. Thomas Jr., "Florence Greenberg, 82, Pop-Record Producer," *New York Times* (4 November 1995), 54.

60. Quoted in notes for *The Scepter Records Story,* Capricorn 9 42003-2 (1992), 7.

61. Quoted in Bruce Pollock, *When Rock Was Young: A Nostalgic Review of the Top 40 Era* (New York: Holt, Rinehart and Winston, 1981), 39.

62. Quoted in Sheila Weller, *Girls Like Us: Carole King, Joni Mitchell, Carly Simon and the Journey of a Generation* (New York: Atria Books, 2008), 49.

63. Jacqueline C. Warwick, "I Got All My Sisters with Me: Girl Culture, Girl Identity, and Girl Group Music," PhD diss., University of California, Los Angeles, 2002, 134.

64. Ren Grevatt, "Gal Singers Make the 'Sick' Scene," *Billboard* (27 February 1961), 5.

65. Grevatt, "Diverse Artists," 2; Grevatt, "Gal Singers," 5. "Sick" refers to what Grevatt called the "'sick' comics," a label applied both to a group of hip stand-up comedians that included Mort Sahl, Jonathan Winters, Shelley Berman, and Lenny Bruce (see "The Sicknicks," *Time* [13 July 1959]) and to such comic books as *Mad, Cracked,* and *Sick.* The sick sound was a reference to the comic books.

66. Quoted in Randy McNutt, *Guitar Towns: A Journey to the Crossroads of Rock 'n' Roll* (Bloomington: Indiana University Press, 2002), 149.

67. "Disk Makers Use More Outside Product as Competition Builds," *Billboard* (16 January 1961), 22.

68. "Indie Producers Pack Potent Sock in Singles Action," *Billboard* (29 September 1962), 4.

69. "Disk Makers Use More Outside Product," 22.

70. Records cut at Gold Star included Ritchie Valens's "La Bamba," the Champs' "Tequila," Miss Toni Fisher's "The Big Hurt," Eddie Cochran's "C'mon Everybody," the Murmaids' "Popsicles and Icicles," Bobby Day's "Rockin' Robin," and the Cascades' "Rhythm of the Rain."

71. Rolling Stones manager Andrew Loog Oldham coined the term "wall of sound," although Spector later registered it as a trademark. His own slogan for the Philles records was "Tomorrow's Sound Today." See Ribowsky, *He's a Rebel,* 187.

72. Bob Rolontz, "New Talent Vies with Vets for Spotlight," *Billboard* (5 January 1963), 6.

73. Paul Ackerman, "Where Do We Go from Here?" *Billboard* (28 December 1963), 21.

74. Paul Gardner, "3,000 Fans Greet British Beatles," *New York Times* (8 February 1964), 25.

75. Beatles, *The Beatles Anthology* (San Francisco: Chronicle Books, 2000), 115.

76. Quoted in Philip Norman, *Shout: The Beatles in Their Generation* (New York: Simon and Schuster, 1996), 220.

77. Beatles, *The Beatles Anthology*, 198.

78. Quoted in Mark Lewisohn, *The Beatles Recording Sessions* (New York: Harmony Books, 1988), 6.

79. George Martin, *All You Need Is Ears* (London: Macmillan, 1994), 141, 76.

80. "The Sound of the Sixties," *Time* (21 May 1965), 84.

81. Ren Grevatt, "The Trend in America," *Melody Maker* (3 September 1960), 2.

82. Quoted in Tony Scherman, *Backbeat: Earl Palmer's Story* (Washington, D.C.: Smithsonian Institution Press, 1999), 90–91.

83. For a detailed study of this rhythmic transition, see Alexander Stewart, " 'Funky Drummer': New Orleans, James Brown, and the Rhythmic Transformation of American Popular Music," *Popular Music* (October 2000), 293–318.

84. For details, see Charles Gower Price, "Sources of American Style in the Music of the Beatles," *American Music* (summer 1997), 208–32.

85. "Solid Revenue Source: Old R&B Hits Pan New Gold in Pop Category," *Billboard* (11 January 1960), 4.

86. Ibid., 4, 52; Ren Grevatt, "Oldie Hit Singles Bloom Anew in LP's," *Billboard* (4 January 1960), 1, 6.

87. June Bundy, " 'Oldie' Programming Move Grows," *Billboard* (23 January 1961), 1.

EPILOGUE

1. "Sinatra's Pioneering Thoughts on LP Pop Tune Production," *Billboard* (31 December 1949), 13.

2. Mark Lewisohn, *The Beatles Recording Sessions* (New York: Harmony Books, 1988), 69.

3. Barney Hoskyns, *Across the Great Divide: The Band and America* (New York: Hyperion, 1993), 138.

4. Rob Bowman, booklet for CD reissue of *Music from Big Pink,* Capitol 72435-25390-2-4 (2000), 5.

5. *Music from Big Pink,* Capitol 2955 (1968).

6. Hoskyns, *Across the Great Divide,* 150.

7. Alfred G. Aronowitz, "Country Soul from Bob's Backup Band," *Life* (26 July 1968), 12.

8. "Down to Old Dixie and Back," *Time* (12 January 1970), 43.

Bibliography

BOOKS

Altschuler, Glenn C. *All Shook Up: How Rock 'n' Roll Changed America*. New York: Oxford University Press, 2003.

Amburn, Ellis. *Dark Star: The Roy Orbison Story*. New York: Carol Publishing, 1990.

Amburn, Ellis. *Buddy Holly: A Biography*. New York: St. Martin's Press, 1995.

Aquila, Richard. *That Old-Time Rock & Roll: A Chronicle of an Era, 1954–63*. Urbana: University of Illinois Press, 2000.

Barlow, William. *Voice Over: The Making of Black Radio*. Philadelphia: Temple University Press, 1999.

Beatles. *The Beatles Anthology*. San Francisco: Chronicle Books, 2000.

Berry, Chuck. *Chuck Berry: The Autobiography*. New York: Harmony Books, 1987.

Bertrand, Michael T. *Race, Rock, and Elvis*. Urbana: University of Illinois Press, 2000.

Betrock, Alan. *Girl Groups: The Story of a Sound*. New York: Delilah Books, 1982.

Biel, Michael. "The Making and Use of Recordings in Broadcasting before 1936." PhD diss., Northwestern University, 1977.

Bjorn, Lars, and Jim Gallert. *Before Motown: A History of Jazz in Detroit, 1920–1960*. Ann Arbor: University of Michigan Press, 2001.

Brackett, David. *The Pop, Rock, and Soul Reader: Histories and Debates*. New York: Oxford University Press, 2005.

Bronson, Fred, and Adam White. *The Billboard Book of Number One Rhythm and Blues Hits*. New York: Billboard Books, 1993.

Broven, John. *Rhythm and Blues in New Orleans*. Gretna, La.: Pelican Publishing, 1978.

Broven, John. *Record Makers and Breakers: Voices of the Independent Rock 'n' Roll Pioneers*. Urbana: University of Illinois Press, 2009.

Brown, Robert J. *Manipulating the Ether: The Power of Broadcast Radio in Thirties America*. Jefferson, N.C.: McFarland, 1998.

Cantor, Louis. *Wheelin' on Beale: How WDIA-Memphis Became the Nation's First All-Black Radio Station and Created the Sound That Changed America*. New York: Pharos, 1992.

Cantor, Louis. *Dewey and Elvis: The Life and Times of a Rock 'n' Roll Deejay*. Urbana: University of Illinois Press, 2005.

Cantwell, Robert. *When We Were Good: The Folk Revival*. Cambridge: Harvard University Press, 1996.

Carlin, Richard. *Country Music: The People, Places, and Moments That Shaped the Country Sound*. New York: Black Dog and Leventhal, 2006.

Carroll, Carroll. *None of Your Business, or My Life with J. Walter Thompson (Confessions of a Renegade Radio Writer)*. New York: Cowles, 1970.

Cateforis, Theo. *The Rock History Reader*. New York: Routledge, 2007.

Chapple, Steve, and Reebee Garofalo. *Rock 'n' Roll Is Here to Pay: The History and Politics of the Music Industry*. Chicago: Nelson-Hall, 1977.

Charles, Ray, and David Ritz. *Brother Ray: Ray Charles' Own Story*. New York: Da Capo Press, 2004.

Chilton, John. *Let the Good Times Roll: The Story of Louis Jordan and His Music*. Ann Arbor: University of Michigan Press, 1997.

Cogan, Jim, and William Clark. *Temples of Sound: Inside the Great Recording Studios*. San Francisco: Chronicle Books, 2003.

Cohn, Nik. *Rock from the Beginning*. New York: Stein and Day, 1969.

Cohodas, Nadine. *Spinning Blues into Gold: The Chess Brothers and the Legendary Chess Records*. New York: St. Martin's Press, 2000.

Coleman, Rick. *Blue Monday: Fats Domino and the Lost Dawn of Rock 'n' Roll*. New York: Da Capo Press, 2006.

Collins, John. *The Story of Chess Records*. New York: Bloomsbury, 1998.

Cotten, Lee. *Shake, Rattle, & Roll: The Golden Age of American Rock 'n' Roll*. Ann Arbor: Popular Culture Ink, 1989.

Crosby, Bing, and Pete Martin. *Call Me Lucky: Bing Crosby's Own Story*. New York: Da Capo Press, 2001.

Curtis, James M. *Rock Eras: Interpretations of Music and Society, 1954–1984*. Bowling Green, Ohio: Bowling Green State University Popular Press, 1987.

Dahl, Bill. *Motown: The Golden Years*. Iola, Wis.: Krause Publications, 2001.

Dannen, Frederic. *Hit Men: Power Brokers and Fast Money Inside the Music Business*. New York: Times Books, 1990.

Deffaa, Chip. *Six Lives in Rhythm and Blues*. Urbana: University of Illinois Press, 1996.

Dempsey, John Mark. *The Light Crust Doughboys Are on the Air: Seventy Years of Texas Music*. Denton: University of North Texas Press, 2002.

Denisoff, R. Serge, and William L. Schurk. *Tarnished Gold: The Record Industry Revisited*. New Brunswick, N.J.: Transaction Books, 1986.

Dickerson, James. *Goin' Back to Memphis: A Century of Blues, Rock 'n' Roll, and Glorious Soul*. New York: Schirmer Books, 1996.

Dixon, Willie, and Don Snowden. *I Am the Blues: The Willie Dixon Story*. New York: Da Capo Press, 1989.

Doherty, Thomas P. *Teenagers and Teenpics: The Juvenilization of American Movies in the 1950s*. Philadelphia: Temple University Press, 2002.

Douglas, Tony. *Jackie Wilson: Lonely Teardrops*. New York: Routledge, 2005.

Doyle, Peter. *Echo and Reverb: Fabricating Space in Popular Music Recording, 1900–1960*. Middletown, Conn.: Wesleyan University Press, 2005.

Dunaway, David King. *How Can I Keep from Singing: Pete Seeger*. New York: McGraw-Hill, 1981.

Early, Gerald. *One Nation under a Groove: Motown and American Culture*. Hopewell, N.J.: Ecco Press, 1995.

Eberly, Philip K. *Music in the Air: America's Changing Tastes in Popular Music, 1920–1980*. New York: Hastings House, 1982.

Eliot, Marc. *Rockonomics: The Money behind the Music*. New York: F. Watts, 1989.

Emerson, Ken. *Always Magic in the Air: The Bomp and Brilliance of the Brill Building Era*. New York: Viking, 2005.

Ennis, Philip H. *The Seventh Stream: The Emergence of Rocknroll in American Pop-

ular Music. Hanover, N.H.: Wesleyan University Press and University Press of New England, 1992.

Escott, Colin, with Martin Hawkins. *Good Rockin' Tonight: Sun Records and the Birth of Rock 'n' Roll.* New York: St. Martin's Press, 1991.

Escott, Colin. *Tattooed on Their Tongues: A Journey through the Backrooms of American Music.* New York: Schirmer Books, 1996.

Floyd, John. *Sun Records: An Oral History.* New York: Avon Books, 1998.

Fong-Torres, Ben. *The Hits Just Keep on Coming: The History of Top 40 Radio.* San Francisco: Miller Freeman, 1998.

Fowler, Gene, and Bill Crawford. *Border Radio: Quacks, Yodelers, Pitchmen, Psychics, and Other Amazing Broadcasters of the American Airwaves.* Austin: University of Texas Press, 2002.

Fox, Ted. *In the Groove: The People behind the Music.* New York: St. Martin's Press, 1986.

Friedwald, Will. *Jazz Singing: America's Great Voices from Bessie Smith to Bebop and Beyond.* New York: Da Capo Press, 1996.

Friedwald, Will. *Sinatra! The Song Is You: A Singer's Art.* New York: Da Capo Press 1997.

Gaar, Gillian G. *She's a Rebel: The History of Women in Rock & Roll.* Seattle: Seal Press, 1992.

Gaisberg, F. W. *The Music Goes Round.* New York: Macmillan, 1942.

Gart, Galen. *Duke/Peacock Records: An Illustrated History with Discography.* Milford, N.H.: Big Nickel, 1990.

Gelatt, Roland. *The Fabulous Phonograph: From Tin Foil to High Fidelity.* Philadelphia: Lippincott, 1955.

Giddins, Gary. *Bing Crosby: A Pocketful of Dreams—The Early Years, 1903–1940.* Boston: Little, Brown, 2001.

Gilbert, James Burkhart. *A Cycle of Outrage: America's Reaction to the Juvenile Delinquent in the 1950s.* New York: Oxford University Press, 1986.

Gillett, Charlie. *Making Tracks: The Story of Atlantic Records.* London: Souvenir Press, 1974.

Gillett, Charlie. *The Sound of the City: The Rise of Rock and Roll.* New York: Da Capo Press, 1996.

Goldberg, Marv. *More Than Words Can Say: The Ink Spots and Their Music.* Lanham, Md.: Scarecrow Press, 1998.

Goldrosen, John. *The Buddy Holly Story.* New York: Quick Fox, 1979.

Gordy, Berry. *To Be Loved: The Music, the Magic, the Memories of Motown.* New York: Warner Books, 1994.

Granata, Charles L. *Sessions with Sinatra: Frank Sinatra and the Art of Recording.* Chicago: A Cappella, 1999.

Greenfield, Thomas Allen. *Radio: A Reference Guide.* Westport, Conn.: Greenwood Press, 1989.

Greig, Charlotte. *Will You Still Love Me Tomorrow?: Girl Groups from the 50s On.* London: Virago Press, 1989.

Gribin, Anthony J., and Matthew M. Schiff. *The Complete Book of Doo-Wop.* Iola, Wis.: Krause, 2000.

Groia, Phillip. *They All Sang on the Corner: New York City's Rhythm and Blues Vocal Groups of the 1950s.* Setauket, N.Y.: Edmund Publishing, 1974.

Grudens, Richard. *The Music Men: The Guys Who Sang with the Bands and Beyond.* Stony Brook, N.Y.: Celebrity Profiles Publishing, 1998.

Guralnick, Peter. *Feel Like Going Home: Portraits in Blues and Rock 'n' Roll*. New York: Outerbridge and Dienstfrey, 1971.

Guralnick, Peter. *Lost Highway: Journeys and Arrivals of American Musicians*. New York: Harper and Row, 1989.

Guralnick, Peter. *Last Train to Memphis: The Rise of Elvis Presley*. Boston: Little, Brown, 1994.

Guralnick, Peter. *Dream Boogie: The Triumph of Sam Cooke*. New York: Little, Brown, 2005.

Hagan, Chet. *Grand Ole Opry*. New York: Henry Holt, 1989.

Halberstam, David. *The Fifties*. New York: Fawcett Columbine, 1993.

Hamm, Charles. *Yesterdays: Popular Song in America*. New York: Norton, 1979.

Hatch, David, and Stephen Millward. *From Blues to Rock: An Analytical History of Pop Music*. Manchester, U.K.: Manchester University Press, 1987.

Havighurst, Craig. *Air Castle of the South: WSM and the Making of Music City*. Urbana: University of Illinois Press, 2007.

Hawkins, Martin. *A Shot in the Dark: Making Records in Nashville, 1945–1955*. Nashville: Vanderbilt University Press, 2006.

Hays, Lee. *Sing Out, Warning! Sing Out, Love! The Writings of Lee Hays*. Amherst: University of Massachusetts Press, 2003.

Helander, Brock. *The Rockin' '50s: The People Who Made the Music*. New York: Schirmer Books, 1998.

Helander, Brock. *The Rockin' '60s: The People Who Made the Music*. New York: Schirmer Books, 1998.

Heylin, Clinton. *Bootleg: The Secret History of the Other Recording Industry*. New York: St. Martin's Press, 1995.

Hirshey, Gerri. *Nowhere to Run: The Story of Soul Music*. New York: Da Capo Press, 1994.

Hopkins, Jerry. *Elvis: A Biography*. New York: Simon and Schuster, 1971.

Horning, Susan Schmidt. "Chasing Sound: The Culture and Technology of Recording Studios in America, 1877–1977." PhD diss., Case Western Reserve University, 2002.

Husing, Ted. *Ten Years before the Mike*. New York: Farrar and Rinehart, 1935.

Ikard, Robert W. *Near You: Francis Craig, Dean of Southern Maestros*. Franklin, Tenn.: Hillsboro Press, 1999.

Jackson, John A. *Big Beat Heat: Alan Freed and the Early Years of Rock and Roll*. New York: Macmillan, 1991.

Jaker, Bill, Frank Sulek, and Peter Kanze. *The Airwaves of New York: Illustrated Histories of 156 AM Stations in the Metropolitan Area, 1921–1996*. Jefferson, N.C.: McFarland, 1998.

Jenkins, Bruce. *Goodbye: In Search of Gordon Jenkins*. Berkeley, Calif.: Frog Books, 2005.

Jorgensen, Ernst. *Elvis Presley: A Life in Music*. New York: St. Martin's Press, 1998.

Kahn, Frank J. *Documents of American Broadcasting*. 3rd ed. Englewood Cliffs, N.J.: Prentice-Hall, 1978.

Kapp, Phyllis. *Ike's Boys: The Story of the Everly Brothers*. Ann Arbor: Popular Culture Ink, 1988.

Katz, Mark. *Capturing Sound: How Technology Has Changed Music*. Berkeley: University of California Press, 2004.

Keil, Charles. *Urban Blues*. Chicago: University of Chicago Press, 1966.

Kelley, Robin. *Race Rebels: Culture, Politics, and the Black Working Class*. New York: Free Press, 1994.

Kennedy, Rick, and Randy McNutt. *Little Labels—Big Sound: Small Record Companies and the Rise of American Music.* Bloomington: Indiana University Press, 1999.

Kenney, William. *Recorded Music in American Life: The Phonograph and Popular Memory, 1890–1945.* New York: Oxford University Press, 1999.

Kraft, James P. *Stage to Studio: Musicians and the Sound Revolution, 1890–1950.* Baltimore: Johns Hopkins University Press, 1996.

Lacasse, Serge. "'Listen to My Voice': The Evocative Power of Vocal Staging in Recorded Rock Music and Other Forms of Vocal Expression." PhD diss., University of Liverpool, 2000.

Laine, Frankie, and Joseph F. Laredo. *That Lucky Old Son: The Autobiography of Frankie Laine.* Ventura, Calif.: Pathfinder, 1993.

Lange, Jeffrey J. *Smile When You Call Me a Hillbilly: Country Music's Struggle for Respectability, 1939–1954.* Athens: University of Georgia Press, 2004.

Lee, Peggy. *Miss Peggy Lee: An Autobiography.* New York: D. Fine, 1989.

Lees, Gene. *Inventing Champagne: The Worlds of Lerner and Loewe.* New York: St. Martin's Press, 1990.

Lehmer, Larry. *The Day the Music Died: The Last Tour of Buddy Holly, the Big Bopper, and Ritchie Valens.* New York: Schirmer Books, 1997.

Levinson, Peter J. *September in the Rain: The Life of Nelson Riddle.* New York: Watson-Guptill, 2001.

Lewisohn, Mark. *The Beatles Recording Sessions.* New York: Harmony Books, 1988.

Loza, Steven. *Tito Puente and the Making of Latin Music.* Urbana: University of Illinois Press, 1999.

Mackenzie, Compton. *My Record of Music.* London: Hutchinson, 1955.

Malone, Bill C. *Country Music, U.S.A.* Austin: University of Texas Press, 1985.

Marcus, Greil, ed. *Rock and Roll Will Stand.* Boston: Beacon Press, 1969.

Marcus, Greil. *Mystery Train: Images of America in Rock 'n' Roll Music.* New York: E. P. Dutton, 1976.

Marcus, Greil. *The Dustbin of History.* Cambridge: Harvard University Press, 1995.

Marmorstein, Gary. *The Label: The Story of Columbia Records.* New York: Avalon, 2007.

Martin, George. *All You Need Is Ears.* London: Macmillan, 1994.

Martin, Linda, and Kerry Segrave. *Anti-rock: The Opposition to Rock 'n' Roll.* Hamden, Conn.: Archon, 1988.

McGowan, James A. *Here Today, Here to Stay: A Personal History of Rhythm and Blues.* Amber, Penn.: Akashic Press, 1983.

McNutt, Randy. *Guitar Towns: A Journey to the Crossroads of Rock 'n' Roll.* Bloomington: Indiana University Press, 2002.

Meltzer, Richard. *The Aesthetics of Rock.* New York: Something Else Press, 1970.

Millard, Andre. *America on Record: A History of Recorded Sound.* New York: Cambridge University Press, 1995.

Miller, Douglas T., and Marion Nowak. *The Fifties: The Way We Really Were.* Garden City, N.Y.: Doubleday, 1977.

Miller, James. *Flowers in the Dustbin: The Rise of Rock and Roll, 1947–1977.* New York: Simon and Schuster, 1999.

Moran, William R., ed. *Herman Klein and the Gramophone.* Portland, Ore.: Amadeus Press, 1990.

Morrison, Craig. *Go Cat Go! Rockabilly Music and Its Makers.* Urbana: University of Illinois Press, 1996.

Newman, Kathy M. "The Forgotten Fifteen Million: Black Radio, Radicalism, and the Construction of the 'Negro Market,'" in *Communities of the Air: Radio Cen-*

tury, Radio Culture, ed. Susan Merrill Squier, 109–33. Durham: Duke University Press, 2003.

Nimmo, H. Arlo. *The Andrews Sisters: A Biography and Career Record.* Jefferson, N.C.: McFarland, 2004.

Norman, Philip. *Rave On: The Biography of Buddy Holly.* New York: Simon and Schuster, 1996.

Norman, Philip. *Shout: The Beatles in Their Generation.* New York: Simon and Schuster, 1996.

Olsen, Eric, Paul Verna, and Carlo Wolff. *The Encyclopedia of Record Producers.* New York: Watson-Guptill, 1999.

Ortizano, G. L. "On Your Radio: A Descriptive History of Rhythm-and-Blues Radio during the 1950s." PhD diss., Ohio University, 1993.

Otis, Johnny. *Listen to the Lambs.* New York: Norton, 1968.

Otis, Johnny. *Upside Your Head: Rhythm and Blues on Central Avenue.* Hanover, N.H.: Wesleyan University Press and University Press of New England, 1993.

Palmer, Robert. *Baby That Was Rock & Roll: The Legendary Leiber and Stoller.* New York: Harcourt Brace Jovanovich, 1978.

Palmer, Robert. *A Tale of Two Cities: Memphis Rock and New Orleans Roll.* Brooklyn: Institute for Studies in American Music, 1979.

Palmer, Robert. *Rock & Roll: An Unruly History.* New York: Harmony Books, 1995.

Passman, Arnold. *The Deejays.* New York: Macmillan, 1971.

Pavlow, Big Al. *Big Al Pavlow's The R&B Book: A Disc-History of Rhythm and Blues.* Providence, R.I.: Music House Publishing, 1983.

Pegg, Bruce. *Brown Eyed Handsome Man: The Life and Hard Times of Chuck Berry.* New York: Routledge, 2002.

Pollock, Bruce. *When Rock Was Young: A Nostalgic Review of the Top 40 Era.* New York: Holt, Rinehart and Winston, 1981.

Porterfield, Nolan. *Jimmie Rodgers: The Life and Times of America's Blue Yodeler.* Urbana: University of Illinois Press, 1979.

Prigozy, Ruth. *The Life of Dick Haymes: No More Little White Lies.* Jackson: University Press of Mississippi, 2006.

Pruter, Robert. *Chicago Soul.* Urbana: University of Illinois Press, 1991.

Pruter, Robert. *Doowop: The Chicago Scene.* Urbana: University of Illinois Press, 1996.

Read, Oliver, and Walter L. Welch. *From Tin Foil to Stereo: Evolution of the Phonograph.* Indianapolis: H. W. Sams, 1959.

Redd, Laurence. *Rock Is Rhythm and Blues: The Impact of Mass Media.* East Lansing: Michigan State University Press, 1974.

Ribowsky, Mark. *He's a Rebel.* New York: E. P. Dutton, 1989.

Roberts, John Storm. *The Latin Tinge: The Impact of Latin American Music on the United States.* New York: Oxford University Press, 1999.

Russell, Tony. *Blacks, Whites, and Blues.* New York: Stein and Day, 1970.

Ryan, John. *The Production of Culture in the Music Industry: The ASCAP-BMI Controversy.* Lanham, Md.: University Press of America, 1985.

Salem, James M. *The Late, Great Johnny Ace and the Transition from R&B to Rock 'n' Roll.* Urbana: University of Illinois Press, 1999.

Sandburg, Carl. *The American Songbag.* New York: Harcourt, Brace and World, 1927.

Sanjek, Russell. *From Print to Plastic: Publishing and Promoting America's Popular Music (1900–1980).* Brooklyn: Institute for Studies in American Music, 1983.

Sanjek, Russell. *American Popular Music and Its Business: The First Four Hundred Years,* vol. 3. New York: Oxford University Press, 1988.

Scherman, Tony. *Backbeat: Earl Palmer's Story.* Washington, D.C.: Smithsonian Institution Press, 1999.

Schicke, C. A. *Revolution in Sound: A Biography of the Recording Industry.* Boston: Little, Brown, 1974.

Schroeder, Richard. *Texas Signs On: The Early Days of Radio and Television.* College Station: Texas A&M University Press, 1998.

Schulenberg, Richard. *Legal Aspects of the Music Industry: An Insider's View.* New York: Billboard Books, 1999.

Schuller, Gunther. *The Swing Era.* New York: Oxford University Press, 1989.

Segrest, James, and Mark Hoffman. *Moanin' at Midnight: The Life and Times of Howlin' Wolf.* New York: Pantheon Books, 2004.

Selvin, Joel. *Ricky Nelson: Idol for a Generation.* Chicago: Contemporary Books, 1990.

Sforza, John. *Swing It! The Andrews Sisters Story.* Lexington: University of Kentucky Press, 2004.

Shaughnessy, Mary Alice. *Les Paul: An American Original.* New York: William Morrow, 1993.

Shaw, Arnold. *The Rockin' '50s: The Decade That Transformed the Pop Music Scene.* New York: Hawthorn Books, 1974.

Shaw, Arnold. *Honkers and Shouters: The Golden Years of Rhythm and Blues.* New York: Macmillan, 1978.

Shea, William. "The Role and Function of Technology in American Popular Music, 1945–1964." PhD diss., University of Michigan, 1990.

Simons, David. *Studio Stories.* San Francisco: Backbeat Books, 2004.

Smith, Wes. *The Pied Pipers of Rock 'n' Roll: Radio Deejays of the 50s and 60s.* Marietta, Ga.: Longstreet Press, 1989.

Spector, Ronnie, with Vince Waldron. *Be My Baby: How I Survived Mascara, Miniskirts, and Madness, or My Life as a Fabulous Ronette.* New York: Harmony Books, 1990.

Stone, Desmond. *Alec Wilder in Spite of Himself.* New York: Oxford University Press, 1996.

Stravinsky, Igor. *An Autobiography.* New York: Norton, 1962.

Swenson, John. *Bill Haley: The Daddy of Rock and Roll.* New York: Stein and Day, 1982.

Symes, Colin. *Setting the Record Straight: A Material History of Classical Recording.* Middletown, Conn.: Wesleyan University Press, 2004.

Taylor, Marc. *The Original Marvelettes: Motown's Mystery Girl Group.* Jamaica, N.Y.: Aloiv Publishing, 2004.

Tosches, Nick. *Hellfire: The Jerry Lee Lewis Story.* New York: Delacorte Press, 1982.

Tosches, Nick. *Country: The Twisted Roots of Rock 'n' Roll.* New York: Da Capo Press, 1996.

Tosches, Nick. *Unsung Heroes of Rock and Roll.* New York: Da Capo Press, 1999.

Tyler, Don. *Music of the Postwar Era.* Westport, Conn.: Greenwood Press, 2008.

Ward, Brian. *Just My Soul Responding: Rhythm and Blues, Black Consciousness, and Race Relations.* Berkeley: University of California Press, 1998.

Ward, Brian. *Radio and the Struggle for Civil Rights in the South.* Gainesville: University Press of Florida, 2004.

Ward, Ed, Geoffrey Stokes, and Ken Tucker. *Rock of Ages: The Rolling Stone History of Rock & Roll.* New York: Summit Books, 1986.

Waring, Virginia. *Fred Waring and the Pennsylvanians.* Urbana: University of Illinois Press, 1997.

Warner, Jay. *American Singing Groups.* Milwaukee: Hal Leonard, 2006.

Warwick, Jacqueline C. "I Got All My Sisters with Me: Girl Culture, Girl Identity, and Girl Group Music." PhD diss., University of California, Los Angeles, 2002.

Warwick, Jacqueline C. *Girl Groups, Girl Culture: Popular Music and Identity in the 1960s.* New York: Routledge, 2007.

Weller, Sheila. *Girls Like Us: Carole King, Joni Mitchell, Carly Simon, and the Journey of a Generation.* New York: Atria Books, 2008.

Wertheimer, Alfred, with Gregory Martinelli. *Elvis '56: In the Beginning.* New York: Collier Books, 1979.

Wexler, Jerry, and David Ritz. *Rhythm and the Blues: A Life in American Music.* New York: Knopf, 1993.

Whitburn, Joel. *Pop Memories, 1890–1954: The History of American Popular Music.* Menomonee Falls, Wis.: Record Research, 1986.

Whitburn, Joel. *The Billboard Book of Top 40 Hits.* 3rd ed. New York: Billboard Publications, 1987.

Whitburn, Joel. *Top R&B Singles, 1942–1988.* Menomonee Falls, Wis.: Record Research, 1988.

Whitburn, Joel. *Top Country Singles, 1944–1988.* Menomonee Falls, Wis.: Record Research, 1989.

Whitburn, Joel. *Joel Whitburn Presents a Century of Pop Music: Year-by-Year Top 40 Rankings of the Songs and Artists That Shaped a Century.* Menomonee Falls, Wis.: Record Research, 1999.

White, Charles. *The Life and Times of Little Richard: The Quasar of Rock.* New York: Da Capo Press, 1994.

White, Roger. *Walk Right Back: The Story of the Everly Brothers.* London: Plexus, 1984.

Whiteman, Paul. *Records for the Millions.* Ed. David A. Stein. New York: Hermitage Press, 1948.

Whiteside, Jonny. *Cry: The Johnnie Ray Story.* New York: Barricade Books, 1994.

Wilder, Alec. *Letters I Never Mailed.* Boston: Little, Brown, 1975.

Wilder, Alec. *American Popular Song: The Great Innovators, 1900–1955.* New York: Oxford University Press, 1990.

Willens, Doris. *Lonesome Traveler: The Life of Lee Hays.* New York: Norton, 1988.

Williams, Gilbert A. *Legendary Pioneers of Black Radio.* Westport, Conn.: Praeger, 1998.

Williams, Richard. *Out of His Head: The Sound of Phil Spector.* New York: Outerbridge and Lazard, 1972.

Williams, Roger M. *Sing a Sad Song: The Life of Hank Williams.* Urbana: University of Illinois Press, 1981.

Zak, Albin J., III. "'Only the Lonely': Roy Orbison's Sweet West Texas Style," in *Sounding Out Pop: Analytical Essays in Popular Music,* ed. Mark Spicer and John Covach. Ann Arbor: University of Michigan Press, 2010.

JOURNALS

Anderson, Tim. "'Buried under the Fecundities of His Own Creations': Reconsidering the Recording Bans of the American Federation of Musicians, 1942–1944 and 1948." *American Music* (22:2, 2004), 231–69.

August, Garry Joel. "In Defense of Canned Music." *The Musical Quarterly* (17:1, 1931).

Denisoff, R. Serge. "The Evolution of Pop Music Broadcasting, 1920–1970." *Popular Music and Society* (2:3, 1973), 202–26.

Eastman, Ralph. "Central Avenue Blues: The Making of Los Angeles Rhythm and Blues, 1942–1947." *Black Music Research Journal* (9:1, 1989), 19–33.

Hesbacher, Peter, Robert Downing, and David G. Berger. "Sound Recording Popularity Charts: A Useful Tool for Music Research." *Popular Music and Society* (4:1, 1975), 3–18.

Hesbacher, Peter, Robert Downing, and David G. Berger. "Sound Recording Popularity Charts II: Some Recommendations for Change." *Popular Music and Society* (4:2, 1975), 86–99.

Kamin, Jonathan. "The White R&B Audience and the Music Industry, 1952–1956." *Popular Music and Society* (6, 1978), 150–68.

Kaplan, Benjamin. "Publication in Copyright Law: The Question of Phonograph Records." *University of Pennsylvania Law Review* (January 1955), 469–90.

Kloosterman, Robert C., and Chris Quispel. "Not Just the Same Old Show on My Radio: An Analysis of the Role of Radio in the Diffusion of Black Music among Whites in the South of the United States of America, 1920 to 1960." *Popular Music* (April 1990), 141–64.

Mackenzie, Compton. "The Gramophone: Its Past, Its Present; Its Future." *Proceedings of the Musical Association* (session 51, 1924–25) (London), 97–119.

Malone, Bill C. "Elvis, Country Music, and the South." *Southern Quarterly* (fall 1979), 123–34.

Manheim, James M. "B-Side Sentimentalizer: 'Tennessee Waltz' in the History of Popular Music." *The Musical Quarterly* (76:3, 1992), 337–54.

Mullin, John T. "Creating the Craft of Tape Recording." *High Fidelity* (April 1976), 62–67.

Peterson, Richard. "Why 1955? Explaining the Advent of Rock Music." *Popular Music* (January 1990), 97–116.

Price, Charles Gower. "Sources of American Style in the Music of the Beatles." *American Music* (summer 1997), 208–32.

Putnam, Milton T. "A Thirty-Five-Year History and Evolution of the Recording Studio." Audio Engineering Society Reprints, no. 1661 (New York: Audio Engineering Society, 1980).

Schultz, Lucia S. "Performing-Right Societies in the United States." *Notes* (March 1979), 511–36.

Shaw, Arnold. "Researching Rhythm and Blues." *Black Music Research Journal* (1, 1980), 71–79.

Stewart, Alexander. "'Funky Drummer': New Orleans, James Brown, and the Rhythmic Transformation of American Popular Music." *Popular Music* (October 2000), 293–318.

Records Cited

Ace, Johnny. "Pledging My Love." Duke 136 (1954).
Ace, Johnny. "My Song." Duke 102 (1952).
Acuff, Roy. "The Tennessee Waltz." Columbia 20551 (1948).
Allen, Rex. "Crying in the Chapel." Decca 28758 (1953).
Ames Brothers. "Rag Mop." Coral 60140 (1949).
Andrews Sisters. "Bei Mir Bist Du Shoen." Decca 1562 (1937).
Andrews Sisters, and Gordon Jenkins. "I Wanna Be Loved." Decca 27007 (1950).
Andrews Sisters, and Gordon Jenkins. "I Can Dream, Can't I?" Decca 24705 (1949).
Angels. "'Til." Caprice 107 (1961).
Animals. "We Gotta Get Out of This Place." MGM 13382 (1965).
Animals. "Bring It on Home to Me." MGM 13339 (1965).
Animals. "House of the Rising Sun." MGM 13264 (1964).
Anka, Paul. "Puppy Love." ABC-Paramount 10082 (1960).
Annette (Funicello). "Tall Paul." Disneyland 118 (1958).
Armstrong, Louis, and Gordon Jenkins. "That Lucky Old Sun" b/w "Blueberry Hill."
    Decca 24752 (1949).
Arnold, Eddy. "The Cattle Call." RCA Victor 6139 (1955).
Baez, Joan. "House of the Rising Sun," on *Joan Baez*. Vanguard 9078 (1960).
Bailey, Mildred. "Rockin' Chair." Vocallion 3553 (1937).
Baker, LaVern. "It's So Fine." Atlantic 2001 (1958).
Baker, LaVern. "Jim Dandy Got Married." Atlantic 1136 (1957).
Baker, LaVern. "Tweedle Dee." Atlantic 1047 (1954).
Ball, Kenny, and His Jazzmen. "Midnight in Moscow." Kapp 442 (1961).
Ballard, Hank, and the Midnighters. "Work With Me Annie." Federal 12169 (1954).
Ballard, Jimmy. "I Want a Bowlegged Woman." King 1118 (1952).
The Band. *Moondog Matinee*. Capitol 11214 (1973).
The Band. *Music from Big Pink*. Capitol 2955 (1968).
Barfield, Johnny. "Boogie Woogie." Bluebird 8272 (1939).
Barker, Blue Lu. "A Little Bird Told Me." Capitol 15308 (1948).
Baxter, Les. "The Poor People of Paris." Capitol 3336 (1956).
Beach Boys. *Pet Sounds*. Capitol 2458 (1966).
Beatles. *The Beatles*. Apple [Parlophone] 7067-7068 (1968).
Beatles. *Sgt. Pepper's Lonely Hearts Club Band*. Parlophone 7027 (1967).
Beatles. *Revolver*. Parlophone 7009 (1966).
Beatles. *Rubber Soul*. Parlophone 1267 (1965).
Beatles. "Till There Was You," on *With the Beatles*. Parlophone 1206 (1963).
Beatles. "Ain't She Sweet" (1961), "The Sheik of Araby," "Besame Mucho" (1962), on
    The Beatles Anthology 1. Apple [Capitol] 7243 8 34445 2 6 (1995).
Bennett, Tony. "Have a Good Time." Columbia 39764 (1952).

Bennett, Tony. "Cold, Cold Heart." Columbia 39449 (1951).

Bennett, Tony. "Because of You." Columbia 39362 (1951).

Berry, Chuck. "Promised Land." Chess 1916 (1964).

Berry, Chuck. "Back in the USA." Chess 1729 (1959).

Berry, Chuck. "Sweet Little Rock and Roller." Chess 1709 (1958).

Berry, Chuck. "Carol." Chess 1700 (1958).

Berry, Chuck. "Johnny B. Goode." Chess 1691 (1958).

Berry, Chuck. "Sweet Little Sixteen" b/w "Reelin' and Rockin'." Chess 1683 (1958).

Berry, Chuck. "Rock and Roll Music." Chess 1671 (1957).

Berry, Chuck. "School Day." Chess 1653 (1957).

Berry, Chuck. "You Can't Catch Me." Chess 1645 (1956)

Berry, Chuck. "Too Much Monkey Business." Chess 1635 (1956).

Berry, Chuck. "Roll Over Beethoven." Chess 1626 (1956).

Berry, Chuck. "Thirty Days (To Come Back Home)." Chess 1610 (1955).

Berry, Chuck. "Maybellene" b/w "Wee Wee Hours." Chess 1604 (1955).

Bilk, Acker. "Stranger On the Shore." Atco 6217 (1962).

Bobbettes. "Mr. Lee." Atlantic 1144 (1957).

Bonds, Gary U.S. "Quarter to Three." Legrand 1008 (1961).

Boone, Pat. "Love Letters in the Sand." Dot 15570 (1957).

Boone, Pat. "Friendly Persuasion (Thee I Love)." Dot 15490 (1956).

Boone, Pat. "I Almost Lost My Mind." Dot 15472 (1956).

Boone, Pat. "I'll Be Home" b/w "Tutti Frutti." Dot 15443 (1956).

Boone, Pat. "Ain't That a Shame." Dot 15377 (1955).

Bowen, Jimmy. "I'm Stickin' With You." Roulette 4001 (1957).

Brenston, Jackie. "Rocket 88." Chess 1458 (1951).

Brown, Charles. "Trouble Blues." Aladdin 3024 (1949).

Brown, Ruth. "Oh What a Dream." Atlantic 1036 (1954).

Brown, Ruth. "So Long." Atlantic 879 (1949).

Bunch of Goodies. Chess 1441 (1959).

Byrds. "Mr. Tambourine Man." Columbia 43271 (1965).

Cadillacs. "Gloria." Josie 765 (1954).

Cash, Johnny. "Folsom Prison Blues." Sun 232 (1956).

Champs. "Tequila." Challenge 1016 (1958).

Chandler, Gene. "Duke of Earl." Vee-Jay 416 (1961).

Chantels. "Well, I Told You." Carlton 564 (1961).

Chantels. "Look In My Eyes." Carlton 555 (1961).

Chantels. "Maybe." End 1005 (1957).

Charles, Ray. "I Can't Stop Loving You." ABC-Paramount 10330 (1962).

Charles, Ray. "Georgia on My Mind." ABC-Paramount 10135 (1960).

Charles, Ray. "What'd I Say (Part 1)." Atlantic 2031 (1959).

Chiffons. "One Fine Day." Laurie 3179 (1963).

Chipmunks. "The Chipmunk Song." Liberty 55168 (1958).

Chords. "Sh-Boom." Cat 3 (1954).

Clark, Buddy. "Peg O' My Heart." Columbia 37392 (1947).

Clark, Claudine. "Party Lights." Chancellor 1113 (1962).

Clooney, Rosemary. "This Ole House." Columbia 40266 (1954).

Clooney, Rosemary. "Come On-A My House" Columbia 39467 (1951).

Clovers. "Love Potion Number Nine." United Artists 180 (1959).

Cochran, Eddie. "Sittin' in the Balcony." Liberty 55056 (1957).

Cole, Cozy. "Topsy II." Love 5004 (1958).

Cole, Nat. "Ramblin' Rose." Capitol 4804 (1962).

Cole, Nat. "Too Young." Capitol 1449 (1951).

Cole, Nat (King Cole Trio). "Straighten Up and Fly Right." Capitol 154 (1944).

Como, Perry. "Ko Ko Mo (I Love You So)." RCA Victor 20-5994 (1955).

Como, Perry. "Cara Cara Bella Bella." RCA Victor 20-4203 (1951).

Contours. "Do You Love Me." Gordy 7005 (1962).

Cooke, Sam. "Bring It on Home to Me." RCA Victor 8036 9 (1962).

Cooke, Sam. "Twistin' the Night Away." RCA Victor 7983 (1962).

Cooke, Sam. "Wonderful World." Keen 2112 (1960).

Cookies. "Chains." Dimension 1002 (1962).

Cowboy Copas. "Tennessee Waltz." King 696 (1948).

Craig, Francis. "Red Rose" b/w "Near You." Bullet 1001 (1947).

Crests. "Sixteen Candles." Coed 506 (1958).

Crew Cuts. "Earth Angel" b/w "Ko Ko Mo (I Love You So)." Mercury 70529 (1955).

Crew Cuts. "Sh-Boom." Mercury 70404 (1954).

Crickets. "Oh Boy" b/w "Not Fade Away." Brunswick 55035 (1957).

Crosby, Bing. "Harbor Lights." Decca 27219 (1950).

Crosby, Bing. "New San Antonio Rose." Decca 3590 (1941).

Crosby, Bing, and the Andrews Sisters. "Ac-Cent-Tchu-Ate the Positive." Decca 23379 (1945).

Crosby, Bing, and the Andrews Sisters. "Pistol Packin' Mama." Decca 23277 (1943).

Crows. "Seven Lonely Days" b/w "No Help Wanted." Rama 3 (1953).

Crows. "Gee" b/w "I Love You So." Rama 5 (1953).

Crudup, Arthur. "That's All Right." RCA Victor 20-2205 (1947).

Crystals. "Then He Kissed Me." Philles 115 (1963).

Crystals. "Da Doo Ron Ron." Philles 112 (1963).

Crystals. "He's Sure the Boy I Love." Philles 109 (1962).

Crystals. "He's a Rebel." Philles 106 (1962).

Crystals. "Uptown." Philles 102 (1962).

Crystals. "There's No Other (Like My Baby)." Philles 100 (1961).

Danny and the Juniors. "At the Hop." ABC-Paramount 9871 (1957).

Dave Clark Five. "I Like It Like That." Epic 9811 (1965).

Dave Clark Five. "Reelin' and Rockin'." Epic 9786 (1965).

Dave Clark Five. "Do You Love Me." Epic 9678 (1964).

Davis, Janette, and Jerry Wayne. "A Little Bird Told Me." Columbia 38385 (1949).

Davis, Jimmie. "You Are My Sunshine." Decca 5813 (1940).

Davis, Skeeter. "I Can't Stay Mad at You." RCA Victor 8219 (1963).

Day, Dennis. "Goodnight Irene." RCA Victor 20-3870 (1950).

Day, Doris. "Secret Love." Columbia 40108 (1954).

Day, Doris, and Buddy Clark. "Love Somebody" b/w "Confess." Columbia 38174 (1948).

Delmore Brothers. "Hillbilly Boogie." King 527 (1947).

Dennis, Clark. "Peg O' My Heart." Capitol 346 (1947).

DeShannon, Jackie. "Needles and Pins." Liberty 55563 (1963).

Dexter, Al. "Pistol Packin' Mama." Okeh 6708 (1943).

Dinning, Mark. "Teen Angel." MGM 12845 (1959).

Dixie Cups. "Chapel of Love." Red Bird 001 (1964).

Domino, Antoine "Fats." "Blueberry Hill." Imperial 5407 (1956).

Domino, Antoine "Fats." "When My Dreamboat Comes Home." Imperial 5396 (1956).

Domino, Antoine "Fats." "My Blue Heaven." Imperial 5386 (1956).

Domino, Antoine "Fats." "Ain't That a Shame." Imperial 5348 (1955).

Dominoes. "Deep Purple." Liberty 55099 (1957).

Dominoes. "Star Dust." Liberty 55071 (1957).

Dominoes. "St. Therese of the Roses." Decca 29933 (1956).

Dominoes. "Rags to Riches." King 1280 (1953).

Dominoes. "These Foolish Things Remind Me of You." Federal 12129 (1953).

Dominoes. "Have Mercy Baby." Federal 12068 (1952).

Dominoes. "When the Swallows Come Back to Capistrano." Federal 12059 (1952).

Dominoes. "Sixty Minute Man." Federal 12022 (1951).

Dominoes. "Harbor Lights." Federal 12010 (1951).

Donegan, Lonnie, and His Skiffle Group. "Rock Island Line." London 1650 (1956).

Doors. *The Doors*. Elektra 74007 (1967).

Drifters. "On Broadway." Atlantic 2182 (1963).

Drifters. "Up On the Roof." Atlantic 2162 (1962).

Drifters. "Save the Last Dance for Me." Atlantic 2071 (1960).

Drifters. "This Magic Moment." Atlantic 2050 (1960).

Drifters. "There Goes My Baby." Atlantic 2025 (1959).

Drifters. "Honey Love." Atlantic 1029 (1954).

Dylan, Bob. *John Wesley Harding*. Columbia 9604 (1968).

Dylan, Bob. *Blonde on Blonde*. Columbia 841 (1966).

Dylan, Bob. *Highway 61 Revisited*. Columbia 9189 (1965).

Dylan, Bob. "House of the Rising Sun," on *Bob Dylan*. Columbia 8579 (1962).

Dylan, Bob, and the Band. *The Basement Tapes*. Columbia 33682 (1975).

Eddy, Duane. "Because They're Young." Jamie 1156 (1960).

Edwards, Tommy. "It's All in the Game." MGM 12688 (1958).

Edwards, Tommy. "It's All in the Game." MGM 11035 (1951).

Everett, Betty. "The Shoop Shoop Song (It's In His Kiss)." Vee-Jay 585 (1964).

Everly Brothers. "Cathy's Clown." Warner Bros. 5151 (1960).

Everly Brothers. "All I Have to Do Is Dream." Cadence 1348 (1958).

Everly Brothers. "Wake Up Little Susie." Cadence 1337 (1957).

Everly Brothers. "Bye Bye Love." Cadence 1315 (1957).

Exciters. "Do-Wah-Diddy." United Artists 662 (1963).

Exciters. "Tell Him." United Artists 544 (1962).

Faith, Percy. "The Theme from *A Summer Place*." Columbia 41490 (1959).

Fisher, Eddie. "Oh! My Pa-Pa." RCA Victor 20-5552 (1953).

Fisher, Toni. "The Big Hurt." Signet 275 (1959).

Fitzgerald, Ella. "Crying in the Chapel." Decca 28762 (1953).

Five Keys. "Glory of Love." Aladdin 3099 (1951).

Five Royales. "Dedicated to the One I Love." King 5098 (1958).

Five Satins. "In the Still of the Nite (I'll Remember)." Ember 1005 (1956).

Five Satins. "All Mine." Standord 100 (1956).

Flamingos. "I Only Have Eyes for You." End 1046 (1959).

Flamingos. "I'll Be Home." Checker 830 (1956).

Fleetwoods. "Come Softly to Me." Dolphin 1 (1959).

Foley, Red, and Evelyn Knight. "My Heart Cries For You." Decca 27378 (1950).

Ford, Tennessee Ernie. "Sixteen Tons." Capitol 3262 (1955).

Ford, Tennessee Ernie, and Kay Starr. "I'll Never Be Free." Capitol 1124 (1950).

Four Knights. "Oh, Baby Mine." Capitol 2654 (1954).

Four Knights. "Oh, Happy Day." Capitol 2315 (1952).

Francis, Connie. "Stupid Cupid." MGM 12683 (1958).
Full Dimensional Sound: A Study in High Fidelity. Capitol 9020 (1953).
Gayten, Paul. "Goodnight Irene." Regal 3258 (1950).
Gene and Eunice. "Ko Ko Mo (I Love You So)." Combo 64 (1954).
Gibbs, Georgia. "Tweedle Dee." Mercury 70517 (1954).
Gibbs, Georgia. "Seven Lonely Days." Mercury 70095 (1953).
Gibbs, Georgia. "Good Morning, Mr. Echo." Mercury 5662 (1951).
Glenn, Darrell. "Crying in the Chapel." Valley 105 (1953).
Gordon, Rosco. "Booted." Chess 1487 (1951).
Grant, Gogi. "The Wayward Wind." Era 1013 (1956).
Guitar Slim. "The Things That I Used to Do." Specialty 482 (1953).
Gunter, Hardrock. "Birmingham Bounce." Island EP7544 (1958).
Gunter, Hardrock. "Birmingham Bounce." Bama 104 (1950).
Gunter, Shirley, and the Queens. "Oop Shoop." Flair 1050 (1954).
Haley, Bill, and the Comets. "Thirteen Women (And Only One Man in Town)" b/w "(We're Gonna) Rock Around the Clock." Decca 29124 (1954).
Haley, Bill, and the Comets. "Shake, Rattle and Roll." Decca 29204 (1954).
Haley, Bill, and the Comets. "Crazy Man, Crazy." Essex 321 (1953).
Haley, Bill, and the Comets. "Stop Beatin' Round the Mulberry Bush" b/w "Real Rock Drive." Essex 310 (1953).
Haley, Bill, and the Saddlemen. "Icy Heart" b/w "Rock the Joint." Essex 303 (1952).
Haley, Bill, and the Saddlemen. "Rocket 88." Holiday 105 (1951).
Haley, Bill, and the Four Aces of Western Swing. "Too Many Parties and Too Many Pals" b/w "Four Leaf Clover Blues." Cowboy 1201 (1948).
Harmonicats. "Peg O' My Heart." Vitacoustic 1 (1947).
Harris, Wynonie. "Bloodshot Eyes." King 4461 (1951).
Hayes, Bill. "The Ballad of Davy Crockett." Cadence 1256 (1955).
Hearts. "Lonely Nights." Baton 208 (1955).
Helms, Bobby. "My Special Angel." Decca 30423 (1957).
Hendrix, Jimi. *Electric Ladyland.* Reprise 6307 (1968).
Herman's Hermits. "Wonderful World." MGM 13354 (1965).
Herman's Hermits. "Silhouettes." MGM 13332 (1965).
Herman's Hermits. "I'm Into Something Good." MGM 13280 (1964).
Holly, Buddy. "True Love Ways," "Moondreams," on *The Buddy Holly Story, Volume 2.* Coral 57326 (1960).
Holly, Buddy. "It Doesn't Matter Anymore" b/w "Raining in My Heart." Coral 62074 (1959).
Holly, Buddy. "Rave On," on *Buddy Holly.* Coral 57210 (1958).
Holly, Buddy. "Peggy Sue" b/w "Everyday." Coral 61885 (1957).
Holly, Buddy. "Words of Love." Coral 61852 (1957).
Holly, Buddy, and the Crickets. "Oh Boy" b/w "Not Fade Away." Brunswick 55035 (1957).
Holly, Buddy, and the Crickets. "That'll Be the Day." Brunswick 55009 (1957).
Homer and Jethro. "Unhappy Day." RCA Victor 20-5214 (1953).
Howard, Don. "Oh, Happy Day." Essex 311 (1952).
Howlin' Wolf. "How Many More Years" b/w "Moanin' at Midnight." Chess 1479 (1951).
Hunter, Ivory Joe. "I Almost Lost My Mind." MGM 10578 (1950).
Ink Spots. "The Gypsy." Decca 18817 (1946).
Ink Spots. "My Prayer." Decca 2790 (1939).
Jackson, Bull Moose. "Why Don't You Haul Off and Love Me?" King 4322 (1949).

Jackson, Bull Moose. "I Want a Bowlegged Woman." King 4189 (1948).

James, Etta. "All I Could Do Was Cry." Argo 5359 (1960).

Jaynetts. "Sally, Go 'Round the Roses." Tuff 369 (1963).

Jelly Beans. "I Wanna Love Him So Bad." Red Bird 10-003 (1964).

Jenkins, Gordon. *Seven Dreams.* Decca DL-9011 (1953).

Jenkins, Gordon. "Bewitched." Decca 24983 (1950).

Jenkins, Gordon. "Homesick, That's All," on *Gordon Jenkins and His Chorus and Orchestra Playing His Own Compositions.* Decca A-786 (1950).

Jenkins, Gordon. *California.* Decca DAU-722 (1949).

Jenkins, Gordon. "My Foolish Heart." Decca 24830 (1949).

Jenkins, Gordon. *Manhattan Tower.* Decca DA-438 (1946).

Jewels. "Hearts of Stone." R&B 1313 (1954).

Johnson, Marv. "Come to Me." United Artists 160 (1959).

Jones, Joe. "You Talk Too Much." Roulette 4304 (1960).

Justis, Bill. "Raunchy." Phillips International 3519 (1957).

K-Doe, Ernie. "Mother-In-Law." Minit 623 (1961).

Kaempfert, Bert. "Wonderland By Night." Decca 31141 (1960).

Kenner, Chris. "I Like It Like That, Part 1." Instant 3229 (1961).

Kenton, Stan. "Laura." Capitol 1704 (1951).

Kenton, Stan. *Mirage* on *Innovations in Modern Music.* Capitol 189 (1950).

King, Carole. "Oh, Neil." RCA Victor 7673 (1960).

King, Carole. "Short Mort." RCA Victor 7560 (1959).

King, Pee Wee. "Slow Poke." RCA Victor 21-0489 (1951).

King, Pee Wee. "The Tennessee Waltz." RCA Victor 20-2680 (1948).

Kingsmen. "Louie Louie." Wand 143 (1963).

Kingston Trio. "Tom Dooley." Capitol 4049 (1958).

Knight, Evelyn. "A Little Bird Told Me." Decca 24514 (1948).

Knox, Buddy. "Party Doll." Roulette 4002 (1957).

Laine, Frankie. "Hey Joe!" Columbia 40036 (1953).

Laine, Frankie. "I Believe." Columbia 39938 (1953).

Laine, Frankie. "The Cry of the Wild Goose." Mercury 5363 (1950).

Laine, Frankie. "God Bless the Child." Mercury 5355 (1950).

Laine, Frankie. "Mule Train." Mercury 5345 (1949).

Laine, Frankie. "That Lucky Old Sun." Mercury 5316 (1949).

Laine, Frankie. "Georgia On My Mind." Mercury 5293 (1949).

Laine, Frankie. "All of Me." Mercury 5048 (1947).

Laine, Frankie. "That's My Desire." Mercury 5007 (1947).

Laine, Frankie, and Jo Stafford. "Settin' the Woods on Fire." Columbia 39867 (1951).

Laine, Frankie, and Jo Stafford. "Hey Good Lookin'." Columbia 39570 (1951).

Lawrence, Steve. "Go Away Little Girl." Columbia 42601 (1962).

Led Zeppelin. *Led Zeppelin.* Atlantic 8216 (1969).

Lee, Brenda. "I Want to Be Wanted." Decca 31149 (1960).

Lee, Brenda. "I'm Sorry." Decca 31093 (1960).

Lee, Peggy. "Just One of Those Things." Decca 28313 (1952).

Lee, Peggy. "Lover." Decca 28215 (1952).

Lee, Peggy. "Be Anything (But Be Mine)." Decca 28142 (1952).

Lewis, Jerry Lee. "High School Confidential." Sun 296 (1958).

Lewis, Jerry Lee. "Great Balls of Fire." Sun 281 (1957).

Lewis, Jerry Lee. "Whole Lot of Shakin' Going On." Sun 267 (1957).

Little Eva. "The Loco-Motion." Dimension 1000 (1962).

Little Jimmy Dickens. "Country Boy." Columbia 20585 (1949).

Little Peggy March. "I Will Follow Him." RCA Victor 8139 (1963).

Little Richard. "Baby Face," "By the Light of the Silvery Moon," on *Little Richard 2.* Specialty 2103 (1958).

Little Richard. "Good Golly Miss Molly." Specialty 624 (1958).

Little Richard. "Keep a' Knockin'." Specialty 611 (1957).

Little Richard. "Lucille." Specialty 598 (1957).

Little Richard. "Long Tall Sally." Specialty 572 (1956).

Little Richard. "Tutti Frutti" b/w "I'm Just a Lonely Guy." Specialty 561 (1955).

Little Richard. "Baby," "All Night Long" (1955), on *Little Richard: The Specialty Sessions.* Specialty 8508 (1989).

Love Those Goodies. Checker 2973 (1959).

Lowe, Jim. "The Green Door." Dot 15486 (1956).

Lund, Art. "Crying in the Chapel." Coral 61018 (1953).

Lund, Art. "Peg O' My Heart." MGM 10037 (1947).

Lymon, Frankie, and the Teenagers. "Why Do Fools Fall in Love." Gee 1002 (1956).

Manfred Mann. "Do Wah Diddy Diddy" b/w "Sha La La." Ascot 2157 (1964).

Mann, Gloria. "Teen Age Prayer." Sound 126 (1955).

Marcels. "Blue Moon." Colpix 186 (1961).

Martha and the Vandellas. "Heat Wave." Gordy 7022 (1963).

Martin, Dean. "Memories Are Made of This." Capitol 3295 (1955).

Martin, Dean. "Return to Me." Capitol 3894 (1958).

Martino, Al. "I Love You Because." Capitol 4930 (1963).

Marvelettes. "Please Mr. Postman." Tamla 54046 (1961).

Mathis, Johnny. "Gina." Columbia 42582 (1962).

Mauriat, Paul. "Love is Blue." Phillips 40495 (1967).

McCrea, "Earl-Jean." "I'm Into Something Good." Colpix 729 (1964).

Mello Kings. "Tonite Tonite." Herald 502 (1957).

Miller, Mitch. "The Yellow Rose of Texas." Columbia 40540 (1955).

Miracles. "Way Over There." Tamla 54069 (1962).

Mitchell, Guy. "My Truly, Truly Fair." Columbia 39415 (1951).

Mitchell, Guy. "My Heart Cries For You" b/w "The Roving Kind." Columbia 39067 (1950).

Modugno, Domenico. "Nel Blu Dipinto Di Blu (Volare)." Decca 30677 (1958).

Monroe, Bill. "Blue Moon of Kentucky." Columbia 37888 (1947).

Monroe, Vaughn. "They Were Doin' the Mambo." RCA Victor 20-5767 (1954).

Moody, Clyde. "I Love You Because." King 837 (1949).

Moonglows. "Sincerely." Chess 1581 (1954).

Morrison, Van. *Astral Weeks.* Warner Bros. 1768 (1969).

Mullican, Moon. "Cherokee Boogie." King (1951).

Mullican, Moon. "Goodnight Irene." King 886 (1950).

Murmaids. "Popsicles and Icicles." Chattahoochee 628 (1963).

Norman Petty Trio. "Mood Indigo." X 0040 (1954).

Nutmegs. "A Story Untold." Herald 452 (1955).

Oldies but Goodies in Hi-Fi. Original Sound 5001 (1959).

Oldies in Hi-Fi. Chess 1439 (1959).

Orbison, Roy. "Only the Lonely." Monument 421 (1960).

Orioles. "Crying in the Chapel." Jubilee 5122 (1953).

Orioles. "It's Too Soon to Know." It's a Natural 5000 (1948).

Page, Patti. "Most People Get Married." Mercury 71950 (1962).

Page, Patti. "Old Cape Cod." Mercury 71101 (1957).

Page, Patti. "Oh, What a Dream." Mercury 70416 (1954).

Page, Patti. "Cross Over the Bridge." Mercury 70302 (1954).

Page, Patti. "And So to Sleep Again." Mercury 5706 (1951).

Page, Patti. "Mister and Mississippi." Mercury 5645 (1951).

Page, Patti. "Mockin' Bird Hill." Mercury 5595 (1951).

Page, Patti. "The Tennessee Waltz" b/w "Boogie Woogie Santa Claus." Mercury 5534 (1950).

Page, Patti. "With My Eyes Wide Open I'm Dreaming." Mercury 5344 (1950).

Page, Patti. "Money, Marbles and Chalk." Mercury 5251 (1949).

Page, Patti. "Confess." Mercury 5129 (1948).

Paris Sisters. "I Love How You Love Me." Gregmark 6 (1961).

Parker, Little Junior. "Feelin' Good." Sun 187 (1953).

Paul, Les. "Carioca." Capitol 2080 (1952).

Paul, Les. "Josephine." Capitol 1592 (1951).

Paul, Les. "Lover" b/w "Brazil." Capitol 15037 (1948).

Paul, Les. *The New Sound.* Capitol H 226 (1948).

Paul, Les, and Mary Ford. "Falling in Love With Love," on *Les and Mary.* Capitol 577 (1955).

Paul, Les, and Mary Ford. "Don'cha Hear Them Bells." Capitol 2614 (1953).

Paul, Les, and Mary Ford. "Vaya Con Dios." Capitol 2486 (1953).

Paul, Les, and Mary Ford. "In the Good Old Summertime." Capitol 2123 (1952).

Paul, Les, and Mary Ford. "Just One More Chance." Capitol 1825 (1951).

Paul, Les, and Mary Ford. "The World Is Waiting for the Sunrise." Capitol 1748 (1951).

Paul, Les, and Mary Ford. "I Wish I Had Never Seen the Sunshine." Capitol 1592 (1951).

Paul, Les, and Mary Ford. "How High the Moon." Capitol 1451 (1951).

Paul, Les, and Mary Ford. "Mockin' Bird Hill." Capitol 1373 (1951).

Paul, Les, and Mary Ford. "The Tennessee Waltz." Capitol 1316 (1950).

Payne, Leon. "I Love You Because." Capitol 40238 (1949).

Penguins. "Earth Angel" b/w "Hey Senorita." Dootone 348 (1954).

Penny, Hank. "Bloodshot Eyes." King 828 (1950).

Perkins, Carl. "Blue Suede Shoes." Sun 234 (1956).

Peter and Gordon. "To Know You Is to Love You." Capitol 5461 (1965).

Peter and Gordon. "True Love Ways." Capitol 5406 (1965).

Peter and Gordon. "I Go to Pieces." Capitol 5335 (1965).

Platters. "I'll Never Smile Again." Mercury 71847 (1961).

Platters. "If I Didn't Care." Mercury 71749 (1960).

Platters. "To Each His Own." Mercury 71697 (1960).

Platters. "Red Sails in the Sunset." Mercury 71656 (1960).

Platters. "Harbor Lights." Mercury 71563 (1960).

Platters. "Smoke Gets in Your Eyes." Mercury 71383 (1958).

Platters. "Twilight Time." Mercury 71289 (1958).

Platters. "My Dream." Mercury 71093 (1957).

Platters. "My Prayer" b/w "Heaven On Earth." Mercury 70893 (1956).

Platters. "(You've Got) The Magic Touch." Mercury 70819 (1956).

Platters. "The Great Pretender." Mercury 70753 (1955).

Platters. "Only You (And You Alone)." Mercury 70633 (1955).

Prado, Perez. "Patricia." RCA Victor 7245 (1958).

Presley, Elvis. "Are You Lonesome Tonight." RCA Victor 47-7810 (1960).

Presley, Elvis. "It's Now or Never." RCA Victor 47-7777 (1960).

Presley, Elvis. "Stuck On You." RCA Victor 47-7740 (1960).

Presley, Elvis. "Jailhouse Rock." RCA Victor 47-7035 (1957).

Presley, Elvis. "(Let Me Be Your) Teddy Bear." RCA Victor 47-7000 (1957).

Presley, Elvis. "All Shook Up." RCA Victor 47-6870 (1957).

Presley, Elvis. "Too Much." RCA Victor 47-6800 (1957).

Presley, Elvis. "Love Me Tender" b/w "Any Way You Want Me (That's How I Will Be)." RCA Victor 47-6643 (1956).

Presley, Elvis. "Don't Be Cruel" b/w "Hound Dog." RCA Victor 47-6604 (1956).

Presley, Elvis. "Heartbreak Hotel." RCA Victor 47-6420 (1956).

Presley, Elvis. "I Forgot to Remember to Forget" b/w "Mystery Train." Sun 223 (1955).

Presley, Elvis. "Baby Let's Play House." Sun 217 (1955).

Presley, Elvis. "That's All Right" b/w "Blue Moon of Kentucky." Sun 209 (1954).

Presley, Elvis. "I Love You Because," "Blue Moon" (1954), on *Elvis Presley*. RCA Victor 1254 (1956).

Presley, Elvis. "My Happiness," "That's When Your Heartache Begins" (1953), "Tomorrow Night," "Harbor Lights," (1954), on *The King of Rock and Roll: The Complete 50s Masters*. RCA 07863 (1992).

Preston, Jimmy. "Rock the Joint." Gotham 188 (1949).

Preston, Johnny. "Running Bear." Mercury 71474 (1959).

Price, Lloyd. "Lawdy Miss Clawdy." Specialty 428 (1952).

Prisonaires. "Just Walkin' in the Rain." Sun 186 (1953).

Raney, Wayne. "Why Don't You Haul Off and Love Me?" King 791 (1949).

Ray, Johnnie. "Cry" b/w "The Little White Cloud That Cried." Okeh 6840 (1951).

Ray, Johnnie. "Whiskey and Gin." Okeh 6809 (1951).

Rays. "Silhouettes." Cameo 117 (1957).

Reed, Jimmy. "Honest I Do." Vee-Jay 253 (1957).

Remember the Oldies. Argo 649 (1959).

Reynolds, Debbie. "Tammy." Coral 61851 (1957).

Riddle, Nelson. "Lisbon Antigua." Capitol 3287 (1955).

Rodgers, Jimmie. "Kisses Sweeter Than Wine." Roulette 4031 (1957).

Rodgers, Jimmie. "Honeycomb." Roulette 4015 (1957).

Rodgers, Jimmie. "Blue Yodel No. 1 (T for Texas)." Victor 21142 (1928).

Rolling Stones. *Let It Bleed*. London 4 (1969).

Rolling Stones. *Beggar's Banquet*. London 539 (1968).

Rolling Stones. "Time Is on My Side." London 9708 (1964).

Rolling Stones. "It's All Over Now." London 9687 (1964).

Ronettes. "Be My Baby." Philles 116 (1963).

Rose, David. "The Stripper." MGM 13064 (1962).

Rosie and the Originals. "Angel Baby." Highland 1011 (1960).

Royal Teens. "Short Shorts." ABC-Paramount 9882 (1958).

Scott, Bobby. "Chain Gang." ABC-Paramount 9658 (1955).

Searchers. "Love Potion Number Nine." Kapp Winner's Circle 27 (1964).

Searchers. "Needles and Pins." Kapp 577 (1964).

Sedaka, Neil. "Oh! Carol." RCA Victor 7595 (1959).

Seville, David. "Witch Doctor." Liberty 55132 (1958).

Shangri-Las. "Leader of the Pack." Red Bird 014 (1964).

Sharp, Dee Dee. "Mashed Potato Time." Cameo 212 (1962).

Shirelles. "Sha La La." Scepter 1267 (1964).
Shirelles. "Will You Love Me Tomorrow." Scepter 1211 (1960).
Shirelles. "Tonight's the Night." Scepter 1208 (1960).
Shirelles. "Dedicated to the One I Love." Scepter 1203 (1959).
Shirelles. "I Met Him On a Sunday." Decca 30588 (1958).
Shore, Dinah. "Buttons and Bows." Columbia 38284 (1948).
Simon and Garfunkel. *Bookends*. Columbia 9529 (1968).
Sinatra, Frank. "Pocketful of Miracles." Reprise 20040 (1961).
Sinatra, Frank. *Come Dance with Me*. Capitol 1069 (1959).
Sinatra, Frank. *Only the Lonely*. Capitol 1053 (1958).
Sinatra, Frank. *In the Wee Small Hours*. Capitol 581 (1955).
Sinatra, Frank. *Songs for Young Lovers*. Capitol 488 (1954).
Sinatra, Frank. "Why Try to Change Me Now." Columbia 39882 (1952).
Sinatra, Frank. "April in Paris." Columbia 39592 (1951).
Sinatra, Frank. "Mama Will Bark." Columbia 39425 (1951).
Sinatra, Frank. "Hello, Young Lovers." Columbia 39294 (1951).
Sinatra, Frank. "I Am Loved." Columbia 39079 (1950).
Sinatra, Frank. "Goodnight Irene." Columbia 38892 (1950).
Sinatra, Frank. *The Voice of Frank Sinatra*. Columbia 112 (1946).
60 Years of Music America Loves Best. RCA Victor 6074 (1960).
Sly and the Family Stone. *Dance to the Music*. Epic 26371 (1968).
Smith, Bessie. "Bleeding Hearted Blues." Columbia A 3936 (1923).
Soul, Jimmy. "If You Wanna Be Happy." S.P.Q.R. 3305 (1963).
Spaniels. "Goodnite Sweetheart, Goodnite." Vee-Jay 107 (1954).
Stafford, Jo. "Goodnight Irene." Capitol 7142 (1950).
Stafford, Jo. "Jambalaya." Columbia 39838 (1952).
Starr, Kay. "Rock and Roll Waltz." RCA Victor 6359 (1955).
Stoloff, Morris. "Moonglow and Theme from *Picnic*." Decca 29888 (1956).
Strong, Barrett. "Money (That's What I Want)." Anna 1111 (1960).
Teddy Bears. "To Know Him Is to Love Him." Dore 503 (1958).
Thomas, Irma. "Time Is on My Side." Imperial 66041 (1964).
Thomas, Rufus. "Bear Cat." Sun 181 (1953).
Thornton, Willie Mae (Big Mama). "Hound Dog." Peacock 1612 (1953).
Three Friends. "Blanche." Lido 500 (1956).
Three Suns. "Peg O' My Heart." RCA Victor 2272 (1947).
Three Suns. "Twilight Time." Hit 7092 (1944).
Todd, Dick. "Oh, Happy Day." Decca 28506 (1953).
Tornados. "Telstar." London 9561 (1962).
Travis, Merle. "Sixteen Tons." Capitol 48001 (1947).
Travis, Merle. "Divorce Me C.O.D." Capitol 290 (1946).
Tubb, Ernest. "I Love You Because." Decca 46213 (1950).
Tubb, Ernest, and Red Foley. "Goodnight Irene." Decca 46255 (1950).
Turner, Ike, and Tina Turner. "River Deep–Mountain High." Philles 131 (1966).
Turner, Joe. "Shake, Rattle and Roll." Atlantic 1026 (1954).
Turzy, Jane. "Good Morning, Mr. Echo." Decca 27622 (1951).
Valens, Ritchie. "Donna." Del-Fi 4110 (1958).
Valentines. "Lilly Maebelle." Rama 171 (1955).
Valentinos. "It's All Over Now." Sar 152 (1964).
Valli, June. "Crying in the Chapel." RCA Victor 20-5368 (1953).
Ventures. "Walk Don't Run." Dolton 25 (1960).

Vincent, Gene. "Be Bop A Lula." Capitol 3450 (1956).

Wakely, Jimmy. "My Heart Cries For You." Capitol 1328 (1950).

Ward, Robin. "Wonderful Summer." Dot 16530 (1963).

Washington, Dinah. "My Heart Cries For You." Mercury 8209 (1951).

Watson, Paula. "A Little Bird Told Me." Supreme 1507 (1948).

Weavers. "The Midnight Special." Decca 28272 (1952).

Weavers. "Around the Corner (Beneath the Berry Tree)." Decca 28054 (1952).

Weavers. "Wimoweh (Mbube)" b/w "Old Paint (Ride Around, Little Dogies)." Decca 27928 (1951).

Weavers. "So Long (It's Been Good to Know Yuh)" b/w "Lonesome Traveler." Decca 27376 (1950).

Weavers. "Tzena Tzena Tzena" b/w "Goodnight Irene." Decca 27077 (1950).

Weems, Ted. "Peg O' My Heart." Mercury 5052 (1947).

Welk, Lawrence. "Calcutta." Dot 16161 (1960).

Welk, Lawrence. "Oh, Happy Day." Coral 60893 (1952).

Whiting, Margaret. "Good Morning, Mr. Echo." Capitol 1702 (1951).

Wilder, Alec. *Frank Sinatra Conducts the Music of Alec Wilder.* Columbia 637 (1946).

Williams, Andy. "Can't Get Used to Losing You." Columbia 42674 (1963).

Wills, Bob, and His Texas Playboys. "New San Antonio Rose." Okeh 5694 (1940).

Wilson, Jackie. "I'll Be Satisfied." Brunswick 55136 (1959).

Wilson, Jackie. "That's Why (I Love You So)." Brunswick 55121 (1959).

Wilson, Jackie. "Lonely Teardrops." Brunswick 55105 (1958).

Wilson, Jackie. "To Be Loved." Brunswick 55052 (1958).

Wilson, Jackie. "Reet Petite (The Finest Girl You Ever Want to Meet)." Brunswick 55024 (1957).

Winterhalter, Hugo. "Canadian Sunset." RCA Victor 6537 (1956).

Wonder, Stevie. "Fingertips—Part 2." Tamla 54080 (1963).

Wooley, Sheb. "Purple People Eater." MGM 12651 (1958).

Wray, Link, and His Ray Men. "Rumble." Cadence 1347 (1958).

Young, Kathy, and the Innocents. "A Thousand Stars." Indigo 108 (1960).

Index